COMRADES

AND

PARTNERS

COMRADES AND PARTNERS

The Shared Lives of
Grace Hutchins and Anna Rochester

Janet Lee

ROWMAN & LITTLEFIELD PUBLISHERS, INC.
Lanham • Boulder • New York • Oxford

ROWMAN & LITTLEFIELD PUBLISHERS, INC.

Published in the United States of America
by Rowman & Littlefield Publishers, Inc.
4720 Boston Way, Lanham, Maryland 20706
http://www.rowmanlittlefield.com

12 Hid's Copse Road
Cumnor Hill, Oxford OX2 9JJ, England

British Library Cataloguing in Publication Information Available

Library of Congress Cataloging-in-Publication Data

Lee, Janet, 1954–
    Comrades and partners : the shared lives of Grace Hutchins and
Anna Rochester / Janet Lee.
        p.   cm.
    Includes bibliographical references and index.
    ISBN 0-8476-9620-0 (cloth : alk. paper)
    1. Hutchins, Grace, 1885–   .   2. Rochester, Anna.   3. Women social
reformers—New England—Biography.   4. Women labor leaders—New
England—Biography.   5. Women communists—New England—Biography.
6. Female friendship—New England.   I. Title.
HQ1412.L44   2000
303.48'4'092274–dc21   99–15412
                                                                                            CIP

Printed in the United States of America

♾™ The paper used in this publication meets the minimum requirements of
American National Standard for Information Sciences—Permanence of Paper for
Printed Library Materials, ANSI/NISO Z39.48—1992.

CONTENTS

ACKNOWLEDGMENTS

I am grateful to the staff of the Special Collections Division of University Archives in Knight Library at the University of Oregon, and especially to Duffy Knaus, Sharla Davis, Will Harmon, Linda Long, and Bernie McTigue for their assistance with Grace Hutchins and Anna Rochester's manuscripts. Thanks also go to Tamiment archivist Peter Filardo, Loret Treese and Kathleen Whalen at Bryn Mawr College, and Wendy Chmielewski of the Swarthmore Peace Collection. I am also grateful to the Fellowship of Reconciliation for their help with this project.

The Women's Writing Group at Oregon State University helped enormously through their perceptive readings of early drafts of this writing. My special thanks go to Becky Warner, Nancy Rosenberger, Joan Gross, Mina Carson, Lisa Ede, Cheryl Glenn, Deltra Ferguson, Anita Helle, Vicki Collins, Annie Popkin, and Susan Shaw for their feedback, support, and encouragement. A Research Grant from the College of Liberal Arts at Oregon State University funded this project at its inception, and a Fellowship at the Center for the Humanities at OSU gave me the release time from teaching to see it to fruition. I am especially thankful to my colleagues at the Center for their support and collegiality.

I appreciate early conversations about this project with Tina Baker, Bettina Aptheker, Gerald Slusser, and Suzanne Sowinska as well as with Rosalyn Baxandall, whose generosity concerning various documents and insight on women of the Old Left were very helpful. Big thanks go to Joan Wallach Scott whose enthusiasm for the project encouraged me to embark in the first place and to Paul Farber for his support. Special thanks go to Mary Carpenter, Lynn Gemmell, Kate Munning, and Steve Wrinn at Rowman & Littlefield for their enthusiasm and vision for this book. As always deep gratitude goes to Gary Barnes for his love and support even while there were many months when Grace and Anna seemed to have moved in with us, and to Fiona and Liam, and to my mother, Letti Halvorsen, and especially to Edyth, who put up with a mother who spent far too much time in front of the computer. I am grateful to all who helped in all the myriad ways with this project.

INTRODUCTION

Life comes to us but once and it should be possible to live one's life in such a way that looking back one would feel no regret for years lived pointlessly; no shame for a petty worthless past—so that as one died one could say: All my life and all my strength has been given to the most beautiful thing in the world—the struggle for the freedom of mankind.[1]

In 1939 GRACE HUTCHINS penned the above quotation from Ostrovski's *The Making of a Hero* in a little spiral-bound notebook filled with her goals and aspirations. It epitomized her creed, shared by life-partner Anna Rochester, for a just and moral life devoted to the improvement of the human condition. Hutchins and Rochester did everything possible to live by such strong ethical principles; they committed themselves to social and economic justice and envisioned a new world order where suffering, want, and greed would have no place. From their privileged beginnings in religious, aristocratic, New England families to their involvement with reformist and then revolutionary politics, the couple lived an intense devotion to this "struggle for the freedom of mankind."

Comrades and Partners is a joint biography that traces the lives of labor reformers and communist intellectuals Grace Hutchins (1885–1969) and Anna Rochester (1880–1966). It weaves the narrative of their personal relationship, and, by giving voice to glimpses of their life stories, hopes to contribute to the history of the intellectual Left. Framed by privileges of race and class, they enjoyed a financial security and independence that allowed them to eschew marriage and share a life together. From this relatively secure base, Hutchins and Rochester were able to commit their lives to social and economic change, use their wealth to support their causes, and embark on an ideological journey from Christianity to communism. Remembered by their fellow comrades as cultured and aristocratic individuals who radiated a refined stoicism and dignified determination, they made their mark as women who opposed injustice against the poor, women, and children through their activism and their prolific writings.

Their journey moved rapidly Left across some diverse ideological landscapes. This journey originated in the late nineteenth century in wealthy New England families where they learned about philanthropy and a responsibility of service to others that helped guide their later lives. These early years, though lived separately, were for both Hutchins and Rochester framed by expectations of women involved in useful and productive work. Educated at Bryn Mawr College, they were among the first generation of women to seek out the company of other women, avoid the constraints of traditional marriage, and have the opportunity to work as change agents in the wider society.[2] This devotional service in the context of reform politics was motivated by their strong affiliation with the Episcopal Church, a faith that undergirded their behavior and anchored their lives. Discovering socialism and pacifism, as well as each other, Hutchins and Rochester moved toward the teachings of Christian socialism that reconciled their growing awareness of social and economic justice with Christian moral ethics. Then a trip around the world helped facilitate their growing convictions about Marxist–Leninist thought, such that by the 1930s Hutchins and Rochester came to be known as committed communist intellectuals.

Central in any joint biography, and no less true for *Comrades and Partners*, is the way personal relationship can provide the backdrop against which professional lives are lived. Hutchins and Rochester were together for over forty-five years and loved each other deeply. They called each other "partner," "pardner," or just "pard," and professed undying love, respect, and admiration for each other. Their romantic friendship exemplifies the choice of educated women of the late nineteenth and early twentieth century when intense female friendships were socially acceptable and women who were privileged enough not to need the financial support of a man were able to build their emotional and professional lives around other women.[3] Indeed, as Aptheker has emphasized, such women were the "cornerstone" of social activism: "The historical verification of this lesbian presence is fundamental to an understanding of the role of women in social movements."[4] Hutchins and Rochester were a part of this cohort of women whose commitment to social activism was integrated with their lesbian orientation.

However, to my best knowledge, Hutchins and Rochester themselves never openly identified as lesbians. They demonstrated the innocence of the golden age of romantic friendships, seeing each other as treasured companions and soul-mates.[5] Yet about the time when Hutchins and Rochester started to live together in the early twenties, romantic friendships were starting to come under scrutiny. This was a result of the work of various sexologists and a push toward the "modern" companionate marriage, which saw lesbianism or "inversion" as abnormal and pathological. Hutchins and Rochester probably thought their romantic friendship had little to do with attachments between "abnormal lesbians" and did not recognize themselves in these descriptions. As cultured and proper maiden ladies, they would most likely have been able to avoid accusations of lesbian pathology, helped perhaps by being well-socialized women who may have seen themselves as relatively asexual. Besides, they lived in Greenwich Village where relationships between women were relatively commonplace and they had many friends who were likewise partnered. As the years passed they most likely understood their relationship as lesbians, but given the homophobia of the Party as well as that of society generally, they would have been keen to disguise this fact.[6] Whether they considered themselves homosexual or not, most likely they would have agreed with the description of "homoaffectionality" in their relationship.[7] As women who dedicated their lives to each other they enrich our understanding of lesbian history.[8]

Hutchins and Rochester were loving partners *and* political comrades. Their politics organized everything about their lives, including their relationship together. This work, "the cause of the working class," was "bigger than [their] friendship";[9] intimacy, in effect, seemed to have been based upon shared work and values. Like many other women active in the Old Left, it was this shared emphasis on public service that was central in the construction of their partnership.[10] Such public service was characterized by strong devotional impulses: they *lived* their faith always, whether it be Christianity, Christian socialism, or communism, and believed in the infallibility of their creed. Always present, it seemed, was their devotion to the improvement of society generally and the lives of working people in particular. These ordered and principled moral positions demanded utmost discipline and personal sacrifice, strong loyalties, and a total commitment of faith; also involved was a certain mysticism and sentiment concerning contemporary miseries and glorious futures. As intellectuals, Hutchins and Rochester understood the abstract theory and leaps of faith necessary in both Christianity and communism, and I believe they were attracted by coherent explanations that made sense of the despair they felt about modern industrial society. Both institutions gave them opportunities for community, be it through the congregation or through comradeship, and both provided a structured system of authority that organized their lives.

Or perhaps I have this all wrong. Because I have been trained to look for continuity and theoretically coherent and seamless narratives, perhaps my argument better reflects the merging between my imagination and their stories, my fictions about their fictions, or perhaps I base an analysis on certain glimpses that support my argument, unconsciously ignoring or leaving uncovered bits and pieces that would suggest otherwise. These thoughts are disconcerting since there is a profound responsibility attached to writing biography: telling someone's story and getting it right.[11] But what does "getting it right" mean? Biographical subjects are constructed and not merely represented, and authorized "facts" might better be seen as fictions that authors utilize out of their own interpretive frameworks. Surrounded by the archival "evidence" of two lives, I am awed by the complexities, gaps, and silences, as well as the contradictions. There are so many layers of intent and meaning in all scraps of information about the lives of Hutchins and Rochester; their own representations of themselves are artful practices that have been selected and produced through a variety of options; my selections of their selections are likewise my own productions: my stories about their stories. And you the reader add another level as you filter the stories about the stories through your own thoughts and experiences. I have to say there are no seamless truths about Hutchins and Rochester, only scraps that are necessarily partial and incomplete. This calls into question the concept of the unified subject. It also points out that representation in the task of writing lives involves various degrees of invention. My understanding of these limits of representation means that this biography is coming from a less confident, and I hope more compassionate, epistemological space.[12]

Addressing this representational crisis does not mean finding better methods to divert the problem since the problem is less methodological than epistemological.[13] We might, to quote Patti Lather, use the ruins of traditional representation as the very site of possibility.[14] By integrating the traditional biographical method, but disrupting and unsettling it to reveal its fictions and uncertainties, perhaps new sites of possibility—of writing a different kind of biography—can be found. With this in mind, there are framed boxes throughout the text of *Comrades and Partners* containing "subtext" that unsettle the narrative. Sometimes they suggest alternative ways of interpreting Hutchins and Rochester's lives and often they give methodological insight to remind the reader who might otherwise be seduced into not questioning a seamless narrative. They also include thoughts about my role as a biographer, mostly in the form of excerpts from my research diary. While such modified split-text narrative might appear to again privilege the traditional academic/expert voice in its relegation of "other" voices to the subtext, this form tries to highlight the necessity of working from within the discipline *while at the same time exposing what that traditional discipline has ignored.* This doubling gesture highlights the traditional narrative at the same time that it complicates it. It also allows you, the reader, to skip the boxes entirely should you desire to read an untroubled narrative, facilitating an intentional act that again highlights the constructed nature of biographical writing.

Certainly this biography assumes agency on the part of Hutchins and Rochester to be less an expression of autonomous individual will and more about the process whereby subjects are formed through historically defined processes. What I mean is that subjects come into being through a complex interplay of sociocultural means that include institutions, practices, and language. As Joan Wallach Scott, who thinks of historical subjects as sites or historical locations or markers, explains: "To figure a person—in this case, a woman—as a place or location is not to deny her humanity; it is rather to recognize the many factors that constitute her agency, the complex and multiple ways in which she is constituted as a historical actor."[15] While Hutchins and Rochester were constituted as political actors across widely differing ideological landscapes, these landscapes molded them in particular ways that I explain throughout the book. Importantly, it is the contradictions and ambiguities implicit in these various contexts that create the rich tapestry of Hutchins and Rochester's lives.

Having become entwined with the lives of this couple, I feel a great fondness for them. They are my friends, they feel like relatives, and they impress me enormously. But they also disappoint me: I especially have wanted them to be feminists and less orthodox communists. These "disappointments" remind me of the difficulties, if not impossibilities, of disentangling this mess of identification and interpretation: my readings of their work and memoirs are interpretive in that they imply as much about me as they do about the authors. In this sense, it is important as writers who write about other writers to acknowledge the situatedness of our/their own interpretations. For me this means that I must be conscious of the feminist lens through which I think and write and all the baggage I bring to this writing. As a white, British woman of working-class origin, married and a mother, born only a little before the last decade of Hutchins and Rochester's lives, and trained as a sociologist, my life experiences have framed this biography and have facilitated a whole host of emotions about the immense bourgeois privilege of Hutchins and Rochester, their life choices and motivations, their strong political passions, and their immense commitment toward social good.

Let me explain how the text is organized. Reflecting Hutchins and Rochester's entanglements with first, traditional Christianity, second, Christian socialism, and third, communism, the text is organized into three parts representing these chronological glimpses into their joint lives. Part one, "Dutiful Daughters," portrays the grounding of Hutchins and Rochester in the privileges of nineteenth-century and early twentieth-century bourgeois Christian culture. Chapters include: one, their New England girlhoods and years at Bryn Mawr College through the turn of the century; two, Rochester's extensive work with social reform organizations, and in particular the National Child Labor Committee and the Children's Bureau up through the second decade of the new century; and three, Hutchins's career as a missionary in China.

The cultural transitions of the early twentieth century found Hutchins and Rochester on the brink of changing times. By the 1920s their growing interest in socialism was challenging notions of religious faith for both of them. Part two, "Christian Socialists," discusses how their understandings of the sheer human misery involved with a rapidly industrializing society, and the lessons of World War I, helped facilitate an integration of socialism and pacifism with commitments to Christianity as an applied politics. It includes three chapters that cover first, their founding of a women's commune in New York City and the co-authoring of their 1922 *Jesus Christ and the World Today*; second, their involvement with the Fellowship of Reconciliation; and third, their "around the world trip" that led them to return in 1927 and join the Communist Party, USA, renouncing Christian socialism as a reformist, and therefore ultimately reactionary, movement.

As the 1930s ushered in a decade of economic depression, New Deal politics at home, and fascism abroad, Hutchins and Rochester's personal faith in God was replaced by a devotional and, they believed, more inclusionary faith in the collective vision of world communism. The Labor Research Association (LRA) claimed their time and energies; they wrote prolifically and gave strong loyalties to the American Communist Party. Part three, "Old Left Loyalists," traverses their involvement with communism from the thirties until the sixties. The first chapter of this section looks at Hutchins and Rochester's activities with the LRA and communist activism during the sectarian politics of the "Third Period," from 1927 to 1935. It explores their lives during these years and analyzes their writing. This period of communist disdain for alliances with noncommunist allies was followed by the years of the "Popular Front," during which coalitions were formed and support for communism was at an all-time high. This popularity was stymied by the Hitler–Stalin pact in 1939 at the start of World War II, although some support was regained after Stalin invaded the Soviet Union in 1941. This second chapter of part three spans the years from 1936 through the end of the war, a period that saw prolific intellectual production, for Rochester in particular. The final chapter examines the postwar period through the Cold War years and into the 1960s. It discusses Hutchins's involvement in Whittaker Chambers's testimony during the Alger Hiss trials and explores this period when government forces virtually decimated the Communist Party. *Comrades and Partners* ends with a focus on Hutchins and Rochester's lives together in their later years.

This couple had the good fortune to enjoy purposeful and principled lives and a loving relationship that lasted almost half a century. They lived through exciting decades and witnessed times of change and transition. Growing up on the historical cusp between nineteenth-century traditions and a rapidly industrializing modern society, they were among the first cohort of women who were able to reconcile their ambitions and the constraints of femininity by publicly committing themselves to a lifetime of service. To live simply, frugally, and committed to the cause of freedom and equality seemed always their hope. I will close with another excerpt from Hutchins's notebook:

> Courage yet, my brother or my sister!
> Keep on—Liberty is to be subserv'd whatever occurs;
> That is nothing that is quell'd by one or two failures, or any
>   number of failures,
> Or by the indifference or ingratitude of the people, or by any
>   unfaithfulness,
> Or the show of the tushes of power, soldiers, cannon, penal statutes.
>
> What we believe in waits latent forever through all the continents,
> Invites no one, promises nothing, sits in calmness and light, is
>   positive and composed, knows no discouragement,
> Waiting, patiently, waiting its time.
>
> Walt Whitman

PART ONE

DUTIFUL DAUGHTERS

CHAPTER ONE

EARLY YEARS

Grace Hutchins and Anna Rochester were born into wealthy New England families seeped in privilege and respectability. They grew up amidst spacious homes and summer cottages, wearing fine clothes and attended by maids and nannies. They had tutors and attended private schools, enjoyed dance lessons and horseback riding, and were able to travel all over the world. These childhoods prepared them for a life of privilege, and indeed, this is what they enjoyed. However, as adults, Hutchins and Rochester did not lead the bourgeois lives of their families and instead used these privileges to live by ethical principles without worry about material concerns and financial need. Yet still this upbringing brought with it profound contradictions that would help mold their later years.

For families such as the Hutchinses and Rochesters, the last decades of the nineteenth century were marked by times of flux and change. The bourgeois values of self-reliance, honesty, and frugality were being

Biography is a practice. It is a conscious product of human action just as *Comrades and Partners* is a retelling, not a realist interpretation of past lives. Nonetheless, how we represent such lives is about the ethical dilemma of finding responsible ways to write of who we/they are and working through how we understand what we understand. Research diary: March 20, 1997: "Problems keeping my imagination in check—who are these women? Are they the proper, cultured maiden ladies they appear or is my imagination meshing with some kind of cultural cover that frames them this way? [Knowledge about them] is piling up—[I feel] like an archaeologist sifting the debris. Or is this more what someone has called a 'reverse archaeology'— it feels like sifting through but really is also about building up?"

stretched by rapid industrialization and the emergence of vast urban centers. Old established families attempted to keep a grip on their moral edge in the face of social, economic, and technological changes through both industrial investments and public roles in religious and charitable organizations. The respectability granted to such wealthy families of this period was not unlike that afforded to European landed gentry; in response these families often acted as though they were the moral guiding forces behind their communities and took their leadership roles seriously. Alongside their philanthropy as leaders of and participants in charity organizations, such roles also included being "upholders of the faith," translated in New England families of the era into strong affiliations with the Anglican or other Protestant denominations. For children such as the young Grace and Anna, being born into these families meant being raised with a strong moral sense of duty to God, family, and community.

During the nineteenth century when boys were expected to go out in the world and perfect such virtues of classical masculinity as strength, honesty, and industry, girls were constrained by the gendered expectations of piety, purity, and domesticity often dubbed the "cult of true womanhood."[1] By the end of the century, however, middle-class women were transposing these virtues to suit themselves, such that the association with the private sphere of the home was broadened to include a nurturing and care for the wider community: "the conscience and the housekeepers of America."[2] These politics of domesticity allowed some women to expand their influence beyond the sphere of their immediate households into a kind of "municipal housekeeping" at the same time that the establishment of women's colleges facilitated the education of middle-class girls in preparation for a life of service to community.[3]

Research for a paper on missionary women first led me to the Grace Hutchins collection housed at the University of Oregon. I read with keen interest about Grace's years as a missionary and admired the adventurousness and spirit she combined with her religious devotion. Moving beyond this folder on her missionary experiences, I found myself engrossed reading about her life and quickly realized how entangled it was with the life story of Anna Rochester. The missionary paper was eventually completed, but my interest in Grace and Anna grew. While other research projects took priority over the next four or five years, I found myself returning again to this biographical work, often "rewarding" myself with a day in the archives on completion of other projects. I thought of it as my "back-burner" research—mostly because as a sociologist I was not sure I was qualified to write biography and was uncertain about my credibility as an author in this genre of writing. I have grown more comfortable as time has passed, but still suffer from the impostor syndrome on a somewhat regular basis.

Hutchins and Rochester were products of this era in being able to access the class privileges and social standing accorded to the offspring of elite families as well as enjoy a space to develop beyond the Victorian expectations for the daughters of such New England "first families." They witnessed the massive social upheavals of a rapidly industrializing society with its economic dislocations and uncertainties and responded with motivations and skills that were a result of their upbringing. Well schooled in the genteel behaviors expected of young upper middle-class women, they displayed a devotion to their families, to God, and, although often expressed in benevolent and patronizing ways, to the wider community. Since their early years followed a pattern of training in femininity with emphasis on service to others, they grew up expecting to be of use to the wider society and engaged in productive work. While this helped provide a basis for their radical humanitarianism as adults and their commitment to the improvement of society, it also gave the foundation for the paradox of their joint lives: how might they disrupt the very society that gave them the privilege to be disrupters in the first place?

Angel of Joy and Comfort

An only child, Anna Rochester was born in 1880 on March 30 to Louise Agatha (Bamman) and Roswell Hart Rochester. While there is less information about Anna's mother, Louise, her father, Roswell, was renowned as the grandson of Colonel Nathaniel Rochester who founded the city that was his namesake. The Colonel died in poverty on the family farm, the same place where Roswell Rochester was raised. Roswell began work as a clerk at the Western Union Telegraph Company in Rochester and eventually became the treasurer of the company, amassing a great deal of wealth along the way. Baby Anna was born in the family home on Fifty-sixth Street and Seventh Avenue, New York City, and moved with her family to Chestnut Cottage in Englewood, New Jersey, when she was three years old. As an only child of older parents (Louise was thirty-five and Roswell forty years old when she was born), Rochester was surrounded by doting family, attendants, and servants. Named after her aunt, the baby was welcomed into a household with all the material securities and comforts of the time.[4]

Louise recorded her daughter's life in a journal called the "AR Annals." Full of sentimental musings, this astonishing journal documented Anna Rochester's life from birth until young adulthood. It reflected a time when motherhood was justified as a full-time commitment and the family was increasingly being seen as a safe refuge from a cruel society.[5] The writing in the journal is sentimental, includes notions of esteem, love, duty, and benevolence, and is heavy on pathos, the rhetoric of sympathy, pity, or compassion.[6] However, even though the "AR Annals" is framed by cultural

Research diary: November 3, 1997: "[The sources I use here are] glimpses
of a larger kaleidoscope; [these sources] are fragments saved and survived
[that are] related in countless ways to fragments tossed and lost. [The motivation for] saving rather than tossing, besides chance and luck, [has in-
volved] realigning our lives in ways that complement who we are at that
present time with how we have imagined ourselves to be in the past. [In
this sense, this biography] is constructed on the fictions of Grace and
Anna's autobiographies, and, in particular, through the autobiographies of
their parents and the ways that they constructed reports of their children's
lives. [The case is then made for] a humble history that says it might have
occurred that way, reminding us that we transform the past by constructing it as the past of a different present."

expectations and clichés of doting mothers and dutiful daughters, it is still
very useful, not only because of the bulk of information about Rochester's
childhood in terms of names and dates and activities, but also because it
gives a glimpse of how an upper middle-class Victorian mother might have
wanted to represent the normative expectations of motherhood. A reader
besides Louise was expected since as the name "AR Annals" implies, it is a
record of her daughter's life, not a personal journal.

With many religious appeals to a higher power, the writing style in the
"AR Annals" is lofty and, interestingly, incorporates British spelling: a reflection of the Rochesters' elite status in New England society or perhaps
Louise's birth origins. Louise refers to her daughter as "the dear child" long
past her daughter's childhood, uses the third person to describe herself, and
alternates between the proud mother, sick wife, and long-suffering widow.
She writes of numerous health problems that included surgery on her eyes
in 1884 and the removal of her left eye a year later in the hope of relief from
headaches. Her health had especially deteriorated after a visit to Bermuda
in 1887, a deterioration that left her fragile and chronically ill. These early
years are full of Louise's domestic responsibilities managing a household
and her daughter's care and education, her religious commitments, and entertaining and visiting. Summers were spent at various summer resorts and
homes with family and friends, and traveling abroad. Roswell diligently
worked long hours at the Western Union Telegraph Company and in philanthropic endeavors in New York and Englewood. Anna's arrival into this
family came as a blessing and a disruption: a coddled, yet stubborn and
willful child.

From the very beginning, Louise Rochester paints a picture of her
daughter as very intelligent and strong willed. Anna was a determined tod-
dler who grew into a bright and opinionated child. Louise reports that
when her daughter was eighteen months old she had very clear convictions

as to her wants and needs, demonstrated a particularly strong will with little patience and perseverance, and was unduly overassertive on many occasions.[7] In response, Louise disciplined Anna in accordance with the expectations of respect and submission accorded to girl children of this era, and tried to bend the will of her determined little daughter with various forms of corporal punishment.[8] Such obedience and respect for parental authority was socialized early into Victorian children by a combination of fear associated with physical punishment and the internalization of strict moral codes. Inappropriate behavior by children, and especially by daughters, who strayed from this path of submission to parental authority was dealt with quickly and sternly. For Anna, discipline was administered through appeal to a strict moral and religious code. Certain passages from the Bible were chosen to illustrate positive behaviors, and recitations were necessary to make sure that the principles of those behaviors were understood.[9] It is not clear whether, by late twentieth-century standards, such "willful" demeanor might barely have evoked comment. For young Anna, however, these were important disciplinary lessons for the future.

Throughout her childhood, Rochester's strength of character continued to be an issue for Louise: it reflected the classic scenario of the mother who marveled at the strength of intellect and opinion of her daughter, yet wanted to mold her in her own image in order that the child and growing woman might avoid the pitfalls of a society that did not reward assertive and independent behavior in girls. Louise often articulated what she saw as a delicate balance of willful determination and stubborn principle in her daughter, exclaiming proudly that while young Anna showed great persistence in trying to carry her own point, there was always firm adherence to principle in all her actions.[10] This principled aspect of her nature was to be a central organizing feature for Rochester's adult life.

The molding of little Anna's character and behavior in accordance with the expectations of upper middle-class daughters was strongly influenced by the family's devout religious faith. Louise documented her daughter's spiritual development carefully since such development was an important and expected part of feminine middle-class gentility. Christened in May 1880 in the Protestant Episcopalian Church of St. Paul's in Englewood, Anna attended her first church service at age five years, and was confirmed a couple of weeks before her fourteenth birthday. Going to Sunday School and saying her prayers were important aspects of her early life; biblical lessons were meant to provide guidance and build an honorable character. At her daughter's confirmation at St. Paul's in 1894, Louise remarked that "for so young a girl, she understands the reality of the sacrifices of the Savior and struggles very hard to overcome her faults."[11] This religious observance of the moral codes of Christianity provided a structure for the "good" (i.e., simple, modest, decent, and in service to others) life: a lesson that was taught to her from a very early age, and, again, one serving as a strong guiding influence for her adult life.

In April 1883, the family moved to Chestnut Cottage in Englewood in order "to try the experiment of country living."[12] Louise Rochester soon discovered that while Anna might be opinionated and willful, she was also very intelligent. When repairs and alterations were being made to the new house, Anna, then three years old, completely astonished her parents by drawing an accurate description of the cess-pool and describing it in an intelligent way.[13] Louise continued to report on the precocious intellectual development of her daughter. One of her concerns was that she might become a mathematician, hardly a respectable occupation for a girl of her class and era: "Arithmetic is postponed because she knows too much of mathematics for her years and exercises her reasoning faculties more than is good for her."[14]

While the reports of Anna's superior intelligence might more accurately have reflected the perceptions of a doting parent upon an only child, Rochester did grow up to become an accomplished scholar. And, despite the lack of encouragement in mathematics, she became a well-respected economist with a penchant for statistics. However, as a child she was definitely encouraged to exercise her analytic capabilities in her study of music. Louise reported her young daughter's love for the piano and her numerous recitals and developing musical expertise.[15]

When Rochester turned nine years old she left the comfort of her private tutor and the local primary school to enter the Dwight School for Girls in Englewood. Here she followed a typical college preparatory course with a focus on the humanities and languages, and a strong emphasis on propriety, feminine decorum, and the social graces. By the time she was fifteen, she had made the decision to attend Bryn Mawr College because of its scholarly reputation, and, from then onwards, her studies were oriented toward the entrance exams, which she took and passed with flying colors.[16] These academic gifts were rewarded by her position as class president during her senior year at Dwight and the winning of a scholarship for Bryn Mawr College: a prestigious academic honor and a substantial sum of money.

The material circumstances of Rochester's family allowed her to travel at a young age. These experiences were probably very formative for her as a

Once I got over the initial embarrassment of being a voyeur of sorts, I found myself immersed in the details of Anna and Grace's lives. I felt like a detective piecing together "the story" from scraps of evidence. But when I had really decided I would write their biography, the research became more charged and more complicated: I was suddenly a biographer. That felt much less comfortable than the previous meddling I had been doing.

Anna Rochester (c. 1895).

child, giving her important educational experiences concerning the world around her and providing confidence and competencies that helped her mature. They also would most likely have reified her privilege as a white bourgeois American since such travel tended not to challenge the late-Victorian sense of world order. Like Hutchins, who also spent time abroad as a girl, Anna Rochester's world was expanded and her pleasures multiplied by the opportunity to travel. On the recorded trip to Great Britain, France, Switzerland, and Germany when Anna was sixteen years old, Louise made some interesting observations about her daughter:

> She proved "a good traveller" in being exempt from sea-sickness, in adapting herself to irrecircumstances, in learning promptly and accurately what to do and how to do it, where to go and how to get there. She acquired a good acquaintance with architecture and the Fine Arts, with History and customs, as could reasonably be expected under the circumstances and in the time available. . . . But, although seriously warned before leaving home of her then gravest fault: imperious disposition, overwhelming confidence in her own judgment—lack of respect for other peoples' opinions if in any way opposed to her own—determination to carry her plans over all opposing opinions and obstacles. She assumed and re-assumed *generalship* in spite of rebukes to a degree exceedingly trying to others and discreditable to herself. It is very pleasant to note that, since her return home—assisted, doubtless by the sense of relief from responsibility!—she has radically reformed her manner in those respects and has suppressed herself in a very encouraging degree. [original emphasis][17]

Rochester's opinionated nature that led her to assume "generalship" was indeed very trying for her mother. Needless to say such behavior might be within the bounds of acceptable behavior, or even perhaps encouraged, should she have been a boy. However, as a girl, her "imperious disposition" contradicted the modesty and delicacies of acceptable feminine behavior. Louise often reported these gendered shortcomings alongside comments on her daughter's strong principles. One gets the impression that while Louise approved of the principle, she disapproved of its forthright expression. Such a tension continued in the relationship between Rochester and her mother throughout the daughter's young adulthood as the strong will and principled character matured, exacerbated most likely by the fact that Rochester took responsibility for a mother whose refined gentility and physical frailty rendered her relatively incompetent much of the time. The following describes young Anna at age eleven:

> When she makes her rather frequent trips to the city with her mother for dentistry and other necessary business, she assumes responsibility which would be ridiculous except for the pathetic apology that her mother is timid in crowded streets on account of her blindness on the left side and Anna is sympathetically conscious of that but too considerate to mention it.[18]

> Of course this mention of "relief from responsibility" might have meant that Anna no longer needed to observe the social customs that dictated her public behavior rather than implying responsibility for her mother's well-being. Given the rhetoric of delicacy in which Louise indulged, it is not clear whether Louise was as dependent and fragile as she made out.

Louise seemed to have given her daughter mixed messages by socializing her in traditional ways and expecting her to undertake all the obligations of a dutiful daughter at the same time that she encouraged her intellectual growth (in certain areas). Years later Rochester recalled her mother giving her incentive for social activism: "Anna," she once said, "if I had your ideas, I'd want to do something about them."[19] Perhaps in some way Louise was living vicariously through Anna since she herself most likely had received little to no education outside of private tutors. While these mixed messages might have bred resentment in Rochester, they seem not to have been publicly articulated. Probably this situation facilitated ambivalence toward Louise on Rochester's part, encouraged no doubt by Louise's own ambivalence about being female in a patriarchal culture. Certainly Rochester took this to heart and lived a life quite different from her mother's.

In *Vera Brittain and Winifred Holtby: A Working Partnership*, Jean Kennard proposes the psychoanalytic theory that romantic friendships like those between British writers Brittain and Holtby, or Hutchins and Rochester, result from an incomplete separation between mother and daughter and the ambivalence toward the mother on the part of the daughter. Following Chodorow's theory that the resolution of this conflict occurs through the reproduction of mothering as women work out their relationships with their mothers in relationships with their daughters,[20] Kennard suggests that in this case the desire for connection is instead resolved through close female friendship:

> A close friend can help to resolve the ongoing struggle of the woman with her mother. The friend as a second self provides a way of separating from the mother without rejecting the female self-image she represents, for the friend is after all a similar image. The friend, like the mother, provides connectedness but not a connection that is an obstacle to independence.[21]

Kennard's suggestion is intriguing but not convincing. I have less faith in psychoanalytic explanations for a whole host of reasons; certainly, the realities of ambivalence on the part of the daughter toward the mother and the rewards of close female friendships are self-evident. The connections between these two are less clear. But female friendship would function to encourage female maturity, and especially autonomy, without breaking the

Feminists love these mother–daughter issues. It has also been suggested that as biographers we recreate our mothers through our relationships with our subjects since we can integrate and separate more effectively from them than from our biological mothers.[22] Sometimes Grace and Anna feel like dead grandmothers to me but consciously I find this theory hard to swallow.

bonds with the mother. A more likely sociological explanation is that women like Rochester and Hutchins experienced the myriad contradictions between the ideals of family life and the realities of the patriarchal family through the ambivalence they felt toward traditional motherhood. These early experiences of dissonance may have ultimately encouraged a rejection of such traditional roles and facilitated a different vision of womanhood, especially when it was a vision that could, and had, materialized for many women of the Progressive era.

Concerning Rochester's nontraditional journey, Louise wrote briefly of her fourteen-year-old daughter's somewhat rocky social development: "she takes as much pleasure in the society of grown people as in those of her own age. She is very critical of her acquaintances and has ceased to have special intimacy with any of her associates."[23] But by Thanksgiving of that same year Louise reported that her daughter had given an evening party for both boys and girls, and, when Anna was sixteen, Louise said that "she is now—and has been for some time past—regarded as having a handsome face and fine carriage, but is apparently devoid of vanity as to her personal appearance. She has many warm friends of her own age and sex but shows little interest in general society."[24] Louise implied here that Anna had girlfriends but displayed little interest in the social whirl of dating and courtship that probably filled the heads of many upper-class girls. Louise was quick to emphasize her daughter's "handsome face and fine carriage" (note she does not use "pretty" here; handsome is usually reserved for an older woman or someone male), and this phrase was juxtaposed with a description of Rochester's lack of vanity. All this paints the picture of a serious young woman, unimpressed perhaps by the superficialities of nineteenth-century femininity. This was in character with the adult whom Anna Rochester would become: an adult who would have little patience for "general society" as it related to the social scene, but much interest in general society meaning social and economic relationships. This latter entry by Louise in the "AR Annals" occurred right after the family had returned from their travels abroad in Europe. It was relatively common among prosperous families like the Rochesters to take a daughter on a grand tour of Europe prior to her "coming out" and entrance on the marriage scene.

There again, another picture paints Anna as awkward and homely, and, rather than rejecting this social scene because of a mature, what we might call feminist analysis, she rejected it because she was not included in it.

A First-Family Boston Daughter

Grace Hutchins was born on August 19, 1885, in Boston, Massachusetts, in a large, gracious Beacon Street home lined with books and portraits. She was the third of three daughters born to Susan Barnes Hurd and Edward Webster Hutchins, although her sisters Louise and Helen died in 1887 when Grace was two years old. The cause of death of these children is not clear, although most likely they succumbed to one of the fatal childhood illnesses so common during this era. Two more children were born, both sons: Henry in 1889 and Edward in 1890, making Grace the eldest child and only daughter. The family was affluent and aristocratic, claiming colonial ancestry on both sides of their lineage. Grace's father was born in 1851 and graduated from Harvard Law School before entering his father's law practice. This firm, founded in 1844 by Henry C. Hutchins and Alex Wheeler, was one of the oldest and most prestigious in New England. Grace's mother, born in Charlestown in 1860, was a Colonial Dame and the daughter of Julia Edwards and Major Charles H. Hurd, a veteran of the Civil War. The Hurd/Hutchins families boasted ancestors who traveled to America prior to 1640 and who fought in both the American Revolution and the Civil War. Susan and Edward were married in Boston in December 1880.

While the folders holding the scraps of material about Grace's childhood provide interesting insights, they do not have the kind of (deceptive) continuity that the "AR Annals" give since they are more fragmented and involve multiple voices. However, because I have more sources for understanding Grace's childhood compared to Anna's, the cumulated "whole" gives a more human picture even while it leaves more gaps in terms of information. This is probably also why Grace's childhood seems more permissive than Anna's. The "AR Annals" is the major source of information for Anna, while for Grace there are a series of affectionate letters written to and from her parents. It is hard to say whether such kinds of letters were lost for Anna or never existed. In addition, this sentimental rhetoric so apparent in the writings associated with Grace and Anna's girlhoods encourages an overprivileging of them as genteel little girls constrained by nineteenth-century femininity. Obviously unclear is how much this discourse reflected actual behavior.

The house at 166 Beacon Street, with its maids and tutors, provided a comfortable and privileged place for Grace to spend her childhood. The Hutchins summer home in Brooksville, Maine, with its fresh air and large garden, gave similar blessings, as well as friendship with the likes of Polly Porter, life-partner of New Deal politician Molly Dewson, who summered close by. Porter was orphaned during adolescence and she developed a close relationship with Hutchins's mother whom she called "Aunt Susy." Porter and Hutchins remained very good friends throughout their lives.[25] As an adult Hutchins was often referred to as gracious and dignified; her roots in respectable upper-class Bostonian society gave her an edge and a quiet confidence. This upbringing provided the training in bourgeois feminine behavior: delicacy, grace, modesty, and piety. Like Rochester, Hutchins's adult life reflected this early training.

Despite their wealth and social prominence, or because of it, Susan and Edward Hutchins were responsible philanthropists as well as upright Bostonians. There was a strong benevolent tradition among privileged Bostonians, which Armory, in *The Proper Bostonians,* quips "is given to settle the well-known ever-gnawing Proper Bostonian conscience."[26] After the deaths of her two elder daughters, Susan volunteered at the Baldwinsville Hospital for Crippled Children and also at the Home for Aged Women. She was active in the Society for Colonial Dames and local gardening clubs. As such she provided young Hutchins with an early role model for civic responsibility. Hutchins's father also provided an example of upstanding civic duty, founding the Legal Aid Society in Boston and working on various boards. Born during the beginning of the Progessive era, a period that historians often mark as the onset of contemporary America, Hutchins witnessed the influx of women into reform work. Like Rochester, but even more so since she was five years her junior, Hutchins was surrounded by women involved in public service.

As a young girl, Hutchins seems to have been a perfect pupil; her Primary Report reads that the eight-year-old had excellent study habits and was an inspiration to her class in always being faithful, reliable, and honest.[27] When she progressed to Miss Folsom's School for Girls in Marlborough Street, Boston, she continued to show herself as a willing and able pupil who received an excellent report, earned by faithful and persistent work.[28] She also showed a penchant for writing at an early age: "The alder by the river shakes out her powdery curls. The willow buds in silver for little boys and girls. The little birds fly over, and oh, how sweet they sing to tell the happy children that once again it's spring."[29] This was penned in the most beautiful handwriting by Hutchins when she was seven years old, and was kept as an example of her "first story." She also created a small magazine entitled *Children's Weekly,* a volume that issued several numbers during the spring and summer of 1896. It contained stories, verse, jokes and riddles, as well as a series of astute remarks about neighboring families and commu-nity events.[30] Hutchins included stories written by her childhood friend Hildegarde Allen as well as her own writing, but saw herself as editor-in-charge. The weeklies show a confident, literate child with a budding sense of humor, as well as a developing social commentary. Having brothers, she no doubt was exposed to the rough and tumble of boys, and, despite her schooling in femininity, seemed to have enjoyed outdoor adventures. She must have been a relatively athletic child given her college career in athlet-ics, and she comes across as energetic and outgoing. Letters written to and

Grace Hutchins in 1900, aged 15 years.

received from her parents during these early years suggest that Hutchins enjoyed a caring and affectionate relationship with both and was especially close to her father.[31]

A girl child born into privileged circumstances might expect nothing less for herself than to be part of the public effort to elevate society; certainly this rapidly changing world offered opportunities the like of which had not been experienced before by women of earlier generations. Surrounded by the genteel comforts and delicacies of nineteenth-century bourgeois life, girl children were expected to develop their empathetic and pious natures toward the elevation of family and society. Femininity was seen as a natural marker of their role as the conscience of industrial-corporate greed and governmental indifference. These were the times of Hutchins's girlhood—times that constrained her clearly within normative standards of femininity, yet gave her permission to do good deeds within a limited public domain in the very name of womankind. These good deeds were circumscribed by Hutchins's religious faith; like many of Boston's social elite, the Hutchinses were members of Trinity Episcopalian Church. As Rochester's father had been a vestryman of their church and president of the local Bible Society, so also Hutchins's father was a vestryman and senior warden of Trinity Church of Boston.

Hutchins also had the good fortune to travel in her youth. This provided invaluable education in the culture, history, art and politics of other societies, and facilitated independence, confidence, and poise. The first recorded trip overseas for Hutchins occurred when she was thirteen years old and gave her over six months away from home. From September 1898 to March 1899 she traveled extensively on this "around the world" trip with her parents. Letters sent to "Aunty Grace" (Hutchins's mother's sister, Grace Hurd Howell) were later typed and bound in a brown leather-covered book with the following inscription: "Letters of Travels, Around the World, by Grace Hutchins, September 11, 1898–March 28, 1899." The letters give a wonderfully detailed travel log written from the perspective of a thirteen-year-old child; they move between naïve wonder and excitement, and arrogant ethnocentric judgment. Even at such a young age, Hutchins's very beautiful prose describing these new surroundings was written with great delicacy.

Actually, there is no *direct* "evidence" from Grace's childhood to explain her later strong religious devotions except these church affiliations of her parents. Affiliation may reflect social custom and desire for respectability as much as authentic spiritual belief. It is possible that her keen religious faith was inspired after she left home and became involved with the Christian Union at Bryn Mawr.

The tone of the writing is interesting; it moves between a feminized rhetoric that takes on a somewhat tentative and often circuitous tone, describing experiences in ways that imply rather than state, and then bold exclamations and judgments that revealed her youth and confidence, and established her individuality as an adventurous young explorer. These exclamations often disrupted the more descriptive writing and suggest a bright child with keen powers of observation and frank insight who was learning to adopt the stylized language appropriate for her gender and class.

This writing also portrays the ethnocentrism and arrogance with which wealthy white travelers observed the indigenous colonized people of the world, and young Hutchins often came across as snobbish, elitist, and racist. Whether she was describing "loafing Indians," the "most hideous monkey looking Chinamen," or the "open mouthed [Japanese] natives, nearly naked,"[32] the enormous race and class privilege of her situation contextualized all this writing. She accepted being the voyeur of all these different cultures, exclaiming that the Chinese steerage passengers were "rather interesting to watch" and the Japanese were "the most unmusical people in the world."[33] They became "others" through her eyes and ears— her glance reflected the privilege of her race and class, and "normality," be it the modalities of music, dress, or aspects of personal hygiene, became squarely centered in her white, upper middle-class reality. The writing also illustrates the strong patriotism Hutchins felt as an American, and, perhaps, as a Boston loyalist. As such, her patriotism was especially directed against the English, whom she perceived as overly stuffy and putting on airs,[34] ironically, perhaps, a first inkling of her intolerance for inherited wealth and power.

Surrounded by servants, agents, and guides, the family traveled from North America to Japan, Hong Kong, Singapore, Ceylon, Egypt and the Nile region, and on to Italy, Central Europe, and England before returning home. Hutchins's father, Edward Sr., appeared to have some business along the way, but the trip was definitely one intended for pleasure and education. Since travel was then, as today, considered a most invaluable education for young people, the trip was most likely timed for Hutchins, positioned as she was on the brink of womanhood.

The "Letters of Travels" begin with a description of the train journey from Boston to Vancouver, where their ship was moored. Grace wrote of the poverty and sheer desolation of the homesteads and settlements crossing the prairies, and the Indians, whom she deprecatingly characterized as wild people and passive loafers, hawking their wares while surrounded by dirty children. Awed by the beauty of the countryside, she captured the majesty of the Columbia gorge area with its "magnificent mountains towering overhead, covered with snow and glistening in the sun. Mountain brooks poured down their sides, leaping precipices and roaring through canyons to join the river.

I wonder how much of the travel log was edited when typed and published, and if it is exhaustive of all the correspondence Grace had with her aunt. Selective editing, retention, or disposal of certain letters or passages would have been very easy at that point. And since there is so much more of this travel log than I can use and I select certain passages, what I've got here is my editing of their (probably) editing.

The train wound round mountains on a narrow ledge, now shooting through a tunnel to rocks and emerging into the sunshine again, now crossing a chasm many feet deep. Far below us ran the Columbia River, rushing over rocks, and tumbling down rapids doing its best to reach the ocean."[35]

Overall, while this travel broadened her horizons and provided a crucial education, it most likely consolidated her sense of privilege and her ethnocentric attitudes. I believe this travel and the other trips she was able to make throughout her childhood whet her appetite for travel and adventure and were an important influence on her decision to work in the overseas mission. An unquestioned sense of her own privilege and a benevolent attitude toward those less fortunate than herself, coupled with a strong sense of adventure and devout Christian beliefs, were all useful, if not necessary, ingredients for her future life as a missionary. After several weeks sailing along the Nile and visiting and sight-seeing in Europe, Hutchins reluctantly prepared for her return to Boston with the strong desire to travel again.[36]

Bryn Mawr Years

Founded in 1885, Bryn Mawr was a very young college when Anna Rochester entered its halls in 1897. Like the other Seven Sisters Colleges, Bryn Mawr was able to provide strong academic training comparable to that received by men of this period. Hutchins and Rochester were among the first women in the United States who were "purposefully educated to be full 'political persons.'"[37] For the most part, Bryn Mawr College provided a supportive environment where young women could be challenged intellectually and create for themselves the foundation for a productive public life. This was the Bryn Mawr that Anna Rochester entered in 1897 and Grace Hutchins in 1903. The college gave women opportunities to form societies and clubs, learn organizational skills, and create networks and mentoring relationships crucial for women's later activities in the political sphere. Such an education also facilitated rhetorical skills through course work in the classics, composition, and elocution, as well as through literary, law, debate and other societies where women were encouraged to practice and fine-tune their skills in speaking and writing. Such instruction was considered essential for maintaining a practice of informed discourse within participatory democracy. Teachers saw educated women as future civic leaders who would exercise their "natural" moral influence.

Martha Carey Thomas (1857–1935), president of Bryn Mawr College from 1894 to 1921, was an exceptional woman who was devoted to furthering the advancement of women in society through education. Having received her B.A. from Cornell and her Ph.D. from the University of Zurich, Thomas became dean and professor of English at Bryn Mawr in 1885 and president of the college in 1894. She believed passionately that women should have the right to education and that they should find their "greatest happiness in congenial work." Hutchins reflected many years later, at her fiftieth class reunion, that Thomas encouraged them to think independently and be open-minded about new ideas and changes: "it helped us, I think, to have what has been called 'the ability to meet whatever comes in the unknown tomorrow.'"[38]

Suffrage clubs were present at all women's colleges, and at least at Bryn Mawr, the president of the college was enthusiastic about their presence. Indeed, Susan Walker Fitzgerald (Bryn Mawr class of 1893) was the recording secretary of the National American Woman Suffrage Association. Many years later it was recalled that Hutchins developed suffragist sympathies while at college, and, even though these views seem not to have been acted upon in any official capacity, they were still distressing to her parents.[39] Yet while young women's education during this period could hardly have avoided such important and timely issues as suffrage, for the most part this education was a classical one. Both Hutchins and Rochester took course work in history, languages, literature, and the classics, with a smattering of

Research diary: March 31, 1998: "[Since I must admit an ongoing wish that Grace and Anna were more feminist, I was] excited to read again about Grace's suffragist leanings, though I wonder how her work with the Christian Union and her religious beliefs would have affected her politics [on the question of women's status in society]. As today, membership in both groups did not necessarily imply a contradiction in beliefs, although the religious and moral training would have had some impact on her beliefs about woman's place. Contacted Bryn Mawr but there was no mention of her formal involvement in any suffrage organizations. Obviously, she could very easily have attended meetings and had suffragist views even though she did not take any formal leadership positions in organizations. [Also possible is that] her memories [of her relationship to feminism during this period] were revised in later life when she was a more politically active woman. [This could be an example of how Grace's memory] better represents her then-self at the age of 77 when these words about suffragist sympathies were spoken than her affiliations at the age of 17."

courses in the social and physical sciences. Hutchins majored in philosophy and English, while Rochester, initially interested in the classics, did not declare a major before she left the college in 1899.

For many students of this era, Christianity provided a moral code of conduct for thought and behavior and was an integral part of their lives. The Christian Union at Bryn Mawr provided a place for devout students to come together, study the Bible, pray, and organize lectures and speakers. When Hutchins entered Bryn Mawr in 1903 she seemed immediately to have found her niche in the Christian Union. Such an organization would have given her an immediate community, allowing an organized outlet for her religious devotion as well as a place for her to develop leadership skills and mature socially. She was an eager member of the union during her freshman year and was elected secretary for the Christian Union in 1904–1905. She then became the treasurer the following year, and president during her senior year.[40] Presidential activities in the union involved making speeches, organizing lectures and sermons, and teaching Bible classes.[41] The *Recorder*, published monthly by the Christian Union, also described its Christian-inspired social reform endeavors.[42]

Hutchins was well known at college as an outstanding all-around athlete and, according to her, known more for her athletic prowess than academic accomplishments.[43] These athletic accomplishments were impressive: avid tennis player and winner of the Tennis Tournament cup in 1906, captain of both the basketball and baseball teams for her class, and captain of the varsity basketball team. She played on her class hockey team all through col-

Grace and friends during tennis, 1919. Grace's friend Polly Parker in the back row, far left, and Grace is in the back row, second left.

lege and, at least in 1905, for the varsity team. She was also a member of the committee for managing varsity practice times. She competed in track, participating in relay and tug-of-war, and threw the shot put 24 feet 6 inches, receiving second place in a 1906 tournament.[44] Alongside athletics, Hutchins also participated in the Law Club, functioned as secretary in 1905, and was a regular debater during their debates.[45] Life for her at Bryn Mawr sounded rich and full. Active in so many extracurricular activities, she seemed to have eagerly accepted leadership positions. She comes across as energetic, confident, and outgoing.

While there are no mentions in any of Hutchins's memoirs of any relationships with boys or potential male suitors during these years before or during Bryn Mawr (which of course does not imply that there were not any), Hutchins seemed to have had strong friendships with women. There is one scrap of a letter left from this earlier period that records an intense friendship with a girl named Margaret Reeve, whom Hutchins met at college. In a letter that dates to the fiftieth class reunion in 1957, Margaret Reeve Carey wrote of Hutchins's upcoming birthday to be spent at Rockport by the sea and recalled some fond memories of their times together at Cape Rosier near Castine, close to Hutchins's summer home, "Fir Cones":

> But I hope for you as for me crying gulls on rocks bring back the wonderful picture of the rocks at Cape Rosier, those rocks scented with blue-berry bushes and sweet fern, and the gulls far below in the bay calling as we prayed and studied together and were in a beautiful communion with one another. Never do I see gulls clustered on rocks and crying their beautiful inimitable cry but I am back there with you. They were the days of a perfect friendship, of completely shared lives and thoughts, and forever they will be one of the most vivid and most precious intervals in my life. Never to be forgotten intervals. So I love to think about you at Rockport, so different from lonely and lovely Cape Rosier, listening to those gulls and remembering, too, remembering with nostalgea [sic] and love the gulls of cold Penobscott Bay.[46]

Compared to Hutchins, there is a distinct silence surrounding Rochester's two years at Bryn Mawr from 1897 to 1899. Rochester did not hold leader-

> I found this letter buried in the "unidentified letters" file of Grace's papers. It was typed and unsigned and Grace had penciled in "Margaret," the Margaret I deduced as Margaret Reeve from her cohort at Bryn Mawr. The letter follows in the tradition of intense emotional relationships between women characteristic of the period and makes me aware of all the letters I am most likely missing. It is easy to romanticize these relationships by constructing a lost time of innocence because, rhetorically, they were presented in this nostalgic way.

ship positions in clubs or organizations, and there is no record of any extracurricular participation. Relatively shy and less outgoing than Hutchins, it seems Rochester invested less in the community.[47] However, her eventual decision to leave Bryn Mawr concerned her mother's well-being when her father died unexpectedly over Thanksgiving, 1897, during one of her first visits home. Roswell's death was very hard on Louise, who, throughout the many years that she wrote the "AR Annals" had commented about her own ill health and loss of sight. Eventually the strains of widowhood were too much for her, and, demonstrating those classic feminine, upper-class, Victorian traits of delicacy and nervous sensibility, she responded with a mental and physical collapse. At first, Rochester stayed on at Bryn Mawr and her mother survived her absence, though only barely. In the journal Louise used many conventionalized appeals to sympathy in reporting this difficult period of her life. Her daughter was the dear child likened to an angel, her departed spouse, the beloved husband. Her own role was that of the grieving, abandoned widow attempting to carry through on her husband's dying wish. There was much intense feeling in her representation of these emotions; the reader is invited to share her feelings of nostalgia and wistful loneliness in being parted from both her husband and her child, and to experience her great joy when she was together again with Anna: "the visit is like that of an angel of joy and comfort."[48] In this writing between 1897 and 1899, Louise comes across as chronically ill, fragile, and dependent: a conventionalized role for middle-class widows of this period.

In the fall of 1898, at the beginning of Anna's sophomore year, Louise had to face seeing her daughter return to college. Then, after the Christmas vacation, Louise suffered a swift emotional and physical deterioration and eventually another nervous collapse.[49] This led to Rochester taking on the classic role of the devoted care-giving daughter, evident in her writing to her mother about leaving Bryn Mawr after the second term of her sophomore year in order to take full responsibility for Louise's care: "I do so wish that you would let me do what I want and not come back to college but devote myself to making you happy."[50] Louise's condition seemed to have been caused more by depression and loneliness than physical factors. In the following quote, the question mark after Louise's use of the term "misfortune" to describe her plight leaves open for speculation whether she eventually saw her collapse as less of a misfortune than a blessing since it led to her daughter's return home:

> Anna's mother had the misfortune (?) to show unmistakable signs of nervous collapse about April first. . . . On the dear daughter's return from college May 7th—the enclosed letter [in the "AR Annals"] was sent to her mother. It is needless, perhaps, to recount that her mother prized that letter above all things that the daughter had ever written before. The solicitation of friends

It is hard from the perspective of today, especially knowing Louise's great class privilege, to give her the sympathy she wants. I find myself having little patience for what in this present historical moment we would probably characterize as neurosis. As is often typical of mothers, Louise disappears as her daughter's life is constructed. This account by Louise, continued for so long, is poignant in its silence about her *own* life, except its construction through very conventionalized rhetoric. There are ethical issues involved in my representing her now as a neurotic woman when that subject position belonged in a completely different historical moment.

and relatives were so strongly in favor of Anna's plan, that with many a pang of being obliged to give up the cherished hope of fulfilling the beloved husband's desires regarding her education, [she] has decided to stay here.... May God who directs our paths, grant that the noble sacrifice made by the dear child may so enrich her character, that the loss of the two subsequent years of college may be as nothing compared with the joy of the sacrifice.[51]

Despite this interruption in her studies and being cast in the role of companion and caretaker, events proved somewhat fortuitous for Rochester as she and Louise left Englewood for extended travels in Europe. The summer of 1899 was spent in England, and then travels continued to Austria, where they spent the winter, and where Rochester was schooled as a concert pianist. Alongside her studies, she "had to be nurse as well as student and performer at the galleries and opera houses, [since] her mother collapsed, utterly, and stayed in bed six full months." After visits to Antwerp, Paris, and several cities in Italy, Louise and Anna returned to their new home at Pine Lodge, Englewood, in November 1900.[52]

Louise continued to express guilt and regret that her daughter was not able to graduate with the class of 1901. Her writings on this issue are loaded with sentimental and nostalgic thoughts. No doubt the journal was a place for her to record feelings of remorse that her daughter had been prevented from receiving her degree, and to assuage any guilt feelings through sentimental expression, attempts to invoke the sympathy of the reader, and appeals to a higher power. In May of 1901, while Rochester was visiting her classmates at the college prior to their graduation, Louise wrote,

As the time for the graduation draws near, she little knows, with what regret and sorrow her mother mourns again that she (the dear child) can not take her place with the others, where she would have shone brightly, and receive her diploma which the dearly beloved husband and father had planned for her to hold—But He knows best.[53]

When Rochester was setting out for Europe with her mother, Hutchins had just returned from European travels with her family. Both were launched into adulthood as dutiful daughters: religious, genteel, educated and well traveled. As the first decade of the twentieth century came to an end, Hutchins and Rochester faced relatively bright futures, even though these futures were bordered by the constraints of nineteenth-century femininity. And they were in good company: thousands of similarly placed women had graduated from women's colleges and were looking forward to productive careers. While, unlike Hutchins and Rochester, most of these women did eventually marry, the precedent had been set for women to anticipate a lifetime of service outside the home in the company of other women. Single women devised new ways of living in community with each other: in settlement houses, religious communities, and women's colleges, as well as in less structured communal arrangements, where they were able to enjoy emotional benefits and an environment conducive for networking and mentoring.[54] In these segregated spaces, women like Hutchins and Rochester learned to live in community with each other, developing bonds of emotional intimacy and important networks for public service. Their desire and ability to live in community with each other were influenced by the frequency and acceptance of same-sex pairing, which, at that time (prior to the 1930s), was not necessarily equated with sexual love.[55] Not yet having met each other, Hutchins and Rochester most likely sought to escape the constraints of marriage and enjoy such companionship of women through their personal ideologies of religious duty and service.

In this way, Hutchins and Rochester emerged into the twentieth century loaded with the gendered and class-related baggage of late-Victorian society. However, at the same time, privileged and educated, they were able to enjoy the precedent set by the hoards of educated, unmarried women who were moving into public life in service of others. This notion of service, inherited from families concerned with philanthropy, was a way of reconciling the contradictions between their personal and professional ambitions and their feminine upbringing. It was a paradox for them to be so situated as religious, devoted, and so thoroughly grounded in the delicacies of middle-class femininity, yet bright, ambitious women who did not (perhaps unconsciously) want to replicate their mothers' lives. The discourses that

> The cultural memory implicit in biography is always shaped in a contested field. In other words, the historical moment is essentially a productive one since it provides the cultural context for autobiography, for biography as the interpretation of someone else's autobiography, and for the act of reading itself at this very moment.

emerged with the unfolding of a new century allowed women like Hutchins and Rochester to be constructed as historical markers for this emerging modern period, integrating the contradictions of the period and working through them by putting energies and ambitions into feminine areas of public service. Rochester began reform work with children and families and Hutchins embarked on missionary work overseas.

CHAPTER TWO

SOCIAL REFORM

In the spring of 1899 when thirteen-year-old Grace Hutchins had returned to Miss Folsom's School in Boston, wiser and more sophisticated on account of her travels abroad, Anna Rochester was preparing to leave Bryn Mawr to care for her widowed mother and to accompany her on travels in Europe. For a little over a year, Rochester traveled extensively and received musical training in some of the most famous musical centers of Europe, fine-tuning her skills as a highly accomplished pianist and musician. The Rochesters were privileged and sheltered women who would have enjoyed the style and comforts of travel expected by the wealthy classes of the time. Alexandra Allen's notes about the "travelling ladies" in her book of the same name most likely described the Rochesters's travel experience:

> A middle-class background seems to have been the common denominator of the travelling ladies. With two or three exceptions, their families had both money and prestige; relatives and near-relatives, friends and acquaintances, British and foreign government officials, opened their doors to them and letters of introduction afforded them comfortable passages en route. In the less rough parts of the globe, land and sea conveyances were arranged without much trouble, and when a short or long stay was needed, there were always cottages, villas, and even luxurious retreats, to be rented for a nominal sum.[1]

In November 1900, when the mother and daughter returned home to Pine Lodge from these extended travels, Rochester continued her musical training at Barnard and at Columbia University, taking classes in musical dictation and the history of music as well as performance. Louise was still physically and emotionally fragile, complaining of "nervous exhaustion." A "cult of invalidism" that labeled well-to-do women delicate and sensitive survived into the first decades of the twentieth century, prescribing rest

> "Biography attracts us as writers and readers because of qualities it shares with literature. Puzzling out the narrative of another woman's life, we recognize dimensions of her character to which she herself is blind and consequently discover new dimensions and possibilities in ourselves. That project of self-discovery is open-ended, for just as we 'remain a mystery to ourselves' so the biographies we write remain incomplete. We have challenged the illusion of objectivity and given up the arrogance of believing that we can, once and for all, get our foremothers right. Second readings thus come with the territory of feminist biography. For only by telling new stories and telling our stories anew can we glimpse the truths that emerge not once and for all but all in their own good time."[2]

cures and encouraging women to forgo certain activities and interests in favor of idleness and "feminine" pursuits. Such nervous exhaustion, termed neurasthenia, was especially linked to middle-class urban existence and was most common among women.[3]

On arriving back home after their travels in Europe, Rochester became involved in some philanthropic work in Englewood, most likely through her church, St. Paul's Episcopalian.[4] She also started teaching Sunday School at St. Paul's and developed a strong religiosity that seemed to provide much personal sustenance during these years of early adulthood. For the first decade of this new century Rochester is said to have divided her time between studying the Bible and teaching Sunday School, tutoring music and piano to private students, and caring for her invalid mother. Alongside her Sunday School classes, Rochester began directing a boy's choir, and, by 1905, was presiding over the Junior Auxiliary, a preparatory religious organization for girls, at St. Paul's. During the summer of 1905 she also worked as an accompanist for the Choral Clubs of Washington and Lichfield in Connecticut.[5] Throughout this period, Rochester's devotion to Christianity deepened and her interest in missionary service was piqued. However, this was most likely stymied by the need to care for her mother, as Hutchins's missionary service, although eventually actualized, seems also to have been constrained by the wishes of her mother.[6]

While Louise would have wanted to represent her unmarried adult daughter in as respectable and devout a light as possible, and therefore may

> Research diary: March 20, 1997: "Imagine to have been able to travel and live like this. What incredible experiences Anna must have had to witness a changing Europe on the brink of a new century. It brings up envy as one of many possible motivations for writing biography."

have overstated her saintly virtues, Rochester appears to have been fully committed to a life of service. Louise wrote:

> Truly this dear child lives a noble life, consecrated to God and His Course of Earth. . . . Her [Sunday School] work is resumed and the enthusiasm of its management, as well as that of the Junior Auxiliary is very gratifying to behold, and very advantageous to the girls. She takes upon herself three small boys, the beginnings of piano playing. She is no laggard. Her days are wellspent working largely for others. She does systematic reading and leads a "simple life" in the midst of much that might lead many another girl to a very different existence. . . . May God bless the darling daughter—who, in the simplicity and grandeur of her faith, thanks Him and rejoices in that which without that faith might have been a sore trial. May He supply all her needs, He sincerely will. . . . Anna's deep interest in Bible study in preparation for the weekly session of her Bible class takes much of her time, but it is time wellspent for her godmother and her mother who know her best, and study her most closely. So many signs of growth and progress in her private life as a Christian woman. The corners are being rubbed down, and she is developing not only into a deeper spiritual growth, but in charm of manner and general attractiveness.[7]

Louise's emphasis on "all" in terms of God fulfilling her daughter's needs might relate to her realization that this daughter of hers would probably never marry. The corners "being rubbed down" tells of the ongoing softening of the assertive personality, with its strong "generalship" that Louise perceived as characterizing Rochester's youth, toward a more compliant and thus more socially acceptable adult femininity. Louise had remarked earlier in the journal about Rochester's lack of interest in high society; now she constructed her daughter's life as one fulfilled by moral and religious passions. It is impossible to say whether and how much Louise overstated these religious motivations in reaction to Rochester's unmarried state or out of a need to write in the particular sentimental way that elevates "the dear child" into a saintly role, thus casting her own self in a role deserving of sympathy: the long-suffering widow. Perhaps Rochester's religious commitments were cultivated in part as a response to her responsibilities as a caregiver, and that without these obligations, she might have led a more secular life. It is also

---

If Anna had kept a journal herself during these years, what might it reveal? I find myself too easily accepting the devoted spinster daughter throwing away her promising young life in order to care for her widowed sick mother stereotype—the stuff of Victorian novels and still somewhat of a cultural cliché. This is again a reflection of the reliance on the heavily rhetoricized "AR Annals."

not clear whether Rochester might have wanted to avoid marriage and potential suitors; in this case the role of the devout, care-taking daughter might
have effectively kept her out of circulation. It is hard to say, although a
poem, unsigned but written in Rochester's hand, sheds some light on this
topic. It is untitled and undated, though written on printed stationery from
Englewood, New Jersey, most likely dating it sometime prior to 1915 when
Rochester moved to Washington, D.C., to work at the Children's Bureau:

> I have no child, no "other self" on whom to pour
> The free forgiveness that we mete ourselves;
> I have no lover whose adoration flatters me,
> No husband, who is part of me,
> To shield and cherish.
> Must I be barren, then, and poor in love and giving?
>
> To friends I give a horrid dole,
> No great largesse, but stinted as I weigh their faults,
> And measured with their love for me.
> I've seen the love that kindles till it leaps beyond the self,
> Consuming judgment,
> Transmuting life to pure and selfless flame
> But still I cherish self.
> Must I be poor and cold forever?[8]

In making sense of this poem it is important to emphasize that Rochester
might not have composed it, but copied it from elsewhere. If that were the
case, then it must still have been a meaningful statement for her, enough to
copy and keep. My sense is that Rochester did write this poem. She is hard
on herself for her judgmental nature, which affected relationships with others, and regretted not having the "joys" of marriage: the lover to flatter, the
husband to shield and cherish, and the child on whom she could shower
love and affection. Despite these regrets, she asserts her own will: "But still I
cherish self," a testimony to her ambitions as well as to the constraints of traditional marriage. I believe this statement reflected her insight concerning

---

I feel hesitant about sharing this poem since it was probably composed
when she felt depressed and lonely and has the power to represent more
than the mood in which it was written. Most of us have written poetry during times of feeling blue and sorry for ourselves, and most would also be
embarrassed to find that a poem written in a dark moment or period came
to illustrate our "true" feelings or general state. I also admit I don't like to
think that this poem implied that Anna was "passed over" or that she was
disappointed not to have experienced traditional marriage. I want to privilege her with a different kind of agency.

the social construction of women's love as necessarily selfless. If "self" was an independent, ambitious woman with strong opinions and hopes for a career, then to be married and a mother during this period would mean, in effect, to give up self. This poem suggests Rochester did regret not having the love and emotional comforts she saw among her married friends and family members, but understood that the price she would have to pay for these was too high. I believe Rochester hoped for love and was pained at this point by its absence, but left it for the record that she understood the context and consequences of such love during this period of history. A final thought concerning this poem is that the work in which Rochester would be involved, with its focus on children and families, most likely would have kept the issue about her own single, childless state at the forefront of her consciousness. It probably facilitated her seeing the worst of family life as well as imagining the best, and helps further explain the context of this poem.

Somewhere between 1905 and 1908 Rochester became very interested in the teachings of socialism, a political ideology that saw much popular support during this period. In the context of mass political upheaval and socioeconomic change, such radicalism was a flourishing political and intellectual force. Rochester was taken by the Socialist Party presidential candidate Eugene Debs and, after hearing him speak during a rally in New York City, was excited by his political platform that promised so much for working people. Rochester supported him in 1908 and again in 1912 and 1920, volunteering during some of his early campaigns. In 1908 she also read Marx's *Das Kapital* and was becoming interested in the writings of Christian socialism after having read several influential books by Walter Rauschenbusch on Christianity and the social order.[9] The other piece in understanding Rochester's movement toward socialism is her involvement with the Society of the Companions of the Holy Cross (SCHC), which maintained a spiritual community dedicated to the pursuit of social justice and ran a retreat center called Adelynrood in South Byfield,[10] and her friendship with Christian socialists Vida Scudder and Florence Converse. Vida Scudder was a settlement worker and outspoken Wellesley English professor, and her romantic partner, Florence Converse, edited the *Atlantic Monthly* for many years. This friendship between Rochester and the couple lasted all their lives and greatly influenced Rochester's growing political consciousness by providing a model not only of devout women concerned about social justice, but also women who loved and had dedicated their lives to other women. Scudder's young adulthood seems to have paralleled Rochester's: both were caretakers for their mothers and both lived and traveled extensively with them in Europe.[11]

In 1908 Louise remarked in the "AR Annals" about her daughter's friendship with Scudder and Converse and her fervor for Christian socialism. Rochester seemed to have been so intensely moved by this new ideology that combined deep religious convictions with practical social change, that

Louise was a little taken aback by her passion. In keeping with what Louise saw as Rochester's tendency to intense affiliation with certain ideas and judgments, she hoped she would balance these zealous passions with reasoned action and perhaps rethink her exalted notions of principle and strive instead for moderation. In terms of upper middle-class femininity, extremes of any kind were rarely encouraged or cultivated. Nonetheless, ideological fervor was destined to be a key part of Rochester's future:

> As one of her chief characteristics is to do thoroughly whatever she undertakes, it is not surprising that in submitting to the rules [of] SCHC to live a simple life and to make her profession of the Christian religion a real thing, she should make the same radical changes in her way of doing things, but like all converts she is led to extremes, which her dearest and nearest hopes may not always be her practice. It is not to be hoped that she will ever stray from principle and live according to it but she may later on relegate some things to expediency which she now places in the category of principle. She is a blessed child, truly of God's own. May all her work begun in Him be continued to her life's end.[12]

Social Activism

As Anna Rochester embarked on a life suffused with concern over the chaos and disintegration of modern industrial cities, she was in good company. In the face of increasing technological change and industrialization, poverty and urban squalor, corporate wrongdoings and economic injustice, middle-class women jumped into volunteer and paid work like never before, changing society, and, through their experiences, changing themselves.[13] Rochester's understandings of service were no doubt broadened by her understandings of social and economic justice implicit in the teachings of Christian socialism. They combined spiritual convictions about duty, commitment, and living a noble life in service of others with political analyses outlining social change programs. Rochester's movement toward social activism was an outgrowth of these ideological commitments for social justice and facilitated by her experiences with socialist colleagues. This agency was also constructed by her attempt to resolve various tensions in her life concerning her bourgeois privilege and her radical politics. For example, some years later Rochester explained to her friend Elizabeth Gurley Flynn how Gurley Flynn's "spunk" had helped orient her (Rochester) as "a newly converted young bourgeois, uncertain about what to do about my Socialist ideas."[14] During this period Rochester was a religiously motivated, wealthy young woman who was beginning to notice both the inequities of the society of which she was a part and the enormous privilege that she enjoyed. Understanding the relational nature of these realities, Rochester's political agency was grounded in new understandings of socialist practice that allowed her to stretch but not go beyond the parameters of femininity and apply her privilege in the service of children and families less fortunate than herself.

By 1909 Rochester was applying the principles of socialism to volunteer work at Denison House, a college settlement house.[15] Part of the larger settlement movement, the college settlement system was championed by Vida Scudder, who initiated such settlements in New York and Philadelphia before opening Denison House on Tyler Street in Boston's South End in 1893. Both Scudder and Converse had worked at Denison and at least Scudder was on the house's Board of Directors. While Scudder eventually resigned from this post in 1919 because of opposition to her politics, for the meantime the friendship she and Converse had with Helena Dudley, headworker at Denison, most likely facilitated Rochester's position there. Denison had become a center for liberal and radical thinkers of all classes and ideologies and was successful as a testing ground and training school for many progressive Christian leaders. Rochester's presence at Denison put her in the midst of women's reform work in Boston at the very same time that Hutchins was involved with the Women's Auxiliary in that same city. There is a good chance that they became acquainted with each other here or perhaps at SCHC or Bryn Mawr alumnae functions, although there is no direct evidence, nor any correspondence, that would suggest that they were friends. My sense is that perhaps their paths crossed, Hutchins left for missionary service, and their friendship was not kindled until a later time.

Settlement work epitomized women's reform work. It combined domestic organization with a passion for social justice and provided emotional nurturance, intimacy and support.[16] Louise Rochester commented on her daughter's work at Denison House in June 1909:

> She realizes her ignorance—and inexperience—but humbly does her best— in visiting, in conducting picnic parties, in actually carrying babies to the hospital or—besides making herself useful in clerical ways at the house. Her defective hearing had grown more noticeable in the Spring, and it was her mother's desire that she should put herself at once, under the care of Dr. McWilliams, a physician in Boston. Her enthusiasm in the work of the settlement and her unwillingness to take any time away from the daily duties, caused her to postpone from day to day this visit to the doctor.[17]

Perhaps Rochester's hearing problem facilitated her departure from a musical career, perhaps not. Either way, the habits of her former life fell away and her new fervor for the teachings of Christian socialism soon became the central organizing principle of her life. By 1911, while Louise was happy to write that this initial zeal had subsided somewhat and her daughter was showing more judgment and temperance in her actions, Rochester's participation in the movement was evolving into a leadership role. Acting

It is unclear whether Anna had a real hearing loss at this time or whether this comment reflected a temporary illness, exacerbated by a mother who was hypervigilant to illness and infirmity. Apart from a piece of music that appears to have been composed by Anna that has survived in the archives, there is no evidence that Anna continued a career as a musician. However, Grace and Anna did have a piano in their apartment, and at least one letter from friends mentioned how beautifully Anna played. Certainly as the two became ardent communists it would have seemed frivolous for Anna to focus on music in the face of economic and social injustice.

as chair for a SCHC conference, Rochester had also accepted leadership roles with the Episcopalian Church, serving as a member of the State Board of Education of the Episcopal Churches in New Jersey.[18]

By 1912 Rochester was working with the New Jersey Consumers' League.[19] She was elected chair of Publicity, and worked for the ten-hour law for women workers. Rochester personally wrote all the press articles that were sent out in connection with the New Jersey campaign: an effort that eventually resulted in the ten-hour law of 1912. Alongside her work with this organization, Rochester sat on the Executive Board of the New Jersey Child Labor Committee. She also represented Englewood Women's Club on the Department of Industrial Conditions and Social Welfare of the New Jersey State Federation of Women's Clubs.[20] All these positions put her in the midst of progressive social reform and gave her invaluable insight and organizing experiences. They also put her into contact with Florence Kelley, the brilliance and energy behind the National Consumers' League, as well as a key player on the National Child Labor Committee, another agency with which Rochester would become involved.

Child Welfare

A focus for white middle-class women's reform efforts was the working conditions and general state of poor children. At the beginning of the century, when the life expectancy of women was barely fifty years and life was harsh for most families, high infant mortality rates were an especially pressing concern. Children died in their early years from all kinds of childhood diseases and most families expected to have to confront a child's death. For example, in *American Women in the Progressive Era*, Dorothy and Carl Schneider quote a woman who remembers her mother losing seven babies in succession: "Our baby was never the same baby two years in succession. The little cradle held a new burden every year, but the former occupant never lived to see its successor. Mother became a mother eleven times. Only the first four children lived."[21] Middle-class women also faced these problems, but to a lesser degree since they had the privileges of domestic help, better nutrition, sanitation, relatively safer environments, and the possibility to escape the city and its plethora of dirt and disease. Nonetheless, most middle-class women reformers of the period were intimately connected to the sadness of infant and child mortality. In the face of these problems and in the context of the increasing professionalization of approaches to childhood and family life, women reformers of the period threw themselves into a moral guardianship for the nation's children. Compared to an earlier time that saw motherhood as a sentimental, infallible, and saintly occupation, now women needed training and education to be good mothers. Social workers and various public health personnel, recently graduated from the new colleges around the country, were hired to instruct the nation's mothers in the raising of their children. As women with a "natural" affiliation with the home, these experts were doubly equipped to assist. This discourse helped construct Rochester's activism: it gave her a moral crusade as well as opportunities to fulfill her ambition for identity and leadership.

Again, a key force behind child labor legislation and protective legislation for working women was the indefatigable Florence Kelley.[22] In early 1902, at the suggestion of Kelley and Lillian Wald (who founded the Henry Street settlement in New York City), the Association of Neighborhood Workers (an amalgam of the thirty-one New York settlement houses of the time) appointed a child labor committee to investigate the problem of working children in New York. Data were collected to show the extent of the problem, and, by the end of that year, the temporary committee was established as the New York Child Labor Committee. Along with such others as Felix Adler, founder of the Ethical Culture movement and a professor at Columbia University, Florence Kelley was a charter member and served on its Executive Committee. Meanwhile, in 1904 the impetus for creating a national organization was in the air and the National Child Labor Committee (NCLC) came into being from its roots in the New York chapter.[23]

Rochester's first paid employment was with the NCLC on a trial basis for six weeks in May and June 1912, although she ended up staying with the organization until 1915. Initially employed as a "special agent" at the salary of $50 a month, she reviewed reports sent in by field agents and state agencies and summarized these into a staff bulletin. By the middle of her second year she had been promoted to secretary of Publications and was responsible for the publicity of the NCLC as well as the publication of the quarterly *Child Labor Bulletin*.[24] The bulletins were very detailed and carefully written; Rochester was a scrupulous editor. She combined numbers, charts, and other kinds of information on child labor with a sentimental appeal to save precious childhoods wasted in the factories and sweatshops of America. Rochester gave numerous speeches and addresses during this period on child labor. One such address included a "Parlor

Conference" to speak on "More Protection for Working Children" as part
of NCLC's ninth annual conference in March 1914. Parlor conferences involved outreach strategies to various organizations such as Mothers' Clubs
and Children's Welfare Associations.[25] A presentation was also given to a
missionary society in the Dorset, Vermont, area (where Louise and Anna
Rochester enjoyed their summer home, Aradyddit). This speech is
Rochester's earliest existing manuscript of her work in the area of child
welfare. Its tone is directed to its feminine audience, using sympathy and
broad appeal to their Christian principles to help prevent the injustices of
child labor. This is a good example of the ways Rochester integrated social
activism with religious devotion; social reform *was* Christian activity and
each fueled the other:

> The working children should have a special appeal to a missionary society, for
> if there was ever in the world an offense to God's little ones that deserved the
> millstone penalty, that offense is child labor. Of course it is only a part of our
> un-Christian order of society, but it is a part which could be abolished to-
> morrow if people willed that it should, and its continuance is a glaring in-
> dictment of the sincerity of our ideals.[26]

In February 1914, Rochester's first published article in the *Child Labor
Bulletin* was "The Eight-Hour Day for Children," an overview of state reg-
ulations with a case for a shortened workday for children. The article is
written in a straightforward, objective tone as a traditional report. As such
it is quite different from an article in her own field of publicity that came
out a few months later. Titled "Newspapers and Child Labor," it encouraged
the public to request that journalists cover a wide range of social problems.
Personal and anecdotal evidence loaded with moral and religious overtones
was used throughout this article, and the result was an inviting and persuasive account that carefully crafted her argument. Writing of the importance of steady dialogue about social reform rather than only during certain campaigns, Rochester wrote: "Even in the days of Elijah, the voice of

I hope you are noticing how the expert academic voice is privileged as a
coherent story unfolds. You are encouraged to follow a linear, mostly
chronological story, to identify with the protagonists and feel empathy, respect, disappointment, etc. It is easy for readers to take for granted the biographical task of assembling "truths" about subjects and the reconstruction of them "as they were." We are encouraged to look forward to the
pleasures of having a coherent self actualize out of a story. But biography,
like all knowledge products, is rhetorically staged and linguistically crafted.
It is a realist fallacy that an authentic subject can emerge from the evidence,
even with the very best intentions.

the Lord did not come in the whirlwind of a fight but in the still, small voice of quiet reading week by week."[27]

The third volume of the *Child Labor Bulletin*, in August 1914, was dedicated solely to Rochester's work. She compiled "Children at Work on Men's Clothing" and "Children at Work in the Glass Industry, New York" from reports by other field agents, giving evidence of poor conditions and low wages, and summarizing child labor laws and potential solutions. She described the health risks associated with the sickness of workers who spit on the floor, were covered in "loathsome rashes," and were otherwise carrying communicable diseases. The appeal to sympathy for the poor afflicted workers was extended to middle-class consumers who might have bought these potentially germ-infested hand-finished garments.[28] This rather victim-blaming stance illustrates the ways in which much reform during this era was linked to middle-class benevolence. Rochester wrote this either from the heart or as a pragmatist who understood how best to frame a plea for immediate results. Like most of us, she probably did a little of both. Finally, several of Rochester's articles were reprinted as small pamphlets and targeted at a more general audience. These writings tended to be among the most sentimental and sensational of her work in their constant appeals to the conscience and sensibility of the reader. One titled "Street Workers" is illustrative of this rhetoric. Written in 1915, it begins with a personalized account of one of America's street children:

> To him the gutter was America. Jack began blacking boots three years ago— at ten. He left school in the primary grade. He learned nothing. He lives in the gutter . . . from seven in the morning until eleven or twelve at night. He rarely goes home at all. He is thirteen years old; his height is four feet.[29]

Louise Rochester felt keenly her daughter's commitment to her work. At one point she commented on Rochester's return to employment "with all the earnestness that real want might have given"[30]—a reminder of Rochester's privileged status that did not require her to work in the public sphere at all. During this period between 1913 and 1915 journal entries are filled with Louise's concern over her daughter's health, reflecting, no doubt, not only a mother's concern for her daughter's well-being and her own preoccupation with health and sickness, but also the nineteenth-century cultural ideologies about the consequences of such public work on women's physical and mental health. Believing in the inherent delicacies of bourgeois women's physical make-up, many assumed that stress resulting from work outside the home would have deleterious effects on women's health and, in particular, their reproductive health. Louise was concerned that summers provide a respite from such toil and believed poor health to be a potential consequence when such recuperation was interrupted. Used to servants, summer homes, and the delicacies of everyday middle-class New England life, Louise Rochester probably

Research diary: April 3, 1997: "There again, maybe Anna really was chronically ill and I misread Louise. However, if she *had* experienced such ill-health, that experience in itself could not possibly be disentangled from the cultural codes of the day about such matters." Can anything exist outside of culture and history?

saw her daughter's commitment to her career as a mixed blessing. Louise would have seen many examples of strong, middle-class, educated women active in the reform efforts of the period, and, as such, her daughter's choice not to marry and to devote herself to the causes of progressivism probably did not come as too much of a shock. There is obvious pride in the subtext of Louise's journal; there is also concern—concern for the well-being of a daughter who has chosen a different life from the mother.

The NCLC had long been involved in the impetus to establish a federal Children's Bureau of the U.S. Department of Labor. The idea came from Lillian Wald and Florence Kelley as early as 1903 and was supported by the NCLC and others.[31] However, a bill to create the bureau introduced into congress in 1905 was not passed and signed by President Taft until April 1912, and then, predictably, with strong opposition from industry since its charge was not only improving infant and child health and welfare, but also regulating child labor. The Children's Bureau provided a place for women to impact policy within the federal government at a time when they still had not received the vote, solidifying networks between settlement houses, the Consumers' League, the Women's Trade Union League, and women's clubs. While it began with a small budget appropriation ($25,640) and a limited staff, the brilliant director Julia Lathrop, the first woman ever to head a federal agency, skillfully emphasized motherhood as "the most essential of employments" and focused on infant health as a way to avoid controversy and build support.[31] She used her extensive networks and worked successfully to protect children and families and support women's role in the government. When Congress tried to reduce and limit the bureau's appropriation to $25,000, Lathrop mobilized her networks and initiated a large public media campaign in support of the bureau. As a result, in 1915 her appropriation had increased fivefold and she was then able to hire additional personnel in all areas of the organization.[33]

Rochester was one of the new hires made by Lathrop in 1915. Having worked closely with Florence Kelley, Lathrop's friend and colleague, Rochester had connections that undoubtedly helped her advance through these circles, placing her within the network of women reformers that provided professional opportunities as well as social and emotional support.

Her class standing, air of prosperous gentility, and well-bred manners were no doubt also a plus. But it was most likely the record of her work with the NCLC that attracted the attention of the bureau's chief. A note on a scrap of paper written in 1939 reported that it was an article written for the Press Bureau of the *Survey* and printed in the *Commonwealth* newspaper in June 1915 that won her Lathrop's merit. The article spoke of the need for a "Children's Charter" to be signed by child welfare leaders and other interested people that would demonstrate commitment and solidarity toward reform in this area. The National Children's Charter had in fact been acted upon as a resolution at the annual NCLC conference in January 1915. Moved by Florence Kelley, seconded by Lillian Wald, and supported by Julia Lathrop, it passed unanimously at the meeting.[34]

In the summer of 1915 Rochester relocated from New York to Washington, D.C., to take up her new position as private secretary to Lathrop. This position was shortly changed to one involving more editorial work: a promotion that seemed to have given her more intellectual freedom as well as prestige within the bureau. Louise Rochester commented on the excitement generated by this new post and the relocation to Washington. She reported that on hearing about the offer, Rochester made a flying trip up to Dorset to consult with her mother and they both decided that a move to Washington would be beneficial for practical as well as professional reasons. Louise was very proud of her daughter's success and exclaimed that "to be associated with a woman of Miss Lathrop's calibre was said by some friends to be a 'Liberal Education in itself.'"[35] After some searching, an apartment in the Westmoreland on California Street was found, within walking distance of Rochester's new office. Rochester lived there with her mother and friend Edith Klein as well as with other employees from the bureau when Louise and Edith were in Dorset. Louise often mentioned Klein, to whom she also seemed very close.[36] Klein stayed connected with Rochester and Hutchins over the years and moved with them to Community House, the women's commune in New York City, in 1921. Louise often referred to Klein as "the devoted Edith," and wrote of Klein accompanying her on various travels and stays at Aradyddit.

The apartment on California Street turned out to be a gathering place for like-minded single women who worked at the bureau. Louise reported that evenings were often spent with someone reading aloud while others worked on their sewing or knitting, and all would discuss the reading and

The "devoted" Edith might just as likely mean devoted to Anna as devoted to Louise, a meaning which changes the picture somewhat.

engage in lively debate. SCHC meetings were held in the apartment, and there seemed to be time set aside for religious study and discussion. With humor Louise also mentioned a class Rochester was taking called "Moto-Mental-Rhythmics":

> To change the current of [Anna's] life, she joined a group of other members of the Bureau in a class for Moto-Mental-Rhythmics. Certainly a title to cause me to take a long breath—(but then long breaths are necessary in this class). However it was a distinct change of occupation and being a thing to improve health by exercising all the body—it has proved a good thing.[37]

Rochester's relationship with her mother remained very close through this period and she seemed to have had much responsibility for the older woman's care until she died sometime after January 1918. On one occasion Louise wrote how Rochester and Klein had taken her to the hospital and stood by her in this hour of need: "In spite of the seventy-one years—many of them full of suffering—the ordeal was passed safely—and much joy reigned in the apartment at the Westmoreland on the return, Oct. 19th. As suffering can call out latent courage on the part of the sufferer—it is equally able to call out loving patience and kindness. So it was in this case. . . . Moreover, one never knows the depths of Divine love and goodness 'til great trials test it.'"[38]

The years at the Children's Bureau were busy ones for Rochester. Her first project involved reviewing legislation affecting children in 1915 and writing a summary with a colleague as well as preparing the summary of Lathrop's Third Annual Report and doing the press work for a report submitted on street trades. In 1916 she worked on the "Summary of the Report on Mental Defectives in New Castle County, Delaware," an article that reported on the dismal provisions for "feeble-minded" children, and also the campaign for "Baby Week," held from March 4 to 11.[39] The intensive publicity for Baby Week focused on the estimated 3,000 babies that died in the United States during their first twelve months of life:

> 1916 is Baby year. The facts about American babies, the needs of American babies, and America's responsibility will this year be known as never before, because the first week in March will be Baby Week throughout the country. . . . During those seven days the needs of babies may be so presented that all the parents of those communities will learn better how to care for their babies, and all the citizens will realize that they have a special obligation to safeguard the conditions surrounding babies.[40]

Rochester wrote press release after press release advertising Baby Week, making suggestions for community involvement and referencing the variety of bureau publications available. Also included that year were releases

Research Diary: April 3, 1997: "Finished a rough draft of Chapter 2—too many silences across large pieces of time—although lots of articles and published writings left behind. I like Anna—I like the way she balances her ambitions with connectedness to her mother and friends. [I have just] read Phyllis Rose's article about her work on Virginia Woolf—her point [about necessary identification with the subject] rings true for me. [She says] biography provides 'psychic food' for the biographer—in the process of writing we work through these issues about independence, ambition, relationship, etc. in our own lives."[41]

about "Taxes and Babies" outlining where tax dollars were spent concerning child welfare, and "Saving Mothers," which talked about high female mortality rates linked to childbirth-related causes and the need to improve services in this area.[42]

By 1917 when the United States entered World War I, Rochester was a strong pacifist. Her politics were informed by Christian ethics as well as by socialist ideology. Pacifist views were shared by other members of the bureau, although not by her mother:

> The entrance of the United States into the horrible war causes a great strain on the pacifist leanings of the whole group, but when work is started in the Bureau—by which investigations into the status of children in the warring countries during the war—an alleviation is felt by them all. A.R. takes charge of the investigation of the French. Others have Russian, German and English. So, in this way . . . bad effects of the war can be modified or even prevented by this action. The declaration of war has caused a great stir in pacifists and those who believe in it. Difference of opinion existing in the very small family of Rochester—the less said on this subject the better. It is now expected that A.R. shall go to Boston on Jan. 19 to address the Women's Club of Boston on "Child Labor in Warring Countries." The paper is very able—and will, I am sure, satisfy even a Boston audience. The scarcity of coal and the withdrawal of many trains between important places may be a cause of delay.[43]

The 1917 Baby Week campaign was less intensive than the 1916 campaign because of the war effort, and the focus instead was on Baby Week as a patriotic act. Indeed, Lathrop was quoted as saying: "No sounder patriotic service can be offered at this time than the practical study of how each community can preserve the welfare of its children, its last line of defense."[44] Rochester was distressed at the politics of war, and the patriotic stance that the bureau had to take most likely would have caused a principled pacifist like herself a certain amount of anxiety. Rochester's major task at this time was the extensive project on the conditions and needs of children in wartime: "Child Labor in Warring Countries: A Brief Review of

World War I was such a turning point in European and U.S. history. We make sense of this war through the historical "facts" about the period; I make sense of it also through the stories I heard from my grandfather who fought in this war, and, as a European, by a real understanding of the incredible loss of life and the mass destruction that occurred then. Knowledge about wars, even more than many other aspects of social life, gets scripted to maintain hegemonic relations in society. We need to remember that historical facts are not just truths in linear arrangement or any more truths than the stories we tell about each other's lives. I think it is important for us to address the politics of the construction of these historical truths about war, especially vis-à-vis the production of knowledge about gender and race. Now, speaking of cultural hegemony, I am editing this chapter against the cultural backdrop of another war in the Middle East.

Foreign Reports." She also undertook the field research on France for this report, while other researchers focused on other countries. Concern over the disorganization of industry and worsening conditions that would affect families, and children in particular, encouraged the researchers to focus on child labor laws and the war exemptions to these laws, policies for school attendance and school leaving, and new plans for industrial education.[45]

The bureau also conducted investigations on infant mortality in various U.S. cities. Rochester headed the research and wrote the report on Baltimore, the city where the most data were collected.[46] This 400-page report was Rochester's most extensive project, the one that was best known of her work at the bureau, and the one most widely cited.[47] It was published in 1922, a year after she and Julia Lathrop left the Children's Bureau. Using social and economic factors such as father's earnings, occupation, and unemployment as explanatory variables alongside such indicators as sanitation, breast-feeding, and general nutrition, the report was important in making the connection between infant mortality and poverty: "It appears, then, that the highest infant mortality was found in the families where the father's earnings were lowest, and the lowest infant mortality where the father's earnings were the highest, and in general the rates for the several causes of death decreased, with the total rate, as the father's earnings rose."[48] This emphasis on the relationship between poverty and infant mortality helped secure the passage of the first social welfare act, the Sheppard–Towner Maternity and Infancy Act, in 1921.

By 1921 both Lathrop and Rochester had departed from the Children's Bureau, and the new chief, Grace Abbott, led the bureau into the next decade. While Rochester was protected by her civil service appointment and could have continued at the bureau, she made the decision to leave. The reasons for her departure are unclear: a changeover in staff would have provided a natural break for someone ready to make a change. Most likely the reformist principles of the bureau would have rubbed against Rochester's deepening socialist political commitments and put her in the uncomfortable position of "insider" with a government against whom she was increasingly displaying "outsider" agitation.[49] For example, while the Children's Bureau did support Rochester's and other researchers' claims that poverty and the gross economic inequities in U.S. society were at the root of high infant mortality rates, they stressed educational solutions rather than systematic structural socioeconomic changes.[50] As a socialist who supported organized labor's interest in child protection, she would also have understood the complexities of child labor among working people. The bureau's inspectors had a difficult time estimating children's ages given that most did not have birth certificates and the dismissal of child earners had important consequences for families at the edge of poverty. Finally, the bureau was often seen by organized labor as too conciliatory with industrialists and factory owners,[51] another concern, no doubt, for Rochester. These ideological differences most likely affected her continuing commitment to the bureau and played a key role in her decision to depart from the organization. Perhaps the timing of Rochester's departure from the Children's Bureau was also connected to the death of her mother, her growing relationship with Hutchins, and their decision to live together in New York City.

Whatever Rochester's reasons for leaving the Children's Bureau, this employment had given her important skills in writing, statistical analysis, administration and networking. As part of a large army of women employed to promote and improve the health and welfare of America's children, she was surrounded by other like-minded women who also worked hard for social betterment. I believe Rochester's life during this period illustrated her growing understanding of the relationship between social and economic inequities and her own class and race privilege. Informed by socialist ideologies for change and Christian values of compassion and service, the decisions that Rochester made during this period were constituted in relation to these historical factors.

CHAPTER THREE

MISSIONARY ZEAL

Trinity Church, Boston, Supplies a Teacher for St. Hilda's, Wuchang

On March 5, a service was held in the chapel of the Church Missions House, to bid God-speed to Miss Grace Hutchins, who goes shortly to join the Hankow mission. Bishop Lloyd celebrated the Holy Communion and made a brief address, emphasizing the fact that Miss Hutchins's departure for distant service represented not only her personal consecration to a higher calling, but the deliberate act of those who remain at home in sending her away. Miss Hutchins is a graduate of Bryn Mawr, where she was president of the Christian Union and taught Bible-classes for younger students. Attendance at the National Convention of the Student Volunteer Movement in 1906 led her to offer herself for missionary service as soon as the way should be open. In the meantime she made herself an effective leader in the Women's Auxiliary, and has been active in various social service enterprises in Boston, winning general regard for her devotion, steadiness and ability.

Miss Hutchins sails from San Francisco March 19, and will be attached to the staff of St. Hilda's School, Wuchang. Here her exceptional ability as a teacher and higher power of personal influence will enable her to render most helpful service as a leader among young Chinese women.[1]

Women's Service in the Foreign Mission

In 1912 Grace Hutchins left for China, propelled by a sincere devotion to Christianity as an applied politic to cure the world's ills. Guided by strong affiliations to her church and the normative constraints imposed on women by this religious body, she was nonetheless able to experience

53

> Lois Rudnick writes: "I am continually struck by the naiveté with which re-
> viewers write about biographies. . . . With rare exception, they evaluate bi-
> ography as a more or less accurate and interesting portrait of the life. They
> compliment or criticize the biographer for bringing, or not bringing, the
> person and his or her times to life. And then they devote their review pri-
> marily to retelling the highlights of the subject's life. What they fail to notice
> is that biographers are active agents. Like fiction writers and historians they
> create their subjects from a particular angle of vision and with a particular
> set of strategies they determine the outcome."[2] But then are all truths rel-
> ative? If facts are only relative to the point of view from which they are con-
> structed and the sign is merely arbitrary, are we left with a kind of "virtual
> biography"? Perhaps as Martin Stannard suggests, "the only real road to
> truth is through doubt and tolerance."[3] While biography is about layers of
> fiction, biographers need to strive for methodological accuracy—knowing
> full well that this is an inventive act.

the adventures of world travel and experience a certain degree of autonomy. Like many other privileged women who joined the ranks of the foreign mission movement, Hutchins's ambitions were framed by a particular historical juncture when women were more easily able to move
outside of the home and into civic duty, yet were still constrained by the
normative standards of nineteenth-century femininity. As such,
Hutchins was able to reconcile these tensions, her missionary career
being a most adventurous example of "municipal housekeeping." It was
an extension of the politics of domesticity where women were able to
bend rather than break the parameters of socially acceptable feminine
behavior. Missionary service provided a positive option for devout yet
adventurous single women in that it provided membership in a strong,
gender-segregated, homosocial community and allowed opportunities
for female leadership, travel, and adventure.[4] Like Rochester, Hutchins's
agency during this period reflects her resolution of the contradictions
between ambition and constraint in the context of a fascinating historical moment at the brink of a new century.

By 1915 there were more than 3 million women on the membership rolls
of over forty denominational female missionary societies, amounting to
one of the largest women's mass movements of the nineteenth and twentieth centuries.[5] This movement had grown substantially since the mid-
nineteenth century and had captured the imagination of thousands of
women who routinely donated to the cause. From the first female missionaries who tended to be wives of men in the field, the mission calling grew
to include thousands of single women ready to serve. As foreign mission
crusader Helen Barrett Montgomery explained in 1910:

We began in weakness, we stand in power. In 1861 there was a single missionary in the field, Miss Marston, in Burma; in 1909, there were 4,710 unmarried women in the field, 1,948 of them from the United States. . . . The women's missionary organizations have built colleges, hospitals, dispensaries, nurses' homes, orphanages, leper asylums, homes for missionaries' children, training schools, and industrial plants. They have set up printing-presses, translated bibles, tracts, and school-books. They have built boats and founded newspapers. They have published missionary magazines, distributed mite boxes, printed millions of lesson leaflets, study outlines, programs, and booklets. They have maintained offices, state and national organizations, yearly and triennial conventions. They have developed a fine network of unpaid helpers with which to cover the entire country. It is an achievement of which women may well be proud.[6]

While these achievements relate to the administrative genius of the movement's leaders, its success was essentially grounded in ideologies that appealed to women's sacred and natural role as mother and "civilizer." Evangelical and feminine traditions reinforced each other in their shared focus on the traditional power of love and feeling, and the emotional aspects of religion, prayer, and conversion.[7] Missionaries would attempt to go into the homes and hearts of potential converts to nurture, teach, and care for the sick, spreading God's word and acting out their maternal responsibility for all God's children. These professional callings tended to be very much grounded in the nineteenth-century expectations of femininity that saw such religious roles as essentially feminine and in keeping with women's innate tendency toward service to God, family, and community.

In the early years of the twentieth century, the primacy of these innate sacred "mothering" attributes as prerequisites for missionary service gave way to a scientific home economic approach. While these developments coincided with the growing cultural acceptance of women's role in the

It is especially in my research for this chapter that I am reminded of the problems associated with this decision I've made to give voice to white upper-class women. Hasn't enough been written about such women already? This is such a paradox: to give voice like this is again to privilege a prosperous white experience, yet to not do this now is to stay silent. It is as if voicing were a zero-sum game and sharing some stories means there is less room for someone else's story. Also, if biography, as Dennis Petrie seems to imply, is "ultimately fiction" (his book has that title), might these new forms of biography neutralize rather than vocalize the articulation of "difference" concerning material, structural conditions as a part of life stories? In other words, does the elimination of the belief in referentiality ignore the referentiality of gender, class, and race?

"municipal housekeeping" aspect of public and religious work, they also reflected a diminishment of the mass moral zeal that had fueled the women's foreign mission movement in its earlier years.[8] With this change in supporting ideologies, women's service in the foreign mission field came to be seen as a career decision, and women were more likely to be professionally trained and to see their role as one similar to social work, nursing, or teaching. This in turn opened up the field to single women. Along with the lure of independence and adventure was a financial compensation (though meager), which often exceeded that available from other options.

In addition, by the time Hutchins served in China in 1912, women's service role had also coincided with developments in the notion of the foreign mission whereby "success" was no longer measured solely by the number of converts but also by an amelioration of the social conditions of indigenous peoples' lives.[9] Unfortunately, such efforts tended to be grounded in ethnocentric beliefs about the superiority of Western religions and society, as well as an understanding of gender relations grounded in patriarchal norms. Ultimately such "progress" was imperialist and capitalist in its outcome, assuming that it was the non-Christian or "heathen" aspect of Chinese culture that was the root cause of these intolerable burdens of savagery forced on women. Christianity was deemed a moral force that would not only convert the individual, but also transform society in accordance with a Western model of civilization, and aims to emancipate "heathen women" were grounded in the racist imperative of colonial ethnocentrism. It is also worth noting that while so many were eager to "save" Chinese peoples abroad, few were doing much to help Chinese immigrants at home.[10] At the same time, however, this imperative concerning the improvement of indigenous peoples' lives did allow women to work independently with other women to bring about changes, and did improve, at least, the material and economic lot of some Chinese women.[11]

In this way, Hutchins's choice to go into missionary service followed the pattern of women's lives during this period: it allowed her to act on her religious upbringing and her belief in Christianity as a progressive force in

> This was my first entrance into the lives of Grace and Anna. When I started researching Grace's foreign mission experiences for my article on missionary women, I had no idea what kind of a woman I was dealing with. I assumed that the person she was then was the same kind of person who lived the rest of her life: I imagined this devout Christian woman aging through the decades. That was an important eye-opener for me and made me question all kinds of assumptions I have made as a result of such brief glimpses into women's lives.

social reform as well as be in the company of other women and experience adventure overseas. Perhaps it also allowed her to avoid marriage.

China, 1912–1916

> Years of the Modern! Years of the unperformed!
> Your horizon rises, I see it parting away for more august dramas,
> I see not America only, not only Liberty's nation but other
>   nations preparing,
> I see tremendous entrances and exits, new combinations, the
>   solidarity of races,
> I see that force advancing with irresistible power on the world's
>   stage,
> The perform'd America and Europe grow dim, retiring in
>   shadow behind me,
> The unperform'd, more gigantic than ever, advance, advance,
>   upon me.
>
>   Walt Whitman[12]

When Hutchins arrived at St. Hilda's School for Girls in Wuchang in the District of Hankow, the revolution of 1911 had initiated a republic and she would have encountered an environment more conducive to missionary activity.[13] At this time reforms were in place and power in China had moved into the provincial assemblies, influence was decentralized, and a revolutionary movement that paralleled the constitutional one demanded a republic. A conference of representatives from all provinces set up a provisional government in December 1911, and by January of 1912 the new republic was officially proclaimed and Yuan Shikai was elected provisional president after the emperor abdicated. The government of Yuan Shikai was not without violence, corruption, and intrigue, and the opposing Nationalist Guomindang Party of Sun Yatsen contended for power with ongoing squirmishes, accompanied by assassinations, and resignations of various prime ministers. Since Yuan Shikai relied heavily on foreign powers and resources, missionary work during this period was relatively safe and open, though certainly not without danger.[14]

A letter written in September 1910 suggests that while Hutchins had made up her mind about her desire to be a missionary as early as 1906, it was resistance from her mother that delayed her departure for six years. The letter is affectionately written by Hutchins's father and addressed to "My dear little daughter." It reads:

I thank you for your letter—I sat down last evening to reply to it, but found I could not do so without dealing with the subject which is uppermost in both our minds and that to expand on this subject would take reams and reams of paper and that, more important still, it was a subject that might better be spoken of face to face to talk frankly about your purposes. My love to you, my dear daughter, all of it that you wish, and above all my sympathy with those plans you have given up for the present for your mother's sake—I understand for I was once like you. Perhaps you can not realize how an old codger like me could be like you but perhaps you will understand some day. . . . I must say that you have all my love and more of my sympathy with your plans than you have any idea of. [15]

This letter reveals the love and caring Edward Hutchins felt toward his daughter and suggests that Hutchins's "plans" had to be put on hold. Her parents had lost two other daughters and had experienced the tragedy of that loss, and they were most likely fearful for Grace's safety in these "foreign lands." The antiforeign sentiment of the period after the Chinese Boxer rebellion of 1898 would probably have caused considerable parental concern. The line in the newspaper article presented at the beginning of this chapter that reads "Miss Hutchins's departure for distant service represented not only her personal consecration to a higher calling, but the deliberate act of those who remain at home in sending her away," suggests some "sacrifice" on her parents' part. Perhaps this coincided with one or the other's ill health. Whatever the feelings associated with her departure, it was just a matter of time until Hutchins's plans were realized. The timing of her departure, after the initiation of a republic, support the argument that the movement toward democracy after 1912 may have helped lower their resistance to her calling, even though the potentiality for extreme civil unrest at this time would have been quite high. Certainly, at almost thirty years old, she would have been able to make a case for her own maturity.

Hutchins's leaving was not only stressful for her parents. There was at least one friend who loved Grace with a passion, and was tearful over her

I puzzled a lot over this letter to Grace from her father. I'm still not sure that the analysis I present is accurate. Grace's "plans" could have been referring to something completely different. But, given the gap between her "decision" about missionary service in 1906 and the departure in 1912, something must have intervened. Alongside the fears associated with Grace's safety in China and perhaps Susan's health, maybe there was another reason for the delay. Is it possible Susan wanted Grace to marry at the appropriate marriageable age during the years after she left Bryn Mawr? If she had gone immediately to China after college, would it have seemed like sending her daughter off to a convent? Maybe by 1912 it was obvious that Grace was not going to lead the domestic life of most first-family Bostonians.

Grace in China (c. 1915).

departure. This friend, who signed herself "Jane" (and included the quotation marks in her signature), was also bereaved when Hutchins departed a second time after a visit home from China in 1914, a visit requested by Hutchins's father. The letter below was written after her second departure and illustrates the intensity and extent of emotional support and solidarity received by women in their relationships with each other during this period. Missionary service in the company of other devoted women would hardly have been an emotional sacrifice for Hutchins, although it is presumed she missed this special friend who saw stars on first encountering Hutchins's dreamlike face and would have married her tomorrow had she been a man. The letter from 1914 reads:

If there was any single thing I could have done to make the getting off any easier, you know, don't you, that I would have been at T—.... If I had been there, however, it would have been with very different feelings from the last occasion. There, it was the first parting for any time since I had come to know you, and despite all I could think to the contrary, there was the wonder as to whether we would meet again at the end of the first China period, our first as familiar a footing as we parted. Now, I know that two or four or any number of years can make no difference whatever, and I look forward with the utmost confidence to the time which will come so soon, when you will walk bodily into my life again, just as you did at Cambridge and the only fire-works that announced the event will be, as there, the stars that flicker before my face as I try to see whether yours is really your own or a dream-face.

Every time I think of this summer, I feel inclined to bless your father on my own account for bringing you back just now. It has meant more than I have any least power to tell you, to be able to talk everything out to you just as it stands. So much of lasting joy and satisfaction was packed into that week at Castine, that I shall still be going over and over it when you come again. I did try to tell you why our friendship meant so much to me in the way of rest and strength. You are literally the only person I know upon whom I dare lean my whole weight, so to speak, without any fears of being a burden. It is partly, I think, because you lean, too, and we prop one another up. Whatever it is, you are the biggest kind of comfort, and if you were a man, I would marry you tomorrow.[16]

This letter was tucked away in a folder in the archives marked "unidentified letters." I assume "Jane" was not the writer's real name; perhaps it was a nickname they used between themselves, or maybe it was chosen just for the writing in order to highlight how poor and lost and ordinary this person would be now that Grace was leaving again, sort of like a "Jane Doe." I later found a letter written to Hutchins in 1944 from Lucy Sturgis that ended "I love you, anyway, and always," which carried the identical handwriting to the one signed "Jane." It appeared that they remained friends, although not with the intensity that "Jane" invoked in this early letter. "Jane"/Lucy's comment about marrying Hutchins tomorrow if she were a man can be interpreted as an innocent remark about their compatibility as friends, a more charged comment reflecting the intensity of the love between them, a reflection of "Jane" putting on the brakes in providing a reminder of heterosexual obligations, or a combination of these. If "Jane" was Lucy, and I think she was, the maturity of the relationship or perhaps its naiveté is demonstrated by the fact that they stayed friends and spoke of the love between them even as years passed.

I loved finding this letter—it was such a treasure after a long day in the archives. It is interesting how the lure of romance really livens up this quest. Attempting to analyze this letter reminds me of reading something Blanche Wiesen Cook wrote, I'm not sure where, about her focus on the private lives of our foremothers. This resulted in an old lesbian being upset that, as a result of Wiesen Cook's probing, no longer was privacy intact and ceremonies unscarred. The mystery and the danger had been penetrated and now it all seemed less romantic. I suppose this is all about the romance of the closet. Whatever the relationships between "Jane" and Grace, the romance and passion were there.

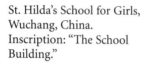
St. Hilda's School for Girls,
Wuchang, China.
Inscription: "The School
Building."

When Hutchins arrived at St. Hilda's she found an orderly and regi-
mented school. While a bulk of the day was spent in individual or community prayer, study at the school was entirely a matter of religious education that centered around such pedagogy as "moral teaching."
Hutchins recalled a typical day at St. Hilda's that involved rising at 6
A.M., followed by private devotion, prayers, and then classes after breakfast until 4 in the afternoon when the girls would do "drill," followed by
singing, supper, study, and bedtime. Saturdays were divided between
sewing in the morning and visits from families in the afternoon. Sundays
of course were devoted to church and prayer. It seems that Hutchins was
remembered for her role in "humanizing" St. Hilda's through a transformation of the school's atmosphere and spirit. She was especially appreciated for her kindly rather than authoritative approach and her efforts
to change the environment of the school toward a more flexible and supportive one.[17]

A pamphlet about St. Hilda's illustrates the missionary goal of evangelism. It addressed the issue "What a Christian School Does for Chinese Girls," and its purpose was fund-raising for the school. A section of the pamphlet titled "St. Hilda's Under Deaconess Phelps" was compiled from letters written before Hutchins arrived in 1908 and 1909. Illustrating the arrogance and elitism that undergirded the colonial mission, this excerpt also underscored the strong devotion missionaries such as Hutchins felt toward their cause:

> It is not that girls are stupid here, far from it. But they have not high standards. How can they, in the midst of heathen surroundings? It is going to be a hard thing for these girls to go out from school, and be better than their surroundings, and yet that is what we are training them for. And our second generation Christians show how the leaven is working. With Christian fathers and mothers the difference is unspeakable. So I feel it to be my deepest responsibility in regard to these girls to give them very thorough religious instruction, in my classes preparing them for Baptism and Confirmation, so that they may feel their responsibility as members of Christ. If only we had workers enough to find and influence the girls of China, waiting and ready to be taught! If people might only realize how critical a time this is, and mass their workers at the front where the battle is to be gained or lost so soon. And if women who have it in their hearts to do things could only see in vision the things that only they can do—the taking the blind, groping, passionate desire which some of these girls in China have and guiding it into the Light and the Truth and the Life! . . . But when the Vision is before us we know that God's will will be done, that the fight is His, and that He will send His reinforcements in due time.[18]

As a passionate and persuasive rhetoric directed toward fund-raising, such writing attempted to play on the hearts and conscience of Christian readers, encouraging them to donate even small amounts to the school. For indeed these schools were a crucial component of the evangelical mission in indoctrinating future mothers who would be central in spreading the Christian faith among their families. While care for indigenous people's well-being may have been genuine by most involved in missionary service, and certainly seemed to have been sincere on Hutchins's part, ultimately missionaries were first and foremost interested in saving and converting foreign peoples to Christianity. This was especially true for women and child converts whom they saw as their special mission. Therefore, strategies for conversion often involved an "intimate evangelism" and the development of a personal relationship within the school.[19]

However, missionaries soon discovered that the low status afforded to Chinese women and female children presented an obstacle for their conversion and they found themselves acting as champions for Chinese women and children's rights as part of their spiritual tactical strategies.[20]

Teachers at St. Hilda's. Grace is in the back row, far right. Inscription: "The teachers again. K. Scott really has 2 eyes."

In 1902, for example, St. Hilda's adopted a policy of requiring Christian Chinese students to unbind their feet since foot-binding was noted as a "heathen practice."[21] Hutchins carried on these reforms as she cared for the girls she taught, and recorded, often in horror, their difficult lives. In her notebook on life at St. Hilda's, Hutchins included several experiences and stories about local people and issues, and shared observations made during visits to various mission stations in the region and in Japan. As part of her intimate evangelism, Hutchins wrote of her "Trip to the Widow's House," an exploit dedicated to improving this woman's life in the name of Christianity:

> Narrow street. Small entrance. Escorted by bound-footed old lady going to visit her daughters. . . . Inside like a vast tenement, each widow with her children living in a tiny room 8 ft by 8, serving as kitchen, dining room, bathroom, bedroom, and sitting-room. No water supply, except the rain. Horrible air. Headache in 2 minutes.[22]

Another story concerned the rescue of a Chinese girl, again illustrating how the improvements in material conditions were linked to indigenous women's conversion to Christianity. Hutchins saw both aspects as success stories:

> Colporteur smoked opium. Had sold his wife for #40. Had bought a little girl at the age of three. Her mother had died in a famine year. Father, poor and sick, accepted #1.50 for his only child. Opium smoker wanted her for a daugh-

ter-in-law but his son died. Rented the 8 year old girl to a theatrical company
for #10 a month. She was to sing indecent songs and do tricks. Had no voice.
Was beaten till she was ill, and was returned to opium smoker. He pawned her
to a house of ill-fame for #160. Was to remain there till 18, and then go back
to the opium-fiend as his slave, to earn money for him. She was 9 when Mr.
Lund rescued her . . . paid #160 for her, and held her papers. In the eyes of the
Chinese law she is still a piece of property. Entered St. Hilda's soon after this.
Now training to be a nurse.[23]

As a teacher and eventually principal of St. Hilda's School, Hutchins had
several occasions to visit other schools on various fund-raising missions.
Much of Hutchins's tours of other mission stations seemed to be organized
around this need; her remarks about different facilities focus on their lack
of resources, understaffing, and general need, and came back time and
again to the material and spiritual needs of the community. Under a journal entry entitled "St. Hilda's Chapel," Hutchins wrote "#5,000 gold," and
scornfully exclaimed that while they had a gymnasium donated by someone who cared about physical education, "Is there not someone who believes in religious education enough to leave a church as a memorial?"[24]
   During a fund-raising visit to Hwai Yuen, she wrote of one day spent at
a missionary Women's Hospital that was understaffed and in need of sup-
plies. While her role there appeared to be observational, it seems she did
pitch in and help deal with the sheer litany of human suffering. She discussed the hard work, the exhausting heat, and the poor material conditions in which they had to work. Amazingly, while resources were inade-
quate and work was never ending, the personal commitment and strong
faith in their duty to "do God's work" still seemed very high: "During the
obstetrical case the leg of the bed on which the patient was lying went
through the floor which was rotten. One of the nurses also went through
the floor. . . . Child had a leg cut off. . . . Woman beaten by her husband with
a club. Woman was a No. 1 wife, husband preferred No. 2."[25]
   Hutchins wrote how the hospital treated a woman who was seriously ill,
calling her account "The Story of the Official's 3rd Wife." It concerned the
wife of the military governor of Hupei, who was very powerful and responsible for the executions of many opponents. He arrived at the mission
hospital with a retinue of sixteen mounted officers and a wife who was in
premature labor. A Chinese midwife had pulled on the umbilical cord and
the uterus had prolapsed outside her body. Hutchins's notes read:

Dr. James (bitten by scorpion so can only use left hand) and Miss Dexter
(help) must be kept sterile and Dr. must scrub left hand with hurt hand. Patient hemorrhaging, rolling over on bed. With left hand forced way into
uterus which then contracted around Dr.'s hand almost paralyzing it. Must
take out placenta freeing it off the wall and taken out in pieces bec. of con-

traction. Miss Dexter had to hold uterus in w. 1 hand and hold abdomen w. other to prevent inversion of the uterus. Woman there all the time pulling away, making it most difficult to keep sheets and towels sterile. Dr. must give intra-uterine douche. Woman refused. Not enough assistants. General came in to persuade her how serious condition was to make her permit it. . . . [Several days later] woman came in to hospital with temperature of 105, streptococcus poison. Been working over her for three days with douches, subcutaneous salt solution, and support. . . . "Sequel": She is much better after 10 days treatment.[26]

The notebook continued with a discussion of the running of a mission clinic and the documentation of a series of acute and chronic medical cases. While Hutchins was moved by the sheer misery of the locals who crowded the clinic, she seemed relatively detached from the pain and humiliation of the patients, and chastised them for their lack of cooperation and their adherence to "superstitions." Her attitude comes across as very matter of fact. This particular clinic at Hwai Yuen had seen 220 people by the end of the month and staff were feeling terribly overworked. Hutchins's detachment reflected their frustration: "Stupid old woman wants yellow medicine not white. . . . After seeing 70 such in one afternoon, Dr. naturally frantic."[27] She wrote that they tried very hard to keep the hospital clean, but it was a full-time job. The patients kept spitting on the floor and as a result, disinfectant had to be used constantly. This was especially hard on the staff in the winter when constant handwashing in cold disinfectant was gruesome. I believe Hutchins's detachment and that of her colleagues reflected the racism and ethnocentrism of missionaries who saw the humanity of the Chinese people as worth less than their own. However, most likely it also served as a survival mechanism for enduring uninterrupted work in stressful conditions when surrounded by such misery.

Despite their dedication and high levels of motivation, life was undoubtedly difficult for Westerners unaccustomed to the heat and Chinese customs. Hutchins wrote in the missionary notebook of "A Typical Night in Summer (June 1st to Sept 15th) in the present quarter of the foreign workers in the Woman's Hospital":

Tiny house surrounded by high Chinese buildings. *No air.* Thermometer 95 in favored spots. Over 100° in feeling. Attic under a low tile roof quite unbearable. Two sides open like large windows but right under eaves of the house. . . . One night Miss Dexter tried the attic but could not sleep for the heat. Came downstairs about 12 or 1 a.m. and tried the bamboo cot, then inside in the airless inside room to escape mosquitoes.

Dr. James hung a hammock between posts in front of the house and lay there till 4 a.m. dozing a little. They tried the attic which had cooled off a little. This

Research diary: May 7, 1997: "I like to think that these efforts [ameliorating the suffering of] Chinese women and children were *the* primary motivators for Grace. Not sure if it's entirely true though—her loyalty to the Church seems so intense that if the Church had said they must bind these women's feet in the name of God, would she have disagreed?"

is the regulation night for summer. Must work all day long. No time to rest during the day time. By 6 a.m. in the attic it is so hot that it wakes a person up even if it were not time to get up and go on duty.[28]

"Duty" was an apt term here; like other missionaries, Hutchins felt it her absolute religious duty to give her all for the foreign mission. While the application of these religious devotions was contextualized by ethnocentrism and a racist colonialist expansion, Hutchins seemed to care deeply about making a difference in the everyday lives of women and girls. As late as 1939 she received a letter from a former pupil in China asking for her help. Martha Li, who signed herself "Now Mrs. Peter Kao," wrote that she remembered Hutchins as a teacher "who really loved me as one of her bright pupils in the English class. You were then very willing to help me through college. Now I wish that, instead of myself, you could help one or two of my children in their education."[29] Hutchins demonstrated strong personal commitments that were governed by Christian values of charity and service; the fact that she kept this letter over the years suggests that she most likely responded with financial help for this ex-pupil.

When the first single women arrived in the missionary field, they boarded with married couples since it was thought that all women needed the protection of a male head of household. As the numbers of single women increased, women's houses were established that fostered a close company of women and a separate women's culture. These communities were especially important in ameliorating the psychosocial needs of indi-

These stories smack of the exotic. How impossible it must have been for Grace to construct their lives in any other way than through the lens of racist ethnocentrism. These women seem so invisible. Trinh T. Minh-ha has said that "a conversation with 'us' about 'them' is a conversation in which 'them' is silenced. 'Them' always stands on the other side of the hill, naked and speechless, barely present in its absence. Subject of discussion 'them,' is only admitted among 'us,' the discussing subjects, when accompanied or introduced by 'us' member, hence the dependency of 'them' and its need to acquire good manners for the membership standing."[30]

viduals uprooted from their homes and communities of origin, and they created new "families" that facilitated a sense of self and identity, providing emotional support and nurturance based upon the sister or mother–daughter models of relationships. As a result of these communities, the potential for a rich women's culture emerged among single missionary women; a culture that could support, nurture, and provide emotional sustenance for them. Ironically, missionary culture, while firmly grounded in religious ideologies that espoused the domestic bliss of subordinate wives, often nourished women in their alternative quest for more fulfilling lives outside of traditional families.

Hutchins wrote briefly of such women as Dorothy Mills, Helen Hendricks, and Katharine Scott with whom she lived and worked. There is no doubt that she enjoyed their companionship and collegiality and that these friendships were very important to her as a young woman displaced in a strange land

Inscription: "Miss Phelps and K. Scott (right) on one of our walks outside the wall."

without immediate family. Alongside her strong faith and devotion to God, the other single women with whom she lived and worked provided immediate and important substitute families. Such networks helped nourish a rich woman–centered space that would have been all too familiar to Hutchins at this point. She was able to maintain a friendship with Helen Hendricks in particular into their old age. Even though within a few decades of leaving China Hutchins found herself on a very different end of the political spectrum than most of her missionary friends, friendships were maintained. A letter from Helen Hendricks confirmed this: "I came away [from a luncheon] admiring you for your charm as a hostess but also your courage in following your convictions. The fact that you gave us a glimpse into how these came to you added much to the zest and the occasion and to my understanding of your point of view. What different roads we have traveled since China Days, but how nice to be able to meet over the luncheon table, as good friends, and talk it over!"[31]

In this way, while Hutchins was part of a religiously conservative and racist movement, this movement did offer her the opportunity for self-fulfillment and self-advocacy. And, while she gave her energy to an institution that she would soon see tied to imperialist forces seeking new resources for colonial expansion and the development of industries at home, I believe her experiences in this movement were empowering. Ironically, in terms of personal agency, she was able to attain leadership roles, develop her administrative and organizational skills and grow professionally in the context of a woman-centered community that was relatively independent of masculine prerogatives.

It is not entirely clear why Hutchins left the mission, except that war was raging in Europe, her health had been suffering, and her parents wanted her to return.[32] Hutchins's acquiescence on this reflects again the filial duty of daughters (especially when that daughter was the oldest child) to cater to the desires and needs of aging parents, and in particular, to the requests of mothers. Despite her return to the United States, her devotion to the cause of Christianity did not diminish, although her thinking would progress markedly left.

Home Again

There is much silence surrounding the activities of Grace Hutchins between 1916 and 1920. She left China a devout missionary and appeared

---

The clue here about her leaving China is a brief mention in a newspaper interview some years later where Grace mentioned that she left China because of ill health and the wishes of her parents. It is not clear whether that meant her ill health or the ill health of her parents; I assumed it implied Grace's ill health, although I'm not sure.

four years later a socialist and a pacifist. While these intervening years are shrouded in relative mystery, the following excerpt from a short biographical update she gave the Bryn Mawr College alumnae magazine, *The Turtle's Progress-Dispatch*, is revealing:

> From a pious missionary in China I became a "Bolshevik," active in the labor movement here in the US. It was the War that turned the tide and made me a Socialist.[33]

Certainly the war years were a centrally defining period for her, as they were for many other Americans. I imagine these years of Hutchins's life to have been similar to Rochester's a decade earlier: pursuing the intellectual analysis of religion and exploring her own faith, staying tuned into the "helping" aspect of her past few years in China in terms of reform work, and responding to the war. I think of her being active in her church, doing charity work, and starting to chafe against the politics of her family concerning the war. And I imagine her starting her relationship with Rochester through a shared devotional spirituality, a spirituality that would more and more reflect a commitment for social justice and move in the direction of Christian socialism.

I do know that on returning from China she became involved with Women's Auxiliary work. She also attended a conference of the Episcopal Conclave in St. Louis in October as a delegate, and, along with friend Helen Hendricks, appeared on the front page of the *St. Louis Star* newspaper.[34] During 1917 she spent a year at the Union Theological Seminary where she was able to enjoy the intellectual pursuits associated with the study of Christianity as well as friendship with one of its faculty, Adelaide Case. Founded in 1836 by a group of "new school" Presbyterian laity and clergy, the Union Theological Seminary was incorporated in 1839 under a charter granted by the legislature of the state of New York. Although denominational, Union welcomed all denominations and aimed to provide a training for teachers of religion, missionaries, and parish ministers, as well as workers in ecclesiastical and benevolent agencies.[35] In the late nineteenth century Union Theological Seminary made a strong commitment to academic freedom through its decision to rescind the prerogative of the General Assembly of the Presbyterian Church on vetoing the appointment of professors. When Hutchins attended in 1917, Arthur C. McGiffert had just been elected as president of the Seminary, and the school was known as a highly credible institution for the study of religion and the Bible.

Between 1917 and 1918 Hutchins took a position as a principal and teacher of a social work training school named St. Faiths. While her opposition to U.S. intervention in the war almost lost her this job, she emerged

Research diary: May 14, 1997: "[I spent a] frustrating morning—what I would give for a firsthand account by Grace about this period of her life. [There are] too many gaps—leads that go nowhere—nothing on St. Faiths. I wish Grace and Anna would come to me in a dream and clear up some of these gaps. Now that would make for one outstanding subtext box.

from this fight doubly energized.[36] In this way it seems that her intellectual interest in religion was pursued at Union at the same time that her political consciousness as a pacifist was developing. Opposed to the war, Hutchins was beginning to get more politically involved. A product of the times, her life was starting to converge with that of soul-mate Anna Rochester.

PART TWO

CHRISTIAN SOCIALISTS

CHAPTER FOUR

SISTERHOOD OF THE SMILING COUNTENANCE

WORLD WAR I changed the world in countless ways. It represented a huge cultural loss of innocence that reverberated throughout U.S. society and moved us into what we often consider the modern era. Amidst the devastation of Europe, the United States emerged with a booming, though as the thirties would show, vulnerable economy. The early 1920s saw the emergence of a new "modern" America as industry and technology advanced, consumption increased, and the expansion of mass culture kept pace with growing advertising and movie industries. While lifestyles with values of consumerism and personal liberation were really only available to an urban middle class, nonetheless, these new ideals had significant impact on the popular imagination for the framing of these modern times. An emphasis on personal gratification characterized the decade as a new materialism gave rise to the equation of democracy with freedom to consume. However, a common description of the twenties as the "Jazz Age" or the "Age of the Flapper" often overlooks the political persecution and repression that also characterized this decade. January 1920 saw Attorney General Mitchell Palmer ordering raids on the homes of alleged radicals, aliens were deported or arrested, and socialists, pacifists, and anarchists endured much persecution without proper legal representation. The Bolshevik Revolution of 1917 fed this "red scare" and drew new lines among the American Left.[1] Much of the reform movements that characterized the Progressive era collapsed and, politically, the period was very bleak.

Women's roles were very much at center stage during this period.[2] While the Nineteenth Amendment had secured the franchise for women, political equality was still a long way away, and organizations committed to im-

"Not only do different writers of biographies of the same people disagree, but also the same biographer holds different opinions, different views, different conclusions, about their subject....The apparent "fact" [of narration] is actually a fabrication of selection and omission, of weaving together contiguously related elements and not directly related ones, for in the time-gaps between the steps outlined lie a host of events, behaviors, persons, not 'seen' in this account.The facts, like the fictions, are a product of their time, place, author, author's frame of mind, reader."[3]

proving women's lot were beginning to face the deceptions associated with women's new "emancipation." Indeed, many came to understand, as they did decades later with the Women's Liberation movement of the 1960s and 1970s, that the "independence" of the "New Woman" was really a farce: the vote had hardly changed anything and it certainly had not improved the structural conditions of most women's lives. This was especially true for the working class, immigrants, and women of color who had always been "free" to work outside the home. But for those who were now liberated to work for paid labor, just like today they did so at lower rates of pay than received by men and still took primary responsibility for work within the home and family. Rising expectations of the new consumer lifestyle kept women working outside the home and a market was maintained for the purchase of these goods and services. Most women kept working as they had always done and life was as difficult as ever.[4]

Given these developments that juxtaposed freedom with consumption and fabricated notions of equality alongside political repressions, it is no small wonder that the 1920s were years that radicalized Hutchins and Rochester and established them as political activists. For them, like many others, the culmination of the period was the trumped-up trial and tragic execution of anarchists Nicola Sacco and Bartolomeo Vanzetti in 1927, an event that coincided with their decision to join the Communist Party.

In 1920 Hutchins and Rochester were still identified with one wing of the Socialist Party, the Christian pacifists. They were ideologically committed to socialism as a blueprint for global equality and strongly believed that Christianity had a role to play in this revolution. The events in Russia and the divisions within the party would no doubt have affected them; at this point in the early 1920s they would not have labeled themselves communists since their commitment to a Christian justice was given a niche by the socialists and not by the atheist communists. The Russian Orthodox Church had slowly been deestablished by the Bolsheviks through antireligious training of children and youth in school and organizations, and the sequestering of church property and expulsion and/or death of those who resisted. In addition, the Bolsheviks had encouraged internal dissension within the church

The article I reference concerning the demise of the Russian Orthodox Church is an *Atlantic Monthly* essay that was most probably read by Grace and Anna. Their friend Florence Converse was editor of this periodical and I feel pretty sure that they subscribed to it. I can only assume that when Grace said that it was the war that made her a Bolshevik, she must have been glossing over what was really a more complicated development in terms of her ideological entanglements. If I am wrong and they thought themselves Bolshevik supporters during this period, then they would have been dealing with some glaring contradictions around their pacifism and their faith. Life of course is full of contradictions and personhood is very complex. Avery Gordon says complex personhood means that all people "remember and forget, are beset by contradiction, and recognize it and mis-recognize themselves and others ... [it means] that people suffer graciously and selfishly too, get stuck in the symptoms of their troubles, and also transform themselves."[5]

among bishops and priests in terms of leadership and practice.[6] Most likely Hutchins and Rochester respected the Bolsheviks' commitment to struggle but did not condone this deestablishment of the church. Through these years of the early 1920s they believed in the power of Christianity to move the revolution forward and keep it on a moral footing. Like other Christian socialists of the period, Hutchins and Rochester protested the economic changes they saw as tearing apart the fabric of humanity.

At this point, our couple had already met and they were deciding to live together. Hutchins in particular was a far different person from the woman who had taught Chinese evangelists less than a decade earlier. She was in-fluenced by her growing socialist consciousness and was increasingly criti-cal of the way a wealthy minority was consolidating power and resources in the face of increasing urban chaos and industrial problems. Passionate to understand the plight of the working class, Hutchins took a temporary job in December 1920 with Seidenberg and Co. of New York, "makers of fine cigars."[7] Since this experience was a requirement of a class at the New York School of Social Work (formerly the New York School of Philanthropy) where she was a student of labor problems, she only worked there a few months. Nonetheless, she credited it as a highly formative experience that helped her apply theories of social and economic practice she had learned in the classroom. Years later Hutchins recalled the injustices of replacing a male tobacco handler at less pay as well as the general poor working con-ditions involved in this job.[8]

From 1920 to 1921 Hutchins continued her study of the relationships between education and social problems at Teachers College of Columbia University. Her social and political analysis was becoming more sophisti-cated and her participation in social justice organizations was increasing.

Research diary: March 31, 1998: "Grace gets a lot of mileage out of these few months at Seidenbergs. [This experience] keeps cropping up and [is] mentioned in various newspaper articles as an example of her commitment to understanding the working class. [I know it must have been quite] a courageous step for such a genteel, aristocratic Bryn Mawr graduate [to join tobacco handlers in the factory]—even if only for a couple of months—but it highlights her contradictions as a wealthy socialist 'choosing' blue-collar work and then using it as an example of her commitment to the struggle. [From the cultural space of my moment it seems] patronizing."

Together with Rochester, they had strong affiliations with the Society of Companions of the Holy Cross (SCHC) and were members of the Executive Committee of the Church League for Industrial Democracy, a group that evolved from the Intercollegiate Socialist Society and was a precursor to Students for a Democratic Society.[9] In addition, they were involved with the Fellowship of Reconciliation, a Christian pacifist organization with socialist leanings, and its journal, the *World Tomorrow*. Nineteen twenty saw Anna Rochester leaving her job at the Children's Bureau and affiliating herself with the Labor Research Committee of the Rand School of Social Science, an institution with which Hutchins also became affiliated. Founded in New York in 1906, the Rand School was the first major workers' school for adult education in the United States. Major intellectual leaders of various progressive social movements taught such classes as trade union policies, music, art, Russian studies, social work and peace education at Rand.[10]

Hutchins and Rochester's desire to live their politics took a practical turn as discussions ensued about creating a living community that reflected their spiritual and ideological beliefs and sustained their activism. They started serious preparations for a shared living space that would allow them to live simply in community with other like-minded women:

> One evening in early December 1920 when three Socialist comrades were dining together, their conversation turned to the topic of shared property, communal living and how one might live radical politics in the everyday sense. Mr. Horace Fort spoke eloquently of the joys of living more usefully and beautifully in the present world in a community of men. It fell to the two women present to mark his comment on the community of men with an asterisk (*), footnoted as "with modification and variation."[11]

And so began the discussion for founding a women's commune, a commune that Hutchins, Rochester and other residents would tongue-in-cheek call "The Sisterhood of the Smiling Countenance and the Merry Laugh." Their experiences of the spiritual community at Adelynrood, the retreat

My first published work on the lives of Grace and Anna was an article on the commune in *Frontiers*.[12] It was another of those glimpses, but more intense than the research on Grace as a missionary. I hadn't realized then the relationship between SCHC and the commune, nor just how radical Grace and Anna were even at this point. As a feminist, of course, I was overjoyed at the notion of a women's commune as I still am, and came down on the side of the homosocial community as one of the last outposts against misogynous modernism. I'm not sure now whether Grace and Anna would have agreed with my characterization, at least in their later years. Ironically, they might have found it overly sentimental. Caring strongly about women's issues, no doubt they would still have thought my obsession with this feminist notion of segregated womanhood overly bourgeois.

center of SCHC, must have undoubtedly affected their desire to live in community this way on a permanent basis. A commune journal documented the following: "After some time spent in this discussion, Grace Hutchins said: 'Why not a community of women?' This thought had been in her mind for some time; for four years, indeed. 'I'm game,' said Anna Rochester, who had not been thinking of it so long."[13]

While this period in the 1920s has so often been described by historians as a marker for modern times, so too these years illustrate a transition point for Hutchins and Rochester. In particular, they were moving out of an era characterized by nineteenth-century language and ideologies into a more modern twentieth-century period. Representative of this earlier nineteenth-century era, the commune they founded was a feminine segregated space that incorporated a sentimental and religious discourse grounded in moral distinctions.

Hutchins and Rochester considered themselves socialists and would have been aware of the affinity between socialism and modernism as well as the modernist critique of feminized sentimental discourse. This critique saw the sentimental representing an outdated social order and as an example of obscene bourgeois life and thought.[14] Budding intellectuals like Hutchins and Rochester could hardly avoid being exposed to the cultural and literary changes characterized by modernism. These changes included the separation of personal self and literature (ultimately obscuring women's voice), authorial transcendence, and the superiority of the rational over the sentimental. Alongside these cultural and literary dilemmas associated with voice and discourse, the contradictions associated with being privileged bourgeois "revolutionaries" loomed large. I suggest that in many ways the writings of Hutchins, Rochester, and their friends during the commune years reflected this situation of being immersed in a historical period that illuminated the juxtaposition of traditional values alongside increasing intellectual and political ferment. In other words, while the commune existed as a place for women to receive support and emotional nourishment, it encompassed a community dedicated to socialism and the disruption of traditional social relations in society, including the very genteel homosocial relations that had nurtured commune members in the first place.[15] The commune's placement then on the brink of this modern era provides a context for exploring the ways Hutchins and Rochester experienced the contradictions and paradoxes of the period. The contradictions and tensions surrounding such a community of privileged women who sought to make progressive changes were great: the modernist paradigms of which these women were a part were simultaneously attempting to erase them. The writings from these commune years of 1921 to 1924 illustrate this dilemma in interesting ways and suggest how Hutchins and Rochester were constructed as historical actors during this period.

The Commune

> The beauty and grace of the house no living person could miss, its lovely comradeship, its burning warmth, its reality of meaning, its truly humble sisterliness. Humor keeps it fresh, respect for differing opinions keeps it sane, vital reverence for life itself prevents it from growing stiff or suspicious of change.[16]

New Year 1921 found Hutchins and Rochester looking for a suitable house for their intentional community. While there was historical precedent for female segregated space, there was also a history of utopian socialist communities that doubtless influenced the creation of the commune.[17] When Hutchins and Rochester first started looking for a house, they were confronted with disappointments caused by the housing shortage in New York. However within a very short time an old friend of Rochester's heard about a house for rent on West Twenty-seventh Street whose tenants had moved to the country. With great anticipation, Rochester arranged to view the house with Hutchins, Edith Klein, and another friend, Josephine Starr. "Unswept and ungarnished though it was, the house enticed her," and it was agreed to rent the house at $150 a month.[18] This was a considerable amount in those days, and even though it was spacious enough to house many tenants, it would have been a large sum of money as initial outlay. Their situation might be contrasted to most working-class New Yorkers who were impacted by both the housing shortage at the time and the cost of living increases that sparked protests across the city during these years.[19] The ability to create a women's house dedicated to spiritual communion and social justice was dependent upon Hutchins and Rochester's class privilege, which enabled their independence and their purchasing power. Note how the situation of wealthy women wanting to live simply and frugally comes across as a noble venture; being poor in the first place and living simply might not attract any special consideration.[20]

The tenants set out to make the house their home by fashioning the rooms and planning their furniture. They cleaned and swept and painted chairs the "soft dark smoke-night-deep-water blue which had been appointed."[21] Some rooms were given such special names as Tweedledee and Tweedledum, Red Sea and the Equator, and, in keeping with the religious devotions of house tenants, one room became the chapel. The house was described as follows:

> American basement, three rooms deep, with hall, and yard—a grassy square with a little paved walk all around it; in the middle room (Tweedledum) gas range and in the back one (Tweedledee) a coal range, and sink: five cupboards

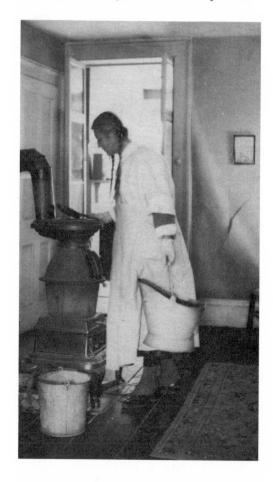

Grace tending the store at Community House (c. 1923).

in all. Above, two living rooms with fireplaces of marble, and two bedrooms opening into the middle room with long glass doors like french windows. (And telephone cupboard at the end of the hall, and Widow's Cruse cupboard at the other. Seven cupboards and closets to date.) Above this story, Oratory, in front, over doorway: the double bedroom; middle (dark) living room called The Equator; and two single bedrooms at back, with bathroom off hall. Six more closets and cupboards, making fifteen to date. Top story, with two bedrooms, trunk room, and bathroom. Four more closets and cupboards, making nineteen in all! [original emphasis][22]

After the renting of the house had been tentatively decided upon, Hutchins and Rochester attended church and took Holy Communion at St. Luke's Chapel. It was January 6, the Feast of the Epiphany. Excited by their plans for a shared community dedicated to prayer and active service, they took their dream to church, "thinking and talking in deepest earnest for this idea."[23] They decided then to carry their plans forward and celebrated this day, January 6, as the founding of the house.

Like Adelynrood, the SCHC retreat center, the commune was founded on a strong religious basis, and religious devotions were focal and unifying aspects of the community. The house was ritually blessed by Rector Fleming James of Rochester's own St. Paul's Church in Englewood, and a room was set aside for individual and community prayers. While ideological contradictions associated with these religious beliefs would plague Hutchins and Rochester by the end of the decade and cause them to reject Christianity, during these years they used the experience of religious community as a model for solidarity, empowerment, and social betterment.[24] The commune documents contain some handwritten pages of script composed by Rochester for communal prayer associated with the SCHC. These pages articulated the strong blending of Christian faith and socialist politics through religious premises based upon justice and equality. The prayers made a strong plea for Christians in political and industrial office to understand their responsibilities to humanity. It also asked that religious leaders understand the ethics of justice associated with their mission. And finally it focused on the individual and the family, asking God to help them overcome avarice and want, prejudice and pride. The following is a short excerpt:

> Help us, O God, to discern the true causes of thankfulness that lie deep in our confusion and suffering today. In the nation's political [and] industrial life. In our relation with Negroes. In our own Church. In the relation of our Church and other Churches. In our communities. In the Companionship. Let us pray for the nations. Let us pray for the sick, the suffering, those in sorrow, and in temptation. May the spirit of joy radiate from the lives of all at Adelynrood and of all Companions everywhere. For the World Conference. For all steps towards Church unity. That bishops, priests, and other ministers may yield their wills to thine and interpret to their people the evils of the world with a clear vision, righteousness, and love.[25]

With great anticipation the first tenants moved in on February 15, 1921. These residents included Hutchins, Rochester, Edith Klein, Stella Lundelins, and Elvira Slack. Josephine Starr arrived in April, and Lucie Myer and Ann Mundelein joined the commune in September. Mundelein, noted as being "as steadfast as a star," was also known as "house treasurer and custodian of the linen closet." In October Mary Ellen Daniels took up residency, followed by Sarah (Sally) Cleghorn in November. Daniels left the following April to join her family in Ohio, and Cleghorn lived at the commune until June 1923. She was a writer and affiliate with the Fellowship of Reconciliation, as well as a teacher at Brookwood, the Fellowship's school. Edith Klein you might remember was the longtime friend of Rochester's who lived with her during the years she had cared for Louise. Klein was reported as working in a cafeteria during the commune years. Nothing is known about Stella Lundelins except that she arrived "fresh with her diploma from St. Lukes." Elvira Slack did not stay long in the commune because she accepted a faculty position at Wellesley College within a few months; Josephine Starr also left that first summer because of her work, and Stella Lundelins left the following summer for unknown reasons. There was much coming and going in the commune as residents relocated over the three years of its existence, and there were also many documented visitors and guests.[26]

One of the initial decisions these first residents had to make concerned the naming of the house. They contemplated such names as "Saint Debs," after socialist Eugene Debs, and the "Unsettlement House" (Rochester's humorous reference to the settlement houses of the time), but mostly it came to be known as "Community House" or just "352." The humor invoked in the naming of the house reflected the general witty atmosphere of the commune where puns were constantly sprinkled through their everyday interactions. Even preparations for cleaning the house before moving in were documented with lighthearted jest and clever puns. Illustrations and cartoons dotted the commune journal and few people seemed to have escaped the tenants' wit and satire. Bishop Jones, for example, secretary of the Fellowship of Reconciliation, visited the commune and must have been involved in some activity that made Cleghorn exclaim about his "ungodly exercises (O! the unecclesiasticalness of such conduct!)."[27]

One summer fresh from Oregon, I spent some time in New York City researching Grace and Anna at Tamiment Library at NYU. I trudged all over trying to locate West Twenty-seventh Street, becoming quite excited when I realized I was only a few blocks away. Camera in hand I stood gaping as the block ended and I saw that a large apartment building stood where my women's brownstone house should have been. How could they?

Community House tenants doing chores (c. 1923).

Central to the commune was the notion of shared housekeeping.[28] In terms of domestic labor, most socialist theory held the mainstream view that women should be involved in productive paid labor and paid little attention to women's reproductive and household labor.[29] Others emphasized that domestic tasks should become public activities with society organized around community kitchens.[30] At Community House, the everyday tasks of housekeeping were carefully divided, and meetings were held every Wednesday so that tenants could talk through ideas and problems, and make plans for the running of the house. Rochester explained the

Community House tenants doing chores (c. 1923).

importance of this shared community in a letter to prospective tenant
Lucie Myer. A former friend of Hutchins, Myer became a lifetime friend
and companion throughout Hutchins and Rochester's lives.

> Dear Lucie Myer,
> I feel that you are already part of the Community but I have settled back on
> that sense of you being with us, quite selfishly, instead of letting you know
> long ago that I am glad. . . . [O]ur life at 352 *is* real, and not playing at sim-

plicity. And I'm glad that you really want a common life and not simply a pleasant, inexpensive way of living together. The possibility of such a Community seems to me so very great—but much depends on our sense of belonging together and taking counsel on all our plans. So I am glad that you want this too. With eager anticipation,

Anna Rochester

And love always from Grace.[31]

Duty, Service, and Solidarity

Central to the commune was commitment to work and service to others. As Rochester's verse suggests below, one of the commune's purposes was to put into action the ideals of duty and service in the context of a loving and supportive community:

> Sick with the world's agony
> Feeble in hope
> Faltering on a lonely road
> Failure and self-clouding the vision of thee
> And then,
> Comrades, articulate, loving,
> The way shining clear,
>
> Adventures and vision and joy,
> And the world?
> May our joy, thy gift in our pain
> Serve.[32]

Hutchins also expressed this sense of duty and commitment in her short verse "When Boston Came to New York":

> Be Brief:
>
> We are not here to spend, to wear, to weep
> It's nearly nine o'clock and we must sleep.
> Let others wear gay furs and silks and lace
> Mine, mine to don an apron and brief-case.[33]

In keeping with the goal of facilitating Christian justice, various organizations met at 352 during its three years of existence. These included many of the groups with which Hutchins and Rochester were affiliated: the Church League for Industrial Democracy, SCHC, Council of the Fellowship of Reconciliation, and staff meetings for the *World Tomorrow*. Hutchins had become associate secretary for the Fellowship in May 1922, and both Hutchins and Rochester were involved in writing and planning for the journal. The presence of these organizations helped increase the

When I knew I wanted to write a biography that tried to disrupt authorial om-nipotence, I thought I might follow Nagel's idea and try to write a "meta-bi-ography"[34]—that is, locate myself as an interacting character within the text. Since I have had no relationship with Grace and Anna outside of this project, I moved beyond what I think Nagel had in mind toward thinking about inten-tionally "fabricating" narrative by creating intentional fiction. And it was this period, the commune years, that gave me inspiration to do that; I could imag-ine myself one of the commune members enjoying the cozy solidarity among friends. This seemed an interesting way to emphasize the impermeable bound-aries between fact and fiction and write something fun and accessible. I tried it without much success and abandoned the idea out of a growing discomfort with what seemed to be an overly melodramatic and self-centered move (not to mention the fact that it stretched my abilities as a creative writer). Research diary: February 12, 1998: "This [putting myself in the text as a fictional charac-ter] is too weird—don't think I can do this—[I feel] too narcissistic, too ex-posed. It might point out authorial authority, but it sure feels like [I'm claim-ing] too much authority—too much on-centre stuff."

sense of commitment and devotion to duty and service on which the com-mune was founded.

Such caring also extended to the neighborhood community. The tenants of 352 seemed well known and liked in the neighborhood, underscoring the aura of womanly virtue and respectability that surrounded the com-mune women, even during these "red scare" years. Helen Hendricks, Hutchins's missionary friend and a visitor to the house, captured in the fol-lowing verse how tenants were able to juxtapose socialist meetings with concern for the local children to create a loving community devoted to service. "352" was indeed a noble venture:

> O' little house of Christmas red
> Who knows what may be born of thee
> In service raise thy modest head
> To share a great world's destiny.[35]

Evoking similar feelings of duty and service as well as deep compassion un-derscored by guilt, Rochester wrote:

> The sunset calls us home to firelight,
> We gather, well content, to dine.
> But they, — its glory mocks their homelessness,
> Hungry they wait in long despair.
> And I am merry
> Having turned a poignant verse
> About their story.[36]

The commune journal records visits and events with local children: caroling at Christmas, baking fudge on April Fool's day, making flower pots at Easter, and trips to the park.[37] The neighbors referred to the tenants as "the Aunts" and seemed to appreciate the time the women spent with their children. The commune journal at one point reported that there was talk of a school that might be founded at 352, but this idea did not come to anything.[38] Community House also provided the women who lived there with the emotional support and security expected of same-sex communities:

> There was a community member
>   who idled from June to September
> She left her dear sisters
> To rats and to blisters
> And yet she did love remember.[39]

The commune journal and correspondence suggest how central and important their friendships were, as well as how much pleasure they took in each other's company. These writings indicate a world of emotional intimacy and richness where friends assumed a centrality in each other's lives. They often referred to themselves as a merry band of "Toug Wullies" complete with various spellings, as in the following anonymous and undated verse. It is still not clear to me what "Toug Wullies" means:

> Four toug wullies
> Happy as could be
> One went to Boston
> Then there were three
>
> Three toug-wu-lis
> Just a little blue
> One went to dinner
> Then there were two
>
> Two toug-wu-lis
> Which shall be our fate;
> A bowl of bread and milk at home
> Or dinner out in state?[40]

Verse seemed to be the preferred way for the women to demonstrate their wit and share their feelings for each other. This same-sex world no doubt alleviated their psychosocial needs and provided a model of woman-to-woman relationships that extended their "family" out into the community, and integrated religious values of commitment and devotion to a compassionate duty toward "sisters," friends, and neighbors. Yet there is a witty, irreverent aspect to much of this verse; a witticism that is evident in the following excerpt from a poem for Lucie Myer's birthday. This one was

> Research diary: March 31, 1998: "[I feel like I'm] getting swallowed up in this chapter—too mushy—too perfect—didn't they just get mad and hate each other sometimes?" Avery Gordon writes about "haunting," about how what appears to not be there is actually a seething presence. Haunting is about how life is and was more complicated than those of us who study it usually have granted. The commune reeks of these ghosts.

written by Rochester. It illustrates the sentimental discourse of intimate affection and respect and then, in the second stanza, moves into social commentary and exaggerated rhyming:

> Elfen spirit and shining eyes
> Laugh that teases, ripples, enriches,
> Soul that does while others prate
> A friend that draws my spirit higher
> That is what I find in Lucie Myer.
>
> But oh! The children know she charms them
> She'll rescue them from the schools that harm them
> And our old-maid stillness will come alive
> She shows the way to a genuine "do," see?
> And we're all ready to follow Lucie.[41]

Unsettling the Sentimental

In much of the writing associated with the commune, the tone moves beyond pathos, the sincere voice of sympathy, to bathos, an exaggerated or overdone sympathy that reflects an abrupt movement from the lofty to the mundane. Bathos is an intentional voice that disrupts pathos. While the sentimental discourse of genteel middle-class femininity was being played out in the writings associated with the commune, there was a distinctive tongue-in-cheek style that simultaneously disrupted that voice.[42] They were of that generation that had grown up with the niceties of nineteenth-century femininity, quoting the poetry of Elizabeth Browning and penning flowery verse to each other, yet they were perhaps beginning to understand that these ways were fast becoming outdated, and, worse still, were identified with bourgeois culture and behavior: I suggest that the "unsettling" of women's traditional voice was one of the ways they dealt with the contradictions of their class and gender in the context of their political affiliation and modernist changes.

Indicative of the love and concern the women had for each other, yet alive with wit and satire, is an account of a day at Community House, written by Ann Mundelein. While it focuses on the domestic duties of the

Community House members and friends "gallavanting [*sic*] at Saddle River, New Jersey" (c. 1923).

house, it unsettles this domestic discourse and offers a redefinition of the notion of a segregated feminine space. Mundelein satirizes the supposed harmony and cheerfulness of women's living groups, especially religious ones, and is quite irreverent in her use of a formal, yet tongue-in-cheek, style:

A Day Full of Little Joys in the Community

The mornings are cold and dark and sleepy on the third floor these December days, and it is oh—so hard to get up—there seems to be no joy at all to life—when suddenly out of the darkness comes the sound of the coal shovel, and saintly Community Consciousness and the draggon [*sic*] Sleepiness have a struggle, and Com. Consciousness wins, although perhaps it is a victory without much glory, and a half awake Community Consciousness finds itself coming down stairs. . . .

We are the Sisterhood of the Smiling Countenance and the Merry Laugh. And as an excellent beginning for a hard working day could anything be better than our breakfast table? Its joys go right on through the day. Sister Grace is sure to be a joy with her never failing enthusiasm, and Sister Sally is sure to bring a happy, poetic interpretation of even the commonplace, and Sister Anna always furnishes the scientific facts and accurate statistics for everything, as well as the glorious vision of the future. And the conversation is certainly delicious. Was there ever a table surrounded by such merriment as ours? If one is trying to edit a book of funny stories he should spend a week in the Community. Or if the conversation is serious it's all about the big job of making this old world all over new and giving everybody a fair chance, and that is a job really worth talking about. Now, next to dinner time, the morning meal is the happiest time of the day.

We have prooved [*sic*] that there can be much housework without drudgery. Our kitchen at 8.15 a.m. sounds as if a birthday party were in progress. The dish pan and the broom and the mop all join in the fun and laugh with us, and by 8.45 when all the work is done, the kitchens shine with a greater glory than just soap and water can give. . . . The crowning joy of the day, however, is the home coming at night, the evening meal and play time around the dish pan, and then the open fire, the book, or the music, or just pleasant conversation—and then night prayers, and bed time comes all too soon. We do not need to label our social hour, and the joy of it all is its spontaneity.[43]

In this writing Mundelein playfully addressed several themes associated with women and women's communities that often were and still are denigrated and trivialized. First, there are many references in this account to traditional feminine and domestic elements such as housework and food preparation; Mundelein also uses birth imagery in reference to the book Hutchins and Rochester were writing, *Jesus Christ and the World Today.* These feminine tasks are appropriated by her exaggerated references to the coal shovel, dishpan, broom and mop, and the women's cheeriness and exuberant embrace of these tasks elevates their mundaneness, therefore dissipating the lack of power associated with the identification of women with household drudgery. In addition, the emphasis here is on shared labor. Mundelein is expressing one of the basic values of Community House at that time: that housework be communal rather than individual, thus transforming its drudgery. As socialists who had read Marx and perhaps learned about his theories of alienation, commune members were trying to replace this traditional form of alienated labor as well as provide a way to move beyond the privatization of domestic tasks.

Second, Mundelein addressed the connotations associated with religious communities. She connoted images of gentle, willing, smiling nuns, embracing the notion of religious sisterhood yet poking fun at traditional devout communities of women. Commune residents playfully called each other "Sister" as did the settlement workers of the time, but the commune members used their first name rather than their last, mimicking the prac-

There is the possibility that rather than reflecting an intentional "unsettling" of the sentimental, these witticisms were actually a component of the sentimental that is not usually seen. Perhaps we have been too keen on reconstructing women's segregated space and the discourse in it as overly serious, thus overlooking such frivolous aspects.

tice of nuns. In a similar fashion, Rochester mocked this formality in her suggestion of "Unsettlement House" as a name for the commune.

Third, Mundelein emphasized the women's mirth, wit, and joviality such that the sheer merriment associated with the house is what shone through in her writing: "We do not need to label our social hour, and the joy of it all is its spontaneity." Traditionally, women's communities had often been seen as serious, prudish, and potentially boring; Mundelein made it very clear that they were quite self-sufficient socially, with each "Sister" bringing something to enrich the community. Her point implied that men did not need to be present for intelligent conversation, meaningful social discourse, and an all-round good time to occur.

Mundelein's writing illustrates the tension that Hutchins and Rochester and other tenants experienced between existing and changing norms. She used the imitative, genteel discourse of nineteenth-century women's writings, invoking and honoring traditional communities at the same time that she satirized them and attempted to carve out a new place for a community of progressive women who sought to make changes in the world: "the big job of making this old world all over new." They were redefining for themselves the meaning of progressive action informed by religious devotion at the beginning of a new modern era. As these writings suggest, there was a tension around the issue of how a progressive community might (re)define itself given the changing norms of the time. The women of the commune wrote with both the sincere voice of the sentimental and a mocking playfulness of that voice. The contradictions here for a group of privileged women engaged in socialist practice must have been enormous, with the commune existing as a microcosm of the larger tensions and contradictions around issues of gender, class, and race.

For Sally Cleghorn, the "archivist" of Community House, this joyous gathering of witty women had its drawbacks. In a letter to Hutchins she voiced her misgivings about the "monastic" character of the community, misgivings that coincided with her departure form the house. The tone of her letter, dated April 1923, was tender and kind. It began "Dearest Grace" and ended with "Goodbye dear and beautiful Grace." Indeed, Cleghorn kept in touch with Hutchins and Rochester throughout their long lives and they continued to be close friends. Cleghorn praised the support and solidarity that she felt in the commune and appreciated the humor, comradeship, and respect for differing opinions. However, at the same time, she articulated what she felt were the drawbacks of living in such an exclusively feminine community, especially one with so little class diversity. In terms of the former, she admits to the freedom they have in the house because of their feminine family and suggests that it would indeed be "curtailed in spots by having a mixed community." Nevertheless, she continued,

I like men around for many reasons which I know, and probably several I don't know; but all the same I feel the siren charm of exclusive femininity. It curiously charms by both its order and by its chance for wildness! But there is a relaxing yet somehow bracing effect from living in the same house with men. . . . It relaxes the precision, and braces the tolerance, of women. They grow less sensitive, perhaps, sometimes. I feel also a sort of sunshine from the company of men. Especially big boys. . . . I feel drawn immeasurably toward community life, but in my dreams of it I find always men and children of assorted ages.[44]

Cleghorn found the "exclusive femininity" both restrictive and empowering: she felt the power and freedom of this community of women but at the same time interpreted this as dangerous and demanding. It seems she preferred a heterosocial world where she felt women could be less "precise" or excessively particular, a seemingly more tolerant world for Cleghorn. While she might have been uncomfortable with the homosocial orientation of the house, Cleghorn may also have been influenced by the modern radical intellectuals who saw this world as repressive and passé. While I suggest that Cleghorn might have been uncomfortable on an unconscious level with the homoerotic tendencies of the house, I really do not believe she was homophobic or consciously opposed to women loving women in the sense we think about it today.

At the point that Hutchins and Rochester became a couple in the early twenties, passionate romantic attachments between women that in earlier times had been a respected social institution were starting to arouse suspicion of pathology. As a result women were increasingly becoming more self-conscious about their romantic identification.[45] I believe Hutchins and Rochester were relatively immune from these suspicions for several reasons. First, they had enormous class privilege and had been raised as very "proper" women. Such privilege would have allowed them to set themselves above and not identify with people whom they saw as different. In addition, they were not young women at this time (Hutchins was in her mid-thirties and Rochester her early forties), and their ages would most likely have allowed them to claim a certain asexual respectability. Second, their love for each other was based upon respect and admiration and was probably felt as a deep moral commitment interpreted as pure and sacred. It would have been easy for them to see their same-sex attachments as having nothing to do with the sexologists' portrait of abnormal and sick lesbians trapped in male bodies or hating men, as identified by the sexologists of the time. They most likely refused to recognize this intense and pure love they felt for each other in the description of lesbianism or inversion.[46] Constructing their relationship this way, no doubt others treated them the way they saw themselves. Finally, Hutchins and Rochester's relationship was nourished and stabilized by the homosocial community within which they lived—a community that represented a former Victorian era of woman identification and affection, characteristic of relative sexual innocence. This community would have helped buffer and solidify their relationship.

However, along with the exclusive femininity of the commune, Cleghorn also disapproved of an "unconscious refinement," or "selected air":

> The sense of dedication to our house at 352 (for go where I may, I feel a child-like sense of proprietorship in the house) is beautiful and great, and how I wish it less I don't know; nor does it lessen the gales of mirth with which we often were childishly carried away—I never laughed more than at 352. But this is true, for better or worse, that in the house the common lazy (moral) sense can't find a footing. . . . One thing that occurs to me, and I think I've said it to Lucie too; namely, that perhaps it's less of a monastic tinge in the house, than an atmosphere of very great, though unconscious refinement. Perhaps if we added to our family one or two women of far less refinement of upbring-ing, whose voices and intonations were louder and coarser than ours, what I have called monastic would prove to have been really something cultural. . . . I do think, too, that the air of the house is a little intellectual; not in the old-fashioned blue-stocking way, but unsolemly so, sufficiently so perhaps to make some of the less self-confident of us (though it's a thing I never feel through my triple cheek) a little timid. . . . In an intellectual house, or with an intellectual person, one feels one's prattling exposed indecently. It seems shocking. I think there is a little high altitude of that sort at 352.[47]

Cleghorn's observations about class are very astute. Hutchins and Rochester's genteel language was an expression of class and gender to-gether: the witty puns and intellectual referencing, the modesty and veiled courtesies. She was reacting to the gendered cultural manifestations of class privilege and was experiencing the intellectual air of the house, the "high altitude," through the witty discourse of Hutchins and Rochester and the other highly educated and privileged tenants. Satire was kept at such a high pitch that Cleghorn seemed to have felt the burden of this de-mand for wit and spontaneity: "one feels one's prattling exposed inde-cently." In the letter she continued with suggestions for weekly or at least fortnightly meetings where "new notions and proposals for experiments of all sorts would be brought forward. If to such alive and active house meetings were added a personnel of some uncongeniality, widely differing social and geographical backgrounds, and even some considerable moral differences, the household would I think assume more of the family and less the selected air."[48]

While Cleghorn's ideas about importing working-class women might make us cringe, it seems a sincere suggestion on her part for more diversity in the house and was written with a real, although naïve, concern for those less fortunate than herself. In another letter to Hutchins and Rochester written while she was doing some work with the YWCA in Troy, New York, she wrote the following:

> It's come off so cold here after a little snowstorm that I am more concerned than ever about the unemployed; and I was suddenly struck with a wonder, this afternoon, whether we could in any way be more hospitable to them at our house? Could we invite 6 of them in for an evening once a week, for example? I would like to give them something not to drink, on my own account. Do you suppose we could?—I mean, [does] something of that (or perhaps some better) [idea] occur to you? One hour, or two of comfort and graciousness would be a real help, I believe, even though we can't keep them all night. But maybe you know reasons which prevent—I'm very featherheaded, I know, and I've only just thought of this—by morning I may remember many reasons myself against it.
>
> Much love, dear Grace and dear Anna! God love *you*!
> Affectionately, Sally N. C.[49]

Cleghorn's ideas about sheltering the unemployed for a couple of hours a week at 352 did not become actualized. Perhaps Hutchins and Rochester and the other tenants were not ready to open their home to the problems of the street, maybe some of them were in favor and others were not, and a group consensus came down on the side of nonsupport for this plan. Perhaps it was understood as patronizing, although probably not. I would have loved to have known how Hutchins and Rochester responded; my sense is that on an intellectual level they would have found the plan to be a good one, and would not have seen it as a patronizing move. Given the focus on philanthropy of the day, a group of genteel women opening their doors to half a dozen unemployed men probably was seen as an informal extension of the YWCA. But my guess is that this idea was too much for Hutchins and Rochester at the time, too much of a risk, too close to home, literally.

Research diary: March 31, 1998: "Re-working [this chapter on the] commune—my favourite chapter—and Sally Cleghorn is one of my favourite characters. She has an astonishing fluency—so articulate yet so beautifully framed in the delicacies of feminine writing." When I first wrote this article for *Frontiers* I did not know much about Sally's long friendship with Grace and Anna nor had I read the essays she wrote that were published in the *World Tomorrow*. And, because this chapter has been reworked so much, more than many others, it reflects the ways biography gets put together out of a series of reflections that are grounded in the context of the moments in which they are written, rather than a seamless or continuous argument.

In order to understand Cleghorn's response to these obvious signs of gendered class privilege at the commune, it is important to consider the historical and sociopolitical context of 1923, which found a breaking down of traditional hierarchies and values, a growth in industrial technologies and consumerism, and the appearance, at least, of a leveling of class differences that supported modernism's rejection of nineteenth-century interpretations of the world. The forces of industrialization and urbanization meant that the physical separation between the classes was breaking down, even though disparities of wealth would increase. Against this cultural backdrop, the class privilege of Hutchins and Rochester was indisputable, and their mannerisms were definitely aristocratic. Cleghorn's response to this "high altitude" must be understood then in light of cultural changes, her awareness of the political contradictions of the commune, and her own desire for a more heterosocial living community. In other words, Cleghorn's critique got right to the heart of the paradox: Hutchins and Rochester's political resistance was one that emerged out of their own privilege, and, as such, posed perhaps an irreconcilable contradiction.

These contradictions may have contributed to the disintegration of the commune in 1924, although there is no clear evidence as to why it disbanded at this time. Hutchins and Rochester moved, with Lucie Myer, to an apartment at 85 Bedford Street in Greenwich Village, New York City, where Hutchins and Rochester lived for the rest of their lives. The Village was a community that nourished them; it provided an atmosphere sympathetic to progressive intellectual thought and unconventional living styles. Also, as Faderman suggests, "If there was anywhere that a non-working-class lesbian community could flourish in the '20s . . . it should have been in an area such as Greenwich Village, where value was placed on the unconventional and the breaking of taboos."[50] Certainly Greenwich Village would have provided a living context that offered community and lessened the contradictions associated with the bourgeois radical intellectual. On one level this quote by Faderman fits, yet it also makes me uneasy. Hutchins and Rochester seem so proper, so very conventional despite their radical politics that I think Greenwich Village was attractive to them primarily because of its intellectual community. I do not believe that they saw themselves as unconventional except in the ideological sense. While they seemed to like to think of themselves as cutting-edge radicals, in their everyday living they probably appreciated the tolerance of the community to include their proper, conventional ways.

This part of Hutchins and Rochester's story serves as a reminder of the ways that political agency is created as the site of critical political and cultural contests. On another level, it is also a reminder of the joys and advantages associated with women's separate space that allowed the merging of culture and politics, provided intimacy, and gave support to women in their public work. It represented a period when Hutchins and Rochester's lives were converging: both were driven by a strong Christian faith and a deep commitment to social justice that undergirded their personal commitments to each other. They sincerely wanted to live their politics and their faith, a combination at this point in their lives that seemed to them to be utterly compatible.

CHAPTER FIVE

CHRISTIAN JUSTICE

WHILE MANY CHRISTIAN socialists left the Socialist Party in order to support World War I, a small section of Christian intellectuals moved closer to socialism as a result of wartime Pacifist commitments.[1] Hutchins and Rochester were included in this group of Pacifists whose experience of U.S. interventionist policy resulted in a strengthening of their commitment to socialism and to Christianity as liberatory social and political forces in the world. This stance was reflected in their book *Jesus Christ and the World Today*, the founding of Community House as an intentional community, and their strong commitments to the Fellowship of Reconciliation and its influential monthly publication, the *World Tomorrow*. This chapter traces the period from 1920 to 1927 and explores Hutchins and Rochester's entanglements with Christian socialism.

The origins of Christian socialism are found in the writings and practices of such Congregationalist ministers as Jesse Jones and George Herron, Episcopalian Rev. Bliss, and writers such as Richard T. Ely, who all helped encourage a cooperative, religiously based brand of socialist politics.[2] The Christian Socialist Fellowship was founded in 1906 and the *Christian Socialist* magazine had wide appeal at the turn of the century. In particular, as a politics that focused on themes of class reconciliation in re-

> "'As for the living,' wrote Villiers de l'Isle-Adam in a phrase that both perturbed and fascinated the modernists, 'our servants will do that for us.' Thus spoke an exemplary fin de siecle decadent of the last century. In this fin de siecle in this differently decaying decade, is it the biographers and not the servants who do the living?"[3]

Grace (c. mid-1920s).   Anna (c. mid-1920s).

ligious understanding, Christian socialism was especially attractive to women reformers. It gave moral and cooperative solutions to urban problems and, as a result, was embraced early on by settlement workers, members of the Women's Christian Temperance Union, and others. Through the years, Christian socialism continued with a relatively broad appeal, helped by the work of Norman Thomas, an influential figure in the Socialist Party during the 1920s and into the 1960s, and Reinhold Niebuhr, a prolific writer, preacher, activist, and teacher whose work also spanned the decades from the 1920s into the Vietnam War era. The antiracist message of Christian socialism was particularly strong and brought support from black Christians in all walks of life, although especially in the south. Indeed, Christian socialists continued to play important roles during the civil rights and antiwar era of the 1960s and have survived in the present era as liberatory theologians.

As Hutchins and Rochester recognized their own privilege, they witnessed the worsening economic plight of the nation's poor and they were caught up by the radicalizing tendencies of the historical moment. Their political agency as Christian socialists brought together their deep affiliation for religious devotion and justice. They strongly believed that Christianity embodied the ethical values of compassion, responsibility, caring, and commitment: all essential aspects of a politics of freedom.

Jesus Christ and the World Today

Hutchins and Rochester's belief that the ethical principles of Christianity provided the framework for the realization of social justice came across loud and clear in the first book that either of them wrote, and their only book to be co-authored: *Jesus Christ and the World Today*. Focusing on the social ethics of Christianity, it was published in 1922 by the George H. Doran Company of New York. In this text Hutchins and Rochester addressed the relationships between individual behavior, morality, and the inequities of industrial life. They considered messages from the teachings of Jesus for society in the 1920s. They believed that Christ was the hope of the world and analyzed these implications for society generally. Since the book was intended as a teacher's guide, each chapter offered material for discussion groups. In the preface, Hutchins and Rochester outlined their general principles and orientation for the text, emphasizing that this was not another book on social and political theory, but rather an ethical discussion of individual and social behavior in light of the teachings of Jesus, the current state of capitalism, and the visions of a socialist agenda:

> We believe that Jesus Christ is the hope of the world; the studies assume this belief and attempt to analyze its implications for the world today. They do not attempt, however to present an economic or political program. We believe that such programs are very definitely the concern of Christians, but intelligent discussion of programs must follow a clear analysis of our personal share in social wrongs and of the kind of relationships we should try to express in our economic and political life.[4]

Jesus Christ and the World Today started out with a chapter called "The Hope." Here Hutchins and Rochester compared the inequities and domination of their current society with life in Palestine during the time of Jesus, citing St. John, among others, who preached a gospel of community sharing. The second chapter, "Within the Family at Nazareth," brought the issues home with a discussion of the necessity for simple living, adequate resources for family stability and participation in the community, and the moral education of children in the home: "A community expresses itself most clearly in the way in which it treats its children. . . . We allow even the babies to pay for their parent's poverty."[5] Chapter Three, "In the Community," critiqued the industrial world of the 1920s: "What would Jesus say about our industrial world to-day? Would He approve of a society that means wealth for a few and poverty for many, power for those on top and the subordination of those underneath?"[6] With strong emphasis they came to the crux of Christian socialism: "Judged then by the principle of Jesus that the life and personality of every individual is of supreme value, any mechanical system that means the subordination of human beings to provide more properly for other human

After the failed attempt at inserting myself as a fictive character as described earlier, I decided to try and organize the book with a series of subtext writings that gave voice to my thoughts about the process of writing biography and gave alternative interpretations to those in the narrative. These were situated at the bottom of pages, separated by a shaded border, and set in a different font. In addition, since I wanted to write a thoroughly contextualized biography, I decided to include what I called "backdrop boxes" that contained alternative primary source material unrelated to Grace and Anna. These either illuminated the narrative by bringing more primary sources to flesh out the analysis or disrupted it through intentional contrast. I searched extensively for other women's voices as primary material against which the voices of Grace and Anna might be understood. In some ways this was quite effective, in other ways it was too messy and complex. I felt I was losing Grace and Anna's story. Instead of not being able to see the forest for the trees, I was losing sight of the trees. Since the boxes seemed to be complicating the narrative far too much, after some hesitation (mostly related to the large investment made over four or five chapters) I decided to abandon the backdrop idea.

beings is unchristian. Any condition of work that leaves the body abnormally tired, the mind dulled and stupified, or the spirit broken, are contrary to the will of God as Jesus understood that will."[7]

From this basis, in later chapters Hutchins and Rochester discussed the possibilities of human development and the inevitable "conflicts" of both Jesus' Palestine and of their time. Comparing race relations of early Palestine to racism and persecution in the United States, they wrote about the ways Jesus dealt with the conflicts that led to his crucifixion and the antagonisms with prominent Jews.[8] They pointed out that in the decade preceding the writing of the book, people such as Eugene Debs had been persecuted for their beliefs just as Jesus was persecuted by the Jews for refusing to uphold the Roman Empire. The final chapters address how all people should face issues of injustice and ends with a final plea to Christians: "go further and desire to assist and have our nations assist (in so far as one nation can assist another without infringing upon its independence) the development in other countries of relations in which human welfare takes precedence of profit."[9]

Much of the collaborative work for the book occurred during Hutchins and Rochester's years living at Community House. Tenants such as Lucie Myer and Sally Cleghorn were no doubt supportive and helpful in producing the text since they were teachers and writers, and, certainly, all residents participated in its creation and felt much joy and combined ownership when it was published in 1922. As Ann Mundelein wrote in "A Day Full of Little Joys in the Community,"

Then there is the excitement of the Postman's ring in the morning. The Book should be heard from at any time now. The community has a sense of ownership even though it is really the child of only two of us, and the Community gets all the reflected glory and most of the thrills of having written a book all its own. So the Postman's coming has a thrill of excitement for all of us.[10]

The women of 352 seemed to have felt a distinct sense of ownership concerning the book. With characteristic satire and good humor, Cleghorn penned the "Biography of a Book" in the commune journal. It began,

July–August	Born in Castine, Maine
September	Disinherited by the Church Committee
October	Flirted with by Macmillan
November	Immured in an oubliette by Harcourt and Brace
January	Seriously addressed by Doran and Co.
January–February	Inquiries as to her Dowry
February	A certain Dowager casts asparagus
February	Grace and Anna call on that dame
February–March	Who Imprisons the ms. incommunicado
March	Thrilling rescue by Postman
March	Seen leaning on arm of Prof. Scott at Assembly
April	Spring outfit planned, with public appearances
May 23	Mounts the rostrum [to] a waiting world, in ceremonial dress of crimson poplin embossed in black, with black panel, alphabetical design; overslip of ecru lace, heavily-decorated in black; begins to address the multitude. Applause begins.[11]

Since I had been proposing this book to publishers, I appreciated the humor of this piece—especially the bit about being immured in the oubliette. (It's a tiny little prison cell, usually beneath the floor, where prisoners, and especially those charged with treason, would be held.) Negative criticism is difficult to swallow.

Even though, as discussed in chapter 4, Cleghorn was the one to complain that the refined witticisms and high altitude of Community House encouraged one's prattling to be indecently exposed, she certainly rose to the occasion in her account here. This account playfully documented how different publishers reviewed the book—some initial interest by Macmillan and negative feedback by Harcourt and Brace. George H. Doran and Co. showed serious interest and it is they who published the book. The thrilling anticipation of the book's publication is evident in this account, as is Community House's pride in the book's splendid appearance and its adoption by E. F. Scott, a professor at the Union Theological Seminary.[12] Note how the Church Committee disinherited the book, probably reflecting an ideological disagreement over the book's socialist orientation.

Reviews of the book were for the most part glowing. *Christian Century* reported that it was "radiant in its Christian idealism as it is relentless in its application to the realities of life; and withal written in a simple, biting style." Editor Charles Clayton Morrison even went so far as to preface this with an exclamation: "If such a book as *Jesus Christ and the World Today*, by Grace Hutchins and Anna Rochester, is a token of the kind of work women are destined to do in religious teaching, then we have a right to thank God and take courage."[13] And Norman Thomas, then associate editor of the *Nation,* had similar high praise: "This is a remarkable piece of work. I have never seen a series of studies dealing with modern social applications of the teachings of Jesus which seemed to me so frank, thoroughgoing, and suggestive. If Christianity is to have any positive influence in the making of a new age, it will have to be the sort of Christianity which this book expounds so well."[14]

More conservative than the *Nation,* the New York Research Department of the Commission on Church and Social Service, affiliated with the Federal Council of the Churches of Christ in America, also reviewed the book. Their positive review commented on the tone of restraint and tolerance that ran through the text, making it accessible to readers outside of the intellectual Christian socialist circle.[15] In addition, this reviewer pointed to Hutchins and Rochester's personal ethics and class privileges to enhance their authority as writers:

> Not the least element of interest in this excellently written book grows out of the fact that it was written by women of culture who have made it their chief aim to approximate the Christian way of life by dwelling among the commonest surroundings and eliminating all semblance of luxury. They have earned their right to this momentous theme.[16]

Jesus Christ and the World Today seemed to have been well accepted by a broad spectrum of Christians. Hutchins and Rochester used reasoned logic and a restrained and genteel style to temper the liberatory message of their text. This persuasiveness was successful; its focus on acceptance and toler-

I mostly use the reviews that Grace and Anna had clipped and kept in their files. It is hard to say whether these represent all the reviews written or a selection of those that the couple wanted to keep. They did retain negative as well as positive reviews, but there is the distinct possibility that favorable reviews were more likely to find their ways into the file. This would bias my analysis in the direction of thinking that their writing was more well received than it might have been.

ation avoided the more controversial assertions of their later professional writings when an orthodox Marxist social and political vision replaced that of Christianity in terms of a method for progressive social change. This book launched Hutchins and Rochester into the world of publishing and gave them confidence in their abilities as writers. And, indeed, the book continued to be praised decades after it was written.[17]

The Fellowship of Reconciliation

One of the most influential left-leaning Christian–pacifist organizations of this era was the Fellowship of Reconciliation (F.O.R.), an institution to which Hutchins and Rochester gave much time and energy between 1921 and 1926. While they contributed to F.O.R.'s maturation, their affiliation with this important organization in its early years also molded their political opinion as religiously trained pacifists and gave them crucial experiences in organization and writing. While not openly socialist, F.O.R. had definite socialist sympathies, giving a political home to such well-known characters as Norman Thomas and A. J. Muste and providing a moderated critique of industrial and labor issues through a decidedly antiwar Christianity. Hutchins and Rochester had become members of F.O.R. prior to moving to Community House; both were listed on the F.O.R. membership roles in 1918, Hutchins in New York and Rochester in Washington, D.C. From being active members in the precommune days, they both started to take on leadership positions in the early 1920s and became influential in helping direct F.O.R.'s mission and politics. Hutchins worked as associate secretary from 1922 to 1924, and both Hutchins and Rochester participated as members of the Executive Committee and the Council. Meetings were held at Community House, often with supper served for a cost of 35 cents per person. F.O.R. offices were located on Broadway in New York City.

During World War I, many pacifist organizations rose to challenge emerging war economies and critique military mobilization.[18] As one of these organizations, F.O.R. was founded in the United States in November 1915 (a year after the organization's initiation in England by Henry T.

Hodgkin). The organization quickly became an outspoken force against war and fascism that has survived to the present era in its work for civil rights and opposition to the Vietnam War and nuclear proliferation. Concerned about the spiritual crises that war presented, the sixty-eight founding members of F.O.R. aimed "to consider the meaning, in a world at war, of the 3 words 'love thy enemies.'" In their statement of purpose these founding members declared the "acceptance of the Spirit of Christ as the only sufficient basis of society."[19] As part of this witness against war, the Fellowship made the cause of conscientious objectors its own and worked closely with the National Civil Liberties Bureau, which was the major support for conscientious objectors. "The Fellowship of Reconciliation: Its Origins and Development" stated that war in Europe initiated the desire to address the conflict between the principles of Christianity and militarism, yet other issues related to the current industrial and racial problems were also at stake.[20] While its agenda was far-reaching and progressive and attracted the support of blacks in the south, the Fellowship for the most part tended to be a white, middle-class, and Protestant organization.[21] The narrative of "Origins and Development" read:

> In its statement of principles emphasis is laid upon the conviction that Christianity is a way of life for the present rather than an ideal for a distant future and that the method of attainment must be in harmony with the goal. Since the members undertake simply to follow the way of Jesus as it applies to social problems no doctrinal or theological differences separate them. In the Fellowship are found members of all different Churches and some of no Church at all, studying and working in close harmony.
>
> The chief aim of the Fellowship has been to convince people of the far-reaching import of the Christian gospel and to gather into a spiritual unity those awakened to the need of this new orientation, rather than to build an organization for accomplishing specific reforms. Thus curious individuals and groups of members have independently undertaken many different projects for working out the Fellowship principle in the fields in which they were most interested.[22]

With the above statement of principles in mind, it is easy to see how well the aims of F.O.R. meshed with the message of *Jesus Christ and the World Today*. This book was written during the most intense period of Hutchins and Rochester's involvement with the Fellowship, and its writing reflected F.O.R. doctrine. In June 1921 F.O.R. held a Council meeting to plan the large fall conference and both Hutchins and Rochester were in attendance and listed as conference planners. Hutchins wrote reports of the conference for the *Survey* and Rochester wrote similar conference details for the *Christian Century*, emphasizing how over 200 people attended from many parts of the United States and abroad out of a growing membership of over

2,000. At the conference, both Hutchins and Rochester were elected onto the F.O.R. Council.[23] By March 1922, the F.O.R. Executive Committee met and appointed Hutchins as associate secretary to the Fellowship, beginning April 15 at a salary of $100 a month, a position she would hold for the next two years. She was to "specialize particularly upon study groups, returned missionaries and the general spreading of the message."[24] She was in attendance at the April 1922 Executive Committee meeting, taking minutes and contributing to the management of the organization. It was voted to send representatives of the American Fellowship to the German Fellowship Conference in July and to the International Conference at Sonntagsberg in Austria in August. Hutchins was instructed as associate secretary to write to the National Council for the Reduction of Armaments for the endorsement of the measures they proposed to write, assuring them of F.O.R. support, yet encouraging more far-reaching action. The Fellowship was also encouraging its members to get involved in the "No More War" demonstrations in July 1922 in their local communities. Finally, there was a discussion about the fall conference of the Fellowship, especially concerning ideas for its theme. Hutchins's suggestion was taken up as the conference theme: "that the thought of the year be centered upon the application of Fellowship principles to all economic and industrial relationships with an appropriate method for bringing this to the attention of individuals and groups."[25] This idea, so closely modeled to the theme of *Jesus Christ and the World Today*, coincided with the book's publication in 1922.

By April 1923, Hutchins was elected to fill the U.S. seat on the International Council and was a most respected and influential member of the Fellowship. June found the Council meeting at Community House, again with afternoon and evening sessions and supper provided in between. A priority on the agenda was a discussion about the Fellowship's need to revise its statement of aims and purposes, brought up by Rochester at an earlier meeting.[26] A letter was sent to Council members reminding them of this upcoming June meeting and announcing that subjects to be discussed included:

> Questions in regard to the DISTINCTIVELY CHRISTIAN EMPHASIS of the Fellowship and our relations to those outside the Christian Church. There will be a report from the Committee on the Consideration of our Aims and Purposes, of which A. J. Muste is Chairman. [original emphasis][27]

A. J. Muste chaired this committee, Rochester was a member, and Hutchins served as secretary.[28] The theme concerning the aims and mission of F.O.R. was an important one because it spoke not only to issues of membership recruitment and retention, but also the ideological commitments of the organization in the context of changing political situations at home and abroad. That both Hutchins and Rochester should be central in this debate at such a point in the history of F.O.R. suggests a convergence of themes:

> Having had the role of secretary in various organizations, I know how often the minutes are sanitized and sometimes reworked. "Off the record" comments are very often the most revealing about an organization and its internal politics and basic principles. It is important to keep this in mind when relying on official minutes as a record of an organization. Yet, the more I read these minutes concerning the revision of the mission statement, the more I see the influence Grace and Anna had on this committee. I can just imagine them explaining their case with a sound and well-reasoned, refined and principled tone. In terms of the mission, the F.O.R. Council agreed that they wanted to make their appeal as wide and intelligible as possible; "it was suggested that the militancy of our policy rather than the exactness of our words would be the best test against weak-hearted people" (Council Minutes, November 3, 1923). The minutes do not record just who suggested this; I like to think that it was Grace or Anna, or both, who said this since the words and phrasing sound so much like them.

F.O.R. was trying to figure out where it stood ideologically at the same time that Hutchins and Rochester were moving left away from the more liberal wing of Christian socialism toward a more radical politics.

Tactically, the dialogue that emerged during the June 1923 meeting of the Council was intended to preempt possible questions and concerns raised at the fall conference. Eventually, it was suggested that a questionnaire to survey members' opinions on this issue would be sent out after the fall conference. Hutchins apparently wrote the questionnaire.[29] It was decided that the Committee on Aims and Purposes would then present a report at the November Council gathering. This meeting again took place at Community House. The report from the Committee on Aims and Purposes attempted to steer between potential factions to emphasize a "no change" policy on F.O.R.'s Christian identity, yet a reinterpretation of what that identity might mean.[30]

As a Christian socialist who had been strongly influenced by his leadership in the 1919 Lawrence Textile strike and the founding of Brookwood Labor College, A. J. Muste was ready to help move the Fellowship away from its more traditional liberal Christian roots toward a more progressive Christian socialist vision.[31] Hutchins and Rochester certainly shared this vision. Understanding the need to retain the support of more traditional Christians and also to respond to its more progressive constituencies, they attempted to advocate a mission that would not be interpreted as a rigid creed, yet reflected their common spirit and basic principles. The "Revised Statement" that was reworked and printed for the membership at large emphasized a statement of purposes rather than principles. It attempted to reflect the diversity of the Fellowship, avoided

Grace and Anna (c. mid-1920s).

mention of God in favor of the more loosely interpreted "Divine," and re-ferred to "Love" as reflected in the teachings of Jesus, rather than Jesus himself, as the basis for human thought and action. It had enough ties to the old Christian message to maintain those affiliations and enough lan-guage reflecting activism in industrial and international relations to re-tain and recruit more progressive members.[32] Again, while this statement of purposes closely resembled the message of *Jesus Christ and the World Today*, and reflected Hutchins and Rochester's collaboration in reframing the vision of the Fellowship, it also demonstrated the strong influence of F.O.R. on their thinking and writing.

Nineteen twenty-three found Hutchins and Rochester involved as am-bassadors for F.O.R. during summer travels in Europe. Since Hutchins had been elected as the U.S. representative for the International Council of F.O.R., she attended the various conferences held that summer. No doubt Rochester was keen to accompany her on these travels as a F.O.R. Council member and delegate. She also had *World Tomorrow* business to attend to. A series of letters home to friends documented the enthusiasm and energy with which the women approached their networking tasks with like-minded F.O.R. delegates in Europe. They were there to spread their message and to learn from colleagues; they also managed to fit in vacation time and seemed to have enjoyed their time away together.

On board *The Majestic*, an ocean liner bound for England at the start of these summer travels, Hutchins and Rochester wrote a "round-robin" letter that was to be passed from friend to friend once read. Hutchins and Rochester had received numerous presents on their departure and were particularly excited about all the food baskets they had been given.[33] Staying in a little hotel off Bloomsbury Square close to the British Museum in London, they had thoroughly enjoyed the opportunity to explore the city and spend time with interesting folks who shared their political visions. In mid-July, after completing arrangements with a new London agent for the *World Tomorrow* and visiting with the British F.O.R. staff, they left for Denmark to attend the Danish F.O.R. conference. The time spent in Denmark proved to be exciting and educational. They boasted how they had not attended even one museum or gallery and had avoided being tourists by mixing with the natives: "who would sacrifice a chance to talk with live Danes in order to see pictures and relics of dead ones?"[34] The Danish conference, begun on July 19 in Copenhagen, gave Hutchins and Rochester the opportunity to dialogue with international delegates and a group of U.S. representatives that included settlement worker Helena Dudley (whom Rochester knew from Denison House days). Hutchins was a featured speaker at this conference, and gave "a fine sincere appeal for simplicity and for an outspoken stand by the international F.O.R. for radical economic change."[35] As part of their education, Hutchins and Rochester also were pleased to be able to visit the International Workingmen's College.

However, it was the time Hutchins and Rochester spent with the Danish F.O.R. leader and writer Andersen Nexö and his family that they seemed to enjoy the most. Rochester found Mr. Nexö to have "a radiant, simple, human kind of spirit that is quite rare . . . and he is, as we heard, a real bolshevik." She continued: "But I couldn't help feeling that his philosophy and his own spirit don't quite match. He deplores humanistic effort (much more broadly interpreted than social work) as a diversion from the main job of changing the economic order. But actually his analysis of the human spirit in individuals is far more generous and warm than his mass-action, rather cynical philosophy."[36] This observation is particularly interesting because it gives some insight into Rochester's understanding of Bolshevism at this point in time. Assuming she implied Nexö's philosophy to be representative of his Bolshevism, she seemed to be saying that his personal ethics and spirit were more pleasing than his philosophy, and that such a human generosity was not often found within the hard-edged cynicism of Bolshevism. It suggested that during the early twenties, while they were moving left ideologically, the couple's support for Bolshevism was still not yet wholehearted.

After Denmark, Hutchins and Rochester attended the Youth Movement conference at Helleran, near Dresden, Germany. Originally they had

During these travels in 1923, Anna was 43 years old and Grace was turning 38. I have found that I constantly imagine them much younger than they actually were. And I imagine them as much like myself even though I am older than Anna was. Very confusing! During this reconstruction of the Community House era it is easy for me to fall into the habit of thinking of them as a group of young women just starting out as adults and sharing a house together rather than as approaching-middle-age women who have made a conscious commitment to form an intentional community that reflected their political values. I recall Barbara MacDonald in one of the essays in *Look Me in the Eye* talking about the lack of public activism expected of old women now and recalling the time when it was older women who were mostly involved in political activity.[37] It is the youth-focused aspects of contemporary culture and the accompanying ageism that sees energy and life more likely attached to the pursuits of young women.

thought of attending the English F.O.R. conference that was also taking place at the end of July. True to form, Hutchins and Rochester were more excited about meeting new people and experiencing a new environment than staying in England. They were especially enthusiastic about learning how young people were approaching national and international problems and looked forward also to discovering how Germany was rebuilding itself politically in the aftermath of World War I.[38] From Germany they departed again for England and enjoyed a vacation in Devonshire on the southwest coast. After this vacation filled with wild walks in the hills along the rugged coastline of Devon and Cornwall, Hutchins and Rochester returned home renewed in mind and spirit. Their vision of the strengths of an international fellowship of progressive Christian socialists was nurtured by these experiences in Europe and they sincerely believed that great strides could be made in industrial relations through F.O.R. activism and communications in the *World Tomorrow*.

Given the relatively precarious financial situation of F.O.R., I expect Hutchins and Rochester paid their own expenses for these travels. That they were able to afford this and devote such energy to organizations for little or no pay also reflected the depth of their resources as well as the privileges of actually being able to live and work their politics without concern for feeding a family or paying the rent. In other words, the strong loyalties given to the Fellowship, like the strong loyalties they gave to every organization with which they found kindred spirit, were possible because of their socioeconomic privilege. They lived their faith because they *could* live their faith: a very enviable position.

Hutchins and Rochester continued their active involvement with F.O.R. through the new year, 1924. At the January meeting of the Council, held at

Community House, Hutchins was elected to a committee for antiwar evangelism while Rochester's work was more cerebral. At the March Council meeting she presented her pamphlet "Am I Doing My Share?" which aimed "to stimulate a deeper interest in supporting the work of the Fellowship. It was approved with certain suggested changes, with the idea that it would be put as a News Sheet, and for wider use."[39] By October 1924, Rochester was listed alongside Hutchins on the Executive Committee of F.O.R., although by the end of the year Hutchins was no longer associate secretary since she was starting to devote more of her time to the *World Tomorrow.*[40] Throughout 1925 the pair stayed active with the Fellowship, although activity was diminishing. Their political journey seemed to be moving left; a direction which would soon be too left for the Fellowship and its vision.

The *World Tomorrow*

Coinciding with their active involvement in F.O.R., Hutchins and Rochester were also heavily invested in the journal the *World Tomorrow,* a journal which by 1923 advertised itself with the subtitle: *"Looking Toward a Social Order Based on the Principles of Jesus."* This socialist-oriented magazine was edited by Norman Thomas at its inception in 1918. Nevin Sayre became involved as editor in 1921, and Devere Allen was the major editor through most of the journal's publication until its closure in 1934. Originally called the *New World,* its name was changed shortly after a Catholic publication objected to the similarity in names. The *World Tomorrow* was a highly influential and widely circulated journal that stayed faithful to the antiwar vision throughout its existence.[41] Norman Thomas wrote that the purpose of the journal was not so much theological or philosophical, but

I want to point out that while I give ownership of this quote to Norman Thomas, the narrative masks the uncertainty of voice actually involved, an uncertainty that frames much biographical writing but is very often presented unproblematically. The quote comes from an undated, unsigned, typed report that has handwritten corrections with similar handwriting as a letter signed by Thomas. It makes sense that as editor of the *World Tomorrow* he would have authored and edited this report, dating it prior to 1921 when Sayre became editor. However, at the 1921 Council meeting Sayre gave a report and proposed a series of developments for the journal and asked permission to be released from F.O.R. duty to work full time with the *World Tomorrow* (F.O.R. Council minutes, November 1921). Another explanation then is that this quote is from this report Sayre gave at that meeting and that Thomas was asked to edit the report from his experience as past editor, explaining his handwriting on the document.

rather "our particular job is to focus and direct ethical and religious feeling toward such social readjustments as will make easier the release of what is noble and God-like in the spirit of man."[42]

Rochester's formal debut in the *World Tomorrow* came with her article "Immigration and Internationalism," published in November 1921. Here she argued that the inconsistencies of immigration laws not only facilitated hardships and inequities for immigrants, but encouraged native-born Americans to project their fears and frustrations, whose root causes lay in the economic order, onto immigrants.[43] This argument, remarkably relevant seventy-five years later in contemporary U.S. relations, continued in the next issue of the journal. It described some of the constructive measures "that challenge the internationalist who is considering the pros and cons of restriction,"[44] and addressed the conditions under which immigrants travel, their treatment at U.S. ports and Ellis Island in particular, and their lives in the United States. By the next month, Rochester was listed as an associate editor of the *World Tomorrow*.

Hutchins was included in the February 1922 issue with a short feature that closely followed the themes and format of *Jesus Christ and the World Today* by crafting pertinent questions and encouraging discussion on the relationship between Christian ethics and present-day life.[45] While Hutchins focused on the relationship between religious and moral education and social and economic problems, Rochester was writing more specifically from a Marxist perspective on capitalist class relations, although her analysis was still grounded in the teachings of Jesus in such a way that she claimed a religious ethical basis for the moral imperatives of socialism. These writings reflected Rochester's growing sophistication with economic theories of society as well as her beautifully eloquent style. While her language was refined and heavily nuanced, and would have appealed to her largely educated, middle-class readership, she displayed a complex and sophisticated analysis of economic and social relations. The following is an excerpt from her article, "The Future in the Present":

> In a world that drives "The God of Vengeance" from the stage and leaves the Winter Garden undisturbed; that punishes communists and rewards Hearsts; that accepts with an Alice in Wonderland solemnity the Treaty that at once demands payments and makes them impossible; that teaches its children sacred phrases about the love of neighbors, while it despises Jews, Germans, Negroes, criminals, radicals, and others—in such a world even a sincere desire for truth seems at times impossible.[46]

Her analysis, however, was never unduly pessimistic. With characteristic idealism, she rejoiced in the principled actions of those who sought to make changes in this world and believed in a ray of hope: "To me the sign is there—not a light flashing across the sky to waken us from our stupor but a tiny shoot of green here and there, rewarding a careful search under the fallen leaves of the dead season."[47]

These writings are also revealing because they spoke about how Rochester, as a bourgeois woman, saw herself in the context of the class struggle. In "What Property Does to the Individual," she addressed the issue of bourgeois privilege and responsibility. Again with characteristic eloquence she introduced the issue, emphasizing that while all lose under oppressive social relations, the complex suffering of most of the world is directly related to the privilege of the few:

> The propertied world, like the world of the poor, is full of an infinite variety of the charming and the disagreeable and the saintly and the brutal. Yet, we range, like the court of the pantomime, from the Ugly Princess to the Lady with a Fan, but all of us are sheltered in the palace while the rest of the world shivers in the portico. And within the palace even the idealist is shaped and crippled by his possessions. It is not the Ugly Princess alone who wears a patch over one eye![48]

Rochester tapped into the difficult and confusing situation of the bourgeois radical—a situation very close to home. She discussed the politics of giving, which is "distorted by the relative security of the giver, by the contrast between his power and the other's need, by the luxurious sentiment of goodness which is yet far from the essence of fellowship when the gift leaves the giver secure and the recipient still gasping in the struggle," and continued, "when we give to our pet causes, whether they are educational or civic, or religious, or revolutionary, we are enjoying the power of money. To have money and use it for crude self-indulgence in a world of injustice and suffering is possible only for those whom property has blinded completely. But those who give from their abundance must struggle against a persistent myopia. Insensibly we magnify the importance of contributions from well-to-do and forget the far greater giving of the poor."[49] Without naming it, the New Testament parable of the widow's mite rang clear. In this essay, Rochester also considered how the opportunity to choose one's activities is a luxury of the privileged bourgeoisie. Raising the issue about whether bourgeois freedom and privilege is ultimately harmful since it maintains class relations, she wrote that once we accept an entitlement to the prerogative of freedom, it has bound us in "deadly slavery."[50] Even when the choice is one of service for the common good, does this freedom, she asked, balance the harm that results from the privilege? Important questions indeed.

Similar issues were raised in another article a couple of months later. "What Eleven Families Spend: The Cost of Comfort That Is Not Luxury" grappled with the real issue of when comfort becomes luxury. Rochester surveyed eleven families, "friends of the *World Tomorrow*," to figure out how it might be possible to "live in a simplicity which includes only that which is essential."[51] The article illuminated the problems associated with the bourgeois privilege of radicals but gave few answers. Articles during this period were written from Rochester's deep personal and political beliefs. She struggled here with all the contradictions of her life concerning socialist activism and her bourgeois status. She came out on the side of principled action: while it was her very bourgeois privilege that gave her the freedom to work for F.O.R. and the *World Tomorrow*, she chose to live a principled life, with all the accompanying contradictions, devoted to the larger struggle for the improvement of the human condition. This was a struggle that was fast taking both Hutchins and Rochester's total allegiance and it was a struggle that helped form them as active subjects. This is an example of the complex and multiple ways that they were constructed as historical actors.

In "The Pacifist's 'Preparedness': How Can We Work for Non-Violent Revolutionary Change?" Rochester focused on the issue of radical social change and preempted the familiar phrase from the sixties that if you are not part of the solution then you are part of the problem, summarizing her stance on this problem.[52] Generally, Rochester assumed a revolution *would* occur; the issue was whether it would be violent or not. She was enough of an orthodox Marxist at this point to have assumed the evolutionary nature of society moving toward class confrontation, but she still believed that Christian principles might head off the violence of class conflict. In addition, Rochester suggested that a greater emphasis on competency, efficiency, and technical skills might help avert a violent revolution. Alongside these increased technical competencies, with increasing idealism, she envisioned "a living nucleus for the renewal of common faith in the power of idealism" among middle-class radicals, accompanied by an active living proof: "by the things he [*sic*] does and the way he lives, that contrary to his own economic interests he is utterly devoted to the cause of the workers."[53] This, she said, is about sacrificing security, power, and personal comfort. Again, reflecting her own principled and ordered life, she emphasized the close relationship between words and deeds, ideologies and everyday living.

Rochester understood that the pacifist who wants a nonviolent revolution cannot judge those who have taken another route; while not condoning the violence of the Bolshevik Revolution, she understood and respected the Russian people's right to attempt to free themselves from oppression. Here she defined a pragmatic pacifism that embraced the self-determination of others to call their own fates: "All who are not pacifists and most of us who are believe that resistance to evil is necessary and right. We disagree as to the method of resistance but we respect as divine that quality in human nature which rises in revolt against wrong. We know that when a mass of people suffering in common from some clear injustice rise against it, they are serving the progress of the race."[54]

More insight into Rochester's developing ideological framework was given in two articles written in 1925. "Sowing the Wind" reflects Rochester's lucid prose and her keen sense of political persuasions, while "Need We Fear Class-Consciousness?" is more insightful concerning Rochester's understandings of Bolshevism.[55] In the latter she commented on the militarism and dictatorships implicit in the communist strategy for change, and suggested that this may not be the best route for the U.S. situation:

> Paradoxically, only a class-conscious labor movement, with a strong political organization, will be able to eliminate class government in the United States. Not class consciousness in the Communist sense, for, at least in the United States, war tactics and dictatorship of the proletariat which the Communists have bound up with the idea of class consciousness are not the way to successful economic change. But class consciousness stripped of the passion and dogmatism with which it has been obscured and restored to its original meaning as awareness of the struggle between the owners in a modern state and the workers.[56]

Rochester's comment about passion and dogmatism is especially interesting since it reflects very much the direction she would move within the next decade. However, while she was writing more about the social and economic relationships involved in the class struggle, Hutchins was continuing to utilize this same framework in her analysis of the New Testament. In a 1924 *World Tomorrow* article, "Prophets and the People," Hutchins wrote about the failures of traditional religious education for a modern society and suggested that attention to such prophets as Jesus, Confucius and Mahatma Gandhi would facilitate important training in democracy. This essay is particularly interesting because it illustrated her scathing critique of traditional institutionalized religious practices in the United States. Having spent decades involved in these institutions she offered a harsh assessment; however, at the same time, she still held out hope for their reform:

> But to most of us, who have a Christian background, the church that taught us our religion was a hierarchy of ordained ministers, laymen and, lowest of all, laywomen. The church was simply reflecting the autocracy or plurocracy of the state. The rich paid for their pews and gave money on one Sunday "for the poor" and on the next "for the missions." The "poor" meant those who were in need and were inferior to the rich. "Missions" meant the heathen, those same yellow, black, red or brown people whose pictures were in the geography book. Jesus Christ was the Master, the Messiah, the King, the Lord, whose commandments were to be obeyed, not because they were found to be the truth of human experience, but because the Lord had given them commandments.[57]

Note how this passage illustrates Hutchins's journey from these very same missions and their saving of the "heathens," the advocacy for the poor within her Episcopalian parish in Boston, and critique of Jesus as the Lord and Master that is so evident in *Jesus Christ and the World Today*, written only two years earlier. Note also her increasing interest in the status of women within traditional institutions (the laywomen of the church as the "lowest of all"), an interest that would come to fruition within the next decade as she investigated the conditions of women in paid labor. In the meantime, her interest in women and feminism was demonstrated by a 1923 *World Tomorrow* article titled "Our Inferiority Complex."[58] It followed a lead article by Freda Kirchwey, managing editor of the *Nation*, titled "Are You a Feminist?"[59] The timing of these essays was undoubtedly motivated by the emergence of Alice Paul's more militant Woman's Party after the ratification of the Nineteenth Amendment in 1920 and the introduction of the Equal Rights Amendment (ERA) in 1923. The ERA was not supported by most people in labor and socialist circles since it was seen as jeopardizing the protective labor legislation for women that had been hard won over the last few decades. However, since the popular imagination of the early twenties created notions of women's independence and liberation and centered on such changing cultural traditions as women's public behavior and dress, feminism became a widely debated topic that the *World Tomorrow* would no doubt want to address.

The article by Kirchwey is brilliant in its blend of humor and strong political analysis. It is a very accessible piece aimed at dispelling the fears surrounding the term "feminist" and introducing the necessity for structural changes associated with the social relations between men and women. Following right after, Hutchins's essay is also very accessible. She also took it as her task to explain the problem:

> Here is a young woman just graduated from a woman's college which has as high academic standing as any college for men. She has been a leader in college. . . . She is fully equipped both in natural gifts and in training to take a position of leadership [now]. But if she is a physician she finds that she is not expected

---

As I re-write this chapter for the umpteenth time, this quote by Clark Blaise rings true for me as much as it speaks about biography as an overworked act of literary reconstruction: "Those of us who compose on word processors are accustomed to shifting vast blocks of type, effectively obliterating traditional notions of narrative in the name of a consistent voice. Narrative therefore surrenders to juxtaposition, plot to non sequitur. After component passages become equivalent, sequences take on open-ended—perhaps even accidental—depth or humor. We begin behaving without the constraints of context. The past, like a compliant corpse, can be 'accessed' or autopsied for accusatory or exculpatory evidence—the remains are eternally contemporary."[60]

to aspire to a profession on a hospital staff unless it be a hospital exclusively for women and children. If she is a lawyer, she finds that the most profitable positions of corporation counsel are open only to men. If she has her graduate degree in social-religious work, she finds that most churches want only men as pastors and rectors, and will at the very most yield the position of church-school director to a woman. In the radical movement she finds that some of the most radical men who accept woman's equality as a fundamental principle are yet the most dominating in relation to women in daily life.[61]

Given the readership of the *World Tomorrow*, this last sentence was undoubtedly an intentional jibe; it was a pertinent remark that reflected her understanding of gender politics. However, Hutchins was not able to analyze the material basis of these politics. With an interesting turn, she described the plight of women in terms of an inferiority complex: "it is mainly we women who must get over this inferiority business."[62] She described men's environment (what we might now call socialization) as the cause of this problem rather than the fault of individual men, but suggested that it would help if men would expect women to have ideas and support their service as leaders. She did not analyze the conditions of men's environment nor demand that men take responsibility for these unequal social relations. Instead she emphasized that when the new democracy arrived (the socialist future), it would not matter whether the leaders were men or women because ability would decide. Interestingly, her understandings of gender were rooted in individualistic liberal ideology: a strong contrast to the material socioeconomic analysis employed to understand class relations. Explaining the absence of any ready-made solution to this problem, with characteristic good humor she wrote,

> I suffer from an inferiority complex myself. I have been the big frog in the little pool, and now I am a little frog in a big pool. But I can see it is no permanent solution that the women frogs should go off and have a pool by themselves. Women who live and work too exclusively with other women miss the balance of life which comes when men and women work together.[63]

With an uncanny resemblance to Cleghorn's critique of Community House, Hutchins spoke against separatist political strategies and toward a more balanced approach. The essay, while mostly quite supportive of feminism, was guarded in several places. For example, she remarked that some women who have good reason to be disgruntled "have become militant feminists, and a few who have become feminists have no sense of humor. Hence the subject of feminism has often been laughed out of court by men and women who do not understand the theory of compensation and who see in it nothing but the grim determination of a few 'mannish' women."[64] Despite the shortcomings in this analysis of gender relationships, that

I was taken by Freda Kirchwey's article and excited to find Grace writing about feminism. The comparison between the two pieces made me feel disappointed with Grace, and, as a result, I rewrote this analysis of her essay several times after deciding I was first being too harsh on her. Research diary: May 27, 1998: "I am amazed that Grace would write about women having an 'inferiority complex' as if it was women's psychological problem when she would never have said the problems associated with capitalism boil down to an inferiority complex among the workers; worse still, they should just get over it! What an interesting liberal take on this issue rather than applying the framework she would have used to understand class relations." This is so very classic in terms of the development of understandings of patriarchy within feminism as ideological rather than based on material–structural systems. Her comment on feminists not having a sense of humor of course shows how old that notion is—it's still going strong as a justification to dismiss women's demands for change. Finally, I've thought quite a bit about this comment of hers concerning being a big frog in a little pool. Perhaps she refers to her presocialist life: time at Bryn Mawr or in the foreign missions when she had held positions of leadership and authority. Being a little frog in a big pool might now reflect her position in the radical movement where she was surrounded by relatively famous and formidable characters. It might also reflect the dictates of feminine modesty that Grace had so well internalized.

Hutchins was willing to take on such a topic reflects her growing understanding of the inequalities associated with gender and her desire to understand the plight of women in modern society.

Before long, Hutchins was using her analysis of gender politics at the office after an altercation with Nevin Sayre. Underused in her position with F.O.R., she hoped to take on a more active role with the development of the journal. She remarked that she was insufficiently challenged by F.O.R. work unless Secretary Paul Jones was away, and, when he was in New York, she had little independent work. As a result, Hutchins took over some of the work of a managing editor of the *World Tomorrow* after Sayre's resignation from his formal position in 1924, and was especially involved in fund-raising. She then had an altercation with Sayre that reflected her principled as well as expressive nature. Hutchins wrote to Sayre apologizing for "exploding so angrily the other day," and, with characteristic humility, asked him to forgive her since "it is the worst of sins" that reveal "pride and other sins beneath the surface." At the same time though, Hutchins did not mince words in explaining the situation that led to her losing her temper. She wrote that given Sayre's resignation and discussion of withdrawal from the organization, it was such a shock for her to find him dictating letters (when she had written all hers by hand) and thanking her for working "on what has, by your pulling out, become as much my project as yours. . . ." She continued:

> It looked to me as if you were going to walk in now and then and spend two or three days censoring other people's work, as if you were super-editor, while the rest of us did what had to be done. . . . We all have a great respect for you, Nevin, for your generosity and sincerity, your faithfulness and your careful thoroughness. The only difficulty is that your criticisms often leave people less free, less spontaneous, less fresh and joyous in their work, and God knows how this old world needs originality and spontaneity and a general cheering-up. The few who can do constructive work (I am not one of them!) ought to be encouraged to the utmost.[65]

It seems that alongside what Hutchins perceived as Sayre's arrogance in terms of ownership of projects, and his masculine prerogatives concerning dictation, he had also criticized Devere Allen and Anna Rochester concerning their roles as editors of the *World Tomorrow*. While Hutchins was quick to assume modesty concerning her talents, she was very protective of her colleagues, and especially when one of them was her dear friend and partner.

This argument (what she called an "explosion") haunted her somewhat as she pursued the possibility of taking on more work with the *World Tomorrow*. Sayre's resignation and then the anticipated departure of the business secretary led Hutchins to suggest she fill the gap. In a letter to Devere Allen written on Christmas Day 1924, from her family home on Beacon Street, Hutchins suggested that she might solve the present office dilemma of the impending resignation of Business Secretary "Alice" by volunteering her assistance in a (nonsalaried) position.[66] With reference to the earlier altercation with Sayre, she addressed what she called "yours and Nevin's impression of me; I remember how I flew out last Spring and how often it must have seemed to you that I did not have very good judgment. There is the danger that I might fly out again as I did that day!"

The letter has a humble and understated tone typical of Hutchins's writings about herself, yet it also has an interesting combination of spunk and humility. She graciously gave them the opportunity for many "outs"; she wanted to avoid their having to feel embarrassed and no doubt wanted to save face herself should they decide she was not the one for the position. Tactically laying out the problems with working at the office on a more regular basis, she wrote about the loyalty of office staff (especially Esther Shemitz) to Alice and the possibilities of their feeling resentful of Hutchins's position, as well as Hutchins's discussion of her competencies vis-à-vis the position itself. Concerning the latter, with overstated humility she suggested they might not think of her as a hard and consistent worker: "you have all known me as a rather impulsive, desultory kind of a worker, not very able or especially skilled in any one line." She suggested she might take over at least part of Alice's position and launched into her prior record of administration and committed and intense work. The other objection she foresaw was her close relationship with Rochester. On this she wrote: "There is the difficulty of my relationship to Anna which would make the work too much of a close corporation if I were taking much more of the responsibility." She suggested this might be the most serious difficulty, "yet with proper safeguarding and keeping to our own respectful fields in the business and the editorial parts of the work, I think we could overcome that difficulty."[67] Their close relationship as romantic partners was obviously an accepted aspect of the F.O.R. and *World Tomorrow* communities. Hutchins's approach paid off: in the September 1925 issue of the journal she was listed as secretary and business executive.

However, 1925 was a year when Hutchins and Rochester seemed to be featured less both in F.O.R. business and in the journal. The *World Tomorrow* was known for drawing the energies of Christian socialist pacifists who traveled the world and wrote interesting articles on the inequities of colonial domination and the potentialities of new social orders. With this in mind, Hutchins and Rochester instead hoped to join this band of veteran travelers and started making plans for their exciting "round-the-world trip" to take place in 1926. It is not clear whether disillusionment with Christian socialism facilitated this travel, although most likely the trip's timing was related to tensions between the couple's growing radical ideology, especially their critique of traditional Christianity, and the mission of F.O.R. and the *World Tomorrow*. The couple's reduced involvement in 1925 plus the strong change of heart and mind in 1927 suggest that these tensions were most likely in the air. But they did travel as journalists under the auspices of these organizations and wrote extensively for the *World Tomorrow* and other magazines. Traveling to such faraway places as India, China, Japan, and Russia, Hutchins and Rochester got to experience firsthand the problems of colonialism and an advancing global capitalism as well as the promises of alternative economic and sociopolitical orders. Their impressions of what they found here would mold their politics for the rest of their life and help move them toward communist commitments.

On their return in 1927, affiliations with F.O.R. and the *World Tomorrow* became strained as they found themselves in disagreement with principles and policies. In a letter to Sayre, who had continued his position on the Board of Directors for the *World Tomorrow*, Rochester declined an invitation to be elected to this board and explained that she needed to resign as a contributing editor since she felt out of sync with their viewpoints and purposes. It seems that Kirby Page's influence as an editor of the *World Tomorrow* after 1926 had exacerbated these ideological differences: "I am sorry," she wrote, "you are all mighty nice folks. But this particular kind of commitment to a paper with which month by month I mostly do not agree is really unfair all around."[68] On this same day Rochester wrote another letter to Devere Allen and Kirby Page that was more explicit in explaining these differences of opinion. With just a hint of intellectual superiority targeted at these "mighty nice folks," Rochester laid out the problems:

> For example, I feel stultified by even nominal association with a paper that is boasting the League of Nations which to me is—and always has been—the alliance of capitalist–imperialist powers for the protection of the old order. In your industrial number, the strike was discussed as a phenomenon which might be controlled and prevented or softened as if it were unrelated to the basic facts of economic conflict and class struggle. Perhaps we failed in the past to make them clear, but frankly I do not feel that either of you in your own thinking analyzes the basic industrial situations today and the problems of the immediate future in a way which lines up your intentions *with* the working class and not against it.

> Then it may seem a small matter, but as further indication of what I have just said, it is pretty significant that the *World Tomorrow* is the only paper I have seen—conservative or liberal—whose November number completely ignores the anniversary of the Russian revolution. I am sorry in many ways to make this break, for the years on the *World Tomorrow* were stimulating. But it is better not to try any longer to maintain a nominal connection which is not fair either to you or to me. I hope this letter—which should have been written months ago—may now reach you in time to take my name off in the December number.[69]

In this way, the ideological differences eventually caused the women to sever formal ties. However, they maintained a friendship with many F.O.R. personnel and with Devere Allen and his wife Marie in particular.[70] These years with the Fellowship prepared Hutchins and Rochester as politicos by giving them experiences in organization, networking, and leadership. Allegiances to this community helped their political ideology coalesce and made them face the contradictions of a radical political identification in the context of bourgeois privilege. They learned to live with these contradictions and live their faith, as well as live with each other; their politics seemed to help foster their intimacy at the same time that their emotional relationship undergirded their political commitments.

CHAPTER SIX

THE HAPPY TRAVELERS

NINETEEN TWENTY-SIX was an exciting year for Hutchins and Rochester. As journalists they ventured on a year-long, round-the-world trip that took them to China, Japan, the Philippines, India, Europe and Russia with the task of observing, analyzing, and writing about these societies. Their focus was on education and the labor movement in the various countries they visited. As already discussed, they were becoming disillusioned with Christian socialism (or at least with the liberal Christian aspect of these politics) and had cut back on their formal involvement with F.O.R. and the *World Tomorrow*. Given these various tensions, it is quite likely that their extensive travels in 1926 were motivated in part by a desire to escape the domestic politics of the particular circles of Christian socialism in which they traveled. However, their affiliation with the mission and principles of these politics was at least still formally intact since they traveled under the auspices of F.O.R. and the *World Tomorrow*. In addition, there is some suggestion that the trip was a way to help Hutchins deal with the physical and emotional problems associated with menopause. It was often thought that a change in air would help mend the body and spirits and provide a respite from the daily grind.[1] Again, their prosperous financial situation gave them the freedom to enjoy these adventures.

Calling themselves "the happy travelers," Hutchins and Rochester sent numerous "round-robin" letters that were passed among friends and colleagues. Some were informally handwritten and others were printed and circulated as formal greetings and informational reports. While published articles written by the pair tended to be based upon these letters and often contained similar information and analyses, all their writings gave detail to their travel experiences and provided analyses of the economic systems and everyday lives of the various societies and people they visited. Focusing on

> It is possible Grace and Anna were more strongly identified with F.O.R. during this trip than I make out, and that my assumption about disillusionment with this organization and Christian socialism is fabricated more from the lack of evidence that suggests they *were* involved as anything else. If so, this would mean the trip was even more of an epiphany. In terms of Grace's experience of menopause, my "evidence" that this helped motivate the travels is a letter written after the fact about the benefits of the trip in helping Grace deal with menopause. How much they would have said this actually motivated their travels is unclear.

education and labor relations, analyses of various cultures were made through the lens of their socialist politics; they were heartened when sociopolitical and economic practices coincided with their own ideological agenda of labor control and workers democracies. This stance was laid out in the first paragraph of possibly their first letter home, written aboard the *Empress of Russia* on the way to Japan:

Crossing the prairies and the Rockies was to me a truly stirring new adventure—but Canada is not spiritually different from the U.S.A. Imperial oil instead of Socony was the label on the tanks which stood at every prairie station as outposts of capitalism. Vancouver is thickly smeared with a mixture of boosters pride and sentimental reminders of Empire. It leaves an unmistakable flavor of our familiar western world on the traveler's tongue.[2]

> This chapter more than any other contains Grace and Anna's personal reflections on their activities. The couple reconstructed their experiences in letters home, crafting their identities through these travel memoirs. This inventive writing reminds me of something by Gertrude Stein about how identity is a very shaky ontological experience:"And identity is funny as you are never yourself to yourself except as you remember yourself ... it could not be yourself because you can not remember right and if you do remember right it does not sound right because it is not right."[3] She was referring to the limitations of autobiography as a representational device for the self. Indeed the inseparability of fact and fiction characterizes autobiography at the very same time that as the "true story" of someone's life it tends to be seen as the opposite of fiction. At this point and amidst this jumble, biography enters the scene: to tell it like it was and to represent again that true story. So if we thought that autobiography and fiction were unmercifully fused, then biography reconstructs the story of the subject's story through her own story, a story that is then filtered through the stories of multiple readers: the layering of many literary acts of reading and writing.

Through their travel memoirs the pair constructed themselves as radical intellectuals with special insight into the various cultures they visited and with a strong sense for indigenous self-determination. In addition, they saw themselves as adventurous and carefree, seemingly enjoying the incongruity between their status as approaching-middle-age maiden ladies and budding radical politicos. It is important to note that their privileges as wealthy, white, experienced travelers smoothed their journey in a material sense and allowed them the freedom to imagine and construct themselves this way. In particular, with their socialist and pacifist political frameworks that recognized global exploitation and the vagaries of colonialism and militarism, Hutchins and Rochester were at great pains not to behave or be seen as enjoying the unconscious pleasures associated with travelers who did not have a keen sense of global history and politics. Theirs was a different mission, above that of inquisitive tourists or proselytizing missionaries. They were especially aware of the ways that Westerners, and especially the British and North Americans, often behaved, that is, in a peculiarly condescending and patronizing manner among people of developing and colonized countries. Hutchins remarked that such Western travelers were blinded by their own ethnocentrism and tended to "get from their travels only what they expect to see."[4] Rochester remarked in a letter to friends that she felt a "shocking intolerant intellectual snobbishness" toward such traveling types and avoided them at all costs.[5] At the Manila Hotel in the Philippines, for example, where they dined and spent time with Filipino friends, they felt and saw the looks of the Americans in the dining room who were hostile to both Philippine independence and the fraternization with local people. Rochester saw this as evidence of the great "racial cleavages" apparent in this country that set whites above all others and encouraged ethnocentrism among foreign travelers.[6] Needless to say, the irony of this stance as it related to their own situation as travelers committed to their point of view was lost on them, and their own condescension toward the Western unenlightened was left unexplored.

While Hutchins and Rochester did indeed demonstrate a certain measure of intellectual snobbery sprinkled throughout their writings, only rarely did it seem to be admitted openly, and then usually under the guise of personal idiosyncrasy rather than connected to their political framework. What appears evident is a considerable ego investment in their political stance; they seemed to have liked the assessment of themselves as radicals and as the intellectual vanguard of the working class. Perceived as genteel spinsters approaching middle age, their power lay in their incongruity. Underneath mild exteriors were politicos who went back to their rented rooms in the evening to type up critical essays for publication in some of the most radical presses of the day. To highlight their differences from other middle-aged women of their class, they wrote how humored

they were by the innocuous description "charming girls devoted to missionary work and travel" that had helped them acquire visas.[7] Another example was their response to a costume ball onboard ship: "We intend to
blossom out in our evening gowns specially acquired for this trip, the first
in ten years for either of us. We shall not attend the ball but the daily radio
press urges every one of us to come to dinner in costume. (How will they
know that for us an evening gown *is* fancy dress!)"[8]

Another example of this incongruity between appearance and identity,
and their desire to separate themselves from ordinary travelers, was a description of their journey from the Philippines to Singapore, travels spent
with a collection of "utterly unradical Americans." After describing a retired
physician from Boston who was "as imperialistic as they make them," they
recounted the experience of sharing a table from Manila to Singapore with
a New York engineer and his "very charming wife":

> Grace mentioned something she had just read in an American paper. "What
> paper was that?" "The *Nation*." The wife had never heard of it, the husband
> with a sinister look "knew it all too well." Later it transpired that he had been
> a million dollar engineer in the War Department in 1917. We did not insist on
> telling them of our connections with the World Tomorrow.[9]

In this way, the couple's investment in not being ordinary American travelers was a central component of their identity. In the Philippines, originally finding themselves in an upscale hotel catering to Americans tourists,
Hutchins and Rochester quickly chose to relocate to a more modest hotel
with "all sorts of Filipinos and a sprinkling of American and European
business men and two or three non-too-respectable-looking-women."[10]
They enjoyed the mixed company and novelty of the place as well as the
moving picture theater in the courtyard of the hotel, which, if they chose
just the right chair in their room, they could watch for free. These writings
are also sprinkled with Hutchins and Rochester's sense of humor; they understood the necessity of entertaining their readers with foreign escapades
and made the most of situations in order to reveal the irony and humor implicit in their predicaments. This more modest hotel in the Philippines to
which they had relocated, for example, had its drawbacks: one day on returning to the room they found the biggest cockroach either had ever seen
crawling out from under the bureau. And then to make matters worse a bat
of huge proportions flew in through their open window, startling the pair
and scaring them half to death. The moral of this story seemed to imply
that they could only go so far in their quest for "going native."[11]

Occasionally though, Hutchins and Rochester's sense of their own importance came across as a little excessive. For example, in India they were
politely quizzed by police officers as to their intentions and whereabouts.
Rochester wrote that in a way they were "gratified by the attention, for the

Grace and Anna, during their travels, 1926.

comfortable neglect of the police testified to our unimportance, once we had passed the half-hour's quizzing at the consulate in New York before they gave us our visas."[12] I interpret this to mean that they were pleased by the attention of the police because it reaffirmed that they were indeed important visitors and fed their egos concerning their special mission.

Eastern Parts

Armed with a strong materialist economic analysis peppered by the Christian ethics of goodwill, charity and tolerance, Rochester and Hutchins left Chicago on Friday the thirteenth of August on the thirteenth train, heading west, in order to board their ship bound for Japan. They considered this an interesting omen for their journey to come.

This intellectual snobbery stemmed from a lifetime of privilege as well as a moral conviction that their analysis of the world was right; that it was *the* most accurate and useful analysis. My gut feeling is that their gracious, bourgeois, nineteenth-century manners prevented them from being too abrasive or dogmatic in everyday interactions. On the other hand, despite being well schooled in the social graces and niceties, they might have been seen by some as exceedingly overbearing and my interpretation of them as almost matronly travelers who publicly showed tolerance could be misguided.

The first port of call for the "happy travelers" was Japan, a country they described as most reactionary and imperialist. There were laws in Japan, such as the Peace Preservation Law, that prevented public demonstrations and other expressions of resistance to the governmental regime and the imperial family. In "Dangerous Thoughts in Japan," Rochester wrote:

> The present government is determined to suppress all revolutionary propaganda, whether in the labor movement or in the universities. Even any explicit recognition of the class struggle apparently is banned as "dangerous thought." . . . A Japanese graduate of an American woman's college told us, for example, that in attending labor meetings even for the discussion of immediate organization problems unrelated to the communist, socialist, or anarchist propaganda, she had several times been quizzed by a policeman at the entrance and the papers in her bag had been minutely searched before she was allowed to go in. Apparently it is only the socialists who have given up even the pinkest shade of Marxism or who are devoting all their activities to immediate labor demands and keeping discreetly still as to their socialist beliefs who are free to continue their work without frequent arrests and breaking up of meetings.[13]

Despite these crackdowns on the part of Japanese imperial forces, there was support for a new Labor Farmers' Party that had the potential to disrupt the old regime. Hutchins captured this force in an article published in the *Christian Century*, in October 1926, titled "Kagawa as Labor Leader." It was a moving "human interest" story that traced the difficult and dangerous living conditions of the organizer for this new party, the Reverend Toyohiko Kagawa. In particular, Hutchins focused on Kagawa's courage, achievements, and ethics as a Christian progressive. The essay begins in the standard format of much of Hutchins and Rochester's writings, with an invitingly descriptive paragraph about Kagawa that set the stage for the economic analysis that would follow. Given that the readers of the *Christian Century* were perhaps not as familiar with a socialist analysis as some of her other readers, this piece was crafted as a persuasive essay that relied heavily on grounding Kagawa's politics in his persona as a moral and compassionate Christian man:

> As he came into the room we saw that his eyes were shaded by heavy dark glasses which he took off only for a moment showing the clouded swollen eyes that mean trachoma in its latest stages. He told us he was going the next morning for an operation that would perhaps arrest the disease, but a day or two later we heard that the operation was not successful. He would be entirely blind in a few months. . . . He and his wife lived in the centre of the worst districts of Kobe—one of the worst in all Japan, among thieves and outcasts, in three tiny rooms, and it was there they contracted the infectious disease of the eyes which is so common in the east. There his oldest child was born. It was there, too, that he wrote the earlier books which roused the students of Japan

to seek him out, and brought at the same time the officers of the government to watch him as a socialist. . . .

True to his principles of identifying himself with the underdog, Kagawa is a leader in the labor movement. He is today president of the cotton mill workers of Osaka, head of the industrial department in the cabinet of the tenant farmers' union, and organizer of the labor farmer party. At the same time he is president of a peasant school, of a labor school, and of an industrial settlement. . . . He cares intensely about each separate part of life and gives himself to each occasion as if it were not merely one of a hundred others. While speaking to a meeting of deaf children, he was so absorbed in the thought of their handicap as interpreted by his own blindness that he shed tears and forgot entirely the grown-ups and officials who were present. He has usually worked eighteen hours a day, getting up before 5 o'clock in the morning and dictating his letters and writings to three young men who help him. He believes in prayer and opened the first meeting of the tenant-farmers' union with a prayer.[14]

Despite the glimmers of hope they saw in the likes of Kagawa and his colleagues, Hutchins and Rochester found Japan a disappointing country where sympathizers of progressive politics faced a difficult existence. By comparison, China was more to their liking; they were impressed by Chinese customs and ideas and encouraged by the presence of the Kuomintang, the Chinese Nationalist Party. Arriving in Peking in early October 1926, they eagerly talked with students and faculty in the universities, public educators and missionaries involved in educational reform, newspaper editors, and as many ordinary Chinese people as possible. They met F.O.R. folks, as well as deans of universities, and attended Bryn Mawr alumnae teas and even a baseball game. American and Chinese contacts welcomed them to their homes, took them sight-seeing, and helped orient them to the political situation.[15] This latter activity was particularly important given the volatile situation in China concerning the struggles between the Chinese Nationalist Party and the northern troops. These contacts arranged interviews with key people in educational and labor reform, and, to Hutchins and Rochester's delight, they were able to meet with two leaders of the Chinese Nationalist Party who were in hiding.

Careful to respect indigenous cultures, Hutchins and Rochester always tried to converse in the language of the country whenever possible. They had been learning Russian for several months prior to the trip and Hutchins had been brushing up on her Chinese. While not completely fluent in Chinese, she was able to communicate with local people. Alongside their language classes, Hutchins and Rochester had been reading profusely about the various sociopolitical situations of the countries they would visit. Hutchins, for example, was deep in Tyler Dennett's *Americans in Eastern Asia* and was also reading, among other things, Bertrand Russell. In particular, she loved to quote Russell's line about why Europeans found the Chinese uncivilized: "The Chinese are a great nation . . . I think they are the only people in the world who quite genuinely believe that wisdom is more precious than rubies. That is why the West regards them as uncivilized."[16] Armored with past experiences of China and political analyses filtered through the various progressive writers of the day, the couple embarked on a demanding schedule of visiting and talking, listening and taking notes about China, its political situation, issues of educational and labor reform, as well as hopes for the future.[17]

Not surprisingly, both women found themselves supportive of the rebel Kuomintang, the Chinese Nationalist Party. These rebels had been fighting against the northern war lords and the armies of Chang Tso Lin and his ally Marshal Wu Pei Pu, both of whom had the support of foreign powers. Peking in the north was under the control of Chang Tso Lin, and the Kuomintang sympathizers were terrorized or in hiding. Writing in October 1926 after just arriving in China, Hutchins gave her opinion on this situation after their meeting with two Kuomintang leaders:

> "Shh. Do not tell anyone where you are going, whom you see, or what they say, but I will lead you to the two leading Nationalists in hiding here in Peking." He led us, and for nearly two hours we talked with men whose lives are sought by the gray soldiers of Chang Tso Lin. Even while we talked we heard that ten of the twenty eight students, arrested for holding a meeting, were condemned to death and might be beheaded within the next few days. . . . Here in Peking the gray Northern soldiers are in undisputed control. They hold up coal trains and levy tribute which drives the price of coal in Peking up to six or seven times what it was two years ago. They fill the street cars and pay no fare. Worst of all, they force the rickshaw men to pull them, and seldom pay even the meager ten cents (American money) an hour which is the coolies' wage. Yesterday on the street a soldier took off his heavy belt and beat a rickshaw man, while the people stood by without daring to intervene. When we asked an American resident the reason for such treatment, she answered, "It happens every day. The soldiers are conscripting the rickshaw men for the army, and if the man resists, he is beaten. They came for my rickshaw man two days ago and only my intervention saved him."[18]

Despite this poverty and the reign of terror on the people of Peking and other northern cities, Hutchins demonstrated optimism and a stirring hope. Common to socialist writing of the day, it was important for her essay to reflect the positive outcome that would necessarily result from the workers' struggle against imperialist forces:

> This is Peking on the fifteenth anniversary of the Chinese Republic. Yet those who look to the Kuomintang believe that the Chinese will someday dismiss the foreigners and proclaim the sovereignty of their country. While the Peo-

ples' Party builds a unified China, the workers are organizing and stirring in the larger industrial centres, and the peasants in the provinces are beginning to resist exploitation. The national post office is functioning with regularity and efficiency. The Mass Education Movement, promoted and organized entirely by the Chinese, is carrying on classes for adult boys and girls in thirty two centres. Scholars are re-writing the history of China from the viewpoint of modern historical criticism. The New Thought Movement is reconstructing and reinterpreting the past. There is a widespread passion for ideas and the beautiful expression of these ideas in literature. The gray soldiers in Peking today cannot touch these underlying movements which are building the future.[19]

Alongside the political analysis of Peking, Hutchins and Rochester were keenly aware of the sights, sounds, and cultural curiosities of this impressive Chinese city. Rochester exclaimed in letters home that every trip was a sight-seeing expedition since the life of the streets was so colorful and endlessly varied. In a "Dear Friends" letter written October 10, 1926, Rochester wrote of the poverty and distress of many communities around Peking where whole villages had been destroyed. Despite these troubles, she found China both beautiful and fascinating: "carvings and odd decorations on house fronts, [an] unexpected gateway, odd vehicles, outlandish loads carried on the shoulder poles or pulled by coolies with two wheeled carts, glimpses of courtyards through open gates in house walls. And animals: camels, donkeys, ponies, sheep, pigs, goats."[20] They visited the Summer Palace, the beautiful park of Pei Hai, and the Temple of Heaven in the magnificent Forbidden City, exclaiming over the beautifully fragile and richly decorated pottery and porcelains of the Sung dynasty.

Two days after writing this letter to friends and colleagues at home, Rochester and Hutchins left Peking for Hankow. As Rochester reported in an article for the *Nation*, the nationalists had taken Wuchang and the way was now clear for the women to travel south into that region.[21] They sent a printed letter titled "Joyous Christmas and New Year Greetings to Our Friends from the Happy Travelers," actually written at the end of October in order for it to arrive in time for the Christmas holidays. Penned during several boat trips on the Yangtze River from Hankow to Nanking, it reported that they had reached Wuchang only eight days after the release of the city from its forty-day siege. Waiting for news in Peking amidst the rumors of violent confrontations, cholera, and starvation, they heard that Wuchang had surrendered and no foreigners had been hurt, although tragically, over fifty women and children were trampled to death or pushed into the river during the panic.[22]

Hutchins and Rochester's writings suggest they thrived on these uncertainties and dangers. However, as writings, they were obviously written after the fact and reflected the bravado that can be safely felt when immediate danger was past and they were back in their room still flushed with the excitement of the event, yet safely home. These writings also remind me of the feelings of "untouchability" I had when reading reports of missionary women, Hutchins's accounts included. There is the arrogant sense that such individuals are inviolate and immune from the dangers that would beset ordinary citizens.

The couple was enamored with the courage, conviction, and quiet perseverance of the Chinese radicals. They found them earnest, vigorous, and sincere in their attempt to try and improve the condition of their lives. In "Seeing Red in Canton," published in the *Survey* in March 1927, Hutchins elaborated on the idea that one of the most crucial messages for Americans, and American religious liberals in particular, was that foreign powers must not become involved in bolstering the present governmental regime out of fear of a communist takeover in China. She emphasized that the Kuomintang regime was nationalist and not communist, and she commented on the tendency of the foreign press to mislabel the nationalist armies "Reds" and "Bolsheviks" with immediate ties to Russia. Sharing the countless interviews she had with Chinese people from different walks of life and from different regions, she explained in this article that even the left wing of the Kuomingtang was distinct from the Communist Party. In a *World Tomorrow* article Hutchins attempted to minimize the radical intent of the Kuomintang for the average U.S. liberal reader by demystifying Bolshevism and by disassociating the Kuomintang from it as well as emphasizing the human aspect of friendships made and trusted.[23] From their tentative support of Bolshevism during the years preceding these travels, Hutchins and Rochester seemed more ready at this point to support the regime. This support would increase dramatically after time spent in Russia.

This visit to China was a kind of homecoming for Hutchins since it brought back memories of her days as a missionary in the Wuchang region. She visited her old school, St. Hilda's in Wuchang, and saw the trees she had planted ten years earlier; she even spent some time with friends, including the indefatigable Dr. Mary James who was still seeing "about two hundred patients at a time."[24] She was happy to be able to share old memories and new exploits with her partner, to visit friends, meet new people, and try her hand at interpreting Chinese again. Both Hutchins and Rochester gave the distinct impression in their various writings that this country was one that left strong and positive memories both personally and ideologically. On November 13, 1926, with cheerful hearts and eager anticipation of the adventures ahead, they left the vibrant and colorful port of Shanghai bound for the Philippine Islands in search of more adventures and political commentary.

Arriving in Manila in early December, Hutchins and Rochester immediately started another demanding schedule of interviewing key people concerning the sociopolitical and economic situation in the Philippines. They

Grace and Anna in China, 1926. Grace is in the back row, right.
Anna is in the back row, left.

heard the extreme viewpoints of both U.S. control and Filipino independence and the many opinions in between, and they witnessed the constant
American corporate and military presence throughout the various communities on the islands. For example, gold mines, operated by U.S. compa-
nies yet paid for by Filipino money, dotted the landscape as gold was lifted
up steep hillsides on small swinging cars on cable hauls, taken overland to
the post office, and, much to Hutchins and Rochester's amazement,
shipped to the United States by parcel post.

Supportive of Filipino independence, Rochester wrote an article, "Notes
from the Philippines," that she characterized as pro-independence but not
uncritical of this position. It was published in the *World Tomorrow* the following March. Here she emphasized the extent of American influence in

Research diary: May 7, 1997: "Did Grace forgive herself for her work [as a
missionary]? Did she integrate these experiences and see them as part of
her journey? Was it accepted as false consciousness [in the Marxist understanding of people taking on positions that enhance cultural hegemony]?
Engrossed [in thoughts about her work] I dreamed last night that Grace
was telling a story about being a missionary. In my dream she spoke with
dignity and authority and came across as proud and strong."

the islands and the overwhelming American opposition to independence. The U.S. Congress had not redeemed the promise of independence, arguing that there was a lack of stable government. As Rochester astutely noted, "the imperialist viewpoint distorts the definition of stability and will prolong the argument into the indefinite future."[25] Yet Hutchins and Rochester did have respect for the U.S. governor, General Woods, whom they found gracious and principled, and they were critical of "trickery" and efforts on the part of some Filipinos. Rochester remarked that the issue of economic imperialism hardly appeared in the Filipino literature on independence and that Filipino leaders often tended to invite, in moderation, U.S. capital. Ultimately, the solution, like the analysis, she believed, was economic and far-reaching.[26]

After Manila, the pair left for Baguio, originally intending to enjoy a three-week holiday there with visits to the southern islands. However, on arriving they decided to return to Manila early and sail for their next port of call, India, two weeks earlier than they had planned. They thought that this margin of time would be helpful if they needed a respite from traveling in the hot Indian climate or for reaching Europe and Russia ahead of schedule. They eagerly anticipated the visit to India and were encouraged by several introductions to Gandhi and the hope of visiting his ashram, as well as by a potentially more obliging moon for their visit to the romantic Taj Mahal. Despite a holiday cut short, they settled down to several days of reading, armed with a miniature library on the history and politics of the Philippines and a demanding schedule for their Russian language study. They also made time for long walks together, exploring the trails through the hillside villages and enjoying the magnificent waterfalls and mountain views. Hutchins worked on some sketches of China and Rochester wrote the bulk of the communications with people at home. Always they wrote with a genuine affection for friends and colleagues left behind. There was concern for Esther Schemitz, office coordinator at the *World Tomorrow*, who had been beaten up on the picket lines at the Passaic strike, and there were inquiries about policies that affected the labor unions throughout the United States. "Absence makes the heart grow fonder," penned Rochester in one letter, "how glad we shall both be to get home again!"[27] Despite these kind words of friendship, returning home seemed the furthest thing from their minds. They were eager to continue their travels, excited about visiting India, and especially looking forward to being in the Soviet Union.

After leaving the Philippine Islands, Hutchins and Rochester landed in Singapore at the end of December. Major activities here included visits to numerous rubber factories, and observations into rubber manufacturing and the trading policies of foreign powers concerning rubber exportation. This commodity had so completely taken possession of the area that rubber and tin were almost the only exports, with trade of coconuts, pineap-

I wrote an article about Grace and Anna for a journal that focused on gender and history. In it I employed two narratives: one that you normally expect when reading an academic writing biography and another that utilized
my subtext idea, the one I had written about earlier where I used this format to voice my thoughts and alternative explanations. This subtext was situated at the bottom of the page below the traditional narrative and was the
format I was then using in the draft of this book. The reviews were mixed:
one had no idea what was going on and didn't want to engage with it, the
other had very insightful ideas about the article and encouraged much
rewriting. Needless to say the article was not accepted without major revi-
sions and it sits here, as I write, on the corner of my desk. What came out
of this was that the long subtext narrative was not working. In particular, I
understood that in the traditional narrative, out of fear of stating truths and
relying on some representational fallacy, I had avoided analysis. Instead I had
used the subtext for analysis rather than using the subtext for an unpacking
of this analysis. Disappointing as it was at the time, this reviewer had really
done me a favor. The six or seven chapters already completed of this book
then got overhauled yet again and I got rid of the long subtext and reinte-
grated much of it back into the traditional narrative. Then I brought back the
framed boxes that I'd originally used as backdrop boxes and used this format for a shortened, more critical subtext. That's what you're reading now.

ple, and bananas having since shrunk dramatically. So disrupted was the
local subsistence economy that almost all food had to be imported. In one
letter Rochester explained that besides being chock full of seeing and
smelling rubber, she was utterly convinced about the completeness of imperialism since at every turn they were confronted by North American and
European corporate and military interests. Even China was involved in
rubber manufacture and exportation: "I can't quite convey the vivid impression of complete control," she exclaimed.[28] Confronted by these constant reminders of foreign intervention and economic imperialism,
Hutchins and Rochester decided to lay low and show discretion about their
travel motives until they were safely in India. It seems that they were
quizzed by the British Consulate about getting travel documents for India
and they were careful not to jeopardize their opportunity to visit the country and see the guru, Mahatma Gandhi, himself.

A Meeting with Gandhi

Arriving in Colombo (in what was then Ceylon, now Sri Lanka), Hutchins
and Rochester eagerly looked forward to four weeks in India. This part of
their travels was exceptionally memorable since they did eventually meet
and spend time with Gandhi, an event that would be recounted with pride

Research diary: February 12, 1998: "[Had a] conversation with ____ [and] left with a hint of an impression that biography was [a] less credible, less scholarly [endeavor than some other kinds of work]. I've heard it referred to as some kind of academic suicide, as impressionistic and not serious study. Had to admit my first thought was I was glad I already had tenure."

over the years that followed. However, despite this highlight, on the whole they found India quite tiresome. Especially irritating were the "superlordly" British whom they found arrogant and condescending. Hutchins and Rochester spoke of meeting a frumpy, "toplofty" Englishwoman going tiger hunting and some "female imperialists" whom they laughingly dubbed "FIs," but mostly they saw Englishmen associated with the government, military, and industry. According to Rochester, the British kept over 60,000 officers and rank-and-file military personnel in India; she was disgusted to recount that these expenses came out of Indian funds. The pair found it remarkable that there had only been one armed revolt to the date of their writing, although there had been violent revolutionary plottings and unrest on the part of the Indian nationalist movements through the years. Nonetheless, despite Hutchins and Rochester's despair over colonial India, they were still able to enjoy the sights and sounds of India, having their "little thrill" over the Taj Mahal and a visit to Agra. They tended to avoid the hustle and bustle of the bazaars, which they felt were completely spoiled by the persistence of the hawkers, perhaps betraying their anglicized reserve and middle-class distaste for these kinds of spontaneous confrontations.[29]

The cherished visit with Mohandas Karamchand Gandhi took a serious amount of planning and letter writing. Central in transforming the demand for independence into a nationwide mass movement that mobilized communities against imperialism, Gandhi was traveling across India speaking in the towns and villages. He was almost constantly on the move and proving difficult to pin down. Hutchins and Rochester had communicated with the secretary of the ashram at Ahmedabad and eventually received word as to Gandhi's whereabouts over the next few weeks. In a "Dear Friends" letter Rochester recalled how, with much excitement, she and Hutchins headed for the villages of the northern province of Bihar between Benares and Calcutta, hoping to meet up with Gandhi. They first arrived at his ashram at Benares, embarrassed at their incongruous arrival in a rented two-horse phaeton along with two male attendants (even though, as they were quick to add, the second attendant was there only to feed the horses). They had hoped to make a simple entrance on foot, but the heat and the distance had made this impossible. They learned where Gandhi was speaking next and retired to a travelers' bungalow at the ashram. Here they discovered how very cold were the nights in the Ganges valley and made trips the next day for blankets and other provisions. While all they could find was tinned soup and Huntley and Palmer's biscuits at a chemist's shop, they enjoyed the adventure nonetheless. They found the followers of Gandhi at this ashram most cordial and charming, and bought some of the famous Gandhi homespun cotton as a table-cover for their dining table at home.[30]

After a couple of days, Hutchins and Rochester took the train to Motihari, a village about a day's ride from Benares. Here they were dismayed to find that they had missed Gandhi himself by a mere few minutes; he took the train from which they had alighted. They had been swept out of the train station by a courteous stationmaster, only realizing afterwards that the crowds on the platform were indeed greater than usual. In their letter home Rochester hated to admit this close encounter and sheepishly relayed the facts of their missed opportunity. They spent the night at Motihara and took the early train the next morning to Bettiah. The weary travelers were happy to be met at the station and appreciated their speedy arrival at another travelers' bungalow in the village as well as a chance to bathe, rest, and eat a simple meal. During this time the crowds were gathering on the dusty road outside their bungalow, all on their way to an immense open green on the outskirts of town where Gandhi was to make his appearance before the waiting throng. Eventually Hutchins and Rochester joined the procession on its way to the green and joined several thousand men who were sitting on the ground in a great circle around a white draped platform. They were the only women in sight. As an aside, it is disappointing that nowhere did Hutchins or Rochester comment on the politics or the absence of women in the crowd, or on the status of women generally in India, or in any of the countries they visited, except Russia where they did comment on Russian peasant women. So deeply entrenched was patriarchy in these societies that they must have hardly thought to comment. Once close to Gandhi's platform, ushers saw them and presented two solitary chairs in a little enclosure next to the platform where the pair felt quite conspicuous. Then they were told they could meet with Gandhi before he spoke to the assembled crowd. This was the moment they had both been waiting for. Rochester described the encounter as follows:

> We had just sat down on the floor when he came—lively, radiantly smiling, as unlike the sombre ascetic of his pictures as one could well imagine. The face is thin, even bony, and the loss of some front teeth is conspicuous, but this you only realize afterwards. Alertness, eagerness, joyousness, serenity—the personality portrait. We talked about religion—I'm afraid we did a little, although we wanted to listen, for Gandhi is one of those sincerely simple folk who do not set lesser folk off at a distance but make you forget "self" and enjoy a genuine fellowship together. We talked about the real meaning of nonviolence and the depths of goodwill and self-discipline that it involves. In no

sense did Gandhi seem ascetic or unnatural—just more keenly interested in human beings and human relationships than in any paraphernalia of things. He wanted to know about Debs of whom he had only heard recently! He wanted to know about pacifism in the United States and was deeply interested in the long-continued non-violent strike in Passaic. We tried to get a prophecy as to whether non-violent measures—and temper of mind—could be developed quickly enough to ward off class wars and other conflicts leading to war, but wisely no guess was forthcoming. Of one thing he spoke with complete conviction: the privileged cannot preach non-violence to the unprivileged until they share the lot of the unprivileged.[31]

In a *World Tomorrow* article Hutchins portrayed the excitement associated with this interview and the splendor of the speech he gave to the great crowd waiting patiently on the grass. She wrote that he spoke to the assembled audience of khadi, the spinning campaign that he felt was not "merely an expedient to relieve Indian poverty, but the way to release from the evils of industrialism."[32] Khadar promotion was reducing the sale of machine-made cloth, and especially of British-produced cloth, in India. Gandhi also spoke about untouchability to the crowds. He believed that there must be a change of attitude toward the untouchables since the domination of caste was seen as a form of violence in Indian life. He did not, however, repudiate the ancient fourfold caste idea. After his speech he remembered to bid the women a special good-bye. Hutchins recalled this in her article: "'He is speaking to you,' one of the disciples said to us, and we turned to find Gandhi with a hand to help us up on the platform. 'You will be safer up here,' he said, with that wide smile, 'but as soon as I go now, the people will go.' He was gone, and the people followed."[33]

Hutchins and Rochester seemed to have relished their meeting with Gandhi and the opportunity to hear him speak. They declared a great affinity with his ideas and were in agreement with almost everything. The one thing on which Rochester disagreed—"we could have had a glorious argument . . . but naturally in one short talk this could not be"—was on the issue of khadi. Rochester felt that it was "a tragedy that he so completely despairs of controlling power machinery and throws all of his tremendous spiritual drive and purifying ethics into the reviving of handicraft."[34] With her Marxist economic analysis that saw industrialization as a necessary part of the evolution of a class society into a socialist one, and, when under worker control,

> Grace and Anna were in India during January 1927, when my mother was born. I keep thinking about this when reading their letters, thinking about my grandmother who would have been birthing my mother at the same time that Grace and Anna were chasing Gandhi across India.

a tool of human progress, Rochester was invariably at odds with Gandhi's notion of hand-spinning. She also despaired at the inability of applying khadi to the contemporary European and North American situation.[35]

This time in India, contextualized by the everyday presence of British imperialism, reminded Hutchins and Rochester of the interconnections between colonial oppression and capitalist exploitation. In the middle of this despair, they found it fitting that a prophet such as Gandhi should have emerged, and they noted that the vows of the Gandhi ashrams were a direct challenge to the ethical standards for individual communists as well as to the ethics of current Christian practice.[36] I understand this mention of "individual communists" to imply a critique of the violent actions of certain Bolsheviks as well as a critique of the ways colonialism and militarism were supported by much Christian practice in the United States. Interestingly, the critique did not focus on the principles of communism nor communist practice but instead on the idiosyncratic tendencies of certain Bolshevik personnel. This most likely was their way of maintaining support for communism as a political philosophy in the face of reports of Bolshevik hostility and genocide.

This interview with Gandhi is interesting also because of the contrasts that can be made between their firsthand accounts here and discussions of this event years later. In 1936 a *Daily Worker* article summarized Rochester's experiences on these travels: "What she saw in her unconducted tour of the Soviet Union, as contrasted with the futility of Gandhi's passive resistance (and his pious quaffing of goat's milk) erased all doubt from her mind [about the infallibility of communism]."[37] Again in another *Daily Worker* article in 1940, reporter Stephen Peabody explained that when Rochester was told by Gandhi that societal change would be extensive and long in coming, she disagreed, knowing that these changes had occurred in one generation in the Soviet Union: "She tried to tell Gandhi what the Soviet people had been able to do, but he did not want to listen."[38] These accounts, published as they were in the major communist press, were at pains to contrast the rational approach of scientific Marxism with the outmoded and idealistic beliefs of Gandhi. As such they might better reflect the authors' desires to praise the Soviet Union more than anything else, although they seem to have been based on interviews with Rochester. It is not clear whether she approved of these accounts; certainly they stood in sharp contrast to the reverent and respectful portrayal of this visit in the letters written at the time.

Russia at Last

February 1927 found Hutchins and Rochester aboard the *President Garfield*, an ocean liner bound for Genoa, reflecting on their travels through the East and talking with eager anticipation about the upcoming trip to the Soviet

Union. They had immersed themselves in the Russian language for quite some time and were eager to observe this great country firsthand. They were also bursting to apply their emerging political understandings to the Russian situation and intent on absorbing all they could from this travel experience. However, the route to Russia lay via western Europe, leaving them with mixed feelings about reminders of capitalist hegemony. But since it was in Germany where they would receive travel documents for Russia, to Germany they were bound. So they landed in Genoa at the end of February and made their way to Berlin, where they stayed with communist friend and writer Kurt Tetzner. Tetzner had already had several works banned and was being named the leading writer of the young proletariat, achievements that marked his conviction and courage. After several weeks of waiting, Hutchins and Rochester decided not to impose on their host any longer, given the cramped conditions, and took up lodging at a hostel in the city. While the wait was frustrating, Hutchins and Rochester never gave up hope that they would get a visa for the Soviet Union. In fact, they were sure they would, and relied upon the word of various communist friends who assured them it was just a matter of time. They avoided making detailed plans until the official signatures arrived and were careful not to show any critique of communist activity through their correspondences, since, as nonparty journalists, they assumed letters would be intercepted and read.[39] Such comments concerning critiques of Bolshevism suggest their lack of complete support for the regime at this time. Within several years it would be impossible to imagine either of them being critical of communism.

In the interim, they diligently studied their Russian language books, took a daily lesson at the Berlitz School, and exposed themselves to all the Russian influences Berlin had to offer. And Berlin had much to offer. Alongside enjoying such Russian influences as drinking tea out of glasses rather than cups, the pair threw themselves into the Russian literary and artistic scene. They watched several films, including Gorky's "Mother," which they found magnificent. They were disappointed to have missed the film "Potemkin," about the Russian revolution of 1905, since it was considered dangerous propaganda and suppressed; likewise they missed an unnamed play that was causing a stir at the Volksbunne, or People's Stage. Apparently the play was written by a peasant who had never seen a play before, involved both acting and moving pictures, and depicted a revolution in an imaginary country. Hutchins and Rochester were eager to report that the director of the Volksbunne had been ordered to withdraw the piece and everyone was up in arms about it. Participating in the Berlin communist scene in this way provided preparation for the pair as they anticipated the next installment of their journey.

The persecution of communists was becoming a regular occurrence during this period of emerging German nationalism. Certain literature and art was banned and individuals had been imprisoned and fined. Rochester recalled an attack on a group of communists returning from a memorial at a soldiers' cemetery by a group of over twenty "steel helmets." After the assault, they proceeded to riot through the city assaulting passers-by who looked like Jews. These steel helmets, the precursors to the nationalist Nazis, were intimidating and hostile; laws against the possession of weapons were enforced against communists, but not against the steel helmets. Demonstrations followed and there was much show of military force throughout the city. Rochester also noted this military presence during an International Women's Week march under communist leadership. Armored vehicles and police officers with hand grenades and machine guns surrounded two squads of women during the march. Both squads, noted Rochester, were hardly intimidating: one was made up of teenage girls and the other of middle-aged women. Hutchins and Rochester were dismayed at this show of force on the part of the German officials.

The last time the women had been in Berlin was during the summer of 1923 when they traveled to the youth conference and met with F.O.R. and *World Tomorrow* personnel. Now, four years later, they found the air of the city quite different. It had a more modern feel with well-dressed people, glittering shops, and private motor cars and taxi cabs racing around: the "feverish dash" of a city on the go. Despite this, there was high inflation, much unemployment, and poverty. Apartments built for workers stood empty because no one could afford to rent them. Morale was low in the city and elsewhere. Hutchins and Rochester found Berlin a city without much soul and remarked that it was headed for crisis. Ironically they were right, although the crisis they anticipated, the workers' revolution, was not the crisis that would be around the corner in the next decade. With a broad understatement, Rochester ended her letter remarking, "Was there ever before such an interesting world to live in!"[40]

Eventually, when the pair had almost given up hope, the travel documents for the Soviet Union arrived. Russia at last! Arriving in Moscow at the end of April 1927 via Poland, they were just in time for the eastern Easter and May Day holidays. Holidays aside, Hutchins and Rochester were immediately taken by what they described as the amazing efficiency of Russian life and found it all tremendously stimulating. So happily pleased and excited were they by these early weeks in Moscow that they described this time as the definite high point of their travels. In a printed letter in the style of a small pamphlet, titled "Tell Us About Russia," Hutchins and Rochester eloquently shared their first impressions. This pamphlet, written as a greeting to friends, was definitely crafted to educate and inform about the wonderful advances of Russian society:

> One would like to say that in crossing the border into Russia one feels an immediate change of atmosphere. But the villages are not unlike the villages of

Lithuania and of Poland. The vast plain rolls on with little variation towards the forests of northern Russia—which we did not touch—and toward the "black earth" of the Ukraine which is clearly richer than the land west of Moscow. When we went into Russia it happened to be a gray day, and the bare trees recalled somber tales and solitudes. But under sunny skies a few weeks later the same country was gay with blossoms, leaves and green fields. . . . Only after we reached Moscow and began to get the feel of the city were the differences apparent. Most marked is the simplicity of dress, and the amazing predominance of earnest faces. It is literally a city of workers. . . . [41]

Unfortunately they were disappointed to find that they had arrived too late to present the documents and letters of introduction for admittance to the Congress of Soviets. But, staying in a small hotel in Moscow where many of the delegates to the Congress were staying, they were able to observe and get a feel for the diversity of nationalities present in the Soviet governing body. Again, this hotel was to their liking in part because there were no Americans there and it allowed them to learn to blend with the locals. They rejoiced that they had so diligently studied the Russian language; their relative fluency meant they were not dependent upon translators and could participate in the everyday life of the city. It seemed to give them a great feeling of independence to be in charge of their own well-being.

The Moscow May Day celebrations were a special treat. In their letter home, Hutchins and Rochester described these festivities, so representative of the new order in Russia.[42] Their descriptions were very sentimental and represented romantic notions of honest, hard-working peasants with wide-open faces ready to lead their people to freedom. They described the masses of intelligent, earnest, and purposeful-looking people on the streets of Moscow, the rivers of singing workers and children pouring through Red Square carrying banners and signs, and the solidarity of the working classes summoning the present industrial order to greater efficiency.[43] They were being swept away by the spirit of it all. This was indeed a pilgrimage for them. The Soviet women wore bright red head scarves tied at the back of the neck rather than the customary knot under the chin, a style Hutchins and Rochester found to be distinctly fetching. The military garrison was drawn up for review and a series of military parades preceded the annual taking of the oath. The pair found it all most impressive and greatly enjoyed these festivities, the spirit of these workers reinforcing their ideas about the glorious potential of the proletariat. Note that these images of hard-working peasant Russians were recycled ones that had captured the Western European imagination for many decades prior to Bolshevism.[44] Hutchins and Rochester seemed to accept these stereotypes without question; all they saw and experienced convinced them of the romantic fate of these honest, frugal people.

Of course, Hutchins and Rochester also observed a little of the underside of the revolution and wrote of beggars and homeless people in the streets of Moscow. But they were so enthralled by the spirit of Bolshevism that they were ready to overlook shortcomings of the Russian system. With optimism they explained these problems in terms of understanding that Russia "is in no sense a finished paradise. . . . We had testimony from several people— Russian and American, Communist and non-Communist—that during the last few years great headway has been made in caring for the vagabond children. As for the peddlers and beggars, the figures on migration into the cities tell the story. Peasants hearing of improved conditions for city workers have flocked in to get their share much more rapidly than can possibly be absorbed. Meanwhile tremendous effort is going into the adjustment of economic relations between village and town. In no other country is the agrarian problem having such concentrated and purposeful study as in Russia."[45]

Just as some problems were explained and justified in terms of work in progress, other problems were explained as resulting from the past inefficiencies of the old czarist regime. This was Hutchins and Rochester's understanding of the frustrations involved with travel: "And you know that the red tape and certain kinds of clumsy inefficiency that annoy you exceedingly are hold-overs from the old regime which the Bolshevik is trying to change. You remember too the efficient air of three of the four factories you have seen, and you marvel, not that the traveler finds cause for annoyance, but that such great things have been accomplished in so short a time."[46] With such goodwill and eager optimism, the pair braved the railway system and set out south from Moscow to visit the Prikumskaya Russian–American Farm Colony in North Caucasus with four days spent also at Rostov-on-Don on their way back to Moscow.

At Prikumskaya Hutchins and Rochester were most impressed by the modern technological advancements of this farm with its machine shop, motor trucks, village cooperative store, and plans for water-powered energy and wireless telegraphing. They described great efficiency and high morale. A visit to a nearby village revealed twenty families who had agreed to share the land and work it in common as a cooperative. Again they perceived things to be in good order but were interested enough to note the discrimination these farm women experienced by the men in the collective.[47] While Hutchins and Rochester were dismayed at these inequities, their concern was for the most part marked by the great possibilities for freedom enjoyed by women as workers in a communist state.

Russia fit the couple's values of frugality and industry. They found the lack of showiness refreshing and the absence of commercial advertising a great relief. The values of parsimony and principled purpose, so central in Hutchins and Rochester's value system, melded well with the simplicity and frugalities of Bolshevik Russia during this period. The principled devotion of the Bolsheviks to communist theory and practice as well as their hard-working diligence and industriousness were regarded by Hutchins and Rochester as most admirable traits. Here was a society that exemplified the pair's central core values. It is no surprise that they found themselves head over heels in love with Russia, or at least the bit of Russia they were able to see. They were happily willing to soak up what they saw as the important advancements made by the Russian people, compare them to the problems associated with the czarist regimes as well as the problems with the U.S. system, and interpret their everyday experiences in a positive light.

Their first "function" in Moscow, not counting revolutionary films, was a funeral in Red Square of an official whose ashes had come via rail through Berlin. Coincidentally, Hutchins and Rochester had seen the small, isolated squad of German comrades gathered in respect for this official on the platform in Berlin, surrounded by attentive police. They compared that memory to the present throngs of people paying their respect and bestowing military honors from the Red Army and concluded that Russia was indeed a civilized nation. Other functions in the city revolved around plays and concerts and social visits with different people, some they were already acquainted with and some who had been introduced to them through friends. So single-minded were they at this point about absorbing Russian politics that they found visits with Americans somewhat tiresome. Recalling one such evening, Rochester wrote in a "round-robin" letter, "It was an interesting evening, but quite remote from our labor and economic interests, and we are trying to specialize on these so far as we can without rudeness."[48] Compared to these acquaintances, Gregory Yarros, whom Rochester had met at Hull House, was more to their liking. Mr. Yarros was working with the Russian Council of Trade Unions and was very helpful in providing a detailed orientation for them on the Russian political situation. His wife, Maria Schkolnick, was equally distinguished and directed the model Clara Zetkin Children's Home in Moscow. She had been a terrorist involved in the revolutionary groups of the early 1900s, had been caught after an unsuccessful attempt to bomb some facility and was sent to Siberia. She managed to escape, and, after hair-raising adventures via China, arrived in Chicago in 1911 and proceeded to write her memoirs:

> She is just Grace's age exactly and in October 1903 when Grace was entering Bryn Mawr and beginning her career in field hockey and basketball, Maria Schkolnick was on trial for belonging to a revolutionary circle in Odessa. The trial resulted in sentence to exile in Siberia.[49]

Now this was more exciting company!

Thanks to Gregory Yarros and to Mr. Melnachansky, member of the Central Executive Committee of the Soviet Union, head of department in the Central Council of Trade Unions, and president of the Textile Union,

If Grace and Anna had been asked to recount these experiences in Russia before they died, how would they have characterized this time? How would their memories have reconstructed this period? *Daily Worker* articles of 1936 and 1940 reported this time in Russia as utterly convincing for them in terms of praise for the Soviet Union. Would Grace and Anna still have said this in 1960? How were these memories fabricated and altered, if they were? To look back on one's life like this and create a story means taking charge of our own experiences; it's what Clark Blaise calls the drama of consciousness gaining sovereignty over its own experience.

doors started opening for Hutchins and Rochester. New York colleague Bob Dunn had given them a letter of introduction to Melnachansky, who, as a high-ranking Russian official, was able to smooth the way for the women's visit. They were especially eager to visit state factories and soon received an appointment through the Society for Cultural Relations to visit a large, impressive cotton mill in Moscow that employed over 8,000 workers. The timing of this tour coincided with a visit by officials from the German Embassy, and, thanks to the Germans' importance, the assistant director of the factory spent three hours taking all of them through the factory and then the director himself met with them and answered questions in his office.[50] Hutchins and Rochester received more detailed information about the mill than would ordinary visitors since the mill directors and the Russian government had a stake in the formation of impressions by foreign dignitaries.

Again, Hutchins and Rochester's descriptions of the factory revealed the romanticism with which they made sense of the Russian experiment. They noted how the workers "looked up in a friendly kind of way, and one or two in each division shook hands with the Assistant Director."[51] They remarked on the workers' "free and self-respecting look" and found that the "unrepressed naturalness with which they were working and talking was a joy." So taken were they with the manner of these workers that they wrote in the visitors' book that they had never before in any country seen workers in any factory look so much alive.[52] One wonders how authentic or how staged these situations were. Like the American tourists they were so quick to critique, Hutchins and Rochester no doubt saw what they wanted to see. Yet despite their apparent gullibility, Hutchins and Rochester's eager curiosity and lack of cynicism comes across as refreshing. These accounts of Russia are rhetorically crafted as persuasive pieces to convince a liberal Christian or Christian socialist readership that Bolshevism was a positive force. This naïve and breathless enthusiasm was part of the rhetorical power of their writing. They seemed to truly believe what they saw and they saw what they believed.

Production levels were described as high in this mill, although, as Rochester noted, it was by no means exceptional. According to her figures for 1926 and 1927, Russian industry had returned to prewar levels of production, had instituted an eight-hour workday or less, and had over three-quarters of the total production coming from state factories or cooperatives. Attention was now centered on technical improvements and increasing efficiency to raise the level of production still higher.[53] In their halting Russian, the pair asked many questions concerning production techniques and social relations in the factory. They learned about the kinds of work employees performed, the levels of pay and the benefits received. In their letter-pamphlet "Tell Us About Russia," Hutchins and Rochester explained that men and women received the same pay for the same work, although machinists made more than spinners or weavers, and engineers made more than all of them. Without being explicit, Hutchins and Rochester left the impression that, overall, women tended to receive less pay than men since they were congregated in the occupations that were remunerated at lower levels. They did not comment on what we now associate with comparable worth, that gendered occupations are renumerated at different levels of pay (even though Hutchins would go on to critique the U.S. system for this very problem). Also absent from Hutchins and Rochester's economic discussion are accounts of the unpaid labor of women in the home. While Hutchins would eventually address this in the context of the U.S. situation in her 1934 book *Women Who Work*, at this point one gets the impression that nothing must be allowed to mar the Russian experiment. The women would have to wait.[54]

The couple explained that employment in the factory was such that no one could earn more than 225 roubles (about $110) a month and anything over that amount was given back to the Communist Party. They wrote that employees worked in two shifts of ten hours one day and six the next. Most office personnel worked six-hour days and workers in trades injurious to health were employed for only six or seven hours a day. Wages were also supplemented by privileges estimated as equal to a third of the wage. There was free medical care, as well as provisions for disability, old age and funeral expenses, and unemployment. Women had two months of leave with full pay both before and after the birth of a child and could apply for more. Each worker had at least two weeks' vacation a year with full pay and those in dangerous trades and under eighteen years of age received a one-month paid vacation. All the workers in the mill, including the engineers and directors, belonged to the Textile Union, and such a union card entitled workers to 50 percent reduction on tickets for the theater and other entertainments. Finally, each wage earner had access to a club, provided partly by the industry and partly by the union.[55] These advancements, Hutchins and Rochester astutely observed, put U.S. industry to shame.

Other factories visited by Hutchins and Rochester included the Red Rose silk factory in Moscow and the Rosa Luxembourg State Tobacco factory in

Rostov-on-Don. Here they found conditions and production similar to the large mill in Moscow. After visiting one of these smaller factories they shared how they spoke with a machinist whose testimony summed up for them the superior nature of Russian industry. Having worked in the United States for twenty years and Russia for two, "give me Russia every time!" he exclaimed. While not earning as much money, his pay went further and his benefits, such as a month's paid vacation, far outstripped those in the United States. "Can you beat it?" he said. "And that director you're talking to—look at him! He was a blacksmith like us, and he's our director now. But he's in the union with us just the same as before."[56] Hutchins and Rochester were pleased with his answer. Comparing what they had seen here in Russia to the poor conditions and rising inflation associated with the United States, they found the choice obvious.

The "Tell Us About Russia" letter-pamphlet included a section titled "Pros and Cons" concerning this great nation, although most "cons" were actually "pros" in disguise. They talked about the drawbacks associated with the Soviet vision by quoting several local Russians who "rail at the Russia of today."[57] Two male workers, an elderly waiter at a hotel and a sleeper car attendant, both spoke fondly of the days when they could expect tips and prices were lower. But, as Hutchins and Rochester reminded the reader, one man admitted that wages had doubled despite tips and the other overlooked shorter hours and increased benefits. They shared how they had heard many stories of people who had lost property and prestige under the new government, but emphasized that it was easy to focus attention on such discontent and to know nothing of the other side.[58] An example of what they considered inappropriate discontent was shared with them by a woman in a restaurant who had been a concert singer and performer and now found life empty, intolerable, and meaningless. Despite their admiration for the Russian people generally, the pair had little sympathy for this woman's plight; they seemed to have found her work nonessential and unrelated to the needs of the working class, bordering on decadent and perhaps epitomizing the problems associated with the troubled czarist regime. They also found it odd that she seemed to have no fear of unbur-

Research diary: June 10, 1998: "Probably overreacted to this relatively small piece of information [about the woman in the restaurant]. But Grace and Anna come across as such snobs and betray a self-righteous classism about how the masses should be and act. Alongside this arrogance and lack of compassion for a fellow woman, I think I am also reacting to their male-identification: "the worker" was constructed as male and employed in factory work. [It seems to be] the standard against which other people were judged."

dening her soul in no uncertain tones to chance acquaintances in public.[59] Hutchins and Rochester seemed quick to support the strong, earnest, "respectable" industrial workers and peasants; they were just as eager to judge and dismiss this woman's losses. And, while they cherished any chance interaction with workers who would speak openly with them, they chided this woman's willingness to speak to them.

In terms of potential drawbacks to the Soviet system, Hutchins and Rochester explained that despite the one-party regime, the leaders "are in no sense tyrants who enjoy autocracy but realistic revolutionaries with a very definite constructive work to do in unifying and organizing Russia's economic life and bringing the people to a high level of education."[60] While the government did not tolerate any organized opposition, "dictatorship is scarcely the word for a rule in which the two great groups—peasants and industrial workers—enjoy a sense of freedom."[61] Noncommunist workers and peasants, the pair emphasized, found a genuine self-expression in the labor unions, the consumers' cooperative, and the political soviets. Indeed, Hutchins and Rochester's ending to their letter-pamphlet summed up their impressions of Russia and their emerging Marxist approach to social life:

> But one need not defend every act of the Russian government in order to recognize that on the whole the economic life of Russia has definitely moved into the next phase of human evolution. And in political structure she is working out a creative experiment.[62]

As you can tell, the happy travelers were completely enamored and absorbed by what they saw in Russia, their experiences there convincing them of the necessity of the communist experiment. Here was a society that was gallantly moving forward with determined, principled action toward worker control. They romanticized the Russian people as robust and hard working, lacking in ostentation and showiness, who toiled incessantly to change the conditions of their lives and participated in society in lively and intelligent ways. Freed from the shackles of alienation that characterized workers under capitalist industry, here wage workers demonstrated a completely different demeanor. The autocracy of the Bolsheviks worried them somewhat; they described the silence concerning political prisoners and spoke earlier of how adherence to Gandhi's principles of nonviolence would benefit adherence by individual communists. But overall, these anxieties were overshadowed by the positive aspects of the Russian regime, which as Rochester explained above, was hardly a dictatorship since it gave freedom to peasants and industrial workers. They compared what they knew about and understood as communist persecutions to the terrible cruelties and hardships of the czarist regime as well as the social and economic

violence of capitalist and colonialist societies. They understood that the
Russian communists needed no interference that might derail this great
human experiment and that a period of proletarian dictatorship, which included the seizure of the state government, was necessary before capitalist
influences could be completely banished. They believed that world revolution was inevitable given the forces of decay inherent in capitalism, the
presence of nationalist movements ready to revolt, and the increasing organization of left-wing forces around the globe.[63] Russia, they believed, was
just the tip of the iceberg.

It is somewhat puzzling that the pair's complete endorsement of Russia
followed so closely after their positive encounter with Gandhi. They
seemed to find his principles of nonviolence sound, yet went on to endorse
a regime that relied upon violent revolutionary activity. However, as
Rochester explained in "The Pacifist's 'Preparedness,'" a pacifist cannot
condemn those who have taken other routes toward self-determination.[64]
It is also possible they saw Gandhian principles as products of Indian culture that stood apart from application in other contexts, just as khadi made
no sense to Rochester outside of Indian society. The Russian situation was
closer to home; these people had experienced feudal oppression and capitalist control, and the class struggle in place in Russia epitomized the inevitable forces of history that were moving across western and eastern Europe. In this sense it might have been possible for Hutchins and Rochester
to endorse both these political strategies as grounded in the immediate
context of history and society rather than as contradictory politics.

It is easy now with the benefits of hindsight to make the case that
Hutchins and Rochester, in modern language, were snowed during their
visit to Russia—being safely allowed to see only what the Russian government wanted foreigners to see and being prevented from understanding
the extent and depths of Bolshevik persecutions and problems. They visited model factories that may or may not have represented the bulk of
Russian industry, and their zealous affinity with worker causes and desire
for the Russian situation to illustrate a positive human experiment no
doubt encouraged their gullibility. Hutchins and Rochester did visit the Soviet Union during a milder period of Stalin's rule, before his more serious
crackdown on opposition from artists and the intelligentsia and others
who disagreed with his single-minded policies, and no doubt there was
contagion in the spirit of a people committed to transforming the conditions of their lives. Indeed, Hutchins and Rochester were most sincere in
their admiration of the Russian people and interpreted this communist experiment as a kind of collective good for the whole nation and indeed the
world. In this way their ideological changes from Christianity to Christian
socialism and then to communism were all grounded in a strong moral

standpoint of bettering humankind. The "cause" itself did not really change, although the means to a better world did. This cause was always one of maintaining the greater good, of facilitating a kinder, more just society in their eyes.

Hutchins and Rochester found their time in Russia to be incredibly inspiring; they truly felt themselves to be a part of the great force of history. With fond memories and high spirits they returned to western Europe and set sail for home on July 9, 1927. Like a pilgrimage where they emerged reborn, these travels had changed their lives. Never again would life in New York be the same.

PART THREE

OLD LEFT LOYALISTS

CHAPTER SEVEN

A NEW FAITH

Returning to the United States after their formative travels abroad, Hutchins and Rochester were buoyed with fresh hope for revolutionary social change. Convinced at this point of a class analysis that positioned the mass of workers against those who owned and controlled the means of production, they no doubt interpreted the rumblings of the capitalist market as evidence for its decay and disruption. Breaking ties with F.O.R., Hutchins and Rochester joined the Communist Party, USA, and turned their backs on Christian socialism. With great diligence and devotion, and intense commitment, they threw in their lot with the communists and set their sights on a world revolution. This chapter explores these years between 1927 and 1935 when communist commitments now became their full-time duty.

Communism in the United States originated in the left wing of the Socialist Party where there was dissent around such issues as electoral versus mass-action politics, foreign versus native-born interests, and importantly, reactions to the October 1917 Russian revolution.[1] The formal split between the Socialist Party and those who formed various factions and would call themselves communists came in 1919 when the Third Communist International (Comintern) was organized, creating affiliated parties or groups around the globe directed by an international committee. In the United States the Comintern attempted to unify the various communist factions

"Biography is too important to become a playground for fantasies, however ingenious; I believe its future is safe with the reading public, who will keep it human, not too solemn."[2]

and broaden its appeal, while at the same time encouraging the American Left to dependency on directives from the Soviet Union. Much infighting and factionalizing characterized these early years when splintered groups functioned mostly underground. Eventually, the Communist Party of America joined with the United Communist Party (itself a merging of a faction of the Communist Party of America and the Communist Labor Party) to form the Workers Party of America as an aboveground organization. This became known as the Workers (Communist) Party until it was changed to the Communist Party of the United States of America (CPUSA, here referred to also as the CP or the Party) in 1929.[3] In an attempt to create a unified leadership, much of its ethnic base was lost, language groups and cultural institutions like clubhouses and theater groups were dissolved, and, through the direction of the Comintern, key players were expelled. Nonetheless, the CP struggled on into the 1930s with about 18,000 members, plus a larger following of nonmember sympathizers.[4]

In her article "Communism: A World Movement," Anna Rochester explained the meaning of communism as a global political movement to a largely left liberal/Christian socialist audience.[5] While she no longer affiliated herself formally with this readership, Rochester understood how it was positioned and wrote a persuasive essay that attempted to spell out in accessible and nonthreatening ways the legitimacy of this world movement. She emphasized a distinction between the socialists and the communists in the sense that the latter emphasized struggle as a basic fact of the capitalist world and as a central method of revolutionary change. Communists perceived the Socialist Party as being in cahoots with capitalism in its policy of class collaboration. They understood that the socialists would nationalize private industries and maintain the state—propping up capitalism and saving its basic structure. They saw the American Federation of Labor (AFL) in particular as a capitalist tool for keeping the workers quiet and as a diversion against the inevitable revolutionary struggle.[6]

Rochester's stance here followed CP doctrine. Closely supervised by the Comintern, the Party during the late 1920s and early 1930s pursued a sectarian path, refusing allegiances with non-CP organizations and eulogizing

---

There is no such thing as being impervious to history. I interpret Grace and Anna through my understandings of their history, understandings fashioned by my own historical moment. Perhaps my account of their communist passions is overly persuaded by Grace and Anna's history. My interpretation might too strongly reflect a desire for continuity from their zealous Christian days—a case of insight concerning their past overprivileging my understandings of this next moment.

the Soviet Union as the ultimate model for socialism. These years after 1928 came to be known as the "Third Period." It was not until 1935, after the Seventh Congress, that the Cominterm redirected this policy and the "Popular Front" strategy of alliance and collaboration came into effect, extending to the years up to the beginning of World War II when the Hitler–Stalin pact of 1939 shattered many alliances and threw the Party into chaos. Later, when the Germans invaded Russia, the Comintern was able to reaffirm its antifascist position. In 1943 the Comintern was formally dissolved. Buhle writes that "this ended the appearance of fraternal parties always acting in concert, but the American Party, like most other communist parties, retained its ideological dependence on Soviet thinking."[7] The communist press and the *Daily Worker* in particular fiercely defended Soviet policy and directives up through the 1940s.

In many ways, the active life of the communist during this period fit Hutchins and Rochester very well and they rose in status as loyal members who worked diligently as writers and Party organizers. They took young radicals such as Grace Lumpkin and Esther Shemitz under their wing, helping them out financially and providing support.[8] Indeed, communism might have seemed especially attractive to them as intellectuals in several ways: first, here was a creed that, alongside its moral ethic, seemed to give a complete and scientific answer at a time when the scientific method was receiving increasing status within the social sciences and disciplines were eager to disassociate themselves from a (feminized) nonscientific, sentimental perspective. Marxism also set science in opposition to religion and the superstitions involved in religious beliefs and rituals. As communist intellectuals only just emerging from espousing Christian socialist beliefs, no doubt Hutchins and Rochester were happy to let science replace religion in anticipation of a society like the Soviet Union where "[r]ows of icons are being supplanted with bookshelves and holy candles with radio tubes."[9] Also, as intellectuals they were probably comfortable with an imprecise and abstract theory concerning the internal contradictions and natural laws of capitalism and a relatively mechanistic and deterministic analysis.[10]

Ironically, while I believe Marxism was attractive to Hutchins and Rochester because it presented a scientific, relatively straightforward "clear-headed" approach that eschewed the sentimental idealism of the past, it was this very idealism and sentimentalism implicit in Marxism that was so seductive to them. It was a great moral adventure that involved the enormous drama between good and evil. While the following words were not spoken by Hutchins and Rochester, I believe they apply to the couple's life in the communist movement:

> With its stress upon inevitable conflicts, apocalyptic climaxes, ultimate moments, hours of doom, and shining tomorrow, it appealed deeply to our

imaginations. We felt that we were always on the rim of heroism, that the mockery we might suffer at the moment would turn to vindication in the future, that our loyalty to principle would be rewarded by the grateful masses of tomorrow.[11]

Second, communism must have been attractive to Hutchins and Rochester since it would help them make sense of the despair they felt at the state of modern industrial society, especially during the Depression years. The Depression would have been a clarifying experience and a key source of their political passions. No doubt their faith was also buoyed during the thirties by their eyewitness experiences of the Soviet Union's economic progress compared to U.S. economic stagnation. Their heightened sensitivity to injustice schooled during those early years as religious Progressive-era reformers and then as devout Christian socialists was rooted in a strong desire that all people should live well and be happy; their commitment to social fairness so evident along the whole span of their ideological journey was acted out here to its logical conclusion: a society for the people by the people. This dedication to the cause emerged in their keen sense of justice and fairness, a commitment that showed itself in particular during the repressive McCarthy years when communists were denied, among other things, civil rights. The CP gave them a politics of activism; it also gave them identity and comradeship.

Third, I believe communism was attractive to Hutchins and Rochester because it required a total commitment of faith bordering on mysticism. Their capacity for an unwavering belief in the absolute power of the deity facilitated the zealous embrace of communism as the hope of the world, the Kingdom of God on earth. Both ideologies required an absolute and uncompromising stance and were seen as infallible. The communist idealism that required a devotion to a pure utopian future and the moral rejection of the present was most probably experienced as a liberating force. Each personal sacrifice for the cause would have bound Hutchins and Rochester closer to the Party and renewed their sense of responsibility and obligation. In her interviews with communist comrades for *The Romance of American Communism*, Vivian Gornick quoted a respondent as saying, "It was exactly like church; every time you experienced a lapse of faith you prayed an extra hour, gave yourself an extra hundred lashes."[12] Discipline, I believe, was a strong motivating factor here. Hutchins and Rochester sought to live disciplined and principled lives and the Party gave them a highly structured organization and demanded a discipline they were willing to deliver.

Finally, communism required of its converts from among the intelligentsia a combination of arrogance and humility vis-à-vis their relationship to the proletariat. Arrogance was encouraged by the positioning of communist intellectuals as the "vanguard," the advanced contingent of the working class. Humility, familiar to these former Christians, was necessary before the often eulogized true-born proletariat. Orthodox Marxists believed that intellectuals had to obtain from theory and observation what the working class learned either "naturally" or in their work roles. As such, communism involved an almost mystical trust in the working class. This was most likely exacerbated by the fact that the Soviet directorate tended to have little respect for Western intelligentsia and treated them rather shabbily, perhaps justifying their humility and encouraging their sacrifice.[13] Certainly, the heroic Russian cultural icon Maxim Gorky had contempt for the capitalist bourgeoisie, calling them "a rich crop of idiots," like "pigmies suffering from megalomania" with their "filthy cynicism."[14] Bourgeois-turned-communist intellectuals such as Hutchins and Rochester might have taken Gorky's words to heart. Perhaps one important aspect of this humility for Hutchins and Rochester was the assaugement of their guilt as privileged individuals in the face of the lives of the "toiling masses." Any "slips" on their part that might have represented a bourgeois mentality would stand as proof of their privilege and perhaps function to revitalize their devotion.

It seemed to have been this monastic, principled approach to communism that kept Hutchins and Rochester on the straight Party track throughout its trials and tribulations. Their published writings throughout the years show a pernicious orthodoxy in support of Soviet politics and Comintern directives.

Editing this chapter, I started to insert "so-to-speak" after my comment on the "straight Party track" because of the double meaning associated with straight. Ironically, it fits either way. They were on the straight track. I am disappointed that they were not able to more publicly resist Party homophobia and were not able to be more openly lesbian—although maintaining their love and commitment to each other as romantic friends must have been a form of resistance in itself given the homophobia of the Party. Of course I sit here with my heterosexual privilege in the late nineties and the picture looks very different than the view they had. I understand the self-censure that came as a by-product of their political ideology. As Monique Wittig explains: "The question of the individual subject is historically a difficult one for everybody. Marxism, the last avatar of materialism, the science which has politically formed us, does not want to hear anything about a 'subject.' Marxism has rejected the transcendental subject, the subject as constitutive of knowledge, the 'pure' consciousness. All that thinks per se, before all experience, has ended up in the garbage can of history, because it claimed to exist outside matter, prior to matter, and needed God, spirit, or soul to exist in such a way. This is what is called 'idealism.' As for individuals, they are only the product of social relations, therefore their consciousness can only be 'alienated.'"[15]

This is not to say, of course, that they had no personal qualms about Soviet policies or CP leadership in the privacy of their personal conversations, only that they presented themselves publicly as loyal CP comrades. I believe that behind the silences associated with Hutchins and Rochester's private reflections concerning the Party and other matters is ambivalence about disclosing private aspects of the self. Marxists believed individualistic or subjectivist problems were bourgeois ones that would disappear with the victory of class struggle. It was considered "petit bourgeois" to be preoccupied with aspects of the self that could not be reduced to the class struggle; self-censure also came from wanting to avoid a security risk for the Party. In this way, as well as being a result of the methodological hodgepodge of recording a life, silences and fragmented self-portraits also represent the couple's complex lives and their unwillingness to assert an independent ego outside of Party confines. The Party was their life.

In trying to make sense of these zealous commitments it is important to emphasize that the peak of their affiliations as communist intellectuals coincided with the height of communist popularity in the United States. While there were such events as the brutal suppression of a sailors' revolt by the Red Army at Kronstadt in the early 1920s, the liquidation of the kulaks who opposed the collectivization of agriculture later that decade, and the Moscow purges of the thirties, that might have unraveled their faith, there was enough popular support of the Party through this period generally, and especially in the New York City districts where they lived and worked, for the pair to accept the various Party explanations and feel justified in their continuing convictions. The Popular Front years after 1935 would have reaffirmed their political choices. They were in good company as the CP gathered in active members and community figures such as Pete Cacchione from Brooklyn and Benjamin Davis from Harlem were elected to the New York City Council. In a letter to Algernon Black, leader of the Ethical Culture Society, chastising him for his position on a right-wing committee of the American Labor Party, Rochester said her communist colleagues showed more "intelligent devotion" and were no less "fine individuals" than the people she had worked with in church circles: "We are not crooks and ballot-box stuffers. We do not aim at minority manipulation of a deluded mass. No political group—and I say this advisedly—is more frank in its statement of purposes and more honest in its efforts at organization and education. Never in many years of active work in church circles did I know finer individuals or more intelligent devotion than I have found within the Communist party."[16]

Since Hutchins and Rochester's intense loyalty to communism meant renouncing all other faiths, they accepted the orthodox understanding of religion as the opiate of the people, a tool for keeping the masses oppressed. Also, the Christian socialists would have been revealed for their part in covering up the role of the churches as aids to capitalism. As Bennett Stevens

explained in one of the International Publishers' pamphlets, "Christian Socialists are always upholders of religion rather than defenders of [the] militant worker. . . . Christian Socialism is counter-revolutionary."[17] I believe,
despite Hutchins and Rochester's apparent critique of Christian socialism
at this point, that they nevertheless projected intrinsic aspects of religious
devotion and practice onto their relationship with the Communist Party.
Their political agency as communist devotees was constructed in part
through the intersection of epistemologies, institutions, and practices associated with Christian idealism.

Faith was the crucial concept here, and I believe it was their devout faith
in communism that kept Hutchins and Rochester so well connected to the
Party. Mystical faith in the workers as a class and the inevitability of world
communism was coupled with the attractions of a movement that expected
service, discipline, and loyalty. Importantly, these attractions as communist
intellectuals were entirely in character; they lived their communist ideology
as they had lived through other periods of their lives: with altruistic commitment and dedication to the cause. In addition, Hutchins and Rochester
lived communism *together*, they were each available to the other for de-
briefing, rationalization, and support against possible anxieties or resistance. Their personal relationship was grounded in their political work and
it bolstered these communist commitments through a kind of internal
feedback loop. This most likely helped keep their faith intact. In this way,
Hutchins and Rochester's shared experiences of communist institutions
and practices, fed in part by a zealous and devotional form of idealism, produced them as political subjects keen to proselytize as Old Left loyalists.

From Grace to Disgrace

It was into New York, a stronghold of communist activity, that Hutchins
and Rochester dived on their return in July 1927. They eagerly anticipated
settling back to life in New York, enjoying a permanent roof over their
heads and the everyday domestic joys of living together in the apartment at
85 Bedford Street in Greenwich Village. The Village provided a progressive
and diverse milieu where radical thought and nontraditional lifestyles
bloomed, and their apartment on the corner of Bedford Street put them
right in the middle of this milieu.[18] It was a stimulating and supportive location at the hub of progressive thought and action. Hutchins and
Rochester's personal relationship, so rooted in shared progressive thought
and action, seemed to flourish here. Their correspondence from various
times apart was heavy with the love and gratitude each had for the other
concerning the little domestic day-to-day intimacies of living together.
"Dear, dear Partner, how lucky we are to have our pleasant apartment and
to be getting it settled so well," wrote Hutchins in a letter to Rochester dur-

Boston Evening American, Wednesday, August 10, 1927. "New York Woman Among Those Arrested"—Grace and a friend being led to the Joy Street police station.

ing a brief separation.[19] And "Beloved Partner, can I ever tell you what your loving care has meant to me?" exclaimed Hutchins in another correspondence during this period.[20]

Part of the couple's reentry to the United States after their time abroad, at least for Hutchins, whose parents were still living, was reacquainting with family. This seemed always a mixed blessing given their widening ideological differences. The first differences of political opinion between Hutchins and her family concerned her pro-suffrage attitudes while at Bryn Mawr.[21] Then they were upset by her pacifism during the war. As patriotic Americans with sons fighting in this war, Edward and Susan Hutchins were horrified at their daughter's stance. While they hoped her pro-suffrage and pacifist ideas were just a phase, these "liberal" inclinations seemed to them beyond belief for one raised, as she had been, a first-family Bostonian.[22] So while Susan and Edward Hutchins were somewhat prepared for their daughter's political activities, they were shocked and distressed that these politics could have resulted in, to them, the following shameful activity. It was the Boston newspapers that broke the news, screaming the headlines about one of its own, a "Mrs. [sic] Grace Hutchins of New York, one of 39 persons arrested in 'death march' parade in front of State House, and friend being led to the Joy Street police station."[23] The event was a demonstration against the execution of Nicola Sacco and Bartolomeo Vanzetti that involved a "death march" past the Municipal Court building in Boston. Hutchins and Rochester were arrested with thirty-seven others on charges of sauntering and loitering.

Sacco and Vanzetti were radical Italian–American anarchists who were framed and arrested for murdering and robbing factory payroll guards in Braintree, near Boston, in May 1920. The trial, coming as it did in the midst of the severe political repression of the "red scare," received much public attention. In particular, the themes of radicalism versus patriotism were polarized and played out throughout the trial, leading to hysteria concerning foreign-born dissidents. When Sacco and Vanzetti were found guilty, a long struggle ensued to help free them, using evidence that included perjury and illegal activities on the part of the prosecution and police as well as a confession of a convicted bank robber. In opposition to these supporters were conservatives who hoped to squash all radical movements and keenly saw such activities as unpatriotic. Despite the evidence in their favor, in April 1927 Sacco and Vanzetti were sentenced to death, and, in the face of such public agitation as the Boston death march, were executed on August 23. The death of Sacco and Vanzetti was an important formative event for Hutchins and Rochester, as it was for many other radicals in America, revealing what they already believed, that American "democracy" was a sham. It was both a distressing and exhilarating event that fulfilled Hutchins and Rochester's prophecy about the corruption and decay of the U.S. system of justice and justified the couple in their radical political commitments. It also provided a "coming out," so-to-speak, of their political beliefs in a public way.

Research diary: February 12, 1998: "This photo of Grace and Anna [being led away by policeman] *must* be the front cover piece for the book. It's perfect...." March 31: "realized the photo must not be of Anna after all. [The woman there] is too short, plus she's wearing different clothes than what I take to be Anna in another photo. Disappointing—it would have been so perfect—I just took it for granted that it was a photo of both of them for the longest time. I literally saw what I wanted to see."

The pair had been following the Sacco–Vanzetti case during their time abroad, devouring, whenever they could get it, news from home about the case. They had been back in the United States barely a month when Rochester wrote a letter that was printed in the *Nation*, chastising the authorities of Boston for their scandalous behavior regarding this case. It was printed the day after the prisoners were executed. Her letter followed one written by John Dos Passos, leftist novelist and cofounder of the *New Masses* and alumnus of Harvard University, angered at the participation of the Harvard president in the verdict against Sacco and Vanzetti.[24] Rochester's letter was in a similar vein, this time directed against the Boston authorities. She referred to a frenzied security that harassed innocent people and persecuted radicals.[25] This was one cause about which Hutchins and Rochester cared deeply; it was also one for which they were willing to commit acts of civil disobedience. They joined the National Committee for Sacco and Vanzetti at the Hotel Bellevue in Boston during the last days of the case and gave considerable personal and financial help to the cause.[26]

When it was revealed to Hutchins's family that she had indeed been arrested on the streets of Boston like a common criminal, they were appalled and in shock. They expressed a combination of embarrassment and shame, and complete and utter disappointment, in what they saw as the disgraceful behavior of their daughter. It was exacerbated by the fact that it seemed Hutchins had refused the professional help of her lawyer brother, Edward Jr. This shock and disappointment was shared in a letter written to Hutchins by her mother almost a week later on August 16. It was in response to a letter, now apparently lost, that Hutchins sent to her parents after the arrest:

My Dear Daughter,

Your letter of Sunday has come this afternoon, as calm as if the dreadful accounts in the *Herald Globe-Post* and *Dispatch* were but this hideous nightmare. We wish they really were. It is no use to attempt to give you any idea of our feelings, and I shall not attempt to do it. You must have some idea of what they are . . . we thought that such events as took place in Boston impossible and so we have both received a real shock from which we never expect to recover. As Father cannot read to himself the fine print of the paper, I was asked to read to him: "Grace Hutchins of 166 Beacon St, daughter of Edward W. Hutchins of the law firm of Hutchins and Wheeler." I guessed the result would be serious and had the nitro-glycerine tablets ready which I gave. Father lowered his head and said the word "disgrace" which sums it all up. I suppose we may find out in the next world why we have to hear such tricks, in this world, but it is certainly a mystery now. I can think of nothing but this heavy load that hangs over me. . . . [I] will not attempt to write more.

Ever yours, Mother[27]

"Lost" could mean anything: misplaced, destroyed in anger, or intentionally removed from the collection, among other things. Rather than pieces of a puzzle, these "facts" about their lives are like crystals in a kaleidoscope that transforms a view by tilting in any direction.

Hutchins's response to her family's disdain was a brief letter that explained her stance concerning the Sacco–Vanzetti case. She made the bold assertion that her arrest, which they called a disgrace, was to her "one of the few real honors" to come to the family and she let them know that she would no longer need to be financially dependent upon them.[28] This was a no-nonsense letter that was neither apologetic nor hoping to gain their approval or affection; it asserted independence, morally and financially. The paid employment of which she spoke was taken up, although it seems Hutchins continued to receive an allowance from her family until she inherited a large sum when her mother died in 1942.[29] In this way bridges were not entirely burned, and, given the continuation of correspondence between Hutchins and other family members, this episode did not appear to cause her complete estrangement. It did, however, position her as the black sheep in the family.

The ties with her father seemed to mend, probably because Hutchins enjoyed a close and affectionate relationship with him and they could not stay angry with each other for too long.[30] Edward Sr. died of heart problems relatively soon after this altercation, in June 1929, at the age of seventy-eight years and Hutchins, her mother, and brother Edward Jr. were with him when he died. Tragedy struck again in May 1937 when Edward, known as "Ned," was killed, along with his friend and colleague Otis T. Russell, in a car accident. They were returning from a fishing trip in Vermont when their car left the highway at a curve in the road and overturned. Russell was killed instantly and Hutchins died half an hour after arriving at the hospital.[31] No doubt Ned's death was a great blow to the family, and especially to Susan Hutchins who had already endured the loss of her husband and two young daughters many years earlier. This event seemed to bring Hutchins closer to her other brother, Henry.

This letter from Grace is more complicated than it appears. First, it is written in Susan Hutchins's hand, an unmistakable, extremely difficult to decipher scrawl. Why would a letter signed by Grace be written (signature and all) by her mother? Did Susan make a copy for herself and send the original to someone else? It makes little sense to believe Susan made up any of this, although it is important to acknowledge what might be missing from this copy.

In Sickness and in Health

The job Hutchins referred to in the above-mentioned letter to her parents in 1927 was a position with the Bureau of Women in Industry at the New York Department of Labor. However, her mind was full of other work closer to her heart. She hoped to help with a local subway strike that was pending, organizing the wives, doing publicity work, or helping out with the picket committee. She was not sure if her efforts would be needed, but was "ready to jump while the jumping's good and see what there is to do."[32]

Nonetheless, at the end of August 1927 she accepted a provisional appointment as an investigator with the Bureau of Women in Industry, an appointment that would become permanent if she passed the dreaded Civil Service exam. With help from Rochester who had been through such exams before, her regular appointment was received in December 1927. Given her commitment to radical politics, and, I would guess, disdain for reformist causes and state bureaucracies, it is difficult to imagine Hutchins being highly motivated for a job such as this. Besides a desire to be financially independent, part of her incentive for working at the bureau may have been that it gave her access to material for two books she was planning: *Labor and Silk* and *Women Who Work*. Concerned about women's employment and labor practices, she could use this job to gather material for these texts. However, her time at the bureau was brief. A letter of resignation to Bureau Director Nelle Swartz, dated February 22, 1928, referred to a serious health problem that had involved surgery the preceding November and then again in January. There is silence here concerning this illness and no clues as to its nature except that Hutchins experienced depression along with physical discomfort.[33] This silence and the fact that Grace was at midlife and had some problems associated with menopause encourage me to tentatively suggest it might have been gynecological, although this is unclear.

This illness was weathered more easily by the deep trust and love that had developed between Hutchins and Rochester, a trust that emerged out of their shared work and values. Indeed, the CP tended to encourage the in-

> The silences here about Grace's illness are frustrating since I cannot get access to such things as hospital records and I know there is so much more to the story than can be safely stated. The comment Grace made to her mother in her letter about the "change of life" may have been relatively insignificant and I could be making too much of it in my explanation here of her illness. I want to reiterate that imagining Grace at the bureau given her politics is difficult. It is possible that the illness, although no doubt real, was a useful excuse to quit the position once her data on women's employment had been gathered.

tegration of comrades' personal and political lives and praised relationships based upon love and mental affinity. As Lenin's widow, Nadezhda Krupskaya, was quoted as saying:

> Family life can bring great happiness if it is based on mutual love. But love should not be regarded solely as the satisfaction of a healthy sexual urge. This feeling . . . must be paired with mental affinity, with the striving for a common aim, with the struggle for a common cause.[34]

Certainly Hutchins and Rochester shared a common cause. When the two were separated by Hutchins's departure to the hospital, they missed each other very, very much. Writing from her bed in the hospital, Hutchins penned a love note to Rochester,

> Beloved Partner,
>
> . . . I see so clearly that all you do in this illness is just a further expression of all you do all the time for me, and have done all these years. Wasn't it 7 years ago this month that we moved to 352? And all those years my love for you has grown and deepened and increased mightily, just because your *goodness* calls it out. I am afraid it is I, by being so trying, who have made you a saint! But oh, dearest, in this quiet here, I make good resolutions, and hope I can keep them.
>
> Your buying that bed is overwhelming, but I look forward to it with glee and thanksgiving to my Anna. If I had only the pen of Wm. Ellery Leonard to tell you of my love and my *admiration* for you.
>
> Your ever more loving, Grace[35]

I have to admit I was excited to find this letter with what might be taken as evidence of the sexual nature of their relationship. However, the question needs to be asked why this knowledge of genital sexuality is important. We don't demand proof of sexual activity as evidence of heterosexuality. As far as I can tell, they never identified as lesbians and I feel keenly the ethical dilemma of exposing them now. They seem to fall so easily into the romantic friendship category perhaps because of the rhetorical devices of the time that framed love in terms of admiration and companionship. This was how Grace and Anna expressed their relationship. I assume (wrongly perhaps) that language of a more sexual nature would have been more or less taboo for these refined, middle-aged women. Either way, leaving behind evidence of sexual innuendo would probably be very unlikely. Because I rely on their writings here, the spirit of romantic friendships as feminist scholars have traditionally written about them comes across more obviously. The "accuracy" here is unclear. It also begs the question of how this letter survived. Did these comments slip by unnoticed or were they innocuous enough to be of little concern or were they left intentionally to make a point?

Scholarship on lesbian feminism in the 1970s and 1980s tended to construct an idyllic age of (nonsexual) nineteenth-century romantic friendship. While this construction has more recently been challenged as idealized and inaccurate,[36] it does seem to capture the spirit of Hutchins and Rochester's love for each other as based upon trust, companionship, and admiration. This letter would suggest that this couple's relationship was also one of a sexual nature, although of course the buying of a bed does not necessarily imply genital sexuality. Even so, the mention of "glee" suggests otherwise.

Within a couple of months Hutchins had recovered enough to be working as a correspondent with the Federated Press, the most comprehensive left-oriented news service in the United States. Rochester also was employed by this news bureau, although the couple almost always had different assignments since only one correspondent covered a story. They traveled to picket lines and meetings, educational circles and demonstrations, anywhere they could find action to write about. In 1928, for example, Rochester covered the founding of the National Miners' Union in Pittsburgh and Hutchins was active in the strike of cotton goods workers in New Bedford against a 10 percent wage cut. When the couple were apart they wrote to each other lamenting their parting and wishing they were together. So often these letters described the admiration and respect the two had for each other, and spoke of their appreciation of the love, care and commitment that each showered on the other.[37] When Rochester was covering the founding of the National Miners' Union, Hutchins wrote to her "Most Precious Anna," concerned about her safety, phoning all over to get news of the event and only feeling better when she received a wire: "Beloved, I long to be with you, but I guess you're glad I'm not around to make any extra complications. Almost I took the train this morning but refrained. . . . Six more days till you come home! How I miss you every minute. . . . Your own always, loving you wholly, Grace."[38]

On another occasion, Hutchins anticipated her partner's leaving and wrote a letter before her departure timed for Rochester to read the following morning:

Dearest of all,

I am sitting opposite you here, but will mail this in the station, as I go through to the train, so you will have word from me in the morning to tell you that I love you. Never was there such a friend as you! Not even Shakespeare could describe it, for his was love, but not the companionship of *years*. Nevertheless, he comes as near expressing it as I can find at the present moment:
"For thy sweet love remembered
Such wealth brings. . . ."
Yours f'rever n'ever, Deepest love, Grace[39]

It was not long before Hutchins was ill again, this time in the New York infirmary having her appendix removed. Writing to Rochester from her hospital bed, she penned the following:

> Dearest of all, why should I write a letter to Dr. Edward in appreciation of her care, when it is *you* who have done most of all? You have been so patient with me, so unfailingly thoughtful and understanding. Truly, it moves me to tears when I think of the beauty of your love and devotion. "In sickness and in health," you never let a friend down.
>
> Here's hoping that with the appendix have gone some of my failings and impatiencies, so I may be truly made over new into something better and more worthy of the work we have to do. . . .
> With all my heart full of love and thankfulness for the fineness of you, Grace[40]

Responding to her partner's frequent expressions of love and devotion, Rochester responded, "My Beloved Darling, You've done everything in the world for me that I need. Nothing could have been more perfect in every way than the love and devotion you give me. I don't deserve it at all and I know it—depend on it—and live for it—literally."[41]

Hutchins and Rochester's devotions for each other combined passion and companionship; they were best friends and lovers in the deepest romantic sense. Hutchins was in the habit of doing little things for Rochester like seeing her off at the station and providing a snack for the journey, which Rochester tended not to reciprocate.[42] It seemed that Hutchins was more romantic in her day-to-day interactions and Rochester more practical. This practicality showed itself in a letter Rochester wrote to Hutchins in the summer of 1931, laying out her will in case of her death:

> My precious Grace,
> I shall not try to make this letter a final word of friendship! For we look forward to many years still of common work and play. And we both know how each depends on the other. But the cause of the working class is bigger than our friendship, and it will give either one of us the stimulus and inspiration to go on alone after the other has died. So this letter is merely a practical note about belongings in the apartment.
>
> I mean it when I say that they are all to be yours. But please have in mind that the Rochester relatives would like to have Father's portrait. . . . Also they would like to have the inherited old Spode cups. If Edith would like to have the piano for her children, I think it would still be worth toting to West Englewood. Also she might care for the few bits of jewelry, in the black leather box. But I want you to take yourself the little round pin that we have passed back and forth.
>
> Please don't feel constrained by any earlier suggestions to bring Lucie here (if she wants to come). You certainly will not want to live alone, but don't decide

hastily! You may quite likely want to close this chapter and move into some other apartment, and that also should not be too quickly decided.

You have had my deepest affection, Anna[43]

This letter was typed, although the last sentence, "You have had my deepest affection," was handwritten. Besides revealing the deep love and commitment the pair had for each other, it illustrates again the way their relationship was grounded in shared political commitments: "the cause of the working class is bigger than our friendship." It is interesting that Rochester was the one initiating a will of sorts rather than Hutchins, since it is the latter who had spent the time in the hospital. However, perhaps all this illness had reminded them of their mortality and Rochester, being five years older and the more practical one, had felt the need to write this letter. A reader who knows their history is happy to remember that the couple was fortunate in being able to spend another thirty-five years together.

While Hutchins and Rochester were deeply bonded, as already mentioned, I do not think they saw themselves as lesbians. They also had strong incentives not to do so. After the early 1930s the official ideology of the Soviet Communist Party, and therefore a CPUSA directive, defined gays and lesbians as symptomatic of bourgeois decadency and as an aspect of counterrevolutionary insurgency. In 1938 CP leader Earl Browder declared:

> We consider sexual immorality, looseness and aberrations as the harmful product of bad social organization, and their increase in America today as largely products of the crisis of the capitalist system, of the demoralization among the upper classes which affects the masses by contagion, and we combat them as we combat all other harmful social manifestations.[44]

Despite the emergence of the Mattachine Society (which was an all-male organization), founded in the early 1950s, a gay and lesbian orientation was not normally sanctioned and supported by the Party.[45] In her discussion of women in the Old Left, Ellen Kay Trimberger recounted an interview with a former CP organizer who related that in the late 1940s, "the Party leadership made a decision to drop all homosexuals from the Party because of their presumed openness to blackmail as state repression increased. A local organizer was asked to speak to several known lesbians to request their resignations. These lesbians were friends of the organizer, although she had never discussed their sexual preference with them. When she met with them, they all cried, but the lesbians 'obeyed' and resigned. Looking back on the incident, this activist says that neither she nor the lesbians, although some may have questioned the assumption, ever considered opposing the Party decision."[46] Similarly, in her article on women in the CPUSA, Rosalyn Baxandall explains that even though the CP was a refuge from bourgeois life, "the U.S. totems of family, monogamy, and het-

erosexuality were never officially questioned."[47] While there were significant numbers of lesbians in the Party, Baxandall writes that they were
mostly closeted since homosexuality was equated with the decadence of
capitalism. This helps clarify how Hutchins and Rochester constructed
their relationship publicly.

Labor Research Association

Another decision that Hutchins and Rochester made upon arriving home
in 1927 was to join forces with friend and colleague Robert Dunn to co-
found the Labor Research Association (LRA), an organization that prepared social and economic material for labor unions. Also involved in this
endeavor were friends Solon DeLeon and Alexander Trachtenberg.[48] Although the LRA was politically close to the CP, there were no formal ties
between them. Located at East Eleventh Street in New York City, a few
blocks south of Union Square on Broadway, the LRA was founded to "conduct investigations and studies of social, economic and political questions
in the interest of the labor and progressive movement and to issue its find-
ings in the form of reports, articles, pamphlets and books." The goal of its
publications was to educate the labor movement about broader economic
and sociopolitical issues from a Marxist approach, and it offered its research and consulting services to local and national unions and other labor
organizations.[49] The LRA took a couple of years to get off the ground, and
Hutchins and Rochester appeared to have timed their termination with the
Federated Press to coincide with increased work at the LRA. By 1929 the
pair's work was devoted full time to the LRA. Many books were written
under LRA auspices and published by International Publishers, including
all the texts by Hutchins and Rochester written after *Jesus Christ and the
World Today*. In addition, during the period between 1927 and 1935
Hutchins and Rochester worked on volumes 1 and 2 of the LRA publication, *Labor Fact Book*, published in 1931 and 1934 respectively. These volumes gave up-to-date information on labor issues and were widely used as
reference books. They were supplemented by the monthly magazines that
kept unions abreast of the most recent economic developments.

A long series of pamphlets on topics pertinent to social and economic
life generally, and industrial relations in particular, were prepared under
the direction of the LRA between 1931 and 1936 and published by International Publishers in several volumes. Hutchins and Rochester wrote at
least eight of the pamphlets between them. Representing the polemical
writings of the Third Period, the pamphlets illustrate intense devotion to
the Party in the context of the economic crises of the Depression and criticize New Deal politics.[50] With the primary intent of educating workers on
the social ills of capitalism, the pamphlets followed a specific format: a sen-

timental, often heart-wrenching personal story about the evils of capitalism was followed by a study of current conditions pertaining to that industry, usually with comparisons of workers' bleak existence to the profits and luxuries of the owners and operators. Then came a short history of the workers' struggle: a damning of conservative, liberal, and socialist organizations as enemies of the working class and a discussion of militant union activity. Finally there was a comparison between U.S. workers and those in the Soviet Union.

Hutchins's first pamphlet, "Youth in Industry," was published in 1932 and documented how thousands of young people, old enough to work yet too young to vote, were displacing older workers in order to maintain capitalist profits. She called them to action: "the future belongs to the working youth."[51] The next year Hutchins wrote "Children under Capitalism," again beginning with a touching comparison of two children, one rich, one poor, born under very different circumstances: "The children of the capitalist class are thus literally fattening off the bodies of workers' children ... [in the Soviet Union] the welfare of children is a *first consideration* [original emphasis]."[52]

Nineteen thirty-two also saw the publication of Rochester's pamphlet "Profits and Wages." While Hutchins's writings presented the touching loss of youth among the working classes, Rochester's focused on the lavish spending and lifestyle among rich families: a significant message coming during the Depression years. "Luxury spending and starvation continue side by side," Rochester emphatically wrote, causing "daily robbery" for the majority of working people.[53] This pamphlet was especially sectarian in its scornful distrust of all non–Communist Party organizations. The communist message was painted as standing alone in its potential for bringing dignity and freedom for the marginalized peoples of the United States.

Rochester's pamphlet "Wall Street" was the companion piece to "Profits and Wages." It explored the fusion of U.S. state apparatus and the banking and industrial enterprises, and overviewed the immense wealth of such key financial magnates as J. P. Morgan, Rockefeller, and Kuhn, Loeb, and company. As such it reflected the research she was engaged in for her forthcoming book, *Rulers of America: A Study of Finance Capital.* In this pamphlet Rochester was especially scornful of the activities of the Socialist Party that would attempt a nationalization of industries and the stabilization of capitalism: "For the Socialist Party is determined to conceal from the workers in the U.S. the one most important contrast: here in the U.S. government is and always has been for the service and protection of the capitalist class. In the Soviet Union, government belongs to the working class.... Less openly but no less truly than the Republicans and Democrats, the Socialist Party is a party of capitalism."[54] The Communist Party, she believed, was the only party whose activities threatened Wall Street.

Almost all the International Pamphlets included discussions of the special plight of the "Negro" worker, the foreign born, and, at least those written by Hutchins and Rochester, women. One of the important aspects of communist ideology during this period was its ability to address the plight of African American workers, and, as a result, the CP had considerable support among black workers in the south as well as in the northern states. This rudimentary analysis of difference was reflected in Hutchins's pamphlet, "Women Who Work," a reflection of the research for her forthcoming book with the same title. In this pamphlet Hutchins discussed how the double burden of being female and black meant earning between a third and a half less than white women, even though they are "among the best fighters in the class struggle."[55] She also spoke of the double day of work for all women who toil by day in the factories and toil into the night in their homes. In classic Marxist fashion, fault here lies with capitalism, which "aims to keep women subordinate," using their [women's] labor power to keep the price of men's labor down.[56]

Representative of Third Period writing, it lambasted reformist labor movement attempts, including the Women's Trade Union League, for pursuing a policy of class collaboration. The Socialist Party and such women's groups as the YWCA, the League of Women Voters, and the National Woman's Party also did not escape condemnation. The only organizational hope, Hutchins reported, was the militant Trade Union Unity League, which, unlike other labor organizations, did have women on its committees and included them as a central part in the struggle for working-class freedom.

The Labor Series

As part of a series of industrial studies prepared by the LRA and published by International Publishers, *Labor and Silk* was Hutchins's first book on industrial relations.[57] She had witnessed the Associated Silk Workers Union strike in Paterson, New Jersey, in 1924 and had spoken at a union meeting there. This was a formative experience that facilitated her interest in labor relations in the textile industries.[58] Published in 1929, *Labor and Silk* described the growth and profits of the silk and rayon industries and the effects of industrial conditions on the spirit and livelihood of the workers in the mills. These industries had low wages, high lay-off and unemployment rates, calculated speed-ups, a large percentage of child workers, and terrible working conditions. With characteristic poignancy, Hutchins painted the picture of the silk worker surrounded by deafening machinery, standing all day long, and with no ventilation lest a breeze might break the delicate silk threads. Using data collected during her travels in 1926–1927, she also discussed overseas silk industries: "Hands of Japanese and Chinese girls and children have plunged silkworm cocoons in practically boiling water . . . hands are cheap in the east."[59] Even though famous strikes had occurred at Passaic, Paterson, and New Bedford, this industry was among the most poorly organized; no surprise, it also employed a disproportionately female labor force. Hutchins was deeply concerned that her writing would be useful for the workers themselves, and that her book would be accessible and of interest to them.[60]

Reviews were favorable and *Labor and Silk* seemed to be well received by a broad segment of people interested in labor issues. The *New Republic* emphasized that this was a book that should be read by consumers of textiles and picked up by the National Consumers' League. Remarking on Hutchins's lucid style, the *Office Worker* exclaimed that the "whole book is packed full of information—and it reads like a novel."[61] Likewise, *The Friend* reported its "clear, incisive style, infused with irony, that holds the attention of the lay reader, even through the appendices."[62] A review by Socialist leader A. J. Muste was more critical, remarking that Hutchins gave a "vivid, sympathetic, at times perhaps slightly sentimental, picture of the conditions under which silk workers toil and live."[63] He went on to add that some of the book must be taken with a grain of salt, particularly Hutchins's endorsement of the left-wing activities of the National Textiles Workers Union, which he felt had not yet demonstrated its worth.[64]

In 1931 Rochester published *Labor and Coal*, a treatise on work and labor in the mining industries that painted their future with her characteristic Marxist–Leninist brush:

> In every other country (besides the Soviet Union), between a dark present and the hopeful future, lies a period of class struggle which will grow steadily sharper. The capitalist class is making a last desperate stand to defend its "right" to exploit the worker.[65]

Labor and Coal was praised for its painstakingly detailed and scrupulously researched data as well as its treatment of important aspects of U.S. industry and labor relations. Some approved of the zealous faith in communist solutions, and others found it overzealous and lacking in concrete suggestions for change.[66] Like Hutchins's aspirations for *Labor and Silk*, Rochester also wanted this book to be read by workers in the industry; she wanted this to be a book *for* the miner's movement.[67]

Rochester was so very caught up in ideas about the inevitable historical progression implicit in Marxist analysis that her commitments border on fanaticism. Certainly a small pamphlet she wrote with colleague Pat Toohey, "The Miners' Road to Freedom in a Soviet America," published by Workers Library in 1936, had such a ring about it. This piece was heavy on sentiment, starting out with a touching story about a miner's family shivering in a cold little wooden house during a mountain winter. It painted the absolute injustice implicit in the present system of coal mining and gave solutions in a Soviet-style system.[68] Throughout this pamphlet, the rhetorical intent was to radicalize the miners, raise their consciousness about the evils of the present system, and encourage them to join the ranks of the CPUSA. All seemed painted black or white: the evils of capitalism are constantly juxtaposed against the glorious potentials of communism. Yet, despite this fanaticism, knowing Rochester's past and present commitments, a reader gets the impression that hers is an ethical position sincerely rooted in the moral position of best serving the greater good.

Women Who Work

The position of women in the 1930s was dismal; women remained subordinate to men in almost every way.[69] State laws endorsed lower wages, often required a husband's consent for a woman to have access to her wages, gave women full responsibility for child care and domestic work, fired married women in certain occupations, and provided little to no legal, social, or economic relief from abusing husbands and male partners. The National Recovery Administration (NRA) of the New Deal codified lower wages for women and many union contracts did the same thing.[70] In addition, birth control was not readily available and public facilities for child care mostly nonexistent.[71] Against the social upheavals of the Great Depression and the relatively limited organized activity on the part of a feminist movement, women's particular burden was rarely questioned.[72]

During this Third Period until the mid-thirties, efforts by the CP to address women's inferior status had relatively low priority. An orthodox Marxist perspective saw women's problems as part of class antagonism and grassroots efforts focused in such industries as mining, auto, and steel, where women were underrepresented. As a result, women's exploitation *as women*, separate from their placement in the working class, had little to no recognition. However, the Party treated women relatively well, gave them opportunities, and made women's rights a part of the CP political program. In addition, the CPUSA set up women's commissions, as well as magazines, *Working Woman* and later *Woman Today*, devoted to women's concerns.[73]

Despite these important measures, sexism was rampant in the CP of the thirties and women were grossly underrepresented in positions of leadership.[74] Some members complained that husbands would not let them attend meetings, yet expected them to cook for and host these meetings as well as take responsibility for child care.[75] Within the Party some believed that special attention should be given to women because females were "backward" as demonstrated by their lack of trade union participation and their relationship to the home, a backwardness that presented them as a liability since they would hold men back from the important struggle at hand.[76] This lack of understanding of women's problems outside of their role as wage earners can be compared to the emphasis on understanding the needs and the organization of blacks (assumed to be men) who received considerably more attention by the Communist Party.[77]

This was the context for the publication of Hutchins's *Women Who Work* in 1934, a text that gave her notoriety within the movement as the "principal writer on wage-earning women for the CPUSA."[78] Comprehensive and well researched, *Women Who Work* analyzed the poor conditions and bleak reality of women involved in paid labor. It discussed their segregation into certain parts of the labor force, their low pay and high unemployment, and the poor working conditions that facilitated deteriorating health and occupational diseases. While she focused on women in the factory and mills, Hutchins also included a chapter on women in nonfactory jobs, analyzing women in teaching, nursing, clerical work, domestic service, switchboard operations, and hotel and restaurant work. A chapter was also devoted to women in agricultural work, and throughout she discussed the additional burdens of women working in the south, "Negro" women, and the foreign born. Importantly, Hutchins also had a chapter titled "The Double Burden," where she wrote how domestic work and constant child care added to the toils of working for wages and completely exhausted countless working-class women. Utilizing data from the 1930 U.S. census and the U.S. Women's and Children's Bureaus, *Women Who Work* demanded women's equality at the same time that it painted a dismal picture of their working and living conditions. Like all of Hutchins and Rochester's texts after 1922, this text was prepared under the auspices of the Labor Research Association and it sold for $2 for the cloth edition and $1 for the paperback. The notoriety of *Women Who Work* was such that it was revised in 1952, discussed later in chapter nine. *Working Woman* summed up Hutchins's approach:

> The inescapable conclusion of Comrade Hutchins's book is that the way of freedom for the exploited working woman masses will be along the line taken by the Soviet workers, that the revolutionary proletariat alone make woman a complete partner in the reconstruction of society on a socialist basis.[79]

Women Who Work followed the mandate of the Third Period in its orthodox Marxist approach, its favorable discussion of the Soviet Union, and its isolationist sectarian approach. Hutchins scorned the NRA Codes established as part of Roosevelt's National Industrial Recovery Act in 1933 and gave evidence as to why these laws did not protect most women.[80] Only militant left-wing trade unions were recognized as having any use for the working class, and the "bourgeois women's organizations" were seen as invariably supporting ruling-class power:

> It cannot be denied that most of the religious, social and educational organizations among women are acting as a sedative to lull the workers of the com-

> *Women Who Work* is impressive. But at the same time, as at other points in my research on Grace and Anna's lives in the thirties I am disappointed by their lack of feminist insight; towing the Party line meant feigning all other but an orthodox Marxist approach. This is true with *Women Who Work*. It's hard to like Grace and Anna during these moments. I feel like I do have an intense relationship with them at this point, but an ambivalent relationship where I often find them too uncompromising and doctrinaire, too formidable and polite, too zealous and rigid in their emphasis on principle. However, they might not have liked me all that much either; they would find me too bourgeois, too undercommitted ideologically, too undisciplined, too sensitive: basically not "clear-headed" enough for their principled tastes.

munity to sleep—misleading them into thinking that the authorities, local, state or national, are really doing something "progressive" to aid the working class.[81]

Indeed, Hutchins believed that upper- and middle-class women had already won rights of citizenship and property on an equal basis with men and that the inequities for working-class women were purely economic.[82] As such she was also scornful of the Equal Rights Amendment, castigated as a bill supported by irresponsible bourgeois women that would remove all hard-won protective legislation for working women. Hutchins was not alone in her assessment of the ERA during this period; most working-class women's organizations also saw the ERA as a threat to their livelihood.[83] While *Women Who Work* also followed the classic Party line in its discussion of working women's problems as rooted in the evils of capitalist production rather than male privilege, it did raise two important issues that would provide crucial insight for later Marxist feminist studies. First, it laid the groundwork for the rejection of the orthodox Marxist idea that housework was marginal to the capitalist system and instead emphasized that the reproductive labor of housework contributed to the accumulation of capital.[84] Second, it emphasized the extra burden of "Negro" women's situation, a precursor to Marxist feminist analyses of the mutually supportive relationship between capitalism and racism.[85] In addition, *Women Who Work* also hinted at the important issue of sexism within the movement. Blame, however, was not laid in the context of male chauvinism but attributed to "ruling class propaganda" which, in the case of women's discrimination, was internalized by men and acted ultimately with the old divide and conquer mentality.[86]

Despite the strong assertive voice that rang clear through *Women Who Work*, Hutchins, like most of us, experienced her share of doubt when it came to her writing. In an undated letter that seemed to refer to *Women Who Work*, although it might possibly have concerned *Labor and Silk*,

Grace (c. early 1930s).

Rochester addressed her "Precious Abused Pardner" and revealed as much about herself as her partner concerning professional anxieties:

> I know how you feel—for I am more dependent than you are (and we are both *too* dependent) on encouragement and praise. And you give it to me—and I lap it up—really *too* ready to think my own work is good. I do give myself sincere self-criticism but I don't welcome it from others. Knowing all this about myself, I don't apply it to you! And my overdose of criticism without the expression of more-than-balancing respect I feel for your first chapter was really a crime. And it is a crime which on smaller points I repeat day after day. I am more responsible than Bob for your depression. Somehow I feel as if we were so close that you must *know* that I have a deep steady underlying respect for you. . . . There's *nothing* the matter with your abilities and they are specialized in practice. . . . You have nothing to lie awake over—And nothing to despair about. . . .
>
> Thine wholly—Anna [original emphases][87]

Despite any initial setbacks, *Women Who Work* was completed and reviews mostly positive. These reviews were predictable in the sense that the left-wing presses were full of praise for this work and the more middle-of-the-road reviewers found the subject matter desirous of attention, the research well done, but the communist subtext off-putting. While the *New York World-Telegram* liked to play up the comparison between Hutchins's aristocratic Boston background and her support for the rank-and-file workers of the day, the *New Masses* were relieved to find a book on women that was *not* written from the point of view of middle-class feminists intent upon "making a sort of artificial heaven for themselves, with Miss Greta Palmer of the *World-Telegram* as the Gabriel who blows their horn, and Mrs. Roosevelt as the official spokesman."[88] As an aside, this review illustrates the misogyny implicit in radical thought and organizations of the period. It also helps clarify Hutchins's position vis-à-vis feminism given her identification with such radical organizations. An unfavorable review of Hutchins's book was reported in the *New York Times*.[89] Hutchins and Rochester tended to refer to this newspaper and others of its ilk as the capitalist press or Hearst press; they might not have expected much more from a review among its pages. Likewise they most likely had low expectations of the *Bryn Mawr Alumnae Bulletin*, even though Hutchins in particular was actively involved with the alumnae society. Mildred Fairchild, professor of social economy, reviewed Hutchins's text.[90] Hutchins was upset by this review and had written to Professor Fairchild, objecting to her use of such terms as "oracle" and "propaganda."[91] Fairchild graciously apologized for causing Hutchins concern, but held fast in her review:

> What I do not approve and therefore can not apologise for criticising, is the confusion between scientific data, based on statistical fact-finding, and

On reading these reviews I wanted Grace to defend her "bias" by address-ing the problems associated with objectivity and value neutrality as a rhetor-ical stance. While she might have pointed out the false neutrality and invalid separation of science and politics claimed by traditional researchers as a way to explain the politicized nature of her own bias, I know it is unlikely given her reliance on scientific socialism. Of course there was also little discussion about these issues then. By stressing the juxtaposition of a scientific ap-proach to defend their work (i.e., it's "truth" as evidenced by scientific ma-nipulation and analysis of data), Grace and Anna were in the ironic position of renouncing bias yet incorporating it through ideological positioning. This is a catch-22 that scientific socialism never really was able to address.

sweeping generalization in principle or theory, flung into the midst of the dis-cussion without qualification or preface.[92]

Hutchins and Rochester's writings during this period were decidedly grounded in Third Period ideology and essentially toed the official Party line. Events around them must have seemed to affirm their devotion to communist politics: the economic crisis of the late twenties stood as evi-dence of capitalism's demise, and fascism blazed abroad. The Great De-pression, which so fundamentally shaped life in the United States during this period, stood as a testament to the decay of the capitalist economic order and as a brutal reminder of its failings. This context was a part of the complex interaction of forces that helped produce Hutchins and Rochester as political subjects. With this social and economic despair framing the pe-riod, Hutchins and Rochester saw the Communist Party as a viable solution toward the glorious future they hoped would be just around the corner.

CHAPTER EIGHT

PARTY INTELLECTUALS

New Year's Resolution For Our Readers

ON THIS, the first day of 1939, I pledge to do all in my power to help MAKE it a truly Happy New Year.

I PLEDGE to do everything possible to arouse my friends and my fellow workers to the need for defending the social and national security of my country.

I PLEDGE to help acquaint everyone I meet, with the danger facing the United States from the Berlin-Rome-Tokyo axis and from its supporters here at home headed by Herbert Hoover.

I PLEDGE to work for the preservation of all NEW DEAL achievements and to strive to have them carried further to the end that American men, women and children, Negro and white, will be better fed, better housed, and in better health.

I PLEDGE that when Congress opens this week, I will start sending letters myself, and get my friends and the organizations to which I belong to do likewise, so that our Congressmen will know how we feel on EVERY issue.

I PLEDGE as my very first job of the New Year to help feed Spain and have the embargo lifted as the best way of saving democracy and peace here at home.[1]

From 1935 to 1939 the Party moved from its sectarian stance of the Third Period into the cooperative Popular Front years. The above New Year's resolution from the *Daily Worker* was written at the end of the Popular Front period when collaboration with progressive organizations was encouraged but the Hitler–Stalin pact had not yet been signed. During this period the Comintern-directed Communist Party, USA (CPUSA), moved away from viewing progressive noncommunist organizations such as the Socialist Party as reactionary "social fascists" and toward a policy of rap-

> The margins of the story mark a border between the remembered and the forgotten.[2]

prochement. This occurred in part because Hitler-style fascism was seen as a threat to the Soviet Union and allies were needed. It also became clear that New Deal politics were salvaging U.S. capitalism and a change of policy was necessary. As a result, in the summer of 1935 the Seventh World Congress of the Communist International placed as the immediate task an "establishment of unity of action amongst all sections of the working class in the struggle against fascism,"[3] the Soviet Union joined the League of Nations and signed a mutual defense pact with France, and the Popular Front era was born. Membership in the CPUSA rose at this point to 65,000 members, and the Party started to earn the respect of liberals.[4] Such support was related to communism's reputation as the "soul of Europe" in the Spanish Civil War against fascism. The communists were alone in their support of the loyalists, Mussolini and Hitler were behind Franco's forces, and Britain, the United States, and France refused to intervene. North American and European intellectuals, liberals, and Left militants joined the international brigades, and the Abraham Lincoln Battalion swelled with many U.S. Loyalist–sympathizers against the forces of fascism.[5]

Hutchins had pasted a clipping of the above New Year's resolution into her small notebook. It is amazing that this was only five years after the publication of *Women Who Work*, where "class collaboration" was decried as the evil that diverted workers from their revolutionary potential.[6] Now Hutchins's writing followed a different tack. An interesting comparison to her sectarian 1932 pamphlet and 1934 book on working women was another pamphlet written by her on this topic and published by the Workers Library in 1935. Focusing on the broad issue of social insurance for unemployment, industrial accident and sickness, old age and maternity, it was written specifically to encourage support of the 1935 Workers' Bill for Social and Unemployment Insurance (H.R. 2827), worked out by the CPUSA and endorsed by a long list of organizations and municipal bodies. Alongside demands for complete social insurance, it also called for maternity benefits. The pamphlet ended with a section that included suggestions for the organizational endorsement of the bill: "To secure endorsements by women workers go where the workers are—whether they are in the Young Women's Christian Association, the Young Women's Hebrew Association, the churches, or any other organization of whatsoever kind."[7] Note that only a year earlier Hutchins had chastised the YWCA, writing: "One of the largest of these organizations (that discourage mass action on the part of the workers) is the Young Women's Christian Association. . . . Its local city

> Did this ideological shift slide by unconsciously so that the transition for them was seamless and unrecognizable—or was it a conscious change in ideology/policy? To what extent did their understandings of the present refashion their memories of this past? Certainly, the ability to rework past experience in light of present policy would have been a helpful attribute for maintaining the infallibility of the Party.

organization in an industrial community is always found on the side of the employers in any industrial struggle. It cannot be otherwise when an organization receives its main financial support from the Rockefellers, the Woolworths, the mill owners and the local magnates of an industrial town."[8]

This heyday of communist popular appeal, second only to the popularity of the "national unity" movement during U.S. involvement in World War II, presented Popular Front ideology as carrying the liberal discussions of democracy and freedom to their logical conclusion: socialism, a nation for the people, a "world brotherhood of man":

> The Communist Party of the United States of America is a working class political party carrying forward the traditions of Jefferson, Paine, Jackson and Lincoln, and of the Declaration of Independence; it upholds the achievements of democracy, the right of "life, liberty, and the pursuit of happiness," and defends the United States Constitution against its reactionary enemies who would destroy democracy and all its popular liberties; it is devoted to the defense of the immediate interests of the workers, farmers, and all the toilers against capitalist exploitation, and to preparation of the working class for its historic mission to unite and lead the American people to extend these democratic principles to their necessary and logical conclusion.[9]

In this way, reflecting a keen desire to gain popular support and build a strong movement, the CPUSA moved from a rhetoric of class struggle to class collaboration, attempting to blur the differences between themselves and Left liberal parties. Their distinctions, they emphasized, were only in the amount of zealous enthusiasm they showed in their commitment to a new society. Indeed, in 1935 Earl Browder, general secretary of the CPUSA from 1930 to 1945, remarked that communism was merely "twentieth-century Americanism."[10] Browder, who was a strong advocate for working with New Deal forces, labored to project the Popular Front image. The presidential election of 1936 (when Browder ran unsuccessfully for president) saw the CPUSA give de facto support to Roosevelt and become an active force in his "Second New Deal."[11]

Hutchins and Rochester worked on volumes 3 and 4 of the *Labor Fact Book* during this period.[12] In 1936 volume 3 reported how the Communist Party had long been seeking rapprochement; in fact, "since early 1933, [it had] made numerous proposals for working class unity," had approached the Socialist Party, although "no response was forthcoming."[13] Now, they asserted, a united front was the only way to beat fascism and gone were the damning reports of government programs and noncommunist labor organizations. The couple was astute in recognizing the forces of fascism worldwide as well as in the United States Hutchins wrote about the growth of the fascist menace in the United States in "It Comes on Cat's Feet," published in the *New Masses* in 1938. A central point of this article was the relationship between European industrialists who supported Hitler and Mussolini and U.S. corporate hegemony, characterized as anti-New Deal:

> American corporation officials who point out the advantages (to business men) of a fascist regime are anti-New Deal Republicans or Democrats.... But in order to advocate anything like a fascist system (under whatever name it might be called) in America, these business men must deny the democratic principles on which the United States government is founded.[14]

Alert; Brisk; Confident; Keen

While both Hutchins and Rochester spent the Popular Front years committed to LRA work and immersed in their research and writing, Hutchins also threw herself into politics. She was becoming well known as a strong communist loyalist and may well have been connected to a variety of underground operations.[15] However, in terms of Popular Front politics, Hutchins ran as alderman from the 10th Assembly District in 1935, as New York State comptroller in 1936, and as lieutenant governor in 1938. She also worked as treasurer of the Communist National Election Cam-

Troubling for me is that despite long affiliations with socialist thought and respect for the strong convictions and dedicated lives of communist intellectuals, my perceptions of the autocracy, hierarchy, and male domination of Party organizations make it difficult for me to attribute other than ulterior motives to their actions. This almost automatic assumption of bad faith on the part of CP bureaucracy and hierarchy encourages a cynical response to the statement that they had been seeking rapprochement but had been rebuffed. How difficult it is to interpret CP activities outside of the contemporary anticommunist rhetoric that has framed discourse about the Party. Obviously this is not a new problem; it affects our understandings and analyses of all issues; attitudes about the CP in a red-phobic society like the United States are just an extreme example.

> Research diary: September 11, 1998: "There's a poignancy in thinking about Grace spouting communist rhetoric in her refined accent reeking of upper-class Boston prosperity. How incongruous it must have been to hear her speak of the toiling masses and corporate privilege from that genteel space. It's her naiveté that seems especially poignant; it makes me feel compassion for her vulnerability out there, exposed, out of place even while I respect her courage and convictions."

paign Committee during Browder's bid for presidential office in 1936. Running for the position of state comptroller, Hutchins explained her platform:

First of all we would press to have relief increased by 40 per cent. The comptroller is responsible for this, selling bonds and auditing accounts, he [*sic*] would have influence in pushing for larger amounts. . . . We say that wages must rise with the rising cost of living. Women are refusing to buy milk at the increased price. We believe in unemployment insurance paid at standard wages.[16]

Despite increased publicity for the communist campaign, due in part to her work with the National Election Campaign Committee as well as a statewide radio address on Columbus Day, she lost this election, receiving 67,000 votes. Tremaine, the incumbent comptroller, was reelected with 3 million votes, and the Socialist Party came in second with 99,000. All Hutchins's bids for electoral office were unsuccessful, but, as she later reminded herself with the words of William Morris, he "who rises every time he falls will sometimes rise to stay."[17]

In 1936 Hutchins gave a brief update to the Bryn Mawr alumnae magazine, *The Turtle's Progress-Dispatch* describing her life. She chose a breezy, informal style:

The LRA, for which I've worked these past 7 years, would have fired me long ago if I hadn't done more reading than I used to in College. . . . If New York has a Farmer-Labor ticket in the coming election I shall vote it and perhaps be a candidate for City office from the lower west side. Politically speaking a street corner in a crowded neighborhood is more exciting and interesting, I find, than a basketball or hockey game used to be. Occasionally one has to dodge a potato or tomato thrown by some Fascist opponent from across the street. But for other exercise I depend on walking and a little gardening. I'm hoping for 25 years more of activity; obviously I'm an optimist.[18]

Despite this public bravado, out in the public eye Hutchins had to deal with the anxieties and insecurities associated with running for political office. Although relatively outgoing in her personal nature, Hutchins was usually described as soft-spoken, genteel, refined, and dignified.[19] She must

Grace speaking at the Communist Convention, Madison Square Garden, New York, November 2, 1936.

no doubt have needed to work on her rhetorical skills to receive the popular appeal required to please the broad-based constituencies from the lower west side of New York City. Hutchins dealt with her anxieties about being up to this political work in a series of positive affirmations penned in her notebook:

Act as if it were impossible to fail. *Clear out all the distrusts and timidities,* all the fears of looking ridiculous. *The first result will be a tremendous surge of vitality, and of freshness* . . . each hour of unhampered activity opens into a promise of others in the future. *By ceasing to let fear hold its frustrating sway* we come into the use of already existing attitudes which we formerly had no energy to explore. Do the thing and you shall have the power; but they who do not the thing have not the power. Alert; brisk; confident; keen. [original emphases][20]

The notebook was not a journal that recorded Hutchins's daily thoughts but a small, condensed record of her aspirations, complete with reminders concerning how she felt she should live her life. This last comment, "alert; brisk; confident; keen," summed up Hutchins's organized and principled approach to life; this is how she wanted to appear to others as well as to herself. Indeed, this phrase became shortened to "a b c k" in her notebook, reiterated throughout the years. No muddled, wishy-washy musings; Hutchins wanted crisp, principled thoughts and actions. Orthodox communist doctrine saw personal feelings as trivial, and bourgeois, and certainly Hutchins's notebook was not a place to record feelings other than affirmations and calls to duty. No doubt she would have hated to have been called sentimental since such thought and action contradicted the direct, rational thought that underlay her notions of social action; nonetheless, the language here evoked sentiment and is reminiscent of someone on a religious quest. "Do the thing and you shall have the power," sounds remarkably like something written during her devout Christian years. She believed in the doctrines of Marx as she had the doctrines of Christianity; her faith comes across as infallible.

In the notebooks, comments for herself were affirmed and then reaffirmed at various later dates, often marking Hutchins's birthday, New Year's day, or Christmas day, and usually including lists that laid out a series of goals. They reflected her very ordered life and her desire for clearheadedness and organization. One such list was written in January 1937:

Promptness in reading F.P. [Federated Press] and weeklies
Theory—at least once a week
Thorough work at L.R.A. office
Articles—once a month
Weight—down by 10 pounds [original emphases][21]

On Christmas day that same year, 1937, the list was reviewed and amended to include more scrupulous study and use of time, including the reading of three weekly papers between Thursday morning and Sunday evening, the *Federated Press* daily, the clearing up and reading of all papers at the office in a prompt manner, and the keeping up on fascist literature, "to *really* know them."[22] Hutchins also told herself that she needed to cultivate her volunteer contacts and more systematically study Marxist theory in order to improve her writing and articulation of these theories. Indeed, at the front of the notebook was a section where she kept a running list of books she had read and those she wanted to read. Titles here spanned the years from 1927 to 1964.

On most pages of the notebook Hutchins listed goals and aspirations. Categories for these goals included "Personal," "Work," "Reading," "Financial," and occasionally "General" with such reminders as "not undermining confidence in others by gossip," and "Physical," concerning checkups and staying well rested. Goals emphasized "steady" and "thorough" work and financial aspirations involved goals for saving and donating (10 percent tended to be the norm), as well as reminders for economic frugality. Under "Personal" Hutchins referred to her desire to reduce her weight: in 1940 wanting to get down to 185 pounds, in 1941 changing this to 180. A little shorter than Rochester, whose passport listed her as 5 feet 9 inches tall, Hutchins seemed to have had an ongoing struggle with her weight.[23] Also under "Personal" Hutchins often starred a capitalized "P," something I at first assumed to stand for "partner," implying the priority she made concerning her relationship with Rochester. However, later I realized that "P" was used with reference to "clubs" and understand it now to refer to "Party." If this is correct, its listing under "Personal" again highlights the way the Party was a way of life. As one of Gornick's respondents in *The Romance of American Communism* emphasized, life as a communist was a condition; there was never a time when you were not a communist.[24] In this way, the Party and its sociopolitical context helped constitute Hutchins as a political actor.

Devoted to the communist cause, Hutchins strove to live a principled though generous life and her notebook reminded her with the prompt: "generous, large-mindedness."[25] For example, the poem, "I Saw a Communist" by Samuel Putnam, clipped from the *Daily Worker*, was pasted into the notebook, illustrating these standards against which Hutchins hoped to live. Note the religious overtones to this verse, exemplifying the idealism implicit in the couple's political yearnings:

> I saw a Communist!
> I saw him walking in the murky mist
> That lies between the darkness and the dawn,
> Clear-brained, clear-eyed, and clear voice ringing
> (It seemed to me—he was!—I heard him singing)
> yes, singing he walked on.
>
> I saw him go with bleeding feet,
> Unflincing, I saw him tread

A path of thorns, as if to meet
Some Vision far ahead.
I saw the serpent's fanged tooth,
I heard the serpent's sting;
Yet still I heard him speak the truth
In spite of everything.

There, in the murky mist
Between the darkness and the dawn.
Yes, he walked on,

Head high, a Communist!
He walked and spoke of Peace, of Peace on Earth
As the money-changers fretted and dealt in death.
And there were some who feigned a bitter mirth;
Their fetid, noisome breath
Was spewed in jets of obscene ink;
But they who dealt in death—
They were more like the ones of old, I think,
More like the ones who cried:
Down with him! Stone him! Silence him!
As a certain Man of Peace, a Carpenter died—
That day seemed far, Oh, very far,
And all the world was dim;
The world was old and dim and cold;
It all seemed like a tale long told,
When through the mist a star—
A star with guiding, heartening ray,
Glowing brighter, redder with the day—
A star shone down on him.

And then I knew, and the Many knew—
For they were the Many, not the few—
What star had led him on;
For out of the mist
The Communist
Was walking toward the Dawn![26]

Communist commitments grounded Hutchins and Rochester's personal relationship as companions and lovers. They worked together as comrades, side by side in the struggle for a Soviet America. Friends admired the couple for this strong committed relationship, happy that Hutchins and Rochester were so seemingly compatible and that each was there for the other. Friends often referred to the vitality and energy that Hutchins and Rochester showed, for life, and for each other, noting how this vitality was rooted in their politics and the shared commitment the two had for their work.[27] Indeed, their relationship was integrally tied to this work; it seemed inseparable. Even the snippets of romantic verse that the two wrote for each other were framed in terms of communist commitments,

> Warm heart, clear brain,
> Straight-back, no pain
> Friend to many, loved by all
> Spring of youth,
> Tho' nearly sixty, heeds the call
>   of truth
> And struggle
>   Dear Grace,
>   Beloved Grace[28]

Rochester wrote this little poem on the occasion of her "precious pard's" birthday. A small inscription in Rochester's handwriting on the back of this card also read, "For Papa's birthday." This may have been a spontaneous private joke between them or it could have been a pet name Rochester was accustomed to using for Hutchins. If the latter, it is somewhat incongruous given that it is Rochester, not Hutchins, who seems to come across as the more "masculine" partner, suggesting that things are not always what they seem. Whether Rochester thought of Hutchins as "Papa" or not, she did think of her partner as her "alter ego" and rejoiced in her love and admiration for her. Hutchins always responded by exclaiming how her love for her partner deepened as the years went by.[29]

While this emotional support helped undergird their political work, it also helped Hutchins deal with the deaths in her family: Edward Sr. in 1929, Edward Jr. in 1937, and then, in 1942, the death of her mother. On September 20, 1942, Susan B. Hutchins died in a Boston hospital following a broken hip after a fall at "Fir Cones," the summer house in Castine, Maine, a week earlier. Hutchins rushed to be with her mother and spent agonizing days watching her mother's health deteriorate. Especially distressing was the deterioration of Susan's mental condition as she relived in her mind the death and

---

Research diary: September 11, 1998: "[This inscription] to Papa really stumped me and makes me rethink how I have subconsciously gender-typed them. Anna's more retiring nature and her scrupulous detailed work on statistics in such trades as mining and finance etc. has [led me to] type her as more masculine than Grace whose specialty was women and work, who did special little things for her partner, and thought of herself as impulsive."

funeral of her two small daughters in 1887 and the accident that took her youngest son fifty years later: "Such tragedy in her face and words."[30] Hutchins shared the routine of these days in a letter to her partner:

> I have my hands full. We get to the Hospital before 10, stay 'till one, go home for lunch for an hour; back 'till 6.30, and then over here again in the evenings, with Henry. Obviously I can't leave 'till she is out of danger and things running more smoothly for the nurses. They have a battle to get her to eat anything. Mother has a few lucid moments, but mostly not.[31]

The next letter to her "Beloved," written later that same evening, was more optimistic as Susan seemed to be doing a little better. However, she took a turn for the worst and died within the next couple of days. Hutchins's reconnection with her family responsibilities aroused the fear for Rochester that her partner's choice of lifestyle and independence from her family might possibly be something she regretted. Hutchins emphatically quelled these fears:

> No dearest Anna, I do not for a moment regret my independent life. Mother came to understand it and herself, thought it better all around. Even the relatives and friends understand it now and think it quite natural in my case that I do not live in Boston. Of course nothing in the world would make me change or regret our precious partnership—life itself to me.
>
> Your own loving—Grace[32]

Friends rallied around Hutchins and offered their condolences during this difficult time. There are no personal entries in her notebook between 1941 and 1945, a fact that may or may not be related to this event in her life; the gap here gives no insight as to how she weathered the period. Old friend Mother (Ella Reeve) Bloor with Elizabeth Gurley Flynn, Elizabeth Johnson, and Clara Bodian wrote a letter and signed themselves "your own loving pals," letting Hutchins know how much they were thinking of her during this difficult period. But it was their knowledge that she was a "true Bolshevik" that encouraged them to know that ultimately she would soar beyond her grief:

> At this moment I would like so much to talk to you and if possible see or do something that could help you, but I know that you are a true Bolshevik and will keep *right on going* and in the "going," and in the work you will find the only solace that could possibly be yours. [original emphasis][33]

Mother Bloor was the oldest member of the CP National Committee and a strong influence in the Party. She lived at April Farm in Coopersburg, Pennsylvania, and corresponded with Hutchins and Rochester over the years.[34] She usually signed her letters to her "dearest faithful comrades" from "lovingly, Mother."

Rulers of America

In 1936 Rochester published her most widely acclaimed and most-cited book, *Rulers of America: A Study of Finance Capital*, updated in 1946 in a second edition. Completed after many years of painstaking research, it was interest aroused from this book that influenced a massive federal research project ordered by President Roosevelt.[35] That Rochester wrote this and subsequent

Anna (c. late 1930s).

texts under the auspices of the LRA, dedicated to gathering and interpreting economic data for the labor movement, rather than through an affiliation with a major academic institution with all the privileges and distinctions of an academic home, illustrates Rochester's commitment to applied knowledge, knowledge that could be used by ordinary people to advance their interests. No doubt she understood how the academy was tied to the interests of capital, and perhaps this explains why she never returned to university to claim the degrees she could so easily have acquired had she been interested. Instead Rochester spent her days at a desk in the New York Public Library.

Speaking at a publishers' dinner shortly after the publication of *Rulers of America*, Rochester acknowledged the book's fruition in "preparing the soil for vigorous revolutionary consciousness."[36] It followed Lenin in arguing that a key aspect of capitalist development was the creation of huge monopolies or finance capital representing the merging of banking and industrial interests. The exportation of capital worldwide paralleled this hegemony, encouraging war and global suffering. However, the insatiable drive for profit meant that monopolies would be unable to coordinate activities and competition would ensue. Contradictions inherent in the progress of capitalist development would mean that the rulers would be unable to control the mechanisms they created, encouraging their use of fascist propaganda to have some measure of control over the masses. In this way, Rochester was particularly interested in the structure of finance capital as a stage of capitalist development and its effects upon everyday life in the United States. Written during the Great Depression years, this book helped explain the apparent decay of capitalism and the growth of fascism.

A key aspect of *Rulers of America* was the intricate documentation of financial empires in the United States. Rochester elaborately documented the assets of J. P. Morgan, the Rockefellers, and the Mellons, emphasizing the ways that finance capital ruled industry, controlled the government, and affected the livelihood of the proletariat:

> As the wealth of the capitalists—both large and small—is piled up by their robbery of the working class, so luxury in a capitalist country is directly related to the poverty and misery of the masses. In the crisis and depression, while the total incomes of the wealthy have been reduced, they are still maintaining their great estates and their expensive cars. They are traveling at will and enjoying the best medical care, *because* they have passed on the burden of the crisis to the working class. [original emphasis][37]

Rochester reviewed such selected industries as steel, railroads, oil, and agriculture and expanded on the current crisis in capitalism. These problems intrinsic to capitalist development, she suggested, were paralleled by another great inner conflict: the sharpened political conflict between the

Research diary: September 20, 1998: "My first thought on reading *Rulers of America* was how such an incredible treatise as this should have become so obscure. During all those years in graduate school when I read Domhoff and others on the topic of ruling elites in the United States, I had never heard this book discussed or seen it tucked away in a footnote somewhere. Interesting how I believed New Left scholarship on ruling elites was mostly original."

capitalist class and the working class. This conflict was exacerbated by New Deal measures "which were frankly aimed to bolster up the capitalist structure and the upper groups of farmers."[38] Since this extensive book was written during the Third Period years, though published just at the beginning of rapprochement with other progressive groups, it carried the orthodox critique of liberal policies as an appeasement for the masses designed to prevent revolutionary mass action. However, unlike the various pamphlets written during the early thirties, this book has a scholarly feel and intent and there is no mass call to join the Communist Party or comparison with life in the Soviet Union. Perhaps these were removed right before publication to reflect changing CP policy. Indeed, even though "the economic structure of capitalism is decaying" and its "historic function is completed,"[39] a revolution, she felt, would not occur in the United States unless it became impossible for the ruling classes to maintain their power unchanged, the wants and suffering of the masses became exceptionally acute, and they were unwilling to be robbed without protest. She agreed that capitalist relations in the United States had not yet reached this stage of crisis and that the rulers of America were still secure in their power. "But present trends foreshadow a revolutionary crisis at some future date."[40]

Rulers of America sold very well and the book went into its second printing within three months. Reviews were for the most part glowing. Even those who found the book too polemical had to admit that it was very well written and painstakingly researched. The *Daily Worker* review by Louis F. Budenz was of course very positive: "[H]er book, based on *economic facts* provides us with ammunition for the battle which we must wage" [original emphasis].[41] Reviews in the *Nation* and the *Communist* gave similar praise.[42] Likewise, Rochester's friend Winifred Chappell writing for the *Christian Century* found the book superb, touching "the daily lives of all of us intimately."[43] Professor Colston E. Warne of the Economics Department of Amherst College called it "[t]he most penetrating analysis of the financial groups that rule America that has yet appeared," while the *Book Union Bulletin* declared it the Book Union choice for February 1936. Even the *New York Post* recommended it as one of the best books that deserved reading.[44]

Several reviews were less positive. The *Saturday Review* accused Rochester of handling her material with "an intemperate emotionalism that prohibits any scientific spirit of inquiry," adding that she eagerly overused the word "notorious" and saw "the capitalist evil only in the oversimplified, melodramatic terms of a physical devil with horns, tail, and pitchfork."[45] The review continued with the assertion that Rochester misused the term "Rulers" since her research implied influences rather than oligarchy. It claimed she had been asked about the choice of using "Rulers" and had replied "with the amazing answer that she had to have a title."[46] Rochester could not resist responding to such bad press that characterized her in a personalized way. In a letter to the editor Rochester disputed his facts and wrote harshly of someone who could so easily misquote from a personal conversation. "I did not fully realize that when he had asked for an interview he was really looking for any stick to beat the dog!"[47] Rhetorically sharp-witted, Rochester usually got the last word.

A similar event that occasioned another quick response from Rochester occurred with a review in the *New York Herald-Tribune*. V. D. Kazakevich, an economist at Columbia University, reviewed *Rulers of America* for this newspaper. He critiqued her statistical analyses and the instability and omission of data concerning certain financial fortunes. He also remarked that the text was strongly reminiscent of Lewis Corey's book *The Decline of American Capitalism* published in 1934: "The arrangement of the text, and especially of the reference notes, is strongly reminiscent of the methods used by Lewis Corey, who deals with a similar subject and covers essentially the same ground, although his name is not even included in the index."[48] This review so upset Rochester that she responded to Kazakevich in a letter to the editor of the *Herald-Tribune*. She accused Kazakevich of trying to discredit the book as a conscious and poor imitation of Corey and protested this by pointing out the differences between the work as well as emphasizing that the outline for *Rulers of America* was worked out early in 1932, several years before the publication of Corey's text. She had not, she retorted, even read Corey's book.[49] This latter admission was illuminated again in a letter, invoked as a "peace offering" from Kazakevich to Rochester, where he emphasized that he did not imply plagiarism on her part. In this letter he recounted a conversation with Rochester's LRA colleague Bob Dunn where the latter also told him that Rochester had avoided Corey's work deliberately. Kazakevich stated that he thought this quite extraordinary.[50] Interestingly, I found a slip of paper attached to the clipping of the *Herald-Tribune* review with the short typed statement: "I was so afraid of being drawn into dependence on Corey's book that I have never read it!!"

This admonition on the part of Rochester is very curious. It *is* extraordinary that a scholar would deliberately avoid a text that promised to address similar issues. You would expect a reading and integration motivated at

It is easy to make too much of this revelation since it shows a chink in Anna's competent veneer. Indeed this note was typed and unsigned and it makes me wonder why Anna would go to the trouble of attaching this (if she was the one who did it), except to go down in posterity as not having plagiarized Corey's book. This admonition reveals a vulnerability on Anna's part that surprises me and makes me wonder about her thoughts and motives at the time. It could have been added years later to set the record straight or it might have been attached in the mood of the moment when Anna was embarrassed at being accused of copying Corey's work.

most by an intellectual curiosity concerning the analysis of such issues covered, at least by a fear of intellectual embarrassment and omission should crucial concepts be missed. Rochester's deliberate avoidance might have come from some notion of intellectual purity whereby original ideas ought to pour forth untainted by competing thought, perhaps facilitated by her many years as an independent scholar. Another explanation is that Rochester was so engrossed by an ownership of this work that she did not want to think about anyone writing and publishing a similar tract after the bulk of her work was done, yet before her book was published. It would certainly have been somewhat of a blow to find such a similar book published at such a crucial time in the preparation of her own work. Ignoring it and remaining in denial about it would certainly be one way to deal with these anxieties.

Nonetheless, Rochester received much flattering personal correspondence concerning the book. Friends exclaimed that it was akin to birthing quintuplets, so astonishing and monumental was her accomplishment. Many wrote how proud they were of her and how excited they were to read the book.[51] Even Hutchins's mother sent Rochester a kind letter, astonishing in that someone seemingly so close in ideology to the rulers of America would so eagerly have endorsed the book. But Susan Hutchins's letter reveals less about whether she had actually read or approved of the book and more about her acceptance of Rochester as Hutchins's partner since she seemed to be proudly basking in the achievements of a family member.[52] With similar warmth, old friend Vida Scudder wrote that she was sending the book to the newly established library of the Helena Dudley Memorial Foundation at Denison House. Proud of her protégé despite the difference in political ideology between the two, Scudder wrote that she must tell of her admiration, awe and gratitude concerning this "splendid and noble and immensely valuable thing."[53] *Rulers of America* was always remembered as Rochester's "crowning achievement"; it certainly was a monumental text that helped Rochester become recognized as one of the leading Marxist scholars in the country.[54]

Hitler–Stalin Pact

In 1936 the American Left had to explain the Moscow purge trials when Stalin systematically exiled and/or executed former Bolshevik leaders. However even this embarrassment and shock was preempted by a Nazi–Soviet pact signed by Hitler and Stalin in August 1939, bringing the end of the Popular Front and sending the CPUSA into disarray. Reeling from the news, yet still following Soviet-controlled Comintern directives, the Party scrambled to find an explanation. They reported that the Soviet Union had outwitted the bourgeois democracies and had signed a pact of nonaggression rather than mutual assistance, and, by doing so, had completed a masterful tactical strategy. Peggy Dennis, wife of CP leader Gene Dennis, explained that Party acceptance of this pact was rooted in the underlying belief that "the needs of the Soviet Union are paramount in the class struggle, that its leaders are always wiser than we."[55]

While the news of the Moscow purges and the Nazi–Soviet pact must have rattled them, like Dennis and other comrades, most likely Hutchins and Rochester believed the means were worth the glorious ends. Indeed, Rochester's small book, *Capitalism and Progress* (discussed in the next chapter), explained the rationale for the pact. In a section on "Fascism or Democracy?" Rochester reported on the buildup to the war, the Soviet Union's warning to European nations about Hitler's aggression, and the responses of the "gentlemen at Geneva" who turned "deaf ears to the facts set forth by [Soviet] Maxim Litvinov"[56]:

> Meantime, France, Czechoslovakia, and the Soviet Union had signed mutual assistance pacts. But when Czechoslovakia was occupied by the Nazis, the French failed to act, and the Polish government's refusal to permit the Red Army to cross a strip of Polish territory cut off the possibility of aid from the Soviet Union. The solid front of capitalist powers against the socialist power was still unbroken. So the Soviet Union in August, 1939, protected itself temporarily by a non-aggression pact with Germany. This gave the Soviet people further time to develop their heavy industry and prepare for almost certain attack from the west. A week later, Hitler moved into western Poland, and as Polish resistance crumpled before the Nazi war machine, the Red Army moved into eastern Poland. This area was heavily populated by Ukrainians and Byelo-Russians who outnumbered the Poles. The people welcomed the Red Army as friends. Only the big land-owners and their associates resented it, and fled. Hitler, temporarily observing his non-aggression pact with the Soviet Union, took possession of western Poland and then marched west instead of east.[57]

Rochester emphasized the strategic and tactical aspect of Stalin's decision: the capitalist nations resisted Soviet help by disallowing passage through Poland, and the Soviet Union needed to temporarily protect itself in order to reorganize and arm itself for future conflict. And, importantly, on invading eastern Poland, the Red Army was welcomed, not feared. She continued, explaining that the Nazis swarmed over Europe and were welcomed by reactionary anticommunist fascists. Democratic forces, including the communists, set up underground resistance until in June 1941 Hitler invaded Soviet territory. This led to Churchill's decision to support the Soviet Union, the beginnings of U.S. involvement, and the Teheran pact in November–December 1943 between these nations.

The explanation held up, especially when juxtaposed with the imperialist motives for militarism among the allies that framed the war period. So strong was Hutchins and Rochester's faith in communism and their loyalty to the Soviet Union that when New Deal official Molly Dewson gave her lukewarm feedback to the couple concerning a pamphlet CP writer Alter Brody had written explaining the Soviet position on Soviet–Polish boundaries, they encouraged Comrade Brody to take this (anonymous) feedback from a "better than average liberal" in order to anticipate and preempt future "cynical tossing aside of the arguments." Their comments about the Soviet Union are also particularly revealing in this letter. Rochester shared the following with Brody: "I was a bit baffled by her [Dewson's] reaction. Of course *I* know that Soviet policy is not, and could not be, of the tricky, thirsty *facts*" [original emphases].[58] Always, the couple's political subjectivities were bolstered by "facts," or, at least, their interpretation of the facts that they seemed to sincerely understand as truth. Perhaps since they were such principled women with strong notions of integrity, they would have found it impossible to imagine anyone not acting with similar gestures of honesty and integrity.

Richard Crossman's anticommunist *The God That Failed* documents the thoughts of several ex-communist authors who came to revoke their communist affiliations. Commenting on the propensity of those involved in the movement to accept unsettling and often contradictory news, novelist Arthur Koestler described how the infallibility of the Party helped him make sense of contradictory information:

> Both morally and logically the Party was infallible: morally, because its aims were right, that is, in accord with the Dialectic of History, and these aims justified all means; logically, because the Party was the vanguard of the Proletariat, and the Proletariat was the embodiment of the active principle in History. Opponents of the Party, from straight reactionaries to Social Fascists, were products of their environment; their ideas reflected the distortions of bourgeois society. Renegades from the Party were lost souls, fallen out of grace; to argue with them, even to listen to them, meant trafficking with the Powers of Evil.[59]

Koestler explained that slanders, lies, intimidations and falsehoods were "so easy to accept while rolling along the single track of faith,"[60] especially

> How much of what we take to be a straightforward "objective" history of
> the CP is actually the result of rewriting the past in light of present disap-
> pointments and embarrassments acutely and personally felt by ex-partici-
> pants in the movement? As Avery Gordon has explained: "Reconstruction
> is American History, but it also must perforce be fashioned by people who
> unavoidably make their long or short way—who remember and forget—in
> the vortex of those spiraling determinations. The inevitable but intrusive
> presence of spiraling determinations creates the haunting effect but also
> sets limits on what can be remembered and what needs to be reckoned
> with now in the very charged present."[61]

when this faith was based upon the belief that a temporary suspension of
freedom enabling the Soviet Union to make rapid economic strides would
eventually be reversed.

In commenting on both the Moscow purges and the war pact, Peggy
Dennis echoed similar thoughts:

> We read of the public trials. True, we read in silence, puzzled and uncompre-
> hending, but we read the accounts and we accepted them. We saw it as part of
> the brutal realities of making revolution, of building an oasis of socialism in
> a sea of enemies. We accepted the belief in the infallibility of our leaders, the
> wisdom of our party. Facts and claims to the contrary were rejected as the
> very proof of that anti-Sovietism that demanded the vigilance Stalin urged.[62]

Since the CP wanted to keep the United States out of the war, a rush of
pacifist sentiment emerged as a strategy of the communist press. Needless to
say, the Party lost popular support, especially among Jews, some notable intellectuals, and many of the rank and file. Party leader Earl Browder was sentenced to four years in prison on a passport violation and other leaders such
as Clarence Hathaway and William Schneiderman were arrested for libel and
other charges. Hutchins and Rochester's faith in the Party seemed not to
waive. Incensed that Browder should be imprisoned this way, Hutchins used
her old ties with Polly Porter to gain access to the Roosevelts. Porter's partner Molly Dewson, who had now retired from public life, relayed a letter on
Hutchins's behalf to Eleanor Roosevelt in 1941 asking her to intervene in
Browder's prison term.[63] Later that year, without endorsing it, Dewson forwarded a petition to the Roosevelts asking that Browder be released from
prison by Christmas.[64] This also coincided with a letter from Rochester to the
president asking him to drop the deportation order hanging over Browder's
foreign-born wife.[65] During these tense years of the Hitler–Stalin pact,
Hutchins also showed her support for the Party by joining four other stockholders of the Daily Worker, the Party newspaper, when ownership of the
paper was passed to the Freedom of the Press Company. Later in 1951 when

ownership shifted to Publishers New Press Inc., again Hutchins was one of fifteen stockholders. In this way Hutchins used her inherited wealth to further the goals of the Party. The *Daily Worker* almost always toed the Party line and tended to be very pro-Soviet in its content.[66]

Meanwhile Rochester was still writing profusely. In 1940 she published *Why Farmers Are Poor: The Agricultural Crisis in the U.S.*, a text that reflected her interest in the transformations in industry and agriculture that had been taking place during the thirties. It explored how the ruins of the American farmer were tied to the progress of capitalism and called for cooperation between farmers and wage workers. The development of global monopolies was paralleled by the rise of agribusiness in U.S. farming, a development that Rochester understood as having dire consequences on the livelihoods of the small independent farmers of the Depression era. No doubt motivated by their distressing plight, Rochester set out to explain their misery in the dynamic of capitalism:

> Starving sharecroppers and refugees from the Dust Bowl have been flashed on the newsreels and pictured in the tabloids. Homeless poor farmers in Oklahoma, trekking desperately to a worse poverty in California, have been immortalised by John Steinbeck in Grapes of Wrath. But publicity and literary immortality do not feed the hungry. The farm problem is both deeper and broader than anything newsreels and novels can convey. . . . To understand the farm crisis of the 1930s, which has persisted in spite of some "recovery" after 1932–33, we must have clearly in mind the trends and economic forces operating against the farmers before these years of crisis throughout the business world. Agriculture must be considered against its general background as part of the capitalist economy, for it is not subject to separate economic laws . . . farmers' problems are tied in with the problems of other classes exploited and impoverished by the present system. The long road toward a solution can be found by farmers only as they move in close cooperation with the working class.[67]

Accompanying Rochester's detailed exploration of the growth of capitalism in agriculture were census and government statistics concerning the size and distribution of farms in the United States, income data, output and product figures, employment statistics, working conditions, and the like. The book explored the growing proletariat of wage laborers on the land and described programs developed by the government to mitigate farmer problems. In this text, Rochester revealed her optimism in modern science and technology as positive forces to free humanity of all ills:

> Today we know that the world has land enough to produce, with the methods of scientific agriculture, an indefinitely expanding volume of grain and textiles and fruit and meat and milk. The fears of Maltheus and his followers are scarcely remembered except as one reminder of the long, difficult road that the human race has traveled.[68]

Even though Rochester appeared to have used Lenin's "Capitalism and Agriculture in the U.S." in preparation of her book,[69] the discussion of the Soviet Union as panacea is tempered. And, while it is critical of New Deal attempts for rural recovery, the particularly harsh judgments present in pre–Popular Front writings are absent. As one reviewer noted, her writings, despite being Marxist, were "documented and tempered."[70] It is probably no surprise that this text was published amidst the anxieties associated with the Nazi–Soviet pact.

In claiming Rochester as "one of America's most competent Marxist scholars," Lem Harris in a *New Masses* review gave the book a sound evaluation.[71] Likewise the *Daily Worker, Christian Century* and the *New Republic* gave positive reviews.[72] The scholarly journal *American Economic Review* even exclaimed that it had a "deserved place on the shelf of books well-nigh indispensable to agricultural economics."[73] Not surprisingly, the professor of political science who evaluated *Why Farmers Are Poor* in the *Bryn Mawr Alumnae Bulletin* was less positive in his evaluation, claiming that while it was timely and contained "great facts," these facts were "highly controversial."[74]

When Hitler invaded the Soviet Union in 1941 it allowed the CP to reaffirm its commitment to antifascism, join the war effort against the Nazis, and throw itself into a wartime unity that insisted on a no-strike pledge and ultrapatriotism. The latter was an ironic position of united front politics that alienated some militant trade unionists, among others.[75] Despite this ideological roller coaster and the disillusionment of key CP personnel, Party membership rose during the war. Public acceptance reached an all-time high, responsibilities associated with Party membership were much decreased, and important inroads were made into Congress of Industrial Organizations (CIO) labor unions. So strong was the tendency for national unity and pro-democratic front policy during this period that General Secretary Earl Browder, released from prison on a special pardon, even encouraged an astonishing resolution to dissolve the Party in favor of a political pressure group called the Communist Political Association in May 1944. Policy now again demanded peaceful collaboration with progressive groups.[76]

> Grace and Anna had moved along the ideological spectrum through their years in political work, so perhaps these shifts of the thirties and forties were relatively easy for them to handle. Or, perhaps privately they experienced great angst concerning this ideological roller coaster. Did they have doubts about Party policy? Did they lose respect for Party officials during these times? Was the record wiped clean for them in the writings that have survived?

It must have been a great relief for Hutchins and Rochester to be able to drop their defensiveness and experience some synchronicity between their politics on fascism and popular opinion concerning the Nazi threat. However, again, it was a stretch to move from a stance that proclaimed war as a maneuver for imperialist finagling, and as a stimulant for capitalist production, to one that embraced the military effort. Their stance here though was less pro-war and more antifascist, and, even as the couple declared the most important issue at hand to be the defeat of the Nazi regime, they were also quick to criticize and point out how corporate profits increase during war time as well as the consequences of "guns before butter."[77] Since they had moved away from their pacifist leanings over a decade ago and now understood that violent revolutionary activity was a necessary part of the eventual creation of a socialist state, so the abhorrence to war as an act in and of itself that came across so strongly in their earlier Christian socialist writings dissipated.

United Front Writings

LRA work was booming during this period of collaboration and both Hutchins and Rochester reported in various correspondences to friends that the *Labor Fact Books* and other writings were all-consuming. By this time they had acquired "Little Acorn," a cottage on Mount Airy Road in Croton-on-Hudson, and were able to spend summers there away from New York City, gardening as time allowed. But they diligently worked on their writing at home and commuted into the office during the week; always their work was a top priority in their lives. The LRA came out with three *Labor Fact Books* between 1941 and 1945, all extensive texts packed full with information about legislation, and labor unions, statistics concerning working conditions during wartime, and constant updates on the fight between fascism and democracy. Volume six of the series was subtitled "Labor and War" and gave an extensive overview of economic trends and social conditions during this "gigantic world struggle."[78] While the staff of the LRA worked to produce these texts with help from volunteers in labor unions and other organizations around the country and abroad, the sheer amount of data they collected and were able to summarize and present in accessible ways was incredible. Hutchins and Rochester's productivity during this period was amazingly high.

During the war years Hutchins wrote numerous book reviews for the LRA publications *Economic Notes, Labor Notes,* and *Railroad Notes,* and for the *New Masses* and various other progressive newspapers and magazines.[79] She kept a running list in her notebook of all books she read and reviewed: she was astonishingly productive. As an expert on East Asia, she was especially asked to review new books that focused on Chinese and Japanese his-

I hope I haven't shortchanged Grace in putting the voluminous number of reviews she wrote in the endnotes. I also know that this list is not exhaustive and there are no doubt other pieces out there I have not found. Unlike Anna, Grace seemed to have been more comfortable writing short, pithy pieces rather than long treatises. What this meant though was that the scope of her scholarship had to be very broad and she must have been well versed in the cutting-edge texts of the day in labor and economic issues.

tory and politics, thus providing her with the format for political commentary concerning these nations.[80] In late 1941, published in a timely fashion after the bombing of Pearl Harbor, Hutchins wrote the pamphlet "Japan Wars on the U.S." Here she outlined the choices between the Allied forces of democracy and the Axis powers of fascism, emphasizing that "Japan's blow at this country parallels Nazi Germany's attack on the Soviet Union."[81] An earlier pamphlet, "Japan's Drive for Conquest," had provided the groundwork for this country's "menacing imperialist advance."[82] Around the same time the LRA came out with "Wages and Profits in Wartime," which, although not explicitly authored by Rochester, seems to have been heavily influenced by her research and her prose.[83] Such wartime writings allowed the couple to wax eloquent on the Soviet Union and at the same time be in sync with U.S. popular opinion concerning the future of democracy.

In comparison to the scholarly *Why Farmers Are Poor* is Rochester's 1942 pamphlet published by Farm Research Inc., titled "Farmers in Nazi Germany." While selling as a five-cent pamphlet rather than a book, it had different rhetorical purposes, its tone is completely different, and its contribution to the war effort undeniable. By this time Hitler had invaded the Soviet Union and the CP was acutely anti-Nazi. This pamphlet was advertised as being based on firsthand "authoritative documentary evidence" that analyzed the step-by-step process whereby farmers are "subjugated under the yoke of fascism, family life destroyed, freedom crushed."[84] The following year Rochester wrote another pamphlet, "Farmers and the War," published by Workers Library. Like "Farmers in Nazi Germany" it sold for five cents and was aimed at educating the general rank-and-file trade unionist by providing a critique of capitalism's role in agricultural production as well as an encouragement for the war effort. Typically, it also followed a popular format by presenting a sentimental story: "As Peter, with his round white cap and flapping navy pants, stepped onto the bus and waved a final goodbye, his father's grim smile brought back memories of that terrible drought year when the boy was only 10 years old. . . ."[85]

Rochester's interest in agricultural economics peaked during this period with her *Lenin on the Agrarian Question*, published by International Publishers in 1942. Written during this period of CP popularity when the Soviet Union was considered a democratic ally, it again dared address the Soviet Union and emphasized this country's placement with the U.S. and European democratic powers against the forces of fascism.[86] This book placed Rochester squarely in the pro-Stalinist, anti-Trotskyist camp, toeing the Comintern line on Soviet policy. Her discussion here of Lenin's ideas that capitalism affects both agricultural and industrial relations and that there must be collaboration and unity between agricultural and industrial workers revealed her keen understanding and admiration for Lenin as a brilliant leader and theorist. Writing in an accessible prose heavy on sentiment that painted the Soviet Union in all its myriad glory, Rochester explained that "the Soviet countryside has risen in less than a generation from the depths of ignorance and poverty, in which little islands of 'progress' were supported by the crudest and most brutal exploitation, to the highest peak of agricultural development yet attained by any section of the human race."[87] Stalin was referred to as a reasonable and caring individual who responded to the necessity for agrarian collectivization with such words as: "We cannot carry on by simply ordering the peasants about. We must learn to explain patiently to the peasants the questions they do not understand. We must learn to convince the peasants, sparing neither time nor effort for this purpose. . . ."[88] Collectives were described in glowing terms and their modern scientific and technological achievements praised.

Lenin on the Agrarian Question began by tracing the history of Russian agriculture and the adoption of Lenin's agrarian program by the Russian Social Democratic Labor Party at the turn of the century. Describing the peasant revolts of 1905 and the 1917 October Revolution, Rochester outlined the decree that guaranteed the abolition of landed proprietorship, the "detour" that pulled back from directly bringing the peasants into the socialist economy, and then his push toward the collectivization of agriculture. Rochester acknowledged the "liquidation" of the kulaks, the better-off peasants who opposed this collectivization, and revealed how she dealt with this knowledge of Bolshevik brutality. Throughout the chapters leading up to the discussion of this agrarian collectivization, Rochester painted the kulaks as hostile to the working class and involved in illegal and unscrupulous trading against the poorer peasants. She explained that this liquidation was instigated locally and carried out by the peasants themselves. Rochester quoted Anna Louise Strong's International Pamphlet "Democracy and Dictatorship in the Soviet Union," which outlined this "removal."[89] Strong's work was widely quoted as a response to Bolshevik cruelty; it seemed to function as an "in-house" text referred to in order to dispel fears.[90] Rochester's brief treatment of this part of history, I believe, stemmed less from oversight and more from an intense faith in Soviet politics generally, and Lenin in particular.

Lenin on the Agrarian Question was no doubt well received by the (then unraveling) Comintern. Certainly the *Daily Worker* praised its contents, with reviewer Louis Budenz telling Rochester that he "stayed up so late [reading it] that I was reminded of the days when I used to read Sherlock Holmes after getting my schoolwork done."[91] The persuasive and accessible tone of this book seemed to tap into that stream of consciousness where Soviet life and policies represent one wonderful hope for the world; one great, glorious vision to stir the spirit of humanity. Ironically, the tone of the book was appreciated by a Bryn Mawr alumna reviewer, even though the content was less to her liking. She was particularly swayed by Rochester's "well-bred" prose that relied heavily on sentiment and sympathy (complete with British spelling), a gift from Rochester's aristocratic roots that facilitated her acceptance as a radical Marxist scholar among a less radical audience:

> Miss Rochester's sympathy with Lenin makes the reader feel that his ideas are being presented in the best possible way. Many partisan books, especially dealing with Soviet matters are strident in tone. This is not. I trust it is not "lese-communiste" to say it's extremely well-bred. I mean it as a compliment because I believe it makes a book much more effective.[92]

Before the war was over, International Publishers came out with yet another of Rochester's texts, *The Populist Movement in the United States*. The subtitle of the book summarized it: *The Rise, Growth, and Decline of the People's Party—A Social and Economic Interpretation*. This book more closely resembled an International Pamphlet in its length and relative lack of endnotes, sources, and appendixes. However, like the couple's other united front writing, *The Populist Movement in the United States* made the most of the mood of the times in riding the waves of popular support for communism, endorsing the political campaign of Henry Wallace (who in 1948 would run for president with the Progressive Party[93]), and framing populism as a foundation for the current anti-Nazi unity. In this book Rochester explained the ties between the (specifically American and appealing) Populist movement and socialism in the United States, legitimizing these movements in a broad-based, intrinsically American desire for individual rights and liberties. She wrote how the Populist movement was primarily a defensive organization of farmers and other small business interests against the advance of finance capital, and, in particular, the relentless expansion of the railroad industry.

In the last chapter she showed her communist colors, reflecting on potential drawbacks of a movement with deep traditions that might "seek a revival of the past instead of looking toward a creative future . . . looking backward and trying to restore the past is futile, if not positively harmful to human progress. . . . Only through social ownership, instead of private ownership, can the immensely valuable mechanism of industry and trade

Being English and used to switching between British and U.S. spelling in my research and in my own writing, I did not at first notice that *Why Farmers Are Poor* and *Lenin on the Agrarian Question* used British spelling. It wasn't until the various quotes I was using came up underlined on the computer spell-check system that I realized it. At first I thought it was because these were among her most scholarly texts; however, if that were the case, *Rulers of America* would also have followed this pattern and it did not. These particular books were not British editions either. Were Anna's roots so aristocratic that she had adopted such language use as an affectation of her scholarly self? I looked back through Louise Rochester's writings and she often used British spellings so perhaps this was the way Anna had been taught to write and it was less of a conscious affectation and more of a "natural" act for her. Then again, going through her documents I see her writing "labor" in her own handwriting without the "u." But if this language use was how she liked to present herself as a scholarly author, surely she would have understood the context of this choice? Why would she, as a communist intellectual, want to accentuate this aspect of herself?

be brought into the service of people as a whole. Only then can political freedom and equality become a reality in our complex society."[94] Two paragraphs on the politics and economics of Soviet democracy follow, but even these are foreshadowed, for Rochester, by the tempered statement: "[But] no responsible group within the United States would propose or support a minority move, an attempt to "set up" socialism before the majority of the American people desire it."[95] Rhetorically, this small book on the Populist movement is essentially populist; it sought to make no waves, only to work as part of the united front effort.

As loyal CP members, Hutchins and Rochester had accepted the various switches in ideology and policy required by Party directives, and had understood, no doubt, the wisdom of these changes. But I sense that this move toward collaboration sat more naturally with them and suited the couple better in terms of how I imagine them wanting to live their lives. Perhaps their acceptance of the strident, dogmatic Party line had been facilitated by the relative newness of their faith during the Third Period. At this time they would have been experiencing the rush associated with finding an ordered doctrine that suited their emerging radicalism just when events around them seemed to echo the direction of their politics. Whatever the motivations and feelings underlying their stance, the couple was certainly devout and committed as communist intellectuals. Their generous and principled lives meant that days were spent in service to the working class, again, a cause bigger even than their friendship.

CHAPTER NINE

WHAT'S PAST IS PROLOGUE

In June 1957 Grace Hutchins was a featured speaker for her fiftieth class reunion at Bryn Mawr College. She gave a short speech titled "What's Past Is Prologue," a quotation from Shakespeare's *Tempest* yet recounted in the speech as "You ain't seen nothing yet!" Hutchins spoke with optimism for the future and fond memories of the past; it is characteristic of her spunk and courage that she would frame history as a new beginning. She wove various classmates' accomplishments into her speech, mentioning herself only as someone who had spent the last thirty years assembling archives on labor and economic subjects. This reflected her grace and humility; no doubt it also represented her inability to speak of her politics and activism in the context of this gathering at that particular historical moment. Friends thanked her after the event, praising her talents in public speaking: "you certainly were most distinguished looking and had such a beautiful expression—full of love and sympathy. What a full life you have lived and how much you have given to others!"[1]

This reference to "love and sympathy" illustrates Hutchins's personal ethics of devotion that came through in her public persona. Those devotional years as a compassionate reformist, Christian, and Christian socialist grounded Hutchins's intense communist politics. Again, how similar was the cause, the devotion to the improvement of society, throughout this

> "No matter what evidence we have access to as biographers, the stories that we tell will always change over time because of our own changing histories and historical moments. Although we may recreate the lives of our subjects more clearly or fairly than they or their peers were able to, our portraits will always be unfinished."[2]

"Let biography be witness to history."[3]

ideological journey from Christianity to communism. It was the vehicle that changed. Yet even the various "vehicles" shared similarities. All demanded principled moral positions, utmost discipline and strong loyalties, and a certain amount of mysticism and sentiment that coalesced in idealism. All gave opportunities for community and solidarity and provided a structured system of authority that organized their lives. The Protestant ideal that there is glory in work and service and the emphasis on abstinence and frugality were central defining features in Hutchins and Rochester's orientation to communist practice. However, I do not sense that Hutchins and Rochester would have agreed with my focus on continuity. As communists they saw religious liberals as part of the problem, not the solution, and had little time for such bourgeois politics. I believe they saw a distinct juncture in their lives after 1927 when they joined the Party, understanding their former politics as examples of false consciousness. These tensions and contradictions account for the multiple and complex ways that Hutchins and Rochester constructed themselves as historical actors.

This sincerity and air of compassion, the almost poignant vulnerability that seems to have surrounded Hutchins in particular, were central components of their political loyalties. However, lest we forget, Hutchins was a major player in Old Left politics. She was no doubt connected to various communist front organizations and to the national leadership. My sense is that while she most probably was cognizant of a variety of communist operations at various levels, she was never put in a position where she might have been vulnerable to indictment. The closest she ever came was during the Alger Hiss trial described later in this chapter. Hutchins was of most use to the Party as someone "above board," with impeccable public demeanor, who could "pass" easily as the respectable, educated, wealthy upright citizen that she indeed was. Knowing Hutchins's substantial personal wealth, the Party would have been keen to always make sure that Hutchins was an independent player, unaffiliated with less secure operations so that she could function without incrimination. This appears to be the role that Hutchins played throughout her affiliation with the CP. Rochester was likewise positioned, although she was a less public person since she was best known as a scholar and writer.

Postwar Communism

At the height of united front politics that had placed the struggle between fascism and democracy as the central issue at hand, Rochester wrote the small condensed book *Capitalism and Progress*. The book reflected the spirit of Teheran where Churchill, Roosevelt, and Stalin pledged cooperation and visioned a period of postwar stability. This historic alliance took place during late November and December 1943; Rochester spent much of 1944 writing the book in time for its March 1945 publication. Unfortunately, as events would show, her timing with this book was a little late. No sooner did it come out than communist politics shifted, Browder and his visions of collaboration fell out of favor, and the Party moved on a more sectarian course under the influence of William Z. Foster. This would mean that the highly acclaimed *Capitalism and Progress* would be revised, expanded, "brought up to date,"[4] and renamed *The Nature of Capitalism* within a year. The revision that took place reflected CP movement away from united front strategy.

Capitalism and Progress is remarkable in being written from the perspective that capitalism, even though it included "serious maladjustments and poverty and crises," was overall a progressive development.[5] Exploring the defeat of fascism and the growth of democratic forces that included peaceful cooperation with the Soviet Union, amazingly Rochester held out the promise for the socially useful existence of U.S. capitalism:

> Capitalism has been, unquestionably, a progressive stage in human development. It has produced technical, physical possibilities for health and universal well-being. It has laid the foundations for further progress, by developing to a high degree the interdependence of human beings and arousing a positive sense of workers' solidarity. The very exploitation which has held the people in poverty while employers and investors piled up wealth has stimulated the people to organized creative activity.[6]

This "organized creative activity" was the socialist future Rochester believed would emerge as capitalism progressed: "the task of creative thinking and planning and organized effort [is] to drive the old capitalist machine toward the goal of popular abundance and fuller democracy."[7] Socialist democracy, she asserted, merely reflected a further development of democratic principles. This future was no longer exclaimed in the crisp, determined manner of earlier Soviet blueprints. In fact, quoting Earl Browder, she wrote that "obviously there can be no question of an immediate socialist solution in the United States":

> [T]here is no existing or potential majority now that can be united on a program of action based upon the socialist perspective for our country. . . . It is my considered judgment that the American people are so ill-prepared, subjectively, for any deep-going change in the direction of socialism that postwar plans with such an aim would not unite the nation but would further divide it. And they would divide and weaken precisely the democratic and progressive camp, at the same time uniting and strengthening the most reactionary forces in the country.[8]

This quote was from Browder's book *Teheran: Our Path in War and Peace,* a book that Rochester reviewed for *Soviet Russia Today.*[9] This Teheran alliance seemed to hold such great promise for Rochester: "The fire of war has revealed the unity of the Soviet people and has burned away the veil of hostile propaganda which concealed from most American eyes the reality of Soviet democracy."[10] That she could possibly have written (given some of her earlier, more polemical work) that the revolutionary movement to socialism should not be pushed because it would divide and weaken the democratic–progressive alliance, demonstrated the level of allegiance Rochester had with united front politics. Reviews of the book were good; lacking the radical stridency of much communist writing, it fit with the popular mood of the times and its short, condensed readability was much appreciated.[11] The *Daily Worker* applauded it too and went to lengths to explain how this small text fit into communist intellectual thought (lest anyone should think Marxism had sold out).[12] Many friends sent Rochester notes and letters thanking her for the book and exclaiming their praise of it.[13]

The Comintern had dissolved in 1943, a few months before the Teheran meeting, asserting that they could not determine policy and strategy for diverse movements operating under divergent conditions. The various communist parties around the globe were told to develop their own tactics based upon their unique situations. CP General Secretary Earl Browder still felt strongly for the spirit of Teheran and its united front cooperation and in his last political stroke he attempted the reorganization of the Party into the Communist Political Association. However his loyalty in supporting bourgeois democratic powers was cause for friction between him and the sectarian William Z. Foster. These antagonisms resulted in Foster writing a letter to the National Committee about Browder's disloyalty in February 1944, a letter that was later made public in 1945 by French communist leader Jacques Duclos, who was also harshly critical of Browder.

Hutchins and Rochester's placement within Party hierarchy would have put them in touch with Party infighting, although I believe Foster's letter

Research diary: October 17, 1998: "Wearying of this project, [it is] tedious, end notes are out of control. Worrying about mistakes and oversights—But when I'm not feeling overwhelmed by the sheer detail involved in this project I can enjoy the familiarity I now feel with Grace and Anna. At this point they feel like dead relatives I have loved. But the more I become absorbed with them, the more I don't want to disappoint them in the ways I have reconstructed their lives. They impress me, surprise and disappoint me—how much more complicated are/were their lives than I could ever have imagined. Now I've been thinking about separating from these two women after intense focus on their lives for the last couple of years."

did not go beyond the National Committee level until it was made public the next year.[14] However, given Rochester's loyalty to Party leadership, I would have expected her to support Browder based upon that loyalty. And in that support she was not alone. While historians of the Left have tended to privilege Party matters over movement issues such that this period is characterized by the disarray of Party factions and fissures at the leadership level, the movement was still intact at the level of the rank and file and no doubt Browder still solicited considerable grassroots support.[15] My gut feeling is that Rochester's loyalty to united front strategy was sincere and reflected her interest in populism. But, importantly, it also reflected her very strong allegiances to Party leadership and policy and, therefore, to Browder. His days in this role, however, were numbered.

Amidst public crisis about the direction of the Party, "The National Board's Resolution on the Present Situation and the Tasks Ahead" was reported in the *Daily Worker* on June 22 and an emergency convention officially rejected the national unity policy in favor of a more sectarian line. In the meantime Rochester had a letter printed in the *Daily Worker* that showed where she stood: she registered her support of the National Committee's new position.[16] Always publicly loyal to Party leadership and policy, Rochester agreed to this change and began a revision of *Capitalism and Progress*. Most likely she received subtle pressure from the Party that encouraged this task; I find it hard to believe that an author would voluntarily begin an ideological rewrite of a book just published, reinforcing the idea that she felt pressure to comply with policy and distance herself from Browder. But her compliance, I suspect, was another example of Rochester believing that the collective wisdom of the Party was more important than individual beliefs. She most likely also responded to the postwar winds of change that were sweeping the country after Roosevelt's death and Truman's accession to power; the coalition and spirit of collaboration would have obviously been wearing very thin in light of the demise of New Deal politics. In the meantime, after Browder continued to obstruct this new political line, he was expelled from the Party in February 1946, and Eugene

Was this revision an example of blind loyalty and would she have taken any stance, within reason, that the Party demanded? She disappoints me; I could imagine it impossible not to feel resentment about revising a just-published book because men at the top decided to change strategy. I will never know how she rationalized these changes in her mind and how her feelings about them were expressed in her relationship with Grace. Was it spoken? I might have this all wrong and perhaps she voluntarily decided to revise the book. Alternatively, maybe the pressure was not subtle at all and the Party demanded a revision.

Dennis replaced him as general secretary. Rochester's revised *The Nature of Capitalism* came out the month before, in January.

After its publication, *The Nature of Capitalism* replaced *Capitalism and Progress*, and references to the latter book were rarely made in discussions of Rochester's work. The major difference between them was that the former included a chapter titled "Socialism: The Next Step." Contrary to Rochester's earlier statement in *Capitalism and Progress* that "obviously there can be no question of an immediate socialist solution in the United States," in this chapter she declared that the "[o]bjective conditions are ripe for the next great step forward."[17] Praise of the Soviet Union then followed with discussions of the steady barrage of anti-Soviet lies rather than fires of war burning away the veils of hostile propaganda:

> One country in the world has advanced to Socialism. Its people are released from poverty and unemployment. And there no man or woman of normal vigor lives idly upon the fruits of other men's labor. But a steady barrage of anti-Soviet lies has concealed from most of the American workers the truth about that great nation.[18]

While Rochester again emphasized capitalism's role in progress, the "serious maladjustments" that were part of this progress in the earlier text became more serious problems and contradictions in the rewrite. And it was this aspect that the *Daily Worker* picked up on in their review of the text:

> Writing on the inner contradictions of capitalism Anna Rochester says: "Capitalism has shown itself essentially unable to relate our productive capacity to the needs of the population. It is unable to provide steady peacetime employment for all able-bodied workers. It is held back by chaotic production for profit and by the wasteful distribution of income to private owners of capital. Technically it has the possibilities of producing abundance for all. But its inner contradictions leave capitalism helpless before the problems of mass poverty and unemployment."[19]

This revised text reflected another new chapter in CP history.

McCarthy Years

Despite the fact that communism was still a vibrant aspect of many communities and continued to influence activism at the grassroots level in a variety of organizations, the CPUSA came out of the war years in relative disarray. The horrors of atomic warfare and Nazi camp experimentations showed that the Left could no longer hold heroic confidence in science, a key aspect of scientific socialism. Doubts about history's progress through science and about Soviet innocence shook the economistic Marxist approach at the same time that a growing mass commodity culture was altering the face of the working class. Even so, ideological problems tended not to directly affect the rank and file who participated in the communist movement at the level of the various front organizations like trade unions, choral societies, summer camps, and workers' education institutes.[20] What would go on to destroy this aspect of the movement would be important events mobilizing from outside.

In 1947 President Truman established a loyalty pact for government workers resulting in the investigations of thousands of federal employees and the hounding of thousands more from federal agencies. In addition, the Taft–Hartley anticommunist affidavits resulted in the removal of communists from the labor movement as National Labor Relations Board Services were denied to any unions not purged of these influences. Such developments were accompanied by congressional bills that limited labor's power and civil rights among workers. However, most notorious of these developments was the establishment of the House Committee on Un-American Activities, designated as a permanent committee in the House of Representatives in 1946. Charged with investigating subversive propaganda activities, it quickly became known as the Un-American Activities Committee (HUAC) for its ability to summon testimony and enforce its power through citations for contempt of Congress with a blatant disregard for due process and civil liberties. The HUAC relied upon the 1940 Smith Act for its punch, an act that made it illegal to teach, advocate, or encourage the forcible overthrow of the U.S. government.[21]

Abroad, Truman's policies envisioned the United States as hegemonic world leader. This "Truman Doctrine," the right of the United States to intervene militarily into other countries, the Marshall Plan, where the United States guided the economic and political development of European nations under the guise of reconstruction, and the North Atlantic Treaty Organization (NATO), which gave the United States various military bases and opportunities overseas, consolidated U.S. power abroad. While such events encouraged characterization of the United States as the only major imperialist nation, this position became increasingly difficult to maintain in light of Soviet expansion into Germany and the creation of a communist bloc out of Eastern European formerly independent nations. In addition, some Old Leftists were continuing to question CPUSA allegiance to the Soviet Union, especially those ethnic communists who were witnessing Soviet hegemony in their homelands. All this military expansion on the part of the United States and the Soviet Union set the stage for the Cold War that was right around the corner.[22]

In 1948 the Communist Party threw its support behind Henry Wallace as the Progressive Party candidate for president. However, two days before this third party opened its nominating convention in Philadelphia, several CP leaders where arrested for Smith Act violations. Peggy Dennis, wife of General Secretary Eugene Dennis, explained what happened next: "Newspaper headlines immediately linked the new third party to the arrested Communists and to the key words 'conspiracy' and 'force and violence.' Simultaneously Truman draped himself vigorously in the Roosevelt mantle and energetically wooed labor back into the Democratic fold."[23] Wallace suffered a broad defeat. The Communist Party, already weakened by its factions and fissions and impelled by Foster's hard-line tactics, moved to isolate itself from the rank and file and from progressive noncommunist allies within the labor movement. The red scare tactics and policies meant that individuals who accepted CP positions faced expulsion from the Congress of Industrial Organizations (CIO) which pushed labor leaders rightward. Constant government targeting of groups and individuals that made up the mass of movement organization decimated communist activity and put CP associations on the defensive, trying desperately to keep afloat and keep members out of jail. Throughout the late forties and through the fifties communist constituent organizations folded and recruitment became almost impossible; local governments and private institutions joined the effort, often out of misguided patriotism, and the Party and its affiliated array of mass organizations were thoroughly discredited and marginalized. This attack on the rank and file took an enormous toll and made the movement ineffective even though the Party itself was surviving. While much orthodox history of the CP has emphasized the internal and ideological struggles that decimated the Party, it is important to understand how the intense battering during the McCarthy years helped destroy the movement.[24]

The decade of the forties came to a close in the midst of mounting public hysteria about the "communist menace." The times created partisan hyperbole and paranoia as right-wing conservatives like Martin Dies, William Jenner, Karl Mundt, Richard Nixon, and the infamous Joseph McCarthy kindled public hysteria and went to all lengths to conduct inquiries about alleged communists and sympathizers. McCarthy was among the most die-hard of the anticommunist forces. In 1950, after he alleged that the State Department was riddled with communists, hearings were initiated to investigate the charges and his political career took off as chairman of the Senate Committee of Government Operations. His often wild unfounded accusations pro-

> It is important to remember that many orthodox Left historians have had trouble with this period, visited by ghosts, their own and others. For some, their disaffection with a politics with which they were once overwhelmingly committed has led them to braid together the unrealities of facts and the realities of fictions in making sense of the era. Many got burned by this period or lost their innocence, bitterly fashioning these "historical facts" through the dense narrative of personal experience.

Serious computer problems with this chapter. Ironically I get the following message on the screen that prevents me opening saved documents: "This program has performed an illegal operation and will be shut down." Does this have anything to do with writing a biography about lesbian communists?

vided a bizarre spectacle of vigilant anticommunism as he berated private citizens and violated civil liberties. Ex-communists Elizabeth Bentley and Whittaker Chambers were prominently featured as the HUAC began a series of hearings in the late forties against many former New Deal government officials who were alleged communists and/or Soviet spies. Chambers in particular was the prosecutor's star witness in the perjury trial against Alger Hiss, a high-ranking member of the State Department who was eventually found guilty. This case is detailed below since Hutchins figured somewhat prominently in Chambers's testimony. By this time Hutchins was well known as a Communist Party official and was listed in government documents as someone most likely to head communist front organizations.[25]

Nineteen forty-eight also saw the arrest of twelve communist leaders and members of the National Committee under the Smith Act. Each was individually charged with being a member of the CPUSA: an organization with intentions to teach and advocate the violent overthrow of the government.[26] The prosecutor's star witness here was ex-communist Louis Budenz, former editor of the *Daily Worker* and ex-colleague of Hutchins and Rochester. In October 1949 the expected guilty verdict on eleven of them was passed, and in 1951 the appeal was lost.[27] Events were moving quickly. As a new decade arrived, the Mundt–Nixon Bill and Internal Security Act created loss of citizenship and denial of passports for the "crime" of being a communist, and required the Party and its organizations to register with the Subversive Activities Control Board. Then the Supreme Court issued a blow by upholding the constitutionality of the Smith Act; seventeen CP leaders were arrested in the summer of 1951 on charges of violating the act. These events caused a profound constitutional crisis in the country; in particular, the constitutional right of defendants to bail became a major civil issue and one with which Hutchins would become intimately involved. Alongside the Smith Act defendants and the Hiss trial, Julius and Ethel Rosenberg were charged with atomic espionage and eventually executed for this crime in 1953.[28] Feigning a violation of tax laws, the *Daily Worker* and CP offices were seized in 1956 by Internal Revenue Service agents, even though the *Daily Worker* had filed complete tax statements yearly that had not been challenged.[29] The Labor Research Association also had its account books examined by the Bureau of Internal Security from 1951–1952.[30] The times were indeed very bleak as the communist movement, once a vibrant force in many communities, was being dissipated.

One of the ways Party leadership responded to these events was by adopting a "last-ditch-stand mentality," which came to be known as "five minutes before midnight."[31] One aspect of this was the creation of an elaborate underground apparatus to hide its cadre. The implication of this move was that instead of maintaining the fight for the legality of the Party and struggling for the constitutional and civil liberties that were being eroded by McCarthyism, the Party had been moved into illegality and only those above ground, like Hutchins and Rochester, were left to continue this fight. Public and above ground again in 1956, intense infighting between sectarianism and revisionism absorbed the Party, although a resolution from the National Committee that year under the leadership of Eugene Dennis "inaugurated a new phase in the struggle between sectarianism. . . . [A]dvances have already been made in unfreezing relations with important center forces in the trade unions, the Negro people's organizations and the communities, as well as in beginning to overcome the Party's extreme isolation in many fields."[32] This resolution was presented for discussion at the Party's National Convention in February 1957. When the National Committee drafted its resolution the news from the Twentieth Congress of the Soviet CP concerning Stalin's crimes had not yet come to light. Soviet Premier Khrushchev's denouncement of Stalin as an enemy of the people sent the Party into turmoil again: who could deny news from such a legitimate source?

Some reconciled Khrushchev's news and continued in the Party unified in their opposition to domestic fascism and anti-Soviet propaganda. Some left the Party but continued in the movement on a grassroots level. Others completely bailed out, horrified at these various turns of events. Of those who left, some became archconservatives who went on to make a living out of anticommunism. The Soviet invasion of Hungary in November 1956 had also caused members to leave and new lines to be drawn. By the end of the decade CP membership had dropped to an all-time low and Gus Hall replaced Eugene Dennis as general secretary. The changes away from isolationism proposed at the CP convention in 1957 were dissipated, and, again, the Party was back in the grip of sectarianism. Ironically, in the face of so much hostility from outside during the fifties, many were willing to support all kinds of misdeeds out of sheer conviction and desire for solidarity, and, in the process, perhaps masked serious miscalculations of CP leadership as well as Soviet motives.

Hutchins and Rochester stayed with the movement and with the Party. It is impossible to know how they responded to Khrushchev's announcement. My guess is that they were greatly disturbed but saw Stalin's crimes as evidence of individual pathology rather than as symptomatic of Soviet communism. I imagine them questioning Stalin's behavior rather than the nature of the system that produced it. Indeed, I suspect they saw Khrushchev's admonition as an expression of Soviet stability: an ability to admit errors, mend ways, create new hope, etc. And at this point I believe anything but loyalty to the Party would have been most unlikely. I do like to believe that they were in sync with *Daily Worker* editor John Gates, who was critical of the hard-line sectarians. Since Hutchins was a stockholder with the paper I assume she supported Gates, who had come of age politically during the Browder era. Paul Buhle writes that "for a moment between 1956 and 1958, the *Daily Worker* became a semi-independent player in the Left, condemning the Russian invasion of Hungary and defending dissent within the Party press."[33] Back copies of the *Daily Worker* reveal Hutchins and Rochester's silence publicly on these issues. I interpret this silence and past evidence of their support of Earl Browder and his politics to suggest that they may have been unhappy with another sectarian turn. However, at the same time, the couple had a long history of support for Soviet actions and politics. Given both these factors that posed a contradiction at least at this particular historical moment, silence was most likely an appropriate response on their part. On the other hand, silence is a tricky concept, and, rather than indicating support for Gates's revisionism, it might have suggested disagreement instead.

As Old Left loyalists, Hutchins and Rochester were among those who made links to the New Left by fighting for the civil liberties of political radicals and through their writing with the LRA. Unlike the roots of the Old Left, the New Left responded to an economic and sociopolitical context of affluence and alienation, disillusionment and powerlessness, and their driving force came from middle-class youth on college campuses.[34] Various factions of the New Left were united in their despair of American "democracy," imperialism abroad, and lack of civil rights for those at home. Commenting on this period, Diggins has noted that "the Old Left died when communist Russia failed to fulfill its prophecies; the New Left was born when democratic America failed to keep its promises."[35] While I believe he overstates his point concerning the Old Left in pinpointing its demise in its overreliance on the Soviet Union rather than also emphasizing the external factors of the McCarthy years that killed the movement, the New Left certainly came into being angry about the state of U.S. democracy.

Research diary: November 14, 1998: "Silences . . . everywhere I turn today there are silences. Tracking these silences gets lonely . . . it's the most difficult aspect of writing biography. I read somewhere that tracking silence is about struggling through the broad ensemble of cultural imaginings [created in] the gaps between this and that."

Whittaker Chambers and the Alger Hiss Trial

As the Republican-controlled HUAC facilitated hearings in August 1948 in the midst of mounting public hysteria about the "communist menace," allegations against several notable communists were made by Whittaker Chambers, a writer, a past editor of *New Masses*, and at that time an editor at *Time* magazine. He said he had worked for the Communist Party between 1924 and 1937 and named Alger Hiss, a high-ranking State Department official under the New Deal, as having also been affiliated with the Party.[36] While Hiss vehemently denied these allegations, a series of cover-up actions on the part of then Senator Richard Nixon, the Federal Bureau of Investigations and other agencies, resulted in Hiss's conviction on perjury charges. All this despite the fact that Chambers's testimony often bordered on the absurd and he was prone to changing his story many times.[37] Hutchins was featured during Chambers's initial testimony when he declared that as an ex-communist, he had had his life threatened by the Party. He stated that Hutchins had called at his brother-in-law Reuben Shemitz's office in April 1938 and she had told him that if he were to surrender to the Party, his wife and children would not be harmed. Hutchins's response was featured in several papers; here I quote the *Daily Worker*:

Quiet-voiced, Grace Hutchins branded as "another pumpkin"[38] the Whittaker Chambers' charge that she had threatened his life. In 1938, Miss Hutchins, 63 year-old editor at Labor Research Association, denied the latest hare-brained story as "categorical nonsense," and noted that "it must be that he is losing his mind. . . . It is the most ridiculous thing" she said. "I categorically deny it, I haven't seen Mr. Chambers for at least 11 years, perhaps 12 or 13. . . . I'm a white-haired woman of 63, but I'm not in the habit of threatening anyone. . . . " The news that Miss Hutchins might threaten anyone's life was met in many circles yesterday with considerable surprise and laughter. Her mild-mannered appearance and unperturbably sweet disposition belie the charge. The pudgy Chambers is no intellectual match for the brilliant Miss Hutchins, whose life has been devoted to the cause of bettering the life of people everywhere. Chambers' attack on Miss Hutchins is part of his mosaic of tales.[39]

Newspaper articles at the time explained that Hutchins knew Chambers's wife, Esther Shemitz, when Shemitz was advertising manager of the *World Tomorrow* magazine. Shemitz had asked Hutchins and Rochester to be witnesses for her marriage to Chambers in 1931, and indeed, according to Chambers, they had given the newlyweds their only wedding present, an electric toaster.[40] It was reported that Hutchins said she visited Reuben Shemitz's office to find out the whereabouts of her friend Esther, from whom she had not heard for quite some time.[41]

However, in 1967 psychiatrist Meyer A. Zeligs published a book that quoted Hutchins giving another story. *Friendship and Fratricide: An Analysis of Whittaker Chambers and Alger Hiss* painted Chambers as a delusional man whose adult behavior was caused by a variety of infantile neuroses linked to his childhood. Zeligs said his account of Hutchins's testimony was based upon interviews with her in 1949, 1951, and 1957, and reported her saying that Chambers had visited her office in 1932, telling her he was doing "highly specialized underground work."[42] She was said to have explained that she was completely taken in by Chambers and did not ask any questions, but understood that the real reason for his visit was to borrow $50 to have his teeth fixed. "Miss Hutchins recalled that his teeth were abominable and Chambers told her that the importance of his work demanded that he make a good appearance."[43] They made plans to meet for lunch so that Hutchins could deliver the money. The visit to Reuben Shemitz, she explained (which she thought was in 1937, not 1938), was an attempt to collect the money that Chambers owed her. Zeligs ended his discussion convinced of her innocence: "Thus Chambers imposed himself on Miss Hutchins. By using real people and real events as material, he fused fact and fantasy. His purpose was to convince the reader, as he was convinced, that the Communist Party clearly intended to kill him."[44]

This story (assuming of course that Zeligs reported it accurately) puts Hutchins's earlier motive for the visit to Shemitz's office into question. It is odd that the story inquiring about Esther Shemitz did not come up in Zeligs's account. I can understand the omission of the loan in the public account of 1948, but wonder why there was no mention of the friendship with Esther in Zeligs's account. Zeligs himself could have omitted it, Hutchins could have decided not to stick with this story anymore, or she might have forgotten that this had been her original story when interviewed in 1957, although these last two seem unlikely. Either way, it is difficult to imagine that Hutchins was motivated to go to so much trouble by a five- or six-year-old debt of only $50, even though she was principled enough to expect payment when it had been agreed upon. It would make sense that she suppress the knowledge that she was intimate enough with Chambers to have lent him money in order not to incriminate herself and

Research diary: November 14, 1998: "I laughed when I read the phrase 'Miss Hutchins recalled that his teeth were abominable,' imagining Grace saying 'abominable' in her refined accent. . . . Really torn about this incident. I can't help but believe Grace—but I think her protestations only concern being accused of threatening Chambers—and she's silent on the rest. . . . But how could you not believe this sincere, principled woman? [She] could easily have snowed me."

the Party concerning underground activities during the Hiss trial. And, since she had indeed been close to Esther Shemitz and she probably was concerned about her well-being, this reason she gave for the visit was most probably not too far from the truth, or at least her truth as she reconstructed the event given the situation of the Hiss trial. My sense is that Hutchins was most likely involved with Party underground operations and had gone to see Reuben Shemitz on Party business. But Chambers probably *had* borrowed money from her, she *was* concerned about Esther, and Chambers's assertion of her threatening him was most likely a figment of his disturbed mind. As a result, Hutchins's denial was honest and her astonished response authentic. Her public conduct during this trial was, as always, impeccable. I assume she knew much more than she told and crafted her story carefully to contain the elements of truth associated with her relationship with Chambers. Revealing these pieces of truth and keeping silent about other things would have allowed her to indeed present herself the way she did. I do find it hard to believe that Hutchins threatened Chambers in the way he reported and imagine these accusations most likely as reflecting Chambers's instability. But I may be taken in by Hutchins's remarkable cover: her class privilege, genteel bearing, and advanced age which so effectively allowed her to deny Chambers's allegations of threats and put his story in doubt: "I'm a white-haired woman of 63, I'm not in the habit of threatening anyone."[45]

The public aspect of this trial no doubt took its toll with the constant harassment of CPUSA members leaving Hutchins and Rochester feeling vulnerable. Both were under considerable stress. A month before the story on the Hiss trial broke, Hutchins penned a letter to "Anna darling," concerned about what she saw as her partner's "constantly anxious, worried expression." Referring to Rochester's back problems, Hutchins most likely was also worried about the general stress in their lives. In this letter she pleaded with her partner to make some changes in her life: "What troubles me so deeply is that your eyes, your whole face, and your carriage speak of a *tiredness* that might easily result in more serious difficulty . . . *please, please,* [double underlined] accept suggestions so that your anxious, troubled, worried expression changes to a more calmly confident one."[46] In April of that year a raid on a Communist Party meeting in Rochester, New York, had resulted in the burning of books. Among those burned was *The Nature of Capitalism.* This event encouraged several newspapers to comment on the irony of the burning of the writing of the great granddaughter of that city's founder, Colonel Nathaniel Rochester.[47] Rochester was featured again in 1953 after she was subpoenaed as a witness to give public testimony before Senator McCarthy's hearing on the use of communist authors in an overseas information program.[48] At one level I can imagine Rochester and Hutchins interpreting these harassments as evidence that they were at the cutting edge of radicalism and perhaps the attention they received was enjoyed as a mark of their commitment. However, at the same time these were the kind of events that must have exhausted the couple in many ways. Such stresses no doubt motivated the following statement by Hutchins that was written in response to Chambers's allegations:

> My personal difficulties have not really mounted to much. I have had no repercussions (as yet!) from the absurd and outrageous statement by Whittaker Chambers.... All that Drew Pearson said of him over the radio, national hook-up, was really true. He (Chambers) was, probably still is, a homosexual pervert, a psychopathic case, who was in an asylum for mental cases for quite a period of time. Just why Chambers wanted to bring me into the picture, I can't understand. However, he was feeling rather desperate that day, expecting to be indicted for perjury, as he should have been. He wanted to spring a new sensation, partly in order to hold the newsmen's attention, they say, while his wife escaped downstairs, and partly to show that he really was married (me as a witness) and therefore not quite as disreputable as people were saying.[49]

That Hutchins could so vehemently call him a "homosexual pervert" given her own relationship with Rochester reflected her acceptance of romantic friendships like her own as distinct from the activities of "homosexuals." She no doubt saw her long-term, committed, and very proper relationship with Rochester as completely different from the casual liaisons Chambers was said to have had with men.[50] Most likely her denial also reflected general CPUSA discomfort with homosexuality, and, in addition, since the government openly linked gay and communist activities, it would have behooved her to distance herself as much as possible from this issue and perhaps explained her choice of words in this statement.

In 1952, Chambers published his book *Witness* and reiterated in more detail a series of allegations against Hutchins. Again she declared her innocence by writing a letter to the editors at Random House, the press who published *Witness*, denying these allegations. "This is absolutely false, without the slightest basis of fact," she declared.[51] In *Witness* Chambers had named her as a loyal communist in touch with many underground operations. He had also

---

This typed statement is interesting because its original circulation is unknown. The fact that it was typed suggests a relatively formal readership for wider circulation, although its somewhat intimate style suggested an address to friends. At the top of the page in capitalized typed font was "Not for Publication," a statement that made me hesitate before sharing here. But of course this context does not have the same meaning as it might have when Grace feared being dragged deeper into the fray concerning Chambers's allegations and having her words misunderstood or misquoted.

> Research diary: November 14, 1998: "[I find myself quite] defensive reread-
> ing Chambers's assertions about Grace [and] feel the poignancy of his at-
> tempts at humiliating her. . . . I feel embarrassed for her. This [reopening of
> the Hiss trial spectacle] must have caused her much distress."

relished making fun of Hutchins, playing on the irony of her bourgeois, high-
brow origins against her commitment to the lowly rank-and-file masses. Describing her manner in the meeting with his brother-in-law where he said
Hutchins threatened him, he wrote that "grand manner is second nature to
Miss Hutchins, a fact which has long made her a butt among more self-con-
sciously proletarian levels of the Communist Party. But it also serves the revolution." And, in describing the drama of the encounter he wrote, "And its
bad melodrama is saved by a comedy, at once low and touching, because the
emissary, Miss Hutchins, even in the moment of trying to make a deal, can
not quite throw off the traditions of a gentle past which have become a part
of her."[52]

All these attacks required energy and defensive posturing on the part of
Hutchins and Rochester. Friends rallied around and sent words of support
and solidarity. Old friend Sally Cleghorn wrote of her love and admiration
for both her friends and characterized the whole Whittaker Chambers af-
fair as "a miserable piece of persecution."[53] And, as always, Hutchins and
Rochester had each other for support and consolation and no doubt their
relationship, which was founded and which flourished on their political
commitments, helped them weather these difficult times. The following
verse illustrates this:

> In storm and sunshine
> —and in *storm*, I come
> under your umbrella!
> How I *do* love you
> more and more as years
> go by.[54]

The couple also had the friendship of Lucie Myer, who lived with them on
and off for several decades. While very little is known about her, Myer
seemed originally to have come from Baltimore and did spend time there
when she was not living with Hutchins and Rochester. So close were
Hutchins and Myer that they had a joint savings account in 1960, although
this might have represented Hutchins's benevolence as much as their friendship. I know a favorite activity for Hutchins, Rochester and Myer was reading aloud and that they read a great many books together this way. In fact,
Hutchins's notebook lists the books she read over the decades between 1941

> Lucie Myer is an enigma. She is always mentioned indirectly in terms of her various minor illnesses or her presence in the apartment. I have found almost nothing written by her or written to her. She just seems there, in the background. After Anna died in 1966 she is not in the picture anymore, since then Grace lived alone with a housekeeper. No doubt Lucie would have some interesting insights and wonderful stories to tell. I entertained the outrageous thought at one point that maybe Lucie Myer was a member of the CP underground with her own set of assignments, and Grace and Anna's memoirs were careful not to contain anything incriminating about her life. This is difficult to imagine since they appear such innocuous, refined maiden ladies.

and 1964. A bulk of the reading was done aloud with Rochester and Myer.[55] No mention is ever made about Myer's politics; most likely she was a "fellow traveler" who endorsed the Party but was not officially involved with it. Good friend and LRA colleague Bob Dunn and his wife Slava (whom Hutchins and Rochester affectionately called "Mrs. Bob")[56] also lived next door to them at their Bedford Street apartment, so Hutchins and Rochester enjoyed a small community of like-minded friends and neighbors.

To Labor

> The world's life hangs on your right hand,
>   Your strong right hand,
>   Your skilled right hand,
> You hold the world in your right hand,
>   See to it what you do.
>   Or dark or light,
>   Or wrong or right,
>   The world is made by you.
>
> Then rise as you never rose before
>   Nor hope before
>   Nor dared before,
> And show as was never shown before
>   The power that lies within you.
>   Stand all as one
>   See justice done
>   Believe, and Dare, and Do![57]

These stanzas from the poem "To Labor," by Charlotte Perkins Gilman, were sent out to friends and colleagues as part of Hutchins and Rochester's Christmas greetings in 1949. They were also pasted into Hutchins's notebook, probably in the New Year 1950. "To Labor" summarized their com-

Anna, a friend, and Grace. Perhaps the
friend is the elusive Lucie Myer (c. early
1930s).

mitment to social change and served as motivator for maintaining the fight
in the midst of this bleak period in Left history. As Hutchins had inscribed
in the notebook, of necessity was "unwavering commitment."[58] Hutchins's
goals for her life continued to be penned in the notebook. In 1945, on her
sixtieth birthday, she had written "patience (gentle)," and encouraged herself to be "more economical in small ways, more useful in club" as well as
more careful in keeping her weight down. In 1951 the list had grown to include a focus on "steady, calm, commitment," and a reminder to be "large-
minded, not over-bearing, arouse the liberals, no fuss." She encouraged
herself to stay healthy, keep her weight "below 165, down to 160," and walk
at least one way to or from work. Saving as always was encouraged with "no
new clothes," and "economy in daily expenses."[59] Curiously absent from the
perspective of today are entries in the notebook about feelings, emotions,
and thoughts concerning these goals. Was she able to reduce her weight
down to 160 pounds? Could she avoid the temptations of buying new
clothes? How easy was it to be alert, brisk, confident, and keen? The notebook was a place where Hutchins could lay out her goals for her principled
life, not analyze how well she was doing in meeting them. While this may
have been written elsewhere, or lost or destroyed, my sense is that such in-
trospection was not part of Hutchins's way of living, nor did it fit with a
political identification suspicious of self-ruminations. The following short,
to-the-point notebook entry said it all: "Plain living; high thinking."[60]
     This plain living did include home help, as the couple employed a woman
named Edith Weaver who helped with household chores and did some cook-

ing. Except for the years at Community House when housework was shared communally, throughout most of their lives they appeared to have employed some household help. One wonders if and how they reconciled these bourgeois habits with their communist politics. Certainly both had grown up in an era when household help was a fact of life for those who could afford it and in families where several servants would have been employed.

By the 1950s Hutchins and Rochester had been together for over thirty years; Rochester was over seventy and Hutchins was in her late sixties. They were still very energetic about their work and committed to labor: labor in terms of their own unceasing work and labor in the sense of their commitment to the cause of the working class. Advancing age did not seem to damper their zealous loyalties. I like to think they lived this poem Hutchins had kept in the notebook; perhaps one of them wrote it:

"How Old Are You?"

Age is a quality of mind—
If you have left your dreams behind.
If hope is lost.
If you no longer look ahead,
If your ambition's fires are dead—
Then you are old.
But if from life you take the best,
And if in life you keep the jest,
If love you hold—
No matter how the years go by,
No matter how the birthdays fly,
You are not old![61]

Another verse, this time one written by Rochester for her partner's birthday, also commented on Hutchins's age and focused on the loving commitment to labor and friends that kept her young:

Warm heart, clear brain,
Straight-back, no pain,
Friend to many, loved by all,
Spring of youth,
Tho' nearly sixty, heeds the call
    of truth
And struggle.
        Dear Grace,
        Beloved Grace.[62]

Calling themselves "old gals," they were still going to exhibits, plays, rallies, and meetings in and around the city and enjoying gardening on weekends and summer at "Little Acorn," their portable cottage at Croton-on-Hudson.

The couple had owned a car for quite some time. In the fifties and early sixties it was a 1951 model Ford, and, even though they tended not to drive in the winter, they enjoyed getting out and about in it. Their relationship seemed strong and playful, built on shared commitments and a loving devotion. Below is a Valentine's Day verse that Rochester composed for Hutchins. Ever the witty one, Rochester seemed to delight in writing verse and making puns:

> I know a gal—the grandest pal
>   That ever walked the earth.
> She keeps such a pace (and her name is Grace)
>   That her energy keeps down her girth.
> It's always of others—like sisters and brothers—
>   She thinks as the hours go by.
> Folks like her a lot, but I know that we're not
>   As thoughtful and warm and devoted
> As such a grand pal sure deserves.
> But we all do our best (though we don't pass that test)
>   And we love that grand gal
>   (And forever we shall)
> Without the slightest bit of reserves.[63]

Grace (c. 1950s). Probably at their summer cottage, "Little Acorn."

In this way, despite their advancing age the couple continued to love and labor. Daily they journeyed to the Labor Research Office below Union Square in New York City, and commuted from "Little Acorn" during the summer. Hutchins continued to write book reviews for the *New Masses* and various LRA publications; this activity must have taken an inordinate amount of time.[64] Rochester also wrote book reviews,[65] although her major writing task was her next, and last, project: *American Capitalism, 1607-1800,* a Marxist political interpretation of U.S. economic history that was published in 1949.

I find it interesting and somewhat fitting that Rochester's last book would be one that looked back rather than forward. I can understand Rochester choosing to write history in the midst of the McCarthy years when the Party was flailing and society seemed to have gone mad. The present was in disarray and the future looked bleak; the past was knowable. It was also much safer. For this reason she probably chose not to write more on the progress of capitalism nor the possibilities of socialist revolution. In fact, when criticized for not responding to William Z. Foster's idea of a third American revolution in his *Twilight of American Capitalism,* Rochester responded by pointing out that since her book was a history of capitalism, she could not discuss the outlook for capitalism in the world of 1950.[66] This "looking back" can be contrasted to Hutchins's more forward-looking approach. I think this illustrates a crucial difference between the two; Hutchins was more optimistic and outgoing while Rochester was more scholarly and retiring. Rochester was also five years older than her partner and was less active generally.

The *Worker* found *American Capitalism* exemplary as did the *Masses and Mainstream*; both agreed Rochester had made an important contribution to Marxist history in this survey of 200 years of capitalist economic relations in the United States.[67] Like all Rochester's books, *American Capitalism* contained an impressive amount of information condensed into 109 pages of text. It showed how capitalism was built on slave trading, profiteering, and exploitation, and described the contributions of Native Americans to the survival and growth of colonial centers. She traced the connections between economic developments and the struggle for self-government in describing how the American Revolution was a prelude to the westward expansion and economic development that had formerly

---

In "Your Nearest Exit May Be Behind You," Clark Blaise makes the point that our immediate futures, our possible survival, is located in the reworking of our past.[68] Life is larger than the circumstances that inhabit it; our past can be reconstructed to provide a safety net for a fragile future.

My library copy of *American Capitalism* contains the following anonymous, handwritten comment on the last page of the book: "Tell me what the dear sweet Russian people think about *central planning?* which is the true economic dictatorship by the power elite in the USSR." The suppressed anger in the tone of "the dear sweet" speaks of the vestiges of the Cold War inscribed as public record in this library book.

been hampered by British rule. She ended the book with a discussion of the "most exploited" of all groups in twentieth-century America, the "negroes" who "still suffer constant persecution and discrimination."[69] Consistently through both Hutchins and Rochester's writing is an understanding and concern for race politics. While race inequities were an issue high on the CP agenda and it would behoove Hutchins and Rochester to be inclusive of racial issues in their writings, Hutchins and Rochester came across as genuinely disturbed by the plight of people of color and always included a discussion of race in their work. Before their time in many ways, they seemed to understand not only that the social and economic conditions of African Americans' lives were morally reprehensible, but that their own privilege as wealthy women was related to these inequities suffered by their black comrades. As was true of their understanding of gender, however, it was class that explained these conditions.

Hutchins's contribution during this era included the revision of *Women Who Work* in 1952. It was shortened, condensed, and updated with 1950 Census Bureau figures. Accessible and to the point, the new edition of *Women Who Work* again focused on women's working conditions in the United States. Hutchins emphasized the double burden of women's work, the need for affordable child care, and the requirement that women be treated fairly on the job. Echoing contemporary themes, "making ends meet" for employed women meant not only equal pay for equal work, it also meant the "principle of equal pay must be applied not only when the work of men and women is the same but also when it is comparable or when comparable skills are involved."[70] A section on the Equal Rights Amendment still maintained that this legislation "would imperil all the hard-won legislation enacted to prevent the exploitation of women employed in industry."[71] Hutchins explained that allowances needed to be made for the physical and functional differences between the sexes, and only by recognizing and providing for these differences could real equality between men and women be achieved. Hutchins was passionately concerned about the lives of working women. Her ideas here represent how the meanings of feminism cannot be limited to those of the contemporary women's movement.

The second half of the book focused on women organizing for change. Hutchins emphasized the necessity for fair employment practices and the need for unity among all workers. Unions, Hutchins pointed out, were overwhelmingly male dominated, even though substantial gains had been made concerning unionization among some segments of working women. A chapter was devoted to women organizing in "fraternal" organizations, and the Progressive Party was praised for its forward-looking ideas and strategies concerning working women. The book ended with a short discussion focusing on the ways women could work together on peace issues. Missing was explicit Marxist economic theory and the chapter on "How it is in the Soviet Union." No mention of the Soviet Union or Communist Party was made, except tangentially in passing. The book was written in 1952 at the height of the McCarthy era, and as such, it is a strong, prolabor text that no one would guess was written by a loyal Old Left CP member. Such were the times. However, when all is said and done, I believe Hutchins's focus on the spirit of collaboration between the ranks of all working women reflected the broader, more populist ideology that best suited Hutchins and Rochester's philosophy. It is also ironic that she ended this last book with a discussion of pacifism; a similar place to where she had begun almost forty years earlier.

Interestingly, Hutchins did not reference an important book published in 1940, although first serialized in the *Daily People's World*, a West Coast CP newspaper. This book, *In Woman's Defense*, by Mary Inman, had a more independently feminist flair than *Women Who Work*. Inman wrote of "male domination under class rule" and suggested that all women are oppressed rather than just those of the proletariat.[72] Not surprisingly, *In Women's Defense* was not well received among the top CP leadership.[73] Hutchins's silence concerning a book on the topic of working women by a fellow CP comrade, a book she must have been familiar with, underlines her allegiances to Party doctrine.

The *Daily Worker* found *Women Who Work* indispensable to the understanding of working women's position in the United States, as did the *Masses and Mainstream*, and the Jefferson School of Social Science adopted the book as a required text for their course "The Woman Question."[74] The *Worker* devoted several articles to the book, praising and featuring it on several occasions. *Women Who Work* was also used in an article against the Equal Rights Amendment in the *Worker*. This article suggested that the effective way to help women workers was to organize them in trade unions and allow them leadership positions and child care. It ended with a reminder of something Hutchins had not explicitly mentioned, although passionately believed: "remember, always, that while many gains can be won for women in a capitalist society, they can attain full equality only under socialism, where no human being is at the mercy of exploitation by another."[75]

After the republication of *Women Who Work*, Hutchins's reputation as someone who understood and cared about the plight of women led to her writing a series of reviews and articles on the topic for the *Worker*. In 1959 Hutchins reviewed Eleanor Flexner's new book *Century of Struggle*, praising it as a "long-awaited story of women's efforts to gain their political rights." True to form, Hutchins emphasized the inequities women currently faced in the labor unions and the need for change, but avoided any comment on bourgeois feminism and instead lauded the text for its "well-rounded story of the woman's suffrage movement and its dauntless leaders."[76] In a fortieth anniversary feature in 1964, the *Worker* published a retrospective series on women's rights written by Hutchins. Starting with the Nineteenth Amendment when women got the vote, Hutchins overviewed the decades leading up to the 1960s, focusing on women in paid labor and featuring key figures in women and labor history.[77]

Hutchins and Rochester were also involved in *Looking Forward*, a volume that featured works-in-progress by International Publisher authors and was timed to mark this publisher's thirtieth anniversary in 1954. *Looking Forward* included a chapter by the LRA staff (Bob Dunn, Hutchins and Rochester, and volunteer researchers and writers) titled "East–West Trade and Jobs" that emphasized a peaceful way to avert economic catastrophe at home through coexistence and trade with the socialist world.[78]

Alongside this prolific writing, work on the LRA *Labor Fact Books* was ongoing. Indeed, ten volumes of the *Labor Fact Book* were published that covered the years from 1945 to early 1965, as well as numerous pamphlets.[79] Like their predecessors, the *Labor Fact Books* overviewed economic trends, social conditions in industry and farming, labor relations and strikes, as well as giving summaries of various political events. Most of the later books included a separate section on conditions of blacks in society and industry as well as labor issues abroad. Women usually got a mention in the context of women's involvement in labor unions and concerning legislation impacting families. Space was given to agencies involved in red-baiting during the late forties and fifties and detailed descriptions were included concerning various legislation and ensuing contempt cases. By 1948 all *Labor Fact Books* contained a separate section on the struggle for civil liberties, a predominant theme for progressive organizations of the era, although, interestingly, there is no mention in the *Labor Fact Book* covering 1948 and 1949 about the Hiss trial. There are, by comparison, detailed accounts of other similar trials including the Rosenberg trial several years later, which was recounted in some detail. I can only imagine that they did not want the publicity if this omission was intentional and/or conscious. Finally, Hutchins also edited *Railroad Notes* from 1937 to 1962.

In 1965, when Hutchins turned eighty years old, she was still going into the office daily. "I can not realize I am that old, but I don't intend to retire," she exclaimed in a letter to friends Ruth Erickson and Eleanor Stevenson.[80] A couple of years prior to making this comment, Hutchins had written to these friends and shared an experience of attending a May Day parade in Union Square when a heckler in the crowd spoke sharply to her. She wrote that he said, "'How long has it been since you've done a days work?' And me with my briefcase in hand just come from the office!"[81]

While Hutchins's stamina seemed strong, in 1950 at the age of seventy, Rochester cut back on her professional duties and resigned as vice president of the LRA so that a younger person with more energy might carry that responsibility. She then suffered a series of heart attacks in her mid-seventies and had to be careful not to overtax herself physically.[82] Maintaining volunteer editorial work, she then decided to work from home and no longer went into the LRA office on a regular basis. By the time Rochester was eighty-four years old, Hutchins reported that her partner was very well in general, although forgetting a little more than before.[83] However, despite her tenacity to maintain a working life, Hutchins was not without her share of ailments. In 1957 she was admitted to the hospital for cataract surgery. As happened when the couple was apart, they wrote letters to each other expressing their love and devotion, letters that otherwise would probably not have been written given the everyday routine and rhythm of their lives together. "To a dear one, most deeply missed, good wishes for complete recovery. Quick and certain; then to be warmly kissed—But always beloved, as a great discovery—from Guess Whom??" wrote Rochester. And again, "[I] see the profound truth in the old saying absence makes the heart grow fonder . . . because it shows (by contrast) all that one is deprived of by the absence."[84] Hutchins's cataract surgery was repeated in February 1962, although this time she contracted a serious eye infection that made her quite ill for some time. She hated taking time off work and was eagerly back at the office as soon as she could to work on *Labor Fact Book*, volume 16.[85]

As Old Left loyalists, Hutchins and Rochester were among those who provided continuity between the Old Left and the New in the prolific writings they left behind. Characteristically, throughout the trials and tribulations of this period Hutchins and Rochester seemed not to have lost faith in their vision of world communism. They were among those who continued to fight for constitutional liberties by remaining active in various civil liberties, civil rights, and defense organizations, using large amounts of their personal inheritances for communist causes. Again characteristically, they rode out the times with principled courage and with strong devotions to the Party.

Civil Liberties

As principled comrades, Hutchins and Rochester's commitment to communism was always rooted in notions of political and economic justice. Just as they were disturbed by the lack of justice in the Sacco and Vanzetti case of years ago and had been involved with the ACLU during the thirties,

> Autobiography celebrates consciousness through a series of self-erasures.
> Biography celebrates autobiography in part through the reconstruction of
> these self-erasures.

so too events in the last decades of their lives kindled strong passions against the lack of justice for and supreme antagonisms against political radicals.[86] In 1947 Rochester had written then President Truman to veto "the anti-union, anti-labor bill which enemies of the people have passed in Congress by a shocking majority." This was the Labor Management Relations Act, called the Taft–Hartley Act after its sponsors, which Truman did in fact veto, but which was enacted over his actions. This act was part of a concerted drive to destroy the National Labor Relations Act of 1935 and to weaken labor through federal legislation. Ever the one to turn a pun, Rochester played on the president's name: "If you veto it, with a vigorous statement, and urge all Democratic leaders and Congressmen honestly to support your veto, you will be recognized by workers today and by all Americans tomorrow as a True Man devoted to our country's welfare."[87]

In 1949, when communists were being indicted under the Smith Act, Rochester wrote to the Department of Justice to plead that the court's action in sentencing imprisonment of the defense lawyers in the New York communist case raised issues that seriously threatened basic constitutional rights: "Since when has it been American procedure to deprive accused persons of counsel or place such counsel in jeopardy?" she wrote.[88] Both Hutchins and Rochester frequently penned letters to the editor that were published in the *Daily Worker* and other presses rallying support for those indicted and asking readers to care and help in the cause.[89]

The way Hutchins and Rochester were most influential in working for civil liberties during this era was their commitment to providing bail for indicted communists under the Smith Act. Rochester is mentioned less in this activism, and, although Hutchins spearheaded these organizations, Rochester was no doubt working with her behind the scenes. Hutchins's most memorable action concerning civil liberties was providing $10,000 cash bail for Elizabeth Gurley Flynn. Gurley Flynn was a radical labor activist who rose quickly through the ranks of the CP. She had been intimately involved with the Sacco and Vanzetti case and was a popular speaker and a moving orator. She also was a regular writer for the *Daily Worker*.[90] Indicted with other communist leadership under the Smith Act, she is remembered for having provided her own eloquent defense during her trial; she eventually served over two years in prison. In terms of securing her bail, the *New York Times* wrote that "Miss Hutchins testified that the money was inherited by her from her father, and promised to produce Miss Flynn whenever required to do so."[91] The *Worker* (wordily) reported that "Miss

Hutchins was questioned, heckled and bullied by the government prosecutor as he tried to swerve her from her purpose, but she stood firm, with rock-like determination and dignity which are two of her outstanding traits, and when the contest of will was over, Miss Flynn was out on bail, the first of the defendants to be released, and the precedent has been set for other citizens to come forward and offer bail."[92] After Gurley Flynn's imprisonment Hutchins worked with others for her release, an event much appreciated by Flynn who wrote to Hutchins expressing her loving appreciation and gratitude.[93] Years later Hutchins worked as secretary on the Elizabeth Gurley Flynn Memorial Committee that planned a tribute and memorial volume. Rochester was also a member of this committee.[94]

Hutchins's generosity and commitment to civil liberties also encouraged her to post $5,000 bail for Alexander Trachtenberg, treasurer of the Jefferson School of Social Science.[95] As director of International Publishers, "Trachty" was a close colleague of Hutchins and Rochester; later, Hutchins would go on to serve as a trustee and board member of the Alexander Trachtenberg Memorial Trust. In addition, Hutchins supplied bail funds for John B. Williams, CP former National Labor secretary, and Jacob A. Stachel, CP Education director. The *New York Times* reported: "The bail for both men was supplied by Miss Grace Hutchins who said she was 70 years old and 'an old American who believed in the right of everyone to bail.' Miss Hutchinson [*sic*], a tall, straight-backed woman wearing a black coat with beaver-fur collar and sleeve cuffs, gave her address as 85, Bedford Street, New York City."[96] During this period Hutchins was involved with the American Committee for the Protection of the Foreign Born, an organization that came to specialize in the defense of alien political radicals against deportation charges after the passage of the Internal Security Act of 1950. The committee was closely affiliated with the CP and endured constant official harassment by authorities for many years.[97] Both Williams and Stachel were foreign-born, a fact that no doubt encouraged Hutchins's actions on their behalf.

Hutchins had also been a member and officer with the International Labor Defense (ILD), an organization founded in 1925 that specialized in the legal representation of political radicals. A crucial aspect of ILD strategy was mass protest where the public was mobilized on behalf of the defendants. In 1946 the ILD merged with the National Negro Congress and the National Federation for Constitutional Liberties to found the Civil Rights Congress (CRC). Hutchins worked with the Bail Fund of the CRC of New York until the CRC itself was liquidated by the Subversive Activities Control Board in 1956. Hutchins was involved with this litigation from 1951 to 1956.[98] Considered one of the most successful communist front organizations, the CRC was a key aspect of movement strategy during the McCarthy years.[99] It was in this capacity with the Bail Fund of the CRC that

Research diary: October 5, 1998: "Had the experience this past weekend of explaining this project to a historian friend of a friend and encountering the Grace Hutchins and Anna Rochester who? response. It reminded me of reading about biographer Dee Garrison's story 'Mary Heaton Who? Vorse, Of Course,' and the 'Mable [sic] Who?' in Lois Rudnick's story about her biography of Mabel Dodge Luhan. Both writers, if I'm correct, received t-shirts with these words blazoned on the front. [The experience] encouraged my sense of how important it is to recover the voices of these little-known women."

Hutchins produced bail for communist defendants. She continued working with various bail funds into the sixties and continued this concern for constitutional liberties with sponsorship of the Citizens Committee for Constitutional Liberties.[100]

In addition, in early 1964 Hutchins was featured by writing a series of articles that surveyed four decades of civil liberties struggles for the *Worker*. The third article in the series dealt with the Smith Act. She explained how in 1957 the government eventually dropped the remaining Smith Act cases when a U.S. Supreme Court ruling "held that advocacy of abstract doctrine was not a crime and there was no proof of forcible action to overthrow the government."[101] An important victory!

Final Years

The 1960s were no doubt a more hospitable decade for Hutchins and Rochester. The New Left were mobilizing and civil rights battles waged for the rights of minority peoples. As far as I can tell, the couple was not involved in any New Left organizations; they were from a different era and most likely had little energy or motivation to work with a new generation of activists who differed so markedly from them in so many ways. Hutchins and Rochester were prolabor and identified with the causes of working people. They would probably have had little in common with the dissatisfactions of privileged youth on college campuses, women claiming sexual freedom, or even gays and lesbians claiming a life outside the closet (although these were still pre-Stonewall days); perhaps these struggles would have seemed to them like bourgeois whining. While Hutchins was very supportive of women's rights (and I believe Rochester was too, even though she was less vocal), she was not ready to support an autonomous women's movement and most likely did not support the Equal Rights Amendment in the 1960s either. I think the couple would have had more affinities with the civil rights movement for black power and were more likely to see it as a legitimate independent movement. No doubt they kept tuned into the huge social and cultural changes of the sixties and experienced the relief that came from seeing the fifties, and much of what that decade stood for, come to a close.

Entries in Hutchins's notebook were scant after the late fifties. "P" (Party commitment) was double underlined and marked with an asterisk in 1961 with work emphasized as "steady and regular." An entry on New Year's day in 1962 read: "purpose: keep the group going; utmost economy," and a year later "contacts" were emphasized and "P" again circled in red. Always the devoted CP member, Hutchins had great loyalty to the Party still. Interestingly, wedged at the very back of her notebook was the following verse by John Greenleaf Whittier. It was a poem that echoed themes from earlier days:

"O Brother Man"

O Brother Man, fold to thy heart thy brother;
Where pity dwells, the peace of God is there;
To worship rightly is to love each other,
Each smile a hymn, each kindly deed a prayer.

Follow with reverend steps the great example
of Him whose holy work was doing good;
So shall the wide earth seem our Father's temple,
Each loving life a psalm of gratitude.

Then shall all shackles fill the stormy clangor
of wild war-music o'er the earth shall cease,
Love shall tread out the baleful fire of anger,
And in its ashes plant the tree of peace.

It seems likely that the placement of this poem in the notebook was intentional, although it is possible it was put in there accidentally since it was not pasted onto the page like some other memorabilia. Either way its survival speaks to its meaning for Hutchins. I imagine this to have been a favorite poem from earlier years that still had meaning for her in her old age by emphasizing the necessity of connection to something larger than her own life. While the Party continued to provide collective solidarity, perhaps this poem represented a yearning for more spiritual meaning, perhaps not.

The couple lived quietly during these later years with friend Lucie Myer. It seems that although she was still living with them in 1964, she had suffered from heart problems since the mid-nineteen fifties.[102] While Hutchins still wrote and attended meetings and events, Rochester's health was more fragile and she did not seem to get out as much. In the spring of 1966 Rochester contracted pneumonia and died in the New York General Infirmary on May 11 at the age of eighty-six. Despite her many years of chronic ill health, her death was sudden and no doubt came as a deep tragedy to Hutchins, who had loved her more than she was able to express.

I wonder if Grace and Anna thought that someone someday might write their biography. Did Grace assemble these manuscripts? What did she intentionally destroy, throw away, give away, edit? On numerous letters and newspaper clippings there is Grace's handwriting in red grease pencil marking a date, a last name, or underlining some point. I assume she did this before her eyesight completely failed her and after Anna's death in anticipation of putting these papers in order. Although the Cold War years had passed and now there would be little threat of a security risk, most likely the habit of caution and care remained. Her conscious selection would have provided a remapping of their lives: a construction of the past through the thoughts and desires of her present.

Losing her partner and finding herself alone after all these years must have been terribly difficult for Hutchins. This was most likely exacerbated by the fact that it seems Lucie Myer must have already died by this time too. Rochester's obituary read that she left no immediate survivors; everyone close to the couple knew how incorrect was this statement.[103]

After Rochester died, Hutchins had a live-in housekeeper, and, as she became more frail, a nurse's aide to help care for her. She still took a keen interest in labor issues, especially those concerning women, and continued to donate money to labor and communist causes. For example, Hutchins sponsored the Ad Hoc Women's Committee for International Women's Day in March 1967, and as late as 1969 donated money to the pro-Soviet *Daily World*, the survivor of the *Daily Worker* newspaper.[104] The fond memories of their visit to the Soviet Union in 1927, I believe, were central in understanding Hutchins and Rochester's long history of support for this struggling nation.

In the spring of 1967 Hutchins suffered a serious heart attack and had a lengthy stay in the hospital. Failing eyesight exacerbated her incapacity and meant that she could no longer indulge in the reading and writing that had been her life for so many years. Since their home on Bedford Street was on the third floor and there was no elevator, Hutchins was mostly confined to the apartment. But she talked on the phone to LRA staff daily and still took an interest in the operation of the organization. Colleague Bob Dunn was very involved with Hutchins's care during this period and personally answered much of her private correspondence when her eyesight made it impossible for her to write.[105] No doubt this confinement was difficult on someone so vital and energetic as Hutchins had been. It must have pained her to miss her sixtieth Bryn Mawr reunion in 1967, among other things.

Research diary: November 14, 1998: "Can't read these various dates without thinking about what I was doing then ... [I would have been] 10 years
old then, that was the summer I broke my arm, that was my birthday when
I was 15, etc. This chapter is interesting because for the first time I was conscious in the world when Grace and Anna were still alive. I could even have
carried on an intelligent conversation with them. [I feel] a great remorse I
missed this opportunity, that nobody did an oral history before they died.
My questions to them would have been endless—my major one that puts
me squarely in the realist camp after all: did I get it right?"

In early July 1969, Hutchins suffered another heart attack. She was released from the hospital but died a week later at home, on July 15.[106] There
was no funeral service, but a memorial service was held for her in the fall,
organized by Bob Dunn. He also became executor of her will and was remembered as a good and most loyal friend who had been with the couple
through almost five decades of their lives. Hutchins's friendship with Dunn
seemed to have steadied her life and helped her cope through Rochester's
failing health and death. Tributes to Hutchins's life and work came from all
over. A letter from friend Clara Colon echoed the phrases of many: a fitting
closure, I think, to this biography.[107]

Dear Bob—The announcement mentioned Grace had a surviving brother,
who is a stranger to me. But somehow I imagine no brother could have been
closer to Grace than you, so I'm conveying my thoughts to you.

I feel deeply grieved on learning of Grace's death. It was no surprise in view of
her long illness, yet when it happened it still was a blow. Grace belonged to that
era of great names represented by Elizabeth Gurley Flynn and Anna Rochester,
among the best that our country has produced. One gratifying thing about re-
membering Grace is that she had a long and rich life. She had the courage to
live her convictions in the best tradition-breaking pioneering tradition of a
long line of plucky American fighting women from Anne Hutchinson on.

Perhaps we shouldn't so much mourn for Grace as be glad she lived among
us. Because she was self-effacing, not many people know the details of her
useful, principled and generous deeds. It would be a boon and an inspiration
to all of us, especially the young from among whom the new heroines and
leaders will come, to know more about Grace. Perhaps someone who knew
and loved her well could write that story?

> Warmest regards, Clara
> P.S. Jesús shared my sentiments.

How appropriate that the last sentence of this biography should cause such consternation. This letter from Clara Colon was typed; however, the "p.s." was in her own handwriting. I liked the circular return to Grace's roots in this possible advocation of Jesus in the postscript and thought it a fitting closure. The accent mark was very faint and I thought it was a smudge. It was a puzzle. Then, several weeks later I was reading back copies of the *Daily Worker* on microfiche and realized that Jesús was actually Clara's husband Jesús Colon, a Puerto Rican specialist who had a column in the *Daily Worker* called "As I See It from Here." How strong is our desire for tidy closures.

NOTES

Notes to Introduction

1. Nikolai Ostrovski, *The Making of a Hero* (New York: Dutton, 1937). Hutchins wrote this quote in her notebook on January 12, 1939. Unless otherwise noted, all archival materials are located in the Hutchins and Rochester collections in the Special Collections Division of University Archives, Knight Library, University of Oregon, Eugene.

2. Nancy Cott and Elizabeth Pleck, eds., *A Heritage of Her Own: Toward a New Social History of American Women* (New York: Simon and Schuster, 1979).

3. Historians have used the concept of gender-specific separate space when describing the experience of nineteenth- and early twentieth-century women, although this tends to be a race- and class-bound concept, most fitting in describing the lives of privileged white women. One of the first works to explore the influence of this private space on women's experience was Carroll Smith-Rosenberg's classic article "The Female World of Love and Ritual: Relationships Between Women in Nineteenth-Century America," *Signs* 1 (Autumn 1975): 1–29. See also her book *Disorderly Conduct: Visions of Gender in Victorian America* (New York: Oxford University Press, 1985), as well as Carl N. Degler, *At Odds: Women and the Family in America from the Revolution to the Present* (New York: Oxford University Press, 1980). In terms of the merging of culture and politics, Blanche Wiesen Cook's "Female Support Networks and Political Activism: Lillian Ward, Crystal Eastman, Emma Goldman," in *A Heritage of Her Own* focuses on the role of women's culture in providing sustenance for their political involvement, as do Ellen DuBois, Mari Jo Buhle, Temme Kaplan, Gerda Lerner, and Carroll Smith-Rosenberg in "Politics and Culture in Women's History: A Symposium," *Feminist Studies* 6 (Spring 1980): 26–64. Another source on the connections between the disintegration of women's culture and the decline of public feminism is Estelle Freedman's article "Separation as Strategy: Female Institution-Building and American Feminism, 1870–1930," *Feminist Studies* 5 (Fall 1979): 512–29.

4. Bettina Aptheker, *Tapestries of Life: Women's Work, Women's Consciousness, and the Meaning of Daily Experience* (Amherst: University of Massachusetts Press, 1989), 101–02.

5. Pathbreaking articles on this topic include, again, Smith-Rosenberg, "The Female World of Love and Ritual," and "The New Women as Androgyne: Social Disorder and

Gender Crisis, 1870–1936," in *Disorderly Conduct*. A major source on romantic friendships of this period is Lillian Faderman, *Surpassing the Love of Men: Romantic Friendships and Love between Women from the Renaissance to the Present* (New York: Morrow, 1981); and *Odd Girls and Twilight Lovers* (New York: Columbia University Press, 1991); also Faderman's chapter, "Nineteenth-Century Boston Marriage as a Possible Lesson for Today," *Boston Marriages: Romantic but Asexual Relationships among Contemporary Lesbians*, ed. Esther D. Rothblum and Kathleen A. Brehony (Amherst: University of Massachussetts Press, 1993). Lesbian History Group's *Not a Passing Phase: Reclaiming Lesbians in History, 1840–1985* (London: The Women's Press, 1989) is an interesting account of the British experience. Other sources include: the "Lesbian Herstory" special issue of *Frontiers* (1979); Sheila Jeffreys, *The Spinster and Her Enemies: Feminism and Sexuality, 1880–1930* (London: Pandora, 1985); Judith Schwartz, "Yellow Clover: Katharine Lee Bates and Katharine Coman," *Frontiers* 4, no. 1 (1979): 56–67; Leila Rupp, "'Imagine My Surprise': Women's Relationships in Historical Perspective," *Frontiers* 5, no. 3 (1980): 61–70; Nancy Sahli, "Smashing: Women's Relationships before the Fall," *Chrysalis* 8 (1979): 17–27; and Martha Vicinus, "They Wonder to Which Sex I Belong: The Historical Roots of the Modern Lesbian Identity," *Feminist Studies* 18, no. 3 (1992): 467–97. See Ann Ferguson, "Patriarchy, Sexual Identity and the Sexual Revolution," *Sign* 7 (1981): 159–72, for a discussion of the history of the definition of lesbianism. Finally, note that Smith-Rosenberg and Faderman have been challenged for overprivileging romantic friendships and removing sexual activity from lesbian lives—see, for example, the 1981 special issue of *Heresies*, and Lisa Moore, "'Something More Tender Still than Friendship': Romantic Friendships in Early-Nineteenth-Century England," *Feminist Studies* 18, no. 3 (1992): 499–520. See also studies of gay history and politics: John D'Emilio and Estelle B. Freedman, *Intimate Matters: A History of Sexuality in America* (New York: Harper & Row, 1988); and John D'Emilio, *Sexual Politics, Sexual Communities*.

6. See also Jonathan Katz's interview of Henry Hay in *Radical America*, July/August 1977. Katz's *The Invention of Heterosexuality* (New York: Dutton, 1995) is also an interesting collection. In "Women and the Communist Party, 1930–40," *Socialist Review* 45 (1979): 106, Robert Shaffer writes that "Communists in the 1930s viewed homosexuality as a sexual aberration or vice brought on by the tensions of life under capitalism." Communist Party (CP) policy did not change very much over the next decades. Other sources that discuss CP policy include: Ellen Kay Trimberger, "Women in the Old Left and the New Left: The Evolution of a Politics of a Personal Life," *Feminist Studies* 5 (1979): 432–50; Rosalyn Baxandall, "The Question Seldom Asked: Women and the CPUSA," in *New Studies in the Politics and Culture of U.S. Communism*, ed. Michael Brown, Randy Martin, Frank Rosengarten, and George Snedeker (New York: Monthly Review Press, 1993): 141–61.

7. Faderman, *Odd Girls and Twilight Lovers*, 86.

8. In "'Women Alone Stir My Imagination': Lesbianism and the Cultural Tradition," *Signs* 4 (1979): 738, Blanche Wiesen Cook writes that "women who love women, who choose women to nurture and support and create a living environment in which to work creatively and independently, are lesbian." *Sexual Politics, Sexual Communities: The Making of a Homosexual Minority in the US, 1940–1970* (Chicago: University of Chicago Press, 1998). Also see work by Allan Bérubé and Terence Kissack.

9. Anna Rochester (hereafter AR) to Grace Hutchins (hereafter GH), August 3, 1931.

10. For a discussion of the contrasts between women in the Old versus New Left, see Trimberger, "Women in the Old Left," 432–50.

11. Texts that explore writing of biography include Sara Alpern, Joyce Antler, Elisabeth Israels Perry, and Ingrid Winther Scobie, eds., *The Challenge of Feminist Biography: Writing the Lives of Modern American Women* (Urbana: University of Illinois Press, 1992); Susan Groag Bell and Marilyn Yalom, eds., *Revealing Lives: Autobiography, Biography and Gender* (Albany: State University of New York, 1990); Tret Lynn Broughton and Linda Anderson, eds., *Women's Lives/Women's Times: New Essays on Auto/Biography* (Albany: SUNY Press, 1997); Ira Bruce Nagel, *Biography: Fiction, Fact and Form* (London: Macmillan, 1984); Marc Pachter, ed., *Telling Lives: The Biographer's Art* (Philadelphia: University of Pennsylvania Press, 1981); Dennis Petrie, ed., *Ultimately Fiction, Design in Modern American Literary Biography* (West Lafayette: Purdue University Press, 1981); Mary Rhiel and David Suchoff, eds., *The Seductions of Biography* (New York: Routledge, 1996); and Liz Stanley, *The Auto/biographical I* (Manchester, U.K.: Manchester University Press, 1992). I have found Carolyn Steedman's work very useful: see *Landscape for a Good Woman* (London: Virago Press, 1986), *Childhood, Culture and Class in Britain: Margaret McMillan, 1860–1931* (London: Virago Press, 1990), and *Past Tenses: Essays on Writing, Autobiography and History* (London: Rivers Oram Press, 1992). Sources on biography in the context of situating subjectivities include Kathleen Barry, "Biography and the Search for Women's Subjectivity," *Women's Studies International Forum* 12 (1989): 561–77; Mary Jean Corbett, *Representing Femininity: Middle-Class Subjectivity in Victorian and Edwardian Women's Autobiographies* (New York: Oxford University Press, 1992); and Regina Gagnier, *Subjectivities: A History of Self-Representation in Britain, 1832–1920* (New York: Oxford University Press).

12. Carl Ginzburg, "Checking the Evidence: The Judge and the Historian," *Critical Inquiry* 18 (1991), calls this less confident history "conjunctural." See also Natalie Davis, *Fiction in the Archive* (Stanford: Stanford University Press, 1987). It is the intellectual climate of postmodernism that has produced this "turning upside down" of traditional biographical methods. See, for example, work by Judith Butler, especially *Gender Trouble: Feminism and the Subversion of Identity* (New York: Routledge, 1990); Jane Flax, *Thinking Fragments: Psychoanalysis, Feminism, and Postmodernism in the Contemporary West* (Berkeley: University of California Press, 1990); Linda Nicholson, ed., *Feminism/Postmodernism* (New York: Routledge, 1990); Linda Nicholson and Steven Seidman, eds., *Social Postmodernism* (Cambridge: Cambridge University Press, 1995); and Chris Weedon, *Feminist Practice and Poststructuralist Theory* (New York: Basil Blackwell, 1987). Postmodernism includes an embrace of difference and attention to the ways Western modernity has facilitated a colonialist "othering." See, for example, Homi Bhabha, "The Other Question," *Screen* 24 (1983): 18–36; and "Of Mimicry and Man: The Ambivalence of Colonial Discourse," *October* 34 (1985): 71–80; Edward Said, *Orientalism* (New York: Pantheon, 1978); and Gayatri Spivak, *In Other Worlds: Essays in Cultural Politics* (New York: Routledge, 1988), and *The Post-Colonialist Critic: Interviews, Strategies, Dialogues* (London: Routledge, 1990).

Postmodernism recognizes the failure of the "grand narratives" of humanist projects and disputes the existence of general or universal laws governing either social formations or academic knowledges (see, for example, Jean-Francois Lyotard, *The Postmodern Condition* [Minneapolis: University of Minnesota Press, 1984]). Postmodernism also recognizes that Western modernity (including economic and bureaucratic rationalization and the apparatus and processes of the capitalist industrial state) has reached its limits and postmodern societies now represent the cultural logic of late capitalism (see Frederic Jameson, "Postmodernism, or the Cultural Logic of Late Capitalism," *New Left Review* 146 [1984]: 53–93, on capitalist logic; also Michel Foucault, *The History of Sexuality,* vol. 1 [Harmondsworth: Peregrine, 1978], on notions of "truth"). This new intellectual framework has resulted in a loss of authority for intellectuals and their sense of mission as well as an increasing disenchantment and anxiety as the historically given certainties and universalities of truth and judgment have dissipated. See, for example, Mary Douglas, "The Social Preconditions of Radical Skepticism," in *Power, Action, and Belief,* ed. J. Law (London: Routledge, 1986).

13. Sociologist Norman Denzin, *Interpretive Ethnography: Ethnographic Practices for the Twenty-First Century* (Thousand Oaks, Calif.: Sage, 1997), p. 3, defines the crisis of representation as the assumption that researchers can no longer capture lived experience; rather such experience is created or reconstructed through the social text written by the researcher. In *The Auto/biographical I,* Liz Stanley writes that an understanding of the limits of representation has transformed biography in the following ways: "First is a rejection of what is seen as the false referentiality of depictions of the modernist self, a rejection of its supposed essentialism 'within' and waiting to be actualised. . . . Second, is an equally severe rebuttal of modernist notions of authorship, the unique mind of the individual writer inscribing some quintessential inner truth. And third, by an insistence on intertextuality and a focus on language in use, particularly on the formation and perpetuation of discourses as sets of 'voices' speaking referentially to and about each other" (14–15).

14. Patti Lather, "Postbook: Working the Ruins of Feminist Ethnography" (paper presented at Feminism(s) and Rhetoric(s) Conference, Oregon State University, August 28–30, 1997). See also Lather's article "Creating a Multilayered Text: Women, AIDS, and Angels," in the collection *Representation and the Text: Reframing the Narrative Voice,* ed. William G. Tierney and Yvonna S. Lincoln (Albany: SUNY Press, 1997), and her book (with Chris Smithies), *Troubling the Angels: Women Living with HIV/AIDS* (Boulder, Colo. Westview Press, 1997).

15. Joan Wallach Scott, *Only Paradoxes to Offer: French Feminists and the Rights of Man* (Cambridge: Harvard University Press, 1996), 16.

Notes to Chapter One

1. Barbara Welter, "The Cult of True Womanhood," *American Quarterly* 18 (1966): 150–74.

2. Carroll Smith-Rosenberg, *Disorderly Conduct: Visions of Gender in Victorian America* (New York: Oxford University Press, 1985), 173.

3. Nancy S. Dye, "Introduction," in *Gender, Class, Race and Reform in the Progressive Era,* ed. Noralee Frankel and Nancy S. Dye (Lexington: University Press of Kentucky, 1991), 5.

4. James Carter, "Daughter of the American Revolution—About Anna Rochester, Author of *Rulers of America*," *Daily Worker*, March 6, 1936. Louise was born on April 16, 1845, and Roswell, August 17, 1839. They were married June 4, 1879, and Anna was born a little over nine months later (genealogy chart of the Daughters of the American Revolution, April 1945).

5. Elliot West and Paula Petrick, eds., *Small Worlds: Children and Adolescents in America, 1850–1950* (Lawrence: University Press of Kansas, 1992).

6. Useful texts for exploring the politics of the sentimental include Suzanne Clark, *Sentimental Modernism: Women Writers and the Revolution of the Word* (Bloomington: Indiana University Press, 1991); Mary Kelley, "The Sentimentalists: Promise and Betrayal in the Home," *Signs* 4 (Spring 1979); Nancy Schnog, "Inside the Sentimental: The Psychological Work of *The Wide Wide World*," *Genders* 4 (Spring 1989): 11–25; Jane Tompkins, *Sensational Designs: The Cultural Work of American Fiction, 1790–1860* (New York: Oxford University Press, 1985); and Janet Todd, *Feminist Literary History* (New York: Routledge, 1988). Henry Nash Smith, "The Scribbling Women and the Cosmic Success Story," *Critical Inquiry* 1 (September 1974), makes the case against the discourse of the sentimental due to its perpetuation of patriarchal relations, as also does Ann Douglas in *The Feminization of America* (New York: Knopf, 1977). Scholars who have interpreted the sentimental as a means for women's resistance and power include Dee Garrison, "Immortal Fiction in the Late Victorian Library," *American Quarterly* 28 (Spring 1976); and Helen Waite Papashvily, *All Happy Endings: A Study of the Domestic Novel in America, the Women Who Wrote It, the Women Who Read It, in the Nineteenth Century* (New York: Harper and Bros., 1957). Finally, Mary Jean Corbett in *Representing Femininity: Middle-Class Subjectivity in Victorian and Edwardian Women's Autobiographies* (New York: Oxford University Press, 1992) provides interesting insights on the tensions between women's private and public selves as illustrated in their writings, and grapples generally with the important question of feminine self-representation during this historical period.

7. "AR Annals," October 1881.

8. Ibid., September 1884.

9. Ibid., October 6, 1886.

10. Ibid., April 28, 1894.

11. Ibid., March 17, 1894.

12. Ibid., April 26, 1882. Preparations for building the house took some time and they moved approximately a year after this initial declaration.

13. Ibid., March 1883.

14. Ibid., October 6, 1886.

15. Ibid., August 1887 and June 1889. When she was nine years old, one of Rochester's piano recitals was so well received that it was noted by the local newspaper, the *Englewood Press*.

16. Ibid., May 1897. In "Daughter of the American Revolution," James T. Carter wrote that Bryn Mawr College was chosen because of its scholarly reputation.

17. "AR Annals," June 6, 1896.

18. Ibid., September 1891.

19. Stephen Peabody, "Rochester Papers, Please Copy!" *Daily Worker*, April 29, 1940.

20. Nancy Chodorow, *The Reproduction of Mothering: Psychoanalysis and the Sociology of Gender* (Berkeley: University of California Press, 1978).

21. Jean Kennard, *Vera Brittain and Winifred Holtby: A Working Partnership* (Hanover: University of New England Press, 1989), 15.

22. Belle Gale Chevigny, "Daughters Writing: Toward a Theory of Women's Biography," in *Between Women*, ed. Carol Ascher, Louise DeSalvo, and Sara Ruddick (Boston: Beacon Press, 1984), 375.

23. "AR Annals," April 28, 1894.

24. Ibid., October 1896.

25. Susan Ware's biography of Molly Dewson, *Partner and I* (New Haven: Yale University Press, 1987), focuses on Dewson's relationship with Polly Porter. Ware writes of the friendship between Porter and Hutchins: "it might seem far-fetched to suggest that Polly became a radical simply because of a childhood friendship, but Polly Porter had always been easily swayed by forceful personalities" (137).

26. Cleveland Armory, *The Proper Bostonians* (New York: Dutton, 1947), 169.

27. GH, Primary II Report, October 1893.

28. GH, Miss Folsom's School Report Card, March 14, 1896.

29. GH, handwritten verse, undated.

30. *Children's Weekly* 1, no. 6 (June 10, 1896). Hutchins must have edited several of these handwritten magazines since the surviving one is number 6.

31. GH to Susan Hutchins, May 30, 1900; Edward Hutchins Sr. to GH, September 20, 1910. He often addressed Hutchins as "dear old Grace" in his letters to her.

32. GH, "Letters of Travels," September 18, 1898, September 30, 1898.

33. Ibid., September 18, 1898, November 22, 1898.

34. Ibid., January 15, 1899, February 8, 1899, November 20, 1898.

35. Ibid., September 11, 1898.

36. Ibid., March 11, 1899.

37. Kathryn M. Conway, "Woman Suffrage and the History of Rhetoric at the Seven Sisters Colleges, 1865–1919," in *Reclaiming Rhetorica: Women in the Rhetorical Tradition*, ed. Andrea A. Lunsford (Pittsburgh: University of Pittsburgh Press, 1995), 222. Higher institutions of learning opened their doors to women in 1833 with the founding of Oberlin Collegiate Institute. Antioch College followed in 1853, and the state universities (beginning with Utah in 1850) started admitting women.

38. GH speech, "What's Past Is Prologue," Bryn Mawr College, class of 1907 fiftieth reunion, June 1957.

39. Sidney Streat, "Grace Hutchins—Revolutionary," *Daily Worker*, September 16, 1936. Hutchins also speaks of this in her fiftieth reunion speech at Bryn Mawr College, June 1957.

40. Bryn Mawr College (BMC), *Tipyn O' Bob* 1, no. 5 (March 1904): 38; no. 6 (April 1904): 31; vol. 2, no. 7 (April 1905): 30; vol. 3, no. 6 (April 1906): 25; and *Lantern*, no. 13 (June 1904): 78, and no. 15 (Spring 1905): 85.

41. BMC, *Tipyn O' Bob* 4, no. 1 (November 1906): 24.

42. Unfortunately, Bryn Mawr's alumni office only has copies of the 1903 editions (February, March, and April) of the *Recorder*—an intervening year between Rochester's time at Bryn Mawr and Hutchins's tenure at the college.

43. BMC, *Turtle Progress-Dispatch* 1, no. 4 (June 1936).

44. Hutchins's diverse athletic accomplishments are recorded in Bryn Mawr College's *Tipyn O' Bob* "Athletic Notes." They are as follows: baseball: vol. 2, no. 4 (January 1905): 33; and vol. 3, no. 4 (February 1906): 26; basketball: vol. 3, no. 3 (January 1906): 26; and vol. 4, no. 7 (May 1907): 32. Hutchins reported that she had been captain of the Bryn Mawr varsity basketball team ("statement by the author," *Women Who Work*, February 23, 1934). Hockey achievements were reported in *Tipyn O' Bob* "Athletic Notes," vol. 3, no. 2 (December 1905): 35; tennis: *Lantern*, no. 16 (Spring 1907): 92; shot put and tug–o–war in vol. 3, no. 6 (April 1906): 28. Committee assignments were mentioned in vol. 4, no. 7 (March 1907): 32.

45. BMC, *Tipyn O' Bob* 2, no. 6 (March 1905): 34–35.

46. Margaret Reeve Carey to GH (1957 penciled on top). Margaret married, had three children and lived in Philadelphia. She became an entomologist who specialized in the hawkmoth and made many trips to the cloud forests of Venezuela to study this species.

47. Rochester's obituary described her as modest and shy (*New York Times*, May 12, 1966) as did many of the newspaper write-ups over the years.

48. "AR Annals," February 3, 1898.

49. Ibid., January 2, 1899.

50. AR to Louise Rochester, May 7, 1899, inserted loosely in "AR Annals."

51. "AR Annals," May 1899.

52. Ibid., May 1901.

53. Ibid.

54. For an account of the merging of culture and politics, see Blanche Wiesen Cook's "Female Support Networks and Political Activism: Lillian Ward, Crystal Eastman, Emma Goldman" in *A Heritage of Her Own: Toward a New Social History of American Women*, ed. Nancy Cott and Elizabeth Pleck (New York: Simon and Schuster, 1979), 412–14.

55. See Christina Simmons, "Companionate Marriage and the Lesbian Threat," *Frontiers* 4 (1979): 54–59; and Rayna Rapp and Ellen Ross, "The Twenties Backlash: Compulsory Heterosexuality, the Consumer Family, and the Waning of Feminism," in *Class, Race and Sex: The Dynamics of Control*, ed. Amy Swerdlow and Hanna Messinger (Boston: Hall, 1983), 93–107. Carroll Smith-Rosenberg in "The New Woman as Androgyne," in *Disorderly Conduct*, p. 274, writes that this generation of women at the heights of "Progressive romanticism" had "merged gentility and eroticism," and adds: "their innocence would not continue much longer." This would change with the advent of a consumer culture and its heterosocial and heterosexist ideologies, the development of Freudian psychology and a growing interest in the "companionate marriage," with its focus on mutual (hetero)sexual satisfaction.

Notes to Chapter Two

1. Alexandra Allen, *Travelling Ladies* (London: Jupiter, 1989), 10–11.

2. Jacqueline Dowd Hall, "Second Thoughts on Jesse Daniel Ames," in *The Challenge of Feminist Biography*, ed. Sara Alpern, Joyce Antler, Elisabeth Israels Perry, and Ingrid Winther Scobie (Urbana: University of Illinois Press, 1992), 155.

3. "AR Annals," January 1902. Originally, neurasthenia was an American disorder, described as "American nervousness" by the neurologist George Miller Beard

in the late 1860s. Beard saw a significant correlation between modern social organization and nervous illness. A deficiency in nervous energy was the price ex-
acted by industrialized urban societies, competitive business and social environments, and the luxuries, vices, and excesses of modern life. Five characteristic
features of nineteenth-century progress: the periodical press, steam power, the telegraph, the sciences, and especially the increased mental activity of women, could be
held to blame for the sapping of American nervous strength. See Elaine Showalter,
The Female Malady: Women, Madness, and English Culture, 1830–1980 (London:
Penguin, 1985), 134–35. For other sources on "the cult of invalidism" see Barbara
Ehrenreich and Deidre English's *Complaints and Disorders: The Sexual Politics of
Sickness* (Old Westbury, Conn.: Feminist Press, 1973) and their *For Her Own Good:
150 Years of the Experts' Advice to Women* (New York: Anchor Press, 1979).

   4. AR, statement accompanying the civil service examination—"Experts in
Child Welfare, Departmental" (September 18, 1917), question 19.

   5. "AR Annals," November 19, 1905, September 11, 1906.

   6. Ibid., November 11, 1905.

   7. Ibid., no month 1907.

   8. Unsigned, untitled, undated poem written in AR's hand.

   9. This information was written in Hutchins's handwriting at the bottom of a
brief typed, undated, unsigned biographical statement about Rochester. It was
probably used by International Publishers when advertising one of Rochester's
books.

   10. See Spencer Miller Jr. and Joseph F. Fletcher, *The Church and Industry* (New
York: Longmans, Green, 1930).

   11. "AR Annals," no month 1908. Rochester must surely have read Scudder's *A
Listener in Babel* (Boston: Houghton and Mifflin, 1903). The plot is autobiograph-
ical on Scudder's part but could easily have reflected Rochester's early journey.
Hilda the heroine grows up in sheltered privilege traveling with her mother. She
works in a settlement house and eventually leaves after a conversion to socialism.

   12. "AR Annals," no month 1908.

   13. There are many texts on women's involvements in the Progressive era. See, for
example, Dorothy Schneider and Carl J. Schneider, *American Women in the Progressive Era, 1900–1920* (New York: Doubleday, 1993). For sources on women's education and social reform work see Joyce Antler, *The Educated Woman and Professionalization: The Struggle for a Feminine Identity, 1890–1920* (New York: Garland,
1987); Jill K. Conway, *The First Generation of American Women Graduates* (New
York: Garland, 1987); Ellen C. Lagemann, *A Generation of Women: Education in the
Lives of Progressive Reformers* (Cambridge: Harvard University Press, 1979); and
Barbara M. Solomon, *In the Company of Educated Women: A History of Women in
Higher Education in America* (New Haven: Yale University Press, 1985).

   14. AR to Elizabeth Gurley Flynn, February 15, 1926. My thanks to Rosalyn
Baxandall for sharing this letter with me.

   15. "AR Annals," June 1, 1909.

   16. For an interesting discussion of settlement work and its role during the Progressive era, see Allen F. Davis, *Spearheads for Reform: The Social Settlements and the
Progressive Movement, 1890–1914* (New York: Oxford University Press, 1967). For
her work on the Hull House settlement in Chicago, see Kathryn Kish Sklar, "Hull

House in the 1890s: A Community of Women Reformers," *Signs* 10 (1985): 658–77.

17. "AR Annals," June 1, 1909.

18. Ibid., no month 1911.

19. The states' Consumers' Leagues (CL) were women's reform organizations that addressed urgent social problems. Initially they were formed out of concern for the poor working conditions of saleswomen in the department stores of urban centers. Known for their ability to mobilize middle-class women's consumer clout and boycotting potential, as well as provide consumer education, the CL created "White Lists" of stores who supported CL's mandate concerning working conditions, minimum wage, and working hours. From this base, the CL championed wage and hour laws and the elimination of child labor. With strong political networks and coherent legislative agenda around the health, general lives and working conditions of women and children, the New York Consumers' League, for example, worked for such protective legislation as the Mercantile Inspection Act of 1896, which limited work hours, prohibited child labor, and required seats behind counters for sales assistants as well as better sanitary facilities for workers generally. Eventually, in 1899, the states' leagues coalesced under the National Consumers' League (NCL) led by Executive Secretary Florence Kelley. Kelley was very effective in organizing middle-class women into groups that fought for the rights of working women and children and she was involved with the NCL until her death in 1932. While the effort to improve working conditions through the use of middle-class women's buying power was generally less successful, ultimately efforts at protective legislation paid off. See, for example, Louis L. Athey, "The Consumers' Leagues and Social Reform, 1890–1923" (Ph.D. Dissertation, University of Delaware, 1965).

20. AR, statement to accompany "Experts in Child Welfare, Departmental" (September 18, 1917), question 19.

21. Schneider and Schneider, *American Women in the Progressive Era*, 8.

22. After schooling at Cornell and the University of Zurich, Kelley (1859–1932) began her career at the Hull House settlement in Chicago in 1891 with founder Jane Addams, working there until 1899 when she moved to Henry House, a settlement in New York's lower east side that was founded by Lillian Wald. Here she lived for almost thirty years, spearheading various reform legislation. For biographies of Florence Kelley, see Josephine Goldmark, *Impatient Crusader: Florence Kelley's Life Story* (Champaign: University of Illinois Press, 1953); and Katherine Kish Sklar, *Florence Kelley and the Nation's Work: The Rise of Women's Political Culture, 1830–1900* (New Haven: Yale University Press, 1995).

23. See Walter Trattner, *Crusade for the Children: A History of the National Child Labor Committee and Child Labor Reform in America* (Chicago: Quadrangle Books, 1970), 58. The committee first turned its attentions to the role of children in the Pennsylvania coal mines. The anthracite coal strike of 1902 had publicized the terrible working conditions of thousands of young boys and, despite some bitter opposition from the industry and state labor officials, the Pennsylvania legislature passed a series of laws between 1905 and 1909 to provide a minimum age limit of sixteen years for mine workers. Glass making was another industry known for its employment of child labor and very harsh conditions, as was the textile industry in the south. Eventually,

after much investigation, lobbying, and negotiation, bills were passed in many states. In 1906 the first national child labor bill was introduced into the Senate by Albert Beveridge of Indiana. Congressman Herbert Parsons of New York forwarded a similar bill in the House that same year. The NCLC supported the legislation although its support was by no means unanimous, with the opposition fearing federal intervention in the affairs of the states. Organized labor was also opposed due to its concern about the dangerous precedent of government interference with labor relations. Finally, President Roosevelt did not support the legislation, preferring more information and investigation into the problem. Needless to say, the bill died and the NCLC reorganized in opposition to federal legislation with a twofold agenda: a renewed focus on the passing of legislation by the states and the establishment of a federal children's bureau (see Trattner, *Crusade for the Children*, chap. 3, 69–93). The political climate would change over the next decade with the establishment of the Children's Bureau and public support for children's welfare. The NCLC then moved to support federal legislation and helped draft the Keating–Owen bill which President Woodrow Wilson signed in September 1916.

24. AR, "Experts in Child Welfare, Departmental" (September 18, 1917), question 19.

25. The NCLC ninth annual conference was held in Jacksonville, Florida. See *Child Labor Bulletin* 2, no. 1 (May 1913): 147–48 and 161. On returning home Rochester gave addresses at the Child Welfare Association of the Unity Church in Brooklyn, Woman's Clubs of Englewood and Ridgefield, and at her home church, St. Paul's of Englewood: *Child Labor Bulletin* 2, no. 3 (November 1913): 30; *Child Labor Bulletin* 3, no. 3 (November 1914): 27.

26. Typed, undated document on protection for working children. Penciled on top of the first page in AR's handwriting is "Dorset summer, probably 1913." Land for the house at Dorset had been acquired by September 1912. Louise mentioned in the "AR Annals" (January 1914) that Aradyddit was built for Rochester, who took over the plans herself. Louise Rochester especially enjoyed this house and spent much time there over subsequent years; Rochester mostly visited on holidays and for summer vacations. There is no mention of the house after the Annals come to an end in 1918, and I assume that it was sold after Louise Rochester died in 1919.

27. *Child Labor Bulletin* 3, no. 1 (May 1914): 140. This successful article was presented at the tenth annual conference on "The Federal Child Labor Bill" in New Orleans in March 1914, and it was undoubtedly central in her promotion within the NCLC Publicity Department (see *Child Labor Bulletin* 3, no. 1 [May 1914]: 167 and 172). Interestingly, while working within the system, Rochester's politics seemed to have made themselves known. On one occasion, for example, Rochester publicly protested the elitism of assuming vocational education was for the "bottom" layer of children and replied that "instead of accepting the fact that there is plenty of room at the top and very little at the bottom, we should also work to get rid of top and bottom," *Child Labor Bulletin* 3, no. 1 (May 1914): 186.

28. *Child Labor Bulletin* 3, no. 2 (August 1914): 93–126.

29. AR, "Street Workers," NCLC Pamphlet #246 (1915): 3. Writing during 1915 also included a co–authored article with Florence Taylor on "What the Government Says about Cotton Mills, New York," *Child Labor Bulletin* 3, no. 4 (February 1915); a book review of *Mental and Physical Measurements of Working Children*, by

Wooley and Fischer, *Child Labor Bulletin* 3, no. 4 (February 1915): 8–9; and a report compiled just before leaving the committee: "What State Laws and the Federal Census Say About Child Labor," NCLC Pamphlet #248 (November 1915). Alongside authoring these works, as secretary of publicity with the NCLC, Rochester also had responsibility for the publication of all the bulletins on child labor as well as other publicity. In this role she reported to the eleventh annual conference in Washington, D.C., in January 1915: *Child Labor Bulletin* 4, no. 1 (May 1915): 12–13.

30. "AR Annals," January 1914.

31. James Alner Tobey, *The Children's Bureau: Its History, Activities and Organization* (Baltimore: Johns Hopkins Press, 1925), 1–2.

32. Molly Ladd-Taylor, "Hull House Goes to Washington," in Frankel and Dye, *Gender, Class, Race and Reform in the Progressive Era*, 112–13.

33. Third Annual Report of the Chief, Children's Bureau to the Secretary of Labor, Fiscal Year Ending June 30, 1915 (Washington, D.C.: Washington Government Printing Office, 1915), 5. Rochester herself prepared the summary of this annual report ("Experts in Child Welfare" [September 18, 1917], question 19). Later, with the passage of federal child labor legislation (the Keating–Owen Act) in 1916, the bureau created a Child Labor Division and this was headed by Grace Abbott, another Hull House settlement worker. Abbott became head of the Children's Bureau itself from 1921 to 1934.

34. *Child Labor Bulletin* 4, no. 1 (May 1915): 55–65. In the *Commonwealth* article (June 12, 1915) Rochester explained that the charter would not be a panacea or another child welfare movement, but would rather allow the articulation of principles on which the activities of the various children's associations could be based. In typical style Rochester launched into her forte, persuasive writing: "The charter will deal with the whole of childhood. It will be of interest to the mother whose heart is wrung by the suffering of poor babies in districts where infant mortality is a shame and a problem. It is of interest to the father who looks out for his children but knows that there are many others who have no guardian. It is of interest to the educators who would see all children enjoy an unfolding of the spirit and development of the best in each. It is of interest to the employer who will see in it the future elimination of the inefficient worker. It is of interest to clergymen, social workers, and state officials, and everyone in any way connected with a child."

35. "AR Annals," September 1915.

36. Ibid., January 1914.

37. Ibid., October 4, 1916.

38. Ibid. Note that the date of entry does not correspond with its content. Perhaps Louise finished the entry at a later date and omitted marking it.

39. Children's Bureau, press release for morning papers, November 15, 1915. These accomplishments are also listed in "Experts in Child Welfare, Departmental" (September 18, 1917), question 19.

40. Children's Bureau, press release to afternoon papers, January 1, 1916.

41. Phyllis Rose, "Confessions of a Burned-Out Biographer," in *The Seductions of Biography*, ed. Mary Rhiel and David Suchoff (New York: Routledge, 1996), 131–36.

42. Children's Bureau, press release for morning papers, October 23, 1916.

43. "AR Annals," no month 1917, January 1918.

44. ·Children's Bureau, "Baby Weeks in War Time," press release, April 30, 1917.

45. AR, "Child Labor in Warring Countries" (Children's Bureau Publication #27, July 1917). Other writing during 1917 included "Summary of Child Welfare Laws" (Children's Bureau Publication #21) and "Facilities for Children's Play in the District of Columbia," written with Howard C. Jenness (Children's Bureau Publication #22). Rochester also compiled a report, "Outline of Suggestions for a Club Study in a Rural-Community" (original, typed document, February 1917).

46. AR, "Infant Mortality: Results of a Field-Study in Baltimore, MD" (Children's Bureau Publication #119, 1922).

47. See, for example, Robert Morse Woodbury, "Economic Factors in Infant Mortality," *Quarterly Publication of the American Statistical Association* (June 1924), which cites Rochester's work.

48. AR, "Infant Mortality," 105.

49. Judith Sealander discusses this insider versus outsider status in *As Minority Becomes Majority: Federal Reaction to the Phenomenon of Women in the Workplace, 1920–1963* (Westport, Conn.: Greenwood, 1983), 3–11.

50. Ladd-Taylor, "Hull House Goes to Washington," 115–16.

51. Ibid., 120.

Notes to Chapter Three

1. Unidentified, undated newspaper clipping—probably *Boston Herald*, 1912. My thanks go to Ms. Gwen Workman for sending this clipping to me.

2. Lois Rudnick, "The Life of Mabel Dodge Luhan," in *The Challenge of Feminist Biography*, ed. Sara Alpern, Joyce Antler, Elizabeth Israels Perry, and Ingrid Winther Scobie (Urbana: University of Illinois Press, 1992), 118.

3. Martin Stannard, "The Necrophiliac Art?" in *The Literary Biography: Problems and Solutions*, ed. Dale Salway (Iowa City: University of Iowa Press, 1996), 37. He cites Janet Malcolm who cites Ann Stevenson.

4. For sources on women's role in foreign missions, see for example, R. Pierce Beaver, *American Protestant Women in World Mission: A History of the First Feminist Movement in North America* (Grand Rapids, Mich.: Eerdmans, 1980); Fiona Bowie, Deborah Kirkwood, and Shirley Ardener, eds., *Women and Missions: Past and Present* (Providence, R.I.: Berg, 1993); Leslie A. Flemming ed., *Women's Work for Women: Missionaries and Social Change in Asia* (London: Westview Press, 1989); Patricia Hill, *The World Their Household: The American Women's Foreign Mission Movement and Cultural Transformation, 1870–1920* (Ann Arbor: University of Michigan Press, 1985); Jane Hunter, *The Gospel of Gentility: American Women Missionaries in Turn-of-the-Century China* (New Haven: Yale University Press, 1984); and Neil Stephen, *A History of Christian Missions* (London: Pelican, 1982). Explorations of colonial power, white femininity, and the relationship of these to the social construction of gender among indigenous women include Nupur Chaudhuri and Margaret Strobel, eds., *Western Women and Imperialism: Complicity and Resistance* (Bloomington: Indiana University Press, 1992); Kumari Jaywardena, *The White Woman's Other Burden: Western Women and South Asia during British Rule* (New York: Routledge, 1995); Anne McClintock, *Imperial Leather: Race, Gender, and Sexuality in the Colonial Context* (New York: Routledge, 1995); Mrinalini Sinha,

Colonial Masculinity: The "Manly Englishman" and the "Effeminate Bengali" in the Late-Nineteenth-Century (Manchester U.K.: Manchester University Press, 1995); and Vron Ware, *Beyond the Pale: White Women, Racism and History* (London: Verso, 1992). A good source on women and postcolonialism is Trinh T. Minh-ha's text, *Women, Native, Other: Writing Postcoloniality and Feminism* (Bloomington: Indiana University Press, 1989). See Lian Xi, *The Conversion of the Missionaries* (State College: Pennsylvania State University, 1997), for a discussion of the ways that missionaries took on critical and progressive attitudes toward Western societies. My article on missionary women is "Between Subordination and She-Tiger: Social Constructions of White Femininity in the Lives of Single, Protestant Missionaries in China, 1905–1930," *Women's Studies International Forum* 19 (1996): 621–32.

5. Hill, *The World Their Household*, 3.

6. Helen Barrett Montgomery, *Western Women in Eastern Lands: An Outline Study of Fifty Years of Woman's Work in Foreign Missions* (New York: Macmillan, 1910), 243–44.

7. Hill, *The World Their Household*, 86; Hunter, *The Gospel of Gentility*, 182.

8. Hill, *The World Their Household*, 191.

9. Hunter, *The Gospel of Gentility*, 130.

10. The Chinese Exclusion Act of 1882, supported by politicians and labor leaders who sought to eliminate Chinese labor during the post–Civil War recession, was not repealed until 1943. It limited Chinese immigration and prevented Chinese immigrants from establishing families in the United States. Those who did arrive between 1910 and 1940 often had to endure humiliating physical examinations and intense interrogations at Angel Island Immigration Station in San Francisco. Prejudice against the Chinese was rampant and life was often painful and difficult. Prostitution was rampant in the Chinese districts of major U.S. cities since many Chinese women came as indentured servants or "mui jai"—sold by poor parents in China and resold in the United States. As a result Chinese women were often looked upon with contempt.

11. Hill, *The World Their Household*, 162.

12. Verse excerpted from Vida Dutton Scudder, *On Journey* (New York: Dutton, 1937), 251.

13. The Boxers, who rebelled at the turn of the century, were nationalistic, antiforeign, and anti-Christian rebels who attacked foreigners, missionaries, and Chinese who had converted to Christianity. While not the case for all those who came to be known as Boxers, they tended to oppose the Manchu or Ch'ing dynasty and helped facilitate its demise. Several years prior to the Boxer uprisings of 1898, China had been at war with Japan over Korea, and this defeat, coupled with pressure from the West and the general decadence of the Manchu dynasty, had led to the increasing disintegration of the old regime. European powers took advantage of this situation and claimed leases on strategic ports, eventually helping form an international army that put down the Boxer rebellion and protected Peking. While the Chinese paid heavily for what scholars call the Boxer catastrophe in terms of increasing and accelerated Western influence, in name the Chinese retained independence and territories.

14. For sources on this period of Chinese history see, for example, Jack Gray, *Rebellions and Revolutions: China from the 1800s to the 1980s* (New York: Oxford Uni-

versity Press, 1990); Victor Purcell, *The Boxer Uprising: A Background Study* (London: Cambridge University Press, 1963); and Mary Clabaugh Wright, *China in Revolution: The First Phase, 1900–1913* (New Haven: Yale University Press, 1968). See also Chung Chun Wang, "A Plea for the Recognition of the Chinese Republic," *Atlantic Monthly* 61 (January 1913): 42.

15. Edward Hutchins Sr. to GH, September 20, 1910.

16. "Jane" to GH, August 14, no year.

17. Dorothy Mills to GH, February 1916.

18. "St. Hilda's Under Deaconess Phelps: Told in Letters from July 1908–May 1909," in pamphlet #278 ("St. Hilda's School for Girls, Wuchang," January 1910), 13. This pamphlet was pasted in the front of a blue hardbacked notebook with the inscription in Hutchins's hand, "St. Hilda's School Notes."

19. A personal relationship was essential for conversion, and a focus on women meant that whole families would be affected. As Helen Barrett Montgomery, *Western Women*, p. 62, declared, "Perhaps today we see more clearly than was seen then the necessity of raising woman if we are to raise the race; know more fully than they the horrors of the servile life in which the majority of women the world over are forced to live."

20. Hunter, *Gospel of Gentility*, 174–75.

21. Pauline Osgood, "Report on St. Hilda's School, Wuchang, China, For the Year Ending Jan. 31, 1903," in "St. Hilda's School for Chinese Girls, Wuchang" (Pamphlet #226, 1903).

22. GH, "St. Hilda's School Notes," 25.

23. Ibid., "Moonlight Shadow—Yuck Yin," 1.

24. Ibid., 69.

25. Ibid., 11–12.

26. GH, "Story of the Chinese Official's Wife," in an envelope pasted in "St.Hilda's School Notes," 15.

27. GH, "St. Hilda's School Notes," 52.

28. Ibid., 18.

29. Martha Li Kao to GH, November 24, 1939.

30. Trinh T. Minh-ha, *Women, Native, Other*, 67.

31. Helen Hendricks to GH, April 14, no year. Hutchins also had a close relationship with the Bishop of Hankow, Logan H. Roots, and his wife Eliza, while in China. They were very fond of Hutchins and praised her commitment to St. Hilda's (Bishop Logan Roots to GH, November 9, 1915, and Bishop Logan Roots to GH, February 29, 1916).

32. Betty Feldman, "Grace Hutchins Tells about Women Who Work," *Worker*, March 1, 1953.

33. Bryn Mawr, *Turtle's Progress-Dispatch*, vol. 1, no. 3 (May 30, 1931).

34. The *Church Militant*, vol. 19, no. 7 (December 1916), wrote that Hutchins was involved with Women's Auxiliary work. *St. Louis Star* (October 13, 1916) reported that Hutchins was among the delegates to the Episcopal Conclave held in St. Louis, those "Who Carry Religion to the Heathen."

35. Union Theological Seminary, on-line catalog, January 15, 1997.

36. Betty Feldman, "Grace Hutchins Tells about Women Who Work." Rochester wrote about Hutchins's tenure at St. Faith's in a letter to Devere Allen. She used this

experience as an example of Hutchins's qualifications for working at the *World To-morrow* (AR to Devere Allen, May 9, 1924).

Notes to Chapter Four

1. The Russian revolution of February 1917 had led to the abdication and assassination of Tsar Nicholas II, ending 300 years of absolutist Romanov autocracy; the revolution also led to the return of Vladamir Lenin from Germany in the midst of an unstable Russian provisional government. Political changes were underway in the factories and in the countryside as workers rallied for change, encouraging the Bolsheviks to make a failed attempt to overthrow the government in July. However, a right-wing coup under the former tsarist chief-of-staff, General Kornilov, resulted in Bolshevik support from the more moderate Mensheviks and Socialist Revolutionary Party. By October, the Bolsheviks were ready to strike again and the October Revolution was born, led by Lenin and Trotsky. An attempted assassination plot against Lenin resulted in terror and purging on the part of the Bolsheviks, and, although they emerged victorious, the position of the Bolsheviks was still precarious. An armistice with the Germans in 1918 at Brest Litovsk helped the Bolsheviks remain in power, although it robbed Russia of considerable land, population, and industrial strength. Again the Red Bolshevik armies emerged victorious over the White forces of their enemies during the civil war of 1918–1920; Moscow and Petrograd remained in Bolshevik hands and Trotsky emerged the military hero. Ultimately, while the peasants might have distrusted the Bolsheviks, they feared a restoration of the old order even more. By 1921 military operations had ceased and while much had been lost, Russia survived as a communist state even though it had not been invited to participate in the earlier peace settlements at Versailles or join the League of Nations. See Lionel Kochan and Richard Abraham, *The Making of Modern Russia* (Harmondsworth: Peregrine, 1983).

2. For overviews of women's lives during this period see, for example, Lois W. Banner, *Women in Modern America: A Brief History* (New York: Harcourt Brace Jovanovich, 1974); Nancy Cott, *The Grounding of Modern Feminism* (New Haven: Yale University Press, 1987); Ellen Carol DuBois and Vicki L. Ruiz, eds., *Unequal Sisters: A Multicultural Reader in U.S. Women's History* (New York: Routledge, 1990); Linda K. Kerber and Jane Sherron De Hart, *Woman's America: Refocusing the Past* (New York: Oxford University Press, 1995); and June Sochen, *Herstory: A History of the American Woman's Past* (Palo Alto, Calif.: Mayfield, 1982).

3. Liz Stanley, *The Auto/biographical I* (Manchester, UK: Manchester University Press, 1992), 149.

4. Teresa Amott and Julie A. Matthaei, *Race, Gender and Work: A Multi-Cultural Economic History of Women in the United States* (Boston: South End Press, 1996); Julie A. Matthaei, *An Economic History of Women in America: Women's Work, the Sexual Division of Labor, and the Development of Capitalism* (New York: Schocken Books, 1982).

5. Avery F. Gordon, *Ghostly Matters: Haunting and the Sociological Imagination* (Minneapolis: University of Minnesota Press, 1997), 4.

6. R. O. G. Urch, "Bolshevism and Religion in Russia," *Atlantic Monthly* 131 (March 1923): 396–406.

7. Seidenberg and Co. to GH, letter of appointment, December 9, 1920.

8. GH, "Statement by the author," *Women Who Work* (New York: International Publishers, 1934), February 23, 1934.

9. See Max Horn, *The Intercollegiate Socialist Society, 1905–1921: Origins of the Modern American Student Movement* (Boulder, Colo.: Westview Press, 1979), for an interesting historical overview of these organizations.

10. The Rand School also had a successful summer workers' school called Camp Tamiment. The school was dissolved in 1956 and reorganized as the Tamiment Institute. It was renamed the Tamiment Library and became part of the Elmer Holmes Bobst Library of New York University in 1963.

11. The Community House records (1920–1922) include a commune journal that documented conversations about initiating the community in December 1920, and recorded commune activities through the end of 1922. These journal entries are mostly undated and are loose-leaf pages that have no page numbers. Most are unsigned, although there is one consistent handwriting that appears to be that of resident Sarah (Sally) Cleghorn, who joined the commune in November 1921. Cleghorn is mentioned in a letter from Hutchins and Rochester to other commune residents (March 21, 1922) as "custodian of the archives" and the handwriting matches signed samples of her writing. Cleghorn's authorship of the early entries that record activities prior to her arrival must have been written retrospectively. All commune journal entries are made by Cleghorn unless otherwise noted. She left the commune permanently in 1923 and her departure could explain why the commune journal had no entries after 1922. The Community House records also include a series of letters, postcards, verse and miscellaneous documents that span 1921–1924. This entry in the commune journal (hereafter CJ) is called "The Definite Beginning."

12. Janet Lee, "'Sisterhood of the Smiling Countenance and the Merry Laugh': Unsettling the Sentimental in a New York Women's Commune, 1921–24," *Frontiers: A Journal of Women Studies* 17 (1996): 1–29.

13. CJ, "The Definite Beginning."

14. For a focus on the relationship between the sentimental and modernism, see Suzanne Clark, *Sentimental Modernism: Women Writers and the Revolution of the Word* (Bloomington: Indiana University Press, 1991), 32. See Marianne DeKoven, *Rich and Strange: Gender, History, Modernism* (Princeton: Princeton University Press, 1991), p. 12, for comments on the relationship between modernism and socialism. Also see *The Aesthetic Dimension: Toward a Critique of Marxist Aesthetics* (Boston: Beacon Press, 1978) by Herbert Marcuse for a discussion of Leftist defenders of modernism. For general discussions of modernism I suggest Malcolm Bradbury and James McFarlane, *Modernism* (Harmondsworth: Penguin Books, 1976); Steve Giles, *Theorizing Modernism: Essays in Critical Theory* (New York: Routledge, 1993); Gillian Hanscombe and Virginia L. Smyers, *Writing for Their Lives: The Modernist Women, 1910–1946* (Boston: Northeastern University Press, 1987); Andreas Huyssen, *After the Great Divide: Modernism, Mass Culture, Postmodernism* (Bloomington: Indiana University Press, 1987); and Bonnie Kime Scott, ed., *The Gender of Modernism: A Critical Anthology* (Bloomington: Indiana University Press, 1990). For a more in-depth analysis of the intersections of gender and feminism with modernism see Alice A. Jardine, *Gynesis: Configurations of Woman and Modernity* (Ithaca: Cornell University Press, 1985).

15. This is a constant theme in the development of women writers and intellectuals throughout the modernist period: a desire for the "freedom and authority of serious members of the avante-garde but also [a need for] the traditions of emotional identity they have been pressed to abandon" (Clark, *Sentimental Modernism*, 13).

16. Sarah (Sally) Cleghorn to GH, April 1923.

17. In England the socialist Owenites of the second quarter of the nineteenth century had developed principles and plans on which to establish self-supporting cooperative communities, emphasizing that people should live and work together for their mutual happiness, assistance, and support, hold all their property in common, and work according to ability, receiving according to need. See Ronald G. Garnett, *Cooperation and the Owenite Socialist Communities in Britain, 1825–45* (Manchester, UK: Manchester University Press, 1972). Fourier and Wright established communitarian experiments at Brook Farm and the Nashoba Colony, while other well-known communities, such as the Oneida Colony and the Shakers, took root in the United States. See Wendy E. Chmielewski, Louis J. Kern, and Marilyn Klee-Hartzell, eds., *Women in Spiritual and Communitarian Societies in the United States* (Syracuse: Syracuse University Press, 1993); John Humphrey Noyes, *History of American Socialism* (New York: Hillary House, 1961); and Ernest S. Wooster, *Communities of the Past and Present* (New York: AMS Press [1924], 1974).

18. CJ, "The House Looms into Sight."

19. See, for example, Dana Frank, "Housewives, Socialists, and the Politics of Food," in *Women and Power in American History*, vol. 2, ed. Kathryn Kish Sklar and Thomas Dubin (Englewood Cliffs: Prentice Hall, 1991), 106–7.

20. In *The Literary Review* (October 20, 1923), Sally Cleghorn reviewed *Jesus Christ and the World Today* in an essay titled "Workday Christians." Here she wrote about the personal ethics of Hutchins and Rochester as a way to enhance their credibility as authors. She described the couple as women who had summered and wintered in the Christian life: that is, living devoutly, simply, and frugally. In addition, a review of the book by the Commission on Church and Social Service is included in the commission's Information Bulletin. It read: "Not the least element of interest in this excellently written book grows out of the fact that it was written by women of culture who have made it their chief aim to approximate the Christian way of life by dwelling among the commonest surroundings and eliminating all semblance of luxury" (Information Service Bulletin of the Research Department of the Commission on Church and Social Service, September 30, 1922).

21. CJ, "Painting Chairs Before Moving In."

22. CJ, "The House."

23. CJ, "The Hope and Dream Carried to Church."

24. The house blessing for the chapel read: "Eternal God . . . as day by day we seek Thy presence in this chapel, remind us, O Father that only as we seek Thee also in the crowded ways and in the market place shall we learn to hear Thy voice here in the stillness; only as we give to the service of Thy kingdom our words, our acts, our common life, and all our relations with our fellows, can we dare to offer intercession. And as we go from this chapel to our daily work, let us carry into the little things of every day a light from the flame of Thy love" (typed, unsigned, undated document, "The Office for the Blessing of the House").

25. AR, untitled manuscript, undated.

26. Some visitors to Community House were documented in a guest book included in the Community House records. They included Lydia Springer, "The House Boat Roomer," and Helen Hendricks, who all resided there during the spring of 1922. A Miss Scott (first name unknown, although I think this may have been Katharine Scott, Hutchins's colleague from St. Hilda's) lived at 352 during the winter and spring of 1921–1922. More short-term visitors included Jessie O. Hawley in January 1922, Anna Reedy in February 1922; Adelaide Case (Hutchins's friend at the Union Theological Seminary) on August 19 (Hutchins's birthday), 1922; Clara Williams in September 1922; Polly James and Margaret Godwin in October 1922; Lucy Sturgis on "the night of the fire," 1922; Vida Scudder on "the night after Marian Savage's service, April 26, 1923; and Helena S. Dudley (Rochester's colleague from Denison College settlement days), Miss Shearman, and Josephine Brown, undated. More complete records of commune members, guests, and visitors were made in the first two years, with less attention after 1923. Cleghorn's departure in 1923 probably affected this record-keeping.

27. CJ, "Visitation of the Community by Bishop Jones," cartoon.

28. Untitled, undated, handwritten document that spelled out all the various household duties of the different residents through a rotation system.

29. See, for example, Friedrich Engels, *The Origins of the Family, Private Property and the State* (New York: International Publishers, 1942); and Vladamir I. Lenin, "Women and Society," in *The Woman Question: Selections from the Writings of Marx, Engels, Lenin and Stalin* (New York: International Publishers, 1938).

30. Charlotte Perkins Gilman, *Women and Economics: The Economic Factor Between Men and Women as a Factor in Social Evolution* (New York: Harper and Row [1898], 1966).

31. AR to Lucie Myer, August 15, no year, but this would be 1921.

32. AR, untitled verse, January 1921.

33. GH verse, "When Boston Came to New York," undated.

34. Ira Bruce Nagel, *Biography: Fiction, Fact, and Form* (London: Macmillan, 1984).

35. Helen Hendricks, verse, "352," undated.

36. Verse, "New York, 1921," AR handwriting, undated.

37. The playfulness with which "the Aunts" approached neighborhood children is demonstrated in this excerpt from the commune journal: "In Feb. invited Anna, Lily and John Reedy to stay while their little brother born. L and J were too bashful; but A came over and stayed 10 days. Aunt Stella or Aunt Mary Ellen gave her her bath, Aunt Anna dressed her, Aunt Sally and Aunt Grace played with her, and Aunt Lucy [*sic*] and Aunt Anne took her out gallivanting. Daily remarks of Anna Reedy, 'Tum upstairs and I'll toe you my bed.' Aunt Grace and Aunt Lucy [*sic*] went to the Christening" (CJ, "Anna Reedy," February 1922).

38. CJ, "Late in January 1922 there was talk of a school at 352."

39. Sally Cleghorn to Community House tenants, June 20, 1922.

40. CJ, anonymous verse, untitled, undated.

41. AR verse, untitled, undated.

42. Of all Hutchins's and Rochester's writing during this period, the most contrived piece that mocks the pathos of traditional religious and feminine discourse is a letter Rochester wrote to commune members while vacationing at Saddle River, New Jersey. It is definitely "over the top" in terms of its language and style. Address-

ing "the saints" left behind at Community House, Rochester mentioned a ring they were going to buy and a visit to the chaplain, perhaps implying commemoration of a commitment between her and Hutchins. However this meaning is by no means clear (AR with postscript by GH to Community House tenants, March 21, 1922).

43. CJ, Ann Mundelein, "A Day Full of Little Joys in the Community," December 1921. This was signed with her initials only.

44. Sally Cleghorn to GH, April 15, 1923.

45. Lillian Faderman, *Surpassing the Love of Men: Romantic Friendships and the Love Between Women From the Renaissance to the Present* (New York: Morrow, 1981).

46. Faderman makes this point in *Odd Girls and Twilight Lovers* (New York: Columbia University Press, 1991), 3.

47. Sally Cleghorn to GH, April 15, 1923.

48. Ibid.

49. Sally Cleghorn to GH and AR, undated.

50. Faderman, *Odd Girls and Twilight Lovers*, 82.

Notes to Chapter Five

1. Paul Buhle and John Cort, "Christian Socialism," in *The Encyclopedia of the American Left*, ed. Mari Jo Buhle, Paul Buhle, and Dan Georgakas (New York: Garland, 1990), 133.

2. For sources on Christian socialism, see John Cort, *Christian Socialism* (Maryknoll, New York: Orbis Press, 1988); Arthur F. McGovern, *Marxism, An American Christian Perspective* (Maryknoll, New York: Orbis Books, 1980); and John J. Marsden, *Marxism and Christian Utopianism: Toward a Socio-Political Theology* (New York: Monthly Review Press, 1991). Earlier books include Herbert Aptheker, *The Urgency of Marxist-Christian Dialogue* (New York: Harper and Row, 1970), and Dale Vree, *On Synthesizing Marxism and Christianity* (New York: Wiley, 1976).

3. Marjorie Garber, "Introduction," in *The Seductions of Biography*, ed. Mary Rhiel and David Suchoff (New York: Routledge, 1996), 177.

4. GH and AR, *Jesus Christ and the World Today*, preface (New York: Doran, 1922).

5. Ibid., 43.

6. Ibid., 47–48.

7. Ibid., 59.

8. Ibid., 85. As far as I know, while no one objected to hints of anti-Semitism in this chapter, some did critique the comparisons made between the socioeconomic inequities of the 1920s with the problems in early Palestine during Jesus' life. Burton S. Easton, a professor at the General Theological Seminary in Chelsea Square, New York, wrote to Hutchins that his own sympathies were "entirely Socialistic." Nonetheless, he felt that it was "a profound mistake in a treatment of Christ's ethics to ally Him unequivocally with a concrete occurrence in recent history on either side unless the case is unambiguously clear. And I think you have rather fallen into that mistake" (Burton S. Easton to GH, July 19, 1922).

9. GH and AR, *Jesus Christ and the World Today*, 138.

10. Commune journal, Ann Mundelein, "A Day Full of Little Joys in the Community," December 1921.

11. Ibid., "Biography of a Book," undated (probably May or June 1922), Sarah (Sally) Cleghorn's handwriting.

12. Prior to its publication, Hutchins and Rochester requested that Scott read over the manuscript and give an initial review, focusing on historical referencing in case of scholarly errors. Scott was keen on historical accuracy, and, though open-minded about interpretation, he did not share their ideological leanings. In this way, he might have been considered an ideal "before press" reviewer. In a letter to Hutchins, Scott wrote that he "read it with much pleasure and interest. It is excellently written, with a mutual earnestness and an eye to reality which one cannot but admire . . . although I belong to a different political camp I found nothing in the book that offended or irritated (except, perhaps, one or two laudatory references to Karl Marx, Debs, and similar scoundrels!). If other books with the same general aim were written with the same sanity and moderation, there would probably be much less bitterness on both sides, and we should have a prospect of arriving at the truth" (Professor E. F. Scott to GH, March 22, 1922).

13. Review of *Jesus Christ and the World Today* in the *Christian Century: An Undenominational Journal of Religion* 39 (June 8, 1922): 1.

14. *"Some Opinions of the Book,"* ordering blank for *Jesus Christ and the World Today* by Doran and Co., undated.

15. Information Service Bulletin of the Research Department of the Commission on Church and Social Service, September 30, 1922. Hutchins and Rochester seemed to have managed to write a radical text that was acceptable to many less radical colleagues. Alice Dillingham, Bryn Mawr alumna and a lawyer, found it excellent: "You have written a really wonderful book. I expected to enjoy reading it, but was not prepared for anything so—shall I say sublime. It has, underlying it, the severity of the truly Christ-like spirit. I shall loan it to all my friends." At the top of this letter Rochester had ironically penciled, "From a *not* radical class mate of AR's who is a lawyer," Alice Dillingham to AR and GH, May 30, 1922.

16. Information Service Bulletin of the Research Department of the Commission on Church and Social Service, September 30, 1922.

17. In September 1936, Mr. Elmer B. Michelson from Dorchester, Massachusetts, wrote to say that he had been using the text in a religious social problems class: "It is difficult to tell you how impressed we are with your eruditions, social knowledge of the ancient world and the world today, and your Christian passion. In short, it seems to us that you two women have admirably combined and solved the problem of the individual and society." In 1936, when this letter was written, Hutchins and Rochester were no longer ideologically aligned with their views in the book and would much rather, I'm sure, have been praised for their later writings. However, I expect they appreciated the last part of the letter: "Indeed, you may be further concerned that as a result of our realization of being reborn in Christ, understanding has become possible, desire immediately followed to become part of the creative force of the universe, and action resulted in our joining the left wing militants of the Socialist Party. 'Repent, for the Kingdom of God is at hand'" (Elmer B. Michelson to GH, September 2, 1936).

18. See Charles Chatfield, *For Peace and Justice: Pacifism in America, 1914–1941* (Knoxville: University of Kentucky Press, 1971).

19. "Historical Introduction," Fellowship of Reconciliation (American Section)

archives index (June 14, 1955), Swarthmore College Peace Collection, Swarthmore College, Pennsylvania (hereafter SCPC). All minutes and reports cited below are from the Fellowship archives in SCPC.

20. "The Fellowship of Reconciliation: Its Origin and Development," pamphlet (Nyack, New York: F.O.R. Publication, 1922). The Fellowship's offices were established in New York City and Gilbert A. Beaver was elected as the first chair. Norman Thomas joined the staff in 1917 as co-secretary with Edward Evans. Then in 1919, after Bishop Paul Jones of Utah was forced to resign his diocese in December 1918 because of his Pacifist politics, Jones was elected secretary to succeed Norman Thomas, who then took over editorship of the *World Tomorrow* magazine. Another religiously trained, antiwar socialist was John Nevin Sayre. A friend of Hutchins and Rochester, he also worked as editor for the *World Tomorrow* and took over Hutchins's position as associate secretary of F.O.R. in 1924. He held this post until 1935 and then again from 1940 to 1946. In the meantime he chaired the organization from 1935 to 1939. Sayre's article, "The Story of The Fellowship of Reconciliation, 1915–1935" (Nyack, New York: Fellowship Publications, 1935), is especially useful for understanding the early years of the organization.

21. Glen Zeitzer, "The Fellowship of Reconciliation on the Eve of the Second World War: A Peace Organization Prepares," *Peace and Justice* 3 (Summer, Fall 1975): 46–51.

22. "The Fellowship of Reconciliation," pamphlet, 1.

23. F.O.R. Council minutes, June 21, 1921.

24. Ibid., March 21, 1922.

25. Ibid.

26. This earlier meeting was in February 1923. F.O.R. Council Minutes, February 6, 1923.

27. Gilbert A. Beaver to Council members, May 25, 1923.

28. F.O.R. Council minutes, September 28, 1923.

29. Ibid., October 16, 1923.

30. A. J. Muste and the Committee on the Consideration of our Aims and Purposes, "Committee on F.O.R. Statement," November 1923, 2–3.

31. For biographies of A. J. Muste, see Nat Hentoff, *Peace Agitator: The Story of A. J. Muste* (New York: Macmillan, 1963); and Jo Ann Ooiman Robinson, *Abraham Went Out: A Biography of A. J. Muste* (Philadelphia: Temple University Press, 1981).

32. A. J. Muste and the Committee on the Consideration of our Aims and Purposes, "Proposed Revised Statement: F.O.R.," November 1923.

33. AR to Lucie Myer, to be passed on to other friends, June 26, 1923. Recipients of the letter included Lucie Myer, Stella Lundelins, Sally Cleghorn and Edith Klein, all past or current residents of Community House, as well as friends Lucy Sturgis, Adelaide Case, and Bishop Fleming Jones's wife, whose first name I do not know.

34. AR to "Dear Friends at Home," to be passed on to other friends, July 21, 1923, 1.

35. Ibid., 5.

36. Ibid., 4. As an aside, this letter also contained a remark made by Rochester that the Nexö maids were the only happy-looking working people they had seen in Denmark. While the patronizing tone of this comment seemed lost on Rochester, it is ironic that as a Bolshevik, Nexö should have had maids, happy or not.

37. Barbara MacDonald and Cynthia Rich, *Look Me in the Eye: Old Women, Aging and Ageism* (San Francisco: Spinsters Press, 1983).

38. AR to Lucie Myer, July 12, 1923.

39. The committee on antiwar evangelism was appointed following discussion of a letter from Sidney Strong suggesting "organizing a group of men [*sic*] who would go into a town and develop the Fellowship point of view as a series of meetings like the old time Evangelists." The committee was assigned the duty to "work out the whole matter" (F.O.R. council minutes, January 12, 1924). Rochester's work on the pamphlet was listed as approved in the Council minutes, March 29, 1924.

40. F.O.R. Executive Committee minutes, October 2, 1924.

41. The postwar crackdown on progressive thought and activism resulted in the September 1918 issue of the *New World* being held up by the postmaster general at the New York Post Office because of an objection to an article by Norman Thomas calling on the president to stop military intervention in Russia, an article by Frederick Libby suggesting that the kaiser and Colonel Roosevelt worshipped essentially the same battlegod, and a parable decrying hate by John Haynes Homes. After Nevin Sayre met with President Wilson on the following day in a cabinet meeting, Wilson overruled the decision of the postmaster general.

42. Norman Thomas, "The Distinctive Place of the *World Tomorrow*," undated report (F.O.R. archives, SCPC). In this report Thomas also offered some interesting insight about the ideological orientation of the magazine by commenting on his feelings about its subtitle. The original subtitle of the *New World* was *"A Journal of Christian Thought and Practice."* On the first page of the report Norman Thomas wrote of the implications of this subtitle: "Both purpose and message are I suppose indicated by our sub-title. Regretfully I am obliged to confess that this sub-title—one I believe of my own choosing—is less and less satisfactory. Experience has proved that it awakens misunderstanding; that in some quarters it is looked upon as camouflage and that in others it raises the question: whose Christianity, Jesus's, Pauls's, Tolstoi's or the official Christianity of the various Churches? Moreover I must confess that I am increasingly doubtful whether the religion which must sweep the hearts of men if our ideals are to triumph will be content merely to take over and reinterpret the vocabulary of categories of Christianity."

43. AR, "Immigration and Internationalism," *World Tomorrow* (November 1921): 336–39.

44. Ibid., 339.

45. GH, "For Group Discussion," *World Tomorrow* (February 1922): 59–60.

46. AR, "The Future in the Present," *World Tomorrow* (July 1923): 203.

47. Ibid.

48. AR, "What Property Does to the Individual," *World Tomorrow* (April 1922): 105.

49. Ibid.

50. Ibid.

51. AR, "What Eleven Families Spend: The Cost of Comfort That Is Not Luxury," *World Tomorrow* (June 1922): 169.

52. AR, "The Pacifist's 'Preparedness': How Can We Work for Non-Violent Revolutionary Change?" *World Tomorrow* (July 1923): 214.

53. Ibid., 215.

54. Ibid., 214.

55. AR, "Sowing the Wind," *World Tomorrow* (November 1925): 330–32; and "Need We Fear Class-Consciousness?" *World Tomorrow* (January 1925): 5–6.

56. AR, "Need We Fear Class-Consciousness?" 6.

57. GH, "Prophets and the People," *World Tomorrow* (June 1924): 182.

58. GH, "Our Inferiority Complex," *World Tomorrow* (December 1923): 362–63.

59. Freda Kirchwey, "Are You a Feminist?" *World Tomorrow* (December 1923): 361–62.

60. Clark Blaise, "Your Nearest Exit May Be Behind You: Autobiography and the Post-Modernist Moment," in *The Seductions of Biography*, ed. Mary Rhiel and David Suchoff (New York: Routledge, 1996), 207.

61. GH, "Our Inferiority Complex," 362.

62. Ibid., 363.

63. Ibid.

64. Ibid.

65. GH to John Nevin Sayre, June 19, 1924.

66. GH to Devere Allen, December 25, 1924.

67. Ibid.

68. AR to Nevin Sayre, November 18, 1927.

69. AR to Kirby Page and Devere Allen, November 18, 1927.

70. AR to Devere Allen, December 6, 1951.

Notes to Chapter Six

1. GH to Susan Hutchins, July 11, 1927. In this letter, written after Hutchins had returned from the trip, she explained that she had been going through menopause, "the change of life," and that it had made her "more nervous than usual." She told her mother that the trip had been more beneficial than doctors and sanatoriums.

2. GH to "Dear Friends," August 27, 1926, 1.

3. Gertrude Stein, *Everybody's Autobiography* (London: Virago [1938], 1985), 53.

4. GH to "Dear Friends," August 27, 1926, 2.

5. AR to "Dear Friends," December 10, 1926, 5.

6. AR to "Dear Friends," December 29, 1926, 4.

7. AR to "Dear Friends," August 27, 1926, 2. At this point Rochester and Hutchins were 46 and 41 years old, respectively, hardly "girls," and certainly not devoted to missionary work. In fact, their estimation of missionaries was relatively low, even though at some level they understood the foreign mission's benevolent, though often misguided, attempts at improving the lives of native peoples. Hutchins in particular must have had strong insight into the contradictions of their lot given her past experiences and no doubt understood the role of the missionary in colonialist expansion. Indeed, Rochester endured silent embarrassment in Baguio, on the Philippine Islands, at a missionary friend's extreme condescension to the indigenous Igorot people whom she saw as her "flock"(AR to "Dear Friends," December 29, 1926, 3).

8. AR to "Dear Friends," August 27, 1926, 2.

9. AR to "Dear Friends," December 29, 1926, 3.

10. AR to "Dear Friends," December 9, 1926, 2.

11. Ibid.

12. AR to "Dear Friends," February 5, 1927, 4.

13. AR, "Dangerous Thoughts in Japan" (original manuscript, September 17, 1926), 1–2.

14. GH, "Kagawa as Labor Leader," *Christian Century* (October 28, 1926): 1328.

15. AR to "Dear Friends," October 10, October 11, and December 9, 1926.

16. GH, "Gray Terror in Peking" (original document, October 10, 1926), 4.

17. Hutchins recorded her time interviewing key people in Chinese educational and social reform issues in a tiny bound notebook. This notebook is densely packed with her notes about literature and conversations with various people.

18. GH, "Gray Terror in Peking," 1–2.

19. Ibid., 3–4.

20. AR to "Dear Friends," October 10, 1926, 3.

21. AR, "The Nationalists Take Wuchang," *Nation* (December 15, 1926): 635–36.

22. GH and AR, "Joyous Christmas and New Year Greetings to Our Friends from the Happy Travelers," October 26, 1926, 2–4.

23. AR to "Dear Friends," October 10, 1926, 1–2. See also AR, "Glimpses of New China," *World Tomorrow* (February 1927): 80.

24. GH and AR, "Joyous Christmas and New Year Greetings to Our Friends from the Happy Travelers," October 26, 1926, 3.

25. AR, "Notes from the Philippines," *World Tomorrow* (March 1927): 133.

26. Ibid.

27. AR to "Dear Friends," December 9, 1926, 5.

28. AR to "Dear Friends," December 29, 1926, 2.

29. AR to "Dear Friends," February 5, 1927, 1–6.

30. Ibid., 2.

31. Ibid., 4.

32. GH, "Gandhi in the Villages, " *World Tomorrow* (May 1927): 203.

33. Ibid., 204.

34. AR to "Dear Friends," February 5, 1927, 4 and 6.

35. In her letter Rochester ended her account of Gandhi's interview and speech with a reflection on what she believed were the three creative forces in the world at that time: the Labour Party in England, the Russian communists, and Gandhi himself. At this point she asked whether "time will bring any kind of synthesis or must there be decades of conflict with one or another predominating and the other values submerged until some later age rediscovers them?" (AR to "Dear Friends," February 5, 1927, 6). Time certainly did not bring a synthesis; one wonders what Rochester would think of the late twentieth-century corporate version of these forces.

36. AR to "Dear Friends," February 5, 1927, 6.

37. James T. Carter, "Daughter of the American Revolution—About Anna Rochester, Author of *Rulers of America*," *Daily Worker*, March 6, 1936.

38. Stephen Peabody, "Rochester Papers, Please Copy!" *Daily Worker*, April 29, 1940.

39. All references to their time in Berlin come from a letter, AR to "Dear Friends," April 3, 1927.

40. Ibid., 4.

41. GH and AR, "Tell Us About Russia," pamphlet addressed to "Dear Friends," June 11, 1927, 4–5.

42. Ibid., 6–7.

43. Ibid.

44. Michael Hunt, *Ideology and U.S. Foreign Policy* (New Haven: Yale University Press, 1987).

45. GH and AR, "Tell Us About Russia," 5–6.

46. Ibid., 9.

47. Ibid., 11.

48. AR to "Dear Friends," May 2, 1927, 3.

49. GH and AR, "Tell Us About Russia," 16.

50. AR to "Dear Friends," May 2, 1927, 2–3.

51. GH and AR, "Tell Us About Russia," 11.

52. AR, "Dear Friends," May 2, 1927, 3.

53. Ibid., 4.

54. Hutchins and Rochester cited a Russian colleague who happened to comment how, despite the simple dress of the Bolsheviks, they were never sloppy or dirty, and how Lenin in particular was always neat in his appearance: "I stood behind him one day in a meeting, and I saw that the collar of his old coat had been carefully patched by his wife." No comment was made on the invisible labor of Lenin's or anyone else's wife in the maintenance of this household labor (GH and AR, "Tell Us About Russia," 16).

55. GH and AR, "Tell Us About Russia," 12–13.

56. Ibid., 15.

57. Ibid., 19.

58. Ibid.

59. Ibid.

60. Ibid.

61. Ibid., 20.

62. Ibid.

63. In January 1930, Anna Rochester had an article published in the *World Tomorrow* called "Communism: A World Movement." It summarized the principles of communism and described the Third Communist International (Comintern) of 1919 and its effects worldwide. It gave these explanations for the presence of a Bolshevik dictatorship.

64. AR, "The Pacifist's 'Preparedness': How Can We Work for Non-Violent Revolutionary Change," *World Tomorrow* (July 1923), 213–15.

Notes to Chapter Seven

1. Sources on American communism include: Philip Bart, Theodore Bassett, William W. Weinstone, and Arthur Zipser, eds., *Highlights of a Fighting History: Sixty Years of the Communist Party, USA* (New York: International Publishers, 1979); Paul Buhle, *Marxism in the USA: Remapping the American Left* (London: Verso, 1987); Maurice Isserman, *Which Side Were You On? The American Communist Party During the Second World War* (Middletown, Conn.: Wesleyan University Press, 1982); and Mari Jo Buhle, Paul Buhle, and Dan Georgakas, eds., *Encyclopedia of the American Left* (New York: Garland Press, 1990). See also William Z. Foster, *The History of the CPUSA* (New York: International Publishers, 1952). The his-

tory of the CP has its own history. This is reviewed in Michael E. Brown's article, "The History of the History of U.S. Communism," in *New Studies in the Politics and Culture of U.S. Communism*, ed. Michael E,. Brown, Randy Martin, Frank Rosengarten, and George Snedeker (New York: Monthly Review Press, 1993), 15–44. "Orthodox" (meaning traditional, often right-wing) histories of communism and the Left include Daniel Bell, *Marxian Socialism in the U.S.* (Princeton: Princeton University Press [1952] 1967); John Patrick Diggins, *The American Left in the Twentieth Century* (New York: Harcourt, Brace, Jovanovich, 1973), and *The Rise and Fall of the American Left* (New York: Norton, 1992); Theodore Draper, *Roots of American Communism* (New York: Viking Press, 1957); and Irving Howe and Lewis Coser, *The American Communist Party: A Critical History* (Boston: Beacon Press, 1957). This orthodoxy has continued with Harvey Klehr, *The Heyday of American Communism: The Depression Decade* (New York: Basic Books, 1984); Harvey Klehr, John Earle Haynes and Fridrikh Igorevich Firsov, eds., *The Secret World of American Communism* (New Haven: Yale University Press, 1995); and Harvey Klehr, John Earle Haynes and Kyrill M. Anderson, eds., *The Soviet World of American Communism* (New Haven: Yale University Press, 1998).

2. Elizabeth Longsford, "Reflections of a Biographer," in *The Literary Biography: Problems and Solutions*, ed. Dale Salwark (Iowa City: University of Iowa, 1996), 148.

3. Paul Buhle and Dan Georgakas, "Communist Party, USA," in Mari Jo Buhle, Paul Buhle, and Dan Georgakas, eds., *Encyclopedia of the American Left*, 148.

4. Ibid., 150. Note that in "Women and the Communist Party, USA, 1930–1940," *Socialist Review* 45 (1979): 73–118, Robert Shaffer reports this number as under 10,000 (p. 75).

5. AR, "Communism: A World Movement," *World Tomorrow* (January 1930): 16–19.

6. Rochester makes this point clearly throughout "Communism: A World Movement." Both she and Hutchins also emphasize these differences in the pamphlets written in 1932 as part of the International Pamphlets series, discussed later in the chapter. See especially, "Profits and Wages" (#16), "Women Who Work" (#27), and "Wall Street" (#30).

7. Paul Buhle, "Third International (Comintern)," in Mari Jo Buhle, Paul Buhle, and Dan Georgakas, eds. *Encyclopedia of the American Left*, 775.

8. Conversation with Tina Baker. Whittaker Chambers wrote about their sponsorship of Lumpkin and Shemitz in *Witness* (New York: Random House, 1952), 266.

9. Bennett Stevens, "The Church and the Workers," International Pamphlets #15 (New York: International Publishers, 1932), 28.

10. The following quotation by Maxim Gorky that was written "To American Intellectuals" is a good example of abstract theory that communist intellectuals were supposed to absorb without question: "The aim of the Party is to convert the maximum quantity of physical energy into intellectual energy in the shortest possible time, in order to give vast scope and freedom to the development of the talents and abilities of every individual in the whole mass of the population" (Maxim Gorky, "To American Intellectuals," International Pamphlets #28 [New York: International Publishers, 1932], 28). Of course not all communists interpreted Marxism as deterministic. One of the most well-known writers of the Left, Sidney Hook, saw Marxism as more a philosophy of freedom than determinism. See Sidney Hook,

From Hegel to Marx: Studies in the Intellectual Development of Karl Marx (Ann Arbor: University of Michigan Press [1936], 1968). In his approach it was human volition and agency rather than the unfolding of mechanical laws that would lead to the revolution. By the time of the Popular Front, Hooks was questioning the necessity of the proletarian dictatorship and came out as an anti-Stalinist Trotskyist involved with the American Workers Party. The Trotskyists were a faction who had been expelled from the CP in the twenties but saw themselves as the true Left after Lenin's death. Their journal, the *New International,* can be contrasted with the CP- and Comintern-directed *Daily Worker* and the *Communist.* Another communist faction of this period were the Lovestonites led by Jay Lovestone and represented by the magazine the *Workers Age.* The *New York Intellectuals* by Alan M. Wald (Chapel Hill: University of North Carolina Press, 1987) provides an insightful account of the transformations of the anti-Stalinist Left under the impact of emerging Cold War anticommunist ideology. Hooks continued to move in a right-wing direction through the next decades, eventually supporting both Richard Nixon and Ronald Reagan's presidential bids (see *New York Intellectuals,* 270).

11. Irving Howe, "A Memoir of the Thirties," in Irving Howe, ed., *Steady Work: Essays in the Politics of Democratic Radicalism, 1953–1966* (New Haven: Harcourt, Brace and World, 1966), 359. Irving Howe is a controversial figure in Left circles. Early a Trotskyist and later a Workers Party member who edited the *Labor Action* newspaper, Howe became critical of communism and turned to democratic socialism. This found him editing the journal *Dissent* in the 1950s. The next decades he moved right, although he still supported such progressive causes as Jewish radical-liberalism. See Irving Howe's autobiography, *A Margin of Hope* (New York: Harcourt, Brace Jovanovich, 1982).

12. Vivian Gornick, *The Romance of American Communism* (New York: Basic Books, 1977), 167.

13. Richard Crossman, ed., *The God That Failed* (Washington, D.C.: Regenery Gateway, 1987), 10.

14. Gorky, "To American Intellectuals," 30–31, 29, 9.

15. Monique Wittig, "One Is Not Born a Woman," in Linda Nicholson, ed., *The Second Wave: A Reader in Feminist Theory* (New York: Routledge, 1997), 269.

16. AR to Algernon Black, March 22, 1944.

17. Stevens, "The Church and the Workers," 14–15.

18. For sources on Greenwich Village life and politics see Rick Beard and Leslie Cohen Berlowitz, eds., *Greenwich Village: Culture and Counterculture* (New Brunswick: Rutgers University Press, 1993), and especially the chapter on "The Radical Women of Greenwich Village: From Crystal Eastman to Eleanor Roosevelt" by Blanche Wiesen Cook (pp. 243–57). Judith Schwarz's book, *Radical Feminists of Heterodoxy: Greenwich Village, 1912–1940* (Norwich, Vt.: New Victoria Publishers, 1986), is also very interesting on the feminist element in the Village. Robert E. Humphrey, *Children of Fantasy: The First Rebels of Greenwich Village* (New York: Wiley, 1978), is another early source.

19. GH to AR, July 25, 1927.

20. GH to AR, February 7, 1928.

21. GH, "What's Past Is Prologue," fiftieth reunion speech, Bryn Mawr College, June 1957.

22. See Sidney Streat's article on Hutchins in the *Daily Worker*, "Grace Hutchins—Revolutionary," September 16, 1936. Indeed, before her first visit with her parents after returning home in 1927 she prepared them by emphasizing that she did not want to get "wrought-up" over certain topics about which they would disagree. At the top of this list was talk about Russia and anticipated responses to her new hairstyle, a short, fashionable cut. She was able to pronounce the visit a success; her father pronounced her hair "not so bad," and mother "says nothing, but seems to survive" (GH to AR, July 26, 1927).

23. *Boston Evening American*, night special, August 10, 1927. This newspaper made a mistake concerning Hutchins's identity, referring to her as a "Mrs. Hutchins, New York society woman" and alternately as the wife and as the daughter of "a prominent New York lawyer." Hutchins had penciled in an exclamation mark by this mistake in identity and crossed out the Mrs. and inserted Miss.

24. John Dos Passos, letter printed in the *Nation*, August 24, 1927. Dos Passos was also arrested for demonstrating on behalf of Sacco and Vanzetti and wrote *Facing the Chair*, a compilation of the articles published in the *New Masses* about this experience. He is known as one of the leading writers of the Depression, known best for his novel *U.S.A.*, an experimental trilogy consisting of *The 42 Parallel* (1930), *1919* (1932), and *The Big Money* (1936). After the 1930s, Dos Passos moved away from his progressive left-wing politics and became involved in conservative, Republican causes. In *The Encyclopedia of the American Left*, p. 200, Alan Wald writes that Dos Passos eventually became an admirer of Barry Goldwater, Richard Nixon, and Ronald Reagan.

25. AR, letter printed in the *Nation*, August 24, 1927.

26. Tom O'Connor (Committee for the Vindication of Sacco and Vanzetti) to GH, October 6, 1964.

27. Susan Hutchins to GH, August 16, 1927. Another letter on this event was received by Hutchins's parents, this time written by Susan's brother, Harold, a prominent lawyer in Roswell, New Mexico. This letter expressed his utter contempt and disgust for his niece's actions and offered sympathies to his sister and brother-in-law. It is insightful in its spontaneous and superlative hatred for causes he considered unpatriotic and disgustingly scurrilous, and for his representation of the upper-class Bostonian take on militant causes. As such it represents those conservative patriots who clamored for Sacco and Vanzetti to be removed from the face of the earth. It also reveals a glimpse at the kind of upper-class Bostonian milieu in which Hutchins was raised (Henry Hurd to Susan Hurd Hutchins, August 20, 1927).

28. GH to her parents, August 21, 1927.

29. When Edward Hutchins Sr. died in June 1929 he left everything to his wife. He did not count Grace out of the will, however, and when Susan died in 1942, Grace received equal shares with her brother, Henry.

30. In a letter to Hutchins after their father's death, brother Henry shared his perception of his sister's relationship with her father: "I know how much he admired you, Grace dear, for you are like him in many ways. You have his determination and will" (Henry Hutchins to GH, June 26, 1929).

31. *Boston Herald*, Monday, May 17, 1937.

32. GH to AR, July 1927.

33. In an undated letter to "My Beloved Darling Partner," Hutchins wrote "apparently discouraged feelings go with this trouble just naturally, because it is so long drawn out. . . . I'd go through even a 4th operation to live for you, my partner."

34. Nadezhda Krupskaya, quoted in *Daily Worker*, September 9, 1935, p. 6.

35. GH to AR, February 7, 1928.

36. See, for example, the 1981 edition of *Heresies*, and Lisa Moore, "'Something More Tender Still than Friendship': Romantic Friendships in Early-Nineteenth-Century England," *Feminist Studies* 18, no. 3 (1992): 499–520.

37. AR to GH, undated—circa late 1920s.

38. GH to AR, September 10, no year—circa 1928.

39. GH to AR, April 18, no year—circa early 1930s.

40. GH to AR, September 21, no year—circa 1928.

41. AR to GH, undated—circa late 1920s.

42. AR to GH, September 15, 1937; AR to GH, April 11, no year; AR to GH, July 26, 1939; AR to GH, November 13, 1939.

43. AR to GH, August 3, 1931.

44. Earl Browder, "A Message to Catholics" (New York: Workers' Library Publication, 1938), 9.

45. Gerald Meyer, "Gay/Lesbian Liberation Movements," in Mari Jo Buhle, Paul Buhle, and Dan Georgakas, eds., *Encyclopedia of the American Left*, 262.

46. Ellen Kay Trimberger, "Women in the Old Left and New Left: The Evolution of a Politics of a Personal Life," *Feminist Studies* (Fall 1979): 438.

47. Rosalyn Baxandall, "The Question Seldom Asked: Women and the CPUSA," in Michael E. Brown, Randy Martin, Frank Rosengarten, and George Snedecker, eds., *New Studies in the Politics and Culture of U.S. Communism*, 151.

48. DeLeon was the son of Daniel DeLeon, founder of the Socialist Labor Party and a friend from the Rand School. Trachtenberg, known as "Trachty" to his friends, was the head of International Publishers and had been the energy behind the Research Division of the International Ladies Garment Workers of America as well as the Research Department of the Rand School of Social Science.

49. LRA records, narrative with index, p. 1. The archives of the LRA are located at Tamiment Library (hereafter Tam) in the Elmer Holmes Bobst Library at NYU. See also Victor Perlo, "LRA—That Stands for Facts That Aid Labor," unidentified clipping, undated [probably *Daily Worker*, circa 1955]. All references to the founding of the LRA date it at 1927, except Robert Dunn says 1928 in the written transcript of a memorial speech to Alexander Trachtenberg (who died in December 1966). Dunn also mentioned Scott Nearing as one of the founding friends (See Robert W. Dunn, "Waiting for Trachty," *New World Review*, February 1967). Nearing does not talk about the LRA in his autobiography, *The Making of a Radical: A Political Autobiography* (New York: Harper and Row, 1972). The LRA is still in existence, located at West Twenty-eighth Street in New York City, and publishes the bimonthly *Economic Notes*, the biweekly *Trade Union Advisor*, and does a considerable amount of consulting for trade unions.

50. Rochester also wrote "Your Dollar Under Roosevelt," an undated pamphlet, though probably circa 1933, published by the Worker's Library, which lambasted New Deal efforts and encouraged workers to resist and join the CP.

51. GH, "Youth in Industry," International Pamphlets #13 (New York: International Publishers, 1932), 31.

52. GH, "Children Under Capitalism," International Pamphlets #33 (New York: International Publishers, 1933), 4, 18.

53. AR, "Profits and Wages," International Pamphlets #16 (New York: International Publishers, 1932), 4. Note that Rochester also wrote an article, "Wages in the US," that was published in *Labor Age* back in February 1928.

54. AR, "Wall Street," International Pamphlets #30 (New York: International Publishers, 1932), 15.

55. GH, "Women Who Work," International Pamphlets #27 (New York: International Publishers, 1932), 8.

56. Ibid., 4.

57. Other books in the Labor Series were Rochester's *Labor and Coal*; Robert Dunn's *Labor and Automobiles*; Robert Dunn and Jack Hardy's *Labor and Textiles*; Charlotte Todes's *Labor and Lumber*, and Horace B. Davis's *Labor and Steel*. All were published between 1929 and 1935 by International Publishers.

58. Betty Feldman, "Grace Hutchins Tells About Why Women Work," *Worker*, March 1, 1953.

59. GH, *Labor and Silk* (New York: International Publishers, 1929), 13.

60. Silk industry union organizers in Paterson liked the book but disputed the chapters on mergers and profits, emphasizing that Paterson was in decline and hardly a booming industry calling big profits (Alice and Louisa Kimball to GH, July 28, 1929). Hutchins responded to union organizers, scrupulously explaining how the data on mergers and profits were collected and how and why the Paterson mill was an aberration to the profitable nature of the silk and rayon industries. Her letter was gracious and cordial and it is obvious that Hutchins cared very much about the responses to her writing by union colleagues (GH to Alice and Louisa Kimball, August 24, 1929).

61. *Office Worker*, May 1929.

62. Cited in a *World Tomorrow* advertisement for *Labor and Silk*, December 1929.

63. Unidentified newspaper clipping, July 6, 1929, possibly *World Tomorrow*.

64. It is interesting to note that Muste's work had resulted in the formation of the Textile Workers of America ten years earlier, and more recently he had tried to unify the small, fragmented unions of the New England textile industries. During this period he was working to organize the Conference for Progressive Labor Action, an alternative to communist unionism.

65. AR, *Labor and Coal* (New York: International Publishers, 1931), 234. Rochester wrote an article for *Labor Unity*, "Two Codes in the Mining Industry," about the powers of industry and strike-breaking tactics. She also wrote a review of *The Plight of Bituminous Coal Miners*, by Homer Lawrence Morris, published in the *New Republic* (October 2, 1934). Supposedly this review was actually collaboration between Hutchins and Rochester since the latter had noted this on top of their copy. Similarly, a typed, original document, "Miners in the USSR," was authored by Rochester with an additional handwritten note on the top that read "and GH." This manuscript was undated, although probably circa 1933.

66. An article titled "Books for Workers: *Labor and Coal*," *Labor Unity* (March 21, 1931), praised the book. Writing for the *World Tomorrow* (May 1931), Harry F.

Ward was more critical in suggesting that polemics were not enough and instead U.S. workers needed a "realistic program, born out of the American situation and based upon the experiences of its labor struggles" (6).

67. Early reviews quoted miners remarking that this was "just the kind of book we need for the miners' movement" (H. Kemenovich, member of the National Board, Mine, Oil and Smelter Workers' Industrial Union, "Early Reviews," International Publishers flyer, undated).

68. A call was given to join the Communist Party: "when you, as a mine worker, know what it really is, you will join the Communist Party" (AR and Pat Toohey, "The Miners' Road to Freedom in a Soviet America" [Workers Library, 1936], 47). Note that the CP slogan of 1934 was "For a Soviet America!" (see Maurice Isserman, *Which Side Were You On?*, p. xi).

69. Susan Ware, *Holding Their Own: American Women in the 1930s* (Boston: Twayne, 1982); and chap. 4, "Crisis years: 1929–1945," of Rosalind Rosenberg's *Divided Lives: American Women in the Twentieth Century* (New York: Hill and Wang, 1992). See also Susan Ware, *Beyond Suffrage: Women in the New Deal* (New York: Cambridge University Press, 1981).

70. Paul K. Conkin, *Tomorrow a New World: The New Deal Community Program* (Ithaca: Cornell University Press, 1964). For statistics on the New Deal, see also *Labor Fact Book*, vols. 2, 3, 4, 5 (New York: International Publishers, 1934, 1936, 1938, 1941, respectively).

71. Linda Gordon, *Woman's Body, Woman's Right: A Social History of Birth Control in America* (New York: Grossman, 1976), chap. 10.

72. For a discussion of the U.S. women's movement in the 1930s see Eleanor Flexner, *Century of Struggle: The Woman's Rights Movement in the United States* (Cambridge: Harvard University Press, 1975), and "Feminism and Social Reform," chap. 4 in Ware, *Holding Their Own*.

73. Shaffer, "Women and the Communist Party, USA, 1930–1940," 79–80. For example, the 1928 Communist Party Platform of the Class Struggle included a section on women. Five resolutions were made that centered on the issues of women in paid labor: first, the prohibition of certain kinds of overtime and night work designed to protect women from exploitation; second, the establishment of nurseries and time for feeding babies at the place of work; third, full maternity insurance benefits; fourth, the prohibition of discriminatory union practices and a drive to organize women workers; and fifth, equal pay for equal work.

74. Paula Rabinowitz, "Women and U.S. Literary Radicalism," in *Writing Red: An Anthology of American Women Writers, 1930–1940*, ed. Charlotte Nekola and Paula Rabinowitz (New York: Feminist Press, 1987), 5.

75. See, for example, the autobiography of Peggy Dennis, wife of CP leader Eugene Dennis: *The Autobiography of an American Communist: A Personal View of Political Life, 1925–1975* (Westport, Conn.: Hill, 1975). Note, however, that the case has been made that the Old Left CPUSA was more supportive of women than were the New Left. In "Women of the Old and New Left," Ellen Kay Trimberger suggests that this differential treatment was related to the cultural context in which these women's concerns arose as well as the development of a threatening autonomous women's movement in the 1960s (*Feminist Studies* 5 [Fall 1979]). Peggy Dennis wrote a rebuttal to Trimberger's article that is in the same issue of *Feminist Studies*.

76. See, for example, *Daily Worker*, February 28, 1934, p. 4; and *Party Organizer*, May–June 1934, p. 60.

77. Shaffer, in "Women and the Communist Party, USA," astutely notices that "While almost every article (in communist magazines) about women included a section on the added oppression of *black* women, few of the many articles on blacks made direction (*sic*) mention of the extra problems of black *women*" (78–79).

78. LRA records, narrative with index, p. 1 (Tam). Shaffer also makes this point, (pp. 81–83).

79. Victor Frederick, review of *Women Who Work*, in *Working Woman* (March 1934), 5.

80. GH, *Women Who Work* (New York: International Publishers, 1934), 108–19.

81. Ibid., 259.

82. In *Women Who Work*, p. 7, Hutchins wrote: "Legal disabilities and disqualifications have for the most part been removed in the United States."

83. See chap. 4, "Equal Rights and Economic Roles," of Nancy F. Cott's *The Grounding of Modern Feminism* (New Haven: Yale University Press, 1987). Also see Cott's article "Historical Perspectives: The Equal Rights Amendment Conflict in the 1920s," in *Conflicts in Feminism*, ed. Marianne Hirsch and Evelyn Fox Keller (New York: Routledge, 1990).

84. See Mariosa Dalla Costa, "Women and the Subversion of Community," *Radical America* 6, no. 1 (January–February 1972), 77. For a reference to articles contributing to the debate on domestic labor within a Marxist feminist and socialist feminist perspective, see Heidi Hartmann, "The Unhappy Marriage of Marxism and Feminism: Towards a More Progressive Union," in *Women and Revolution*, ed. Lydia Sargent (Boston: South End Press, 1981), 34–35. Also see Paul Smith, "Domestic Labour and Marx's Theory of Value," in *Feminism and Materialism*, ed. Annette Kuhn and Ann Marie Wolpe (London: Routledge and Kegan Paul, 1978), 198–219.

85. See Angela Y. Davis, *Women, Race, and Class* (New York: Random House, 1981).

86. GH, *Women Who Work*, 18. Columnist Mike Gold of the *Daily Worker* included a letter in the paper from Hutchins that light-heartedly pointed out Party sexism. She referred to an article written by National Miners' Union leader Tony Minerich about the necessity of organizing Women's Auxiliaries. It seemed that Minerich had been laughed at by some members of the Marine Workers' Industrial Union for having brought up such a topic. Referring to her book, Hutchins (courageously, I think, given the times and the strength of Party dogma) wrote: "Men comrades like those marine workers who razzed Comrade Tony will find themselves described in the book as follows: 'As a result of ruling class propaganda, among some of the men workers who should know that their strength lies in working class solidarity, there still exists an attitude of superiority toward women workers'" (Michael Gold, "Change the World!" *Daily Worker*, February 12, 1934).

87. AR to GH, undated.

88. Grace Lumpkin, "Emancipation and Exploitation," *New Masses*, 1934. Lumpkin was a friend and protégé of Hutchins and Rochester. Geraldin Sartain wrote "Sweatshops for Women Survive Despite NRA Codes: Says Woman Who Quit Social Whirl to Aid Workers" for the *New York World-Telegram* (June 25, 1934), which

focused on Hutchins's elite family origins. The copy read: "It's unusual that this Boston girl of such stock should have specialized in labor problems and should speak with so great iconoclastic freedom." Illustrative of both how inaccurate the headline was in terms of Hutchins's involvement in high society as well as her own discomfort with such a label, she had written on the newspaper clipping and had crossed out the subheading starting "Says Woman. . . ." Hutchins would most likely never have wanted to be represented as an ex-society dame given the bourgeois implications of such a role.

89. "Women and Work," review of *Women Who Work,* in the *New York Times,* June 17, 1934.

90. Mildred Fairchild, review of *Women Who Work,* in the *Bryn Mawr Alumnae Bulletin,* May 1934, p. 16.

91. Mildred Fairchild to GH, May 18, 1934.

92. Ibid. A similar critique of *Women Who Work* was voiced by the *Nation:* "When she departs from the realm of science and enters that of politics, the affirmation which becomes her argument has no place for caution, qualification, or weighting." In this write-up the reviewer also astutely noted that "surely the desire of women to please men arises from something more than capitalist propaganda; and surely, too, such indiscriminate disparagement as Miss Hutchins heaps on all who fight in the same battle but with different weapons is itself conscious machination" (Sylvia Kopald Selkman, "Eleven Million Strong," review of *Women Who Work,* in the *Nation* 139 [July 1934], 80).

Notes to Chapter Eight

1. "New Year's Resolution For Our Readers," *Sunday Worker,* January 1, 1939.

2. Frigga Haug and others. *Female Sexualization: A Collective Work of Memory* (London: Verso, 1989), 68.

3. LRA, *Labor Fact Book,* vol. 3 (New York: International Publishers, 1936), 147.

4. Paul Buhle, "Communist Party, USA," in Mari Jo Buhle, Paul Buhle, and Dan Georgakas, eds., *The Encyclopedia of the American Left* (New York: Garland, 1990), 151.

5. At the same time that the Soviet Union and the CPUSA received popular applause for their courageous struggle, there were reports of violent squirmishes between the communist and anarchist forces in Spain as well as Stalin's brutal actions there. For some, idealism was drained and they left the CP disenchanted. See John Patrick Diggins, *The Rise and Fall of the American Left* (New York: Norton, 1992), 175–78.

6. See especially chap. 12 of GH, *Women Who Work* (New York: International Publishers, 1934), where Hutchins focuses on bourgeois organizations that oppose the class struggle.

7. GH, "What Every Working Woman Wants," pamphlet (New York: Workers Library, February 1935), 14.

8. GH, *Women Who Work,* 257–58.

9. "Preamble to the Constitution," Communist Party of the United States of America, undated.

10. Malcolm Sylvers, "Earl Browder," in Mari Jo Buhle, Paul Buhle, and Dan Georgakas, eds., *The Encyclopedia of the American Left,* 112. In 1946, Browder was

eventually expelled from the Party because of Moscow-inspired lack of support abroad, even though, as Sylvers writes, "Browder's positions seem to have corresponded to a widespread desire of members for full political integration and acceptability and to have been in step with the Party's general direction" (113). William Z. Foster, chair of the CPUSA from 1932 to 1957, played a key role in Browder's expulsion, and he led the movement to a more sectarian policy after the war. For a biography of Foster, see Arthur Zipser, *Working-Class Giant: The Life of William Z. Foster* (New York: International Publishers, 1981).

11. During Earl Browder's 1936 presidential campaign, Hutchins wrote an interesting little pamphlet, "The Truth About the Liberty League," which explained the origins of the American Liberty League as a corporate-sponsored attempt to avoid governmental control of private business, especially munitions, and as antagonistic to labor and social relief legislation. In particular, she emphasized how the League was supporting the Republican candidate Alf Landon, governor of Kansas and wealthy oil operator. She showed the "deadly parallel" between the Republican platform and the League on a variety of issues and encouraged readers to work toward forming a Farmer–Labor Party and to vote for Browder in the upcoming election. While the pamphlet stated that the Democrats did not represent a bulwark against fascism, it avoided critiquing Roosevelt or the problems associated with the National Recovery Administration. It did not claim that all parties other than the communists were cut from the same cloth, and by slamming the Republicans, by default she gave endorsement to the Democrats. This was an example of the "lesser evil" strategy of the communists during this Popular Front period. (GH, "The Truth About the Liberty League," International Pamphlets #50 [New York: International Publishers, 1936]).

12. LRA, *Labor Fact Book*, vols. 3 and 4 (New York: International Publishers, 1936 and 1939, respectively).

13. LRA, *Labor Fact Book*, vol. 3, 150.

14. GH, "It Comes on Cat's Feet: Growth of Fascist Menace in America," *New Masses* (December 1938).

15. In his book *Witness* (New York: Random House, 1952, p. 49), Whittaker Chambers alleges that Hutchins was known by British intelligence as a trusted communist contact, as someone who was connected to the operation to screen Japanese students in the United States for communist work in Japan, and as a courier on other underground operations. Chambers was unstable and his accounts were untrustworthy. Nonetheless, there is a good chance that Hutchins was involved in various covert activities for the CP. The FBI also interviewed Hutchins in 1964 concerning the disappearance of Juliet Poyntz, educational director of the International Ladies' Garment Union and a communist whom some suspected had been removed by the Party. Hutchins had responded to police inquiries saying she had absolutely no idea as to Poyntz's whereabouts (*New York Herald*, December 20, 1944).

16. Sidney Streat, "Grace Hutchins: Revolutionary," *Daily Worker*, September 16, 1936.

17. GH notebook, January 12, 1938.

18. The *Turtle Progress-Dispatch* 1, no. 4, June 1936.

19. Streat, "Grace Hutchins—Revolutionary."

20. GH notebook, "3/36–11/13/37" at top of page.

21. Ibid., January 1, 1937.

22. Ibid., December 25, 1937.

23. Ibid., August 19, 1949, and January 1, 1941. Concerning her commitment to her work, in 1941 Hutchins remarked in the Bryn Mawr's *Turtle's Progress-Dispatch* that activities with the LRA were still so absorbing that she put in more than seven hours a day, summer and winter. "But it still doesn't make me any thinner," she quipped (*Turtle's Dispatch-Progress* 1, no. 5, June 1941).

24. Vivian Gornick, *The Romance of American Communism* (New York: Basic Books, 1977), 113.

25. GH notebook, February 11, 1937.

26. Samuel Putnam, "I Saw a Communist," verse clipping from the *Daily Worker*, November 15, 1939.

27. Anna Murdock to Lucie Myer, October 30, no year (probably the early 1940s).

28. AR to GH, August 19, no year. The phrase "tho' nearly sixty" in this verse suggests that the year was probably 1943 or 1944.

29. AR to GH, August 30, 1929; GH to AR, Christmas 1942.

30. GH to AR, September 17, 1942.

31. Ibid.

32. GH to AR, September 14, 1942.

33. Ella Reeve Bloor to GH, September 30, 1942.

34. Ella Reeve Bloor to GH, January 3, 1939; April 20, 1943; January 30, 1944; February 25, 1949; May 14, no year; July 3, no year; October 5, no year; Christmas card, no year.

35. James S. Allen, "Anna Rochester—Marxist Scholar," obituary in the *Worker*, May 24, 1966. Rochester's skill and reputation also encouraged a request she teach at the Jefferson School of Social Science, although she turned this down.

36. Original typed speech given at the Publishers' Dinner for International Publishers, March 1936, p. 2. During this speech she also acknowledged that the many appendixes in the book represented several years of steady part-time work on the part of volunteers at the LRA and much collaboration with LRA colleagues and her "wise comrade Trachtenberg" (head of International Publishers).

37. AR, *Rulers of America: A Study of Finance Capital* (New York: International Publishers, 1936), 153–54.

38. Ibid., 295.

39. Ibid., 301.

40. Ibid., 306.

41. Louis F. Budenz, review of *Rulers of America*, in the *Daily Worker*, April 6, 1936, p. 7.

42. George Marshall, "Directors of Finance," *Nation* (June 27, 1936). Harry Gannes, "A Scientific Study of American Imperialism," *Communist* (April 1936): 376–80.

43. Winifred Chappell, review of *Rulers of America*, in the *Christian Century* (April 1, 1936). Chappell was a friend of Hutchins and Rochester who was devoted to social justice issues and was serving with the Methodist Federation of Social Services. She was involved in the preparation of the federation's monthly *Social Questions Bulletin*, and was considered an influential speaker with strong ties to pro-

gressive social agencies and labor unions (letter of recommendation for Winifred Chappell, written by Henry F. Ward of the Union Theological Seminary, June 3, 1941). In the early forties, Hutchins helped raise a subsidy to allow Chappell to do research and speaking in the south, an act that Chappell received with much appreciation (Chappell to GH, June 13, 1941).

44. Warne's comment was listed in an International Publishers press release on *Rulers of America*, March 18, 1936. The Book Union choice was paraphrased in a LRA flyer sent out with *Economic Notes* (a monthly LRA publication) in April 1936. It cited Herschel Brickell of the *New York Post*.

45. E. D. Kennedy, "Directors and Misdirectors," *Saturday Review* (March 7, 1936), p. 18.

46. Ibid., 19.

47. AR to editor, printed in *Saturday Review*, May 23, 1936, pp. 9 and 19. This last quote is from page 19.

48. V. D. Kazakevich, "Masters by Money Power," *New York Herald-Tribune*, March 15, 1936.

49. AR to editor, printed in *New York Herald-Tribune*, March 17, 1936.

50. V. D. Kazakevich to AR, July 1, 1936.

51. Letters or postcards included: Lucie Myer to AR, February 19, 1936; anonymous to AR, February 19, 1936; Hy Kravif to AR, "Thursday evening"; Miriam Bonner to AR, April 20, 1936; William Floyd to AR, June 7, 1936; L. H. Turner to AR, April 24, 1936; James O'Brien to AR, May 11, 1936; Vida Scudder to AR, April 11, 1936; Susan B. Hutchins to AR, February 21, 1936; and Devere Allen to AR, April 1, 1936. Molly Dewson thanked Hutchins and Rochester for the gift of the book. But Dewson added, "I cannot lie to my friends," and spoke of how the polemics of this kind of writing was off-putting. This disagreement in ideology did not seem to dampen the friendship between the two couples (Molly Dewson to AR, May 3, 1946).

52. Susan B. Hutchins to AR, February 21, 1936.

53. Vida Scudder to AR, April 11, 1936.

54. James S. Allen, AR obituary.

55. Peggy Dennis, *The Autobiography of an American Communist: A Personal View of a Political Life, 1925–1975* (Westport, Conn.: Hill, 1977), 136.

56. AR, *Capitalism and Progress* (New York: International Publishers, 1945), 93.

57. Ibid., 93–94.

58. AR to Alter Brody, December 12, 1943. The pamphlet was one entitled "Behind the Soviet–Polish Break."

59. Arthor Koestler in Richard H. Crossman, ed., *The God That Failed* (Washington, D.C.: Regnery Gateway [1949], 1987), 34.

60. Ibid., 61.

61. Avery Gordon, *Ghostly Matters: Haunting and the Sociological Imagination* (Minneapolis: University of Minnesota Press, 1997), 173.

62. Dennis, *The Autobiography of an American Communist*, 117–18.

63. In *Partner and I: Molly Dewson, Feminism, and New Deal Politics* (New Haven: Yale University Press, 1987), the biography of Molly Dewson and Polly Porter, Susan Ware writes that "[t]heir friendship with Grace Hutchins and Anna Rochester came as close as they came to suspicion in the McCarthy era. . . . She

[Dewson] had passed a letter from Grace Hutchins to Eleanor Roosevelt in 1941. She made the gesture in the spirit of friendship, not out of familiarity with the case: to her, Earl Browder 'was only a newspaper name'" (249) (letter from Eleanor Roosevelt to Molly Dewson, April 17, 1941).

64. Ware, *Partner and I*, 249.

65. AR to President Roosevelt, December 19, 1943.

66. GH, obituary, *New York Times*, July 16, 1969. As an example of the *Daily Worker's* pro-Soviet perspective, when Stalin died in March 1953 the paper eulogized his life and wrote of the deep mourning in the Soviet Union, where "Stalin lives in the heart of humanity" (Joseph Clark, "Joseph Stalin's Heritage, Part II," *Daily Worker*, March 26, 1953).

67. AR, *Why Farmers Are Poor: The Agricultural Crisis in the U.S.* (New York: International Publishers, 1940), 9, 16.

68. AR, *Why Farmers Are Poor*, original manuscript, chap. 11, p. 1.

69. A copy of "Capitalism and Agriculture in the U.S." was in the archives along with research and correspondence concerning *Why Farmers Are Poor*.

70. Russell Lord, "Why We Have Rural Poverty," *New York Herald-Tribune*, August 11, 1940.

71. Lem Harris, "Poverty and the Countryside," *New Masses*, June 25, 1940.

72. Louis F. Budenz, "*Why Farmers Are Poor* Reveals Depths of America's Rural Crisis," *Daily Worker*, May 30, 1940; "Rochester's Book Shows War Increases Impoverishment of U.S. Farmers," *Daily Worker*, June 7, 1940; Winifred Chappell, "Farmers and Workers, Unite!" *Christian Century* (August 21, 1940); Russell Lord, "Farmers in the Red," *New Republic* (August 12, 1940).

73. Rupert B. Vance, "Agriculture, Mining, Forestry, and Fisheries," *American Economic Review* 30, no.4 (December 1940): 856.

74. Roger H. Wells, *Bryn Mawr Alumnae Bulletin* (January 1941): 16–17.

75. Joel Seidman, "Labor Policy During World War II," *Industrial and Labor Relations* (October 1950). See also Earl Browder, "Hold the Home Front," *Communist* (July 1943).

76. AR to Alter Brody, December 12, 1943. Rochester encouraged Brody to write so that he could reach a broad democratic audience. She said: "And I do believe that for future peaceful collaboration, it is extremely important to have influential Democratic circles convinced of the reasonableness of the Soviet position on Polish, etc. boundaries."

77. LRA, "Wages and Profits in Wartime," Pamphlet Series (New York: International Publishers, 1941), 18.

78. LRA, *Labor Fact Book*, vol. 6 (New York: International Publishers, 1943), 9. The other two *Labor Fact Books* are vols. 5 and 7, published in 1941 and 1945, respectively.

79. Hutchins wrote many reviews during this period. During 1937 she reviewed *On Journey*, by Vida Scudder, for the *New Masses* as well as several other books for *Economic Notes* and *Social Work Today*. Nineteen thirty-eight included reviews of *Fashions in Wage Theories*, by Jurgen Kuczinski, and *Labor's New Millions*, by Mary Heaton Vorse, for the *New Masses*; and *A New Deal for Youth*, by Ernest Lindley, for *Labor Notes*. The next year's reviews included *What Price Mills?*, by Caroline Whitney, and *Dividends From Defense*, by the Labor Research Department, for *Economic*

Notes; Organized Labor in Four Continents, by H.A. Marquand and others, *What Is Collective Bargaining?,* by Mollie Ray Carroll, and *Labor Marches,* by Chester M. Wright, for the *New Masses; An Autobiography,* by Ida M. Tarbell, for the *Book Union Bulletin; The House of Mitsui,* by Oland D. Russell, for *China Today; Railroads in Crisis* (LRA pamphlet) for the *Sunday Worker; Factories in the Field: The Story of Migratory Farm Labor in California,* by Carey McWilliam, for *Labor Notes;* and *Dividends to Pay,* by E. D. Kennedy, for *Steel and Metal Notes.* Reviews during 1940 included *Organized Labor and Productivity,* by Morris L. Cooke and Philip Murray, and *Trade Union Press,* edited by John P. Commons, for the *New Masses;* and *Labor and Democracy,* by William Green, and *Mobilizing Civilian America,* by Harold J. Tobin and Percy W. Bidwell, for *Labor Notes.* In 1941 Hutchins published the following reviews: *Full Employment,* by John L. Pierson, for the *New Masses;* the *Social Work Yearbook, 1941,* for the *Daily Worker* and *Labor Notes;* the *Statistical Year Book, 1939–40,* by the League of Nations, for *Economic Notes;* and *Fatigue of Workers: Its Relation to Industrial Production,* by the National Research Council, *The Presidents and Civil Disorder,* by Bennett M. Rich, and *Women for Defense,* by Margaret Culkin Banning, for *Labor Notes.* Nineteen forty-two included reviews of *Japanese Imperialism Exposed: The Secret Tanaka Document,* for the *Worker; From Relief to Social Security,* by Grace Abbott, for the *New Masses; Women for Defense,* by Margaret Culkin Banning, and *Women in War Production,* by the War Production Board, for *Labor Notes; The Setting Sun of Japan,* by Carl Randau and Leane Zugsmith, for the *Sunday Worker;* and *The Economy of Barbarism and Hitler's New Economic Order,* by J. Kuczynski and M. Witt, for *Economic Notes.* Hutchins published reviews of *Exploring the Dangerous Trades; The Autobiography of Alice Hamilton, M.D.;* and *Out of the Kitchen* for the *New Masses* in 1943. During 1944 Hutchins published reviews of *Total War,* by John Dunham. Finally, 1945 reviews included: *Organized Labor and the Negro,* by Herbert R. Northerup, *Justice in Transportation,* by A. C. Wifried, and *Organized Labor,* by Harry A. Millis and Royal E. Montgomery, all for *Railroad Notes; The Chinese Labor Movement,* by Nym Wales, and *Labor Unions in the Far East,* by Eleanor H. Lattimore, for the *New Masses;* and *American Labor Unions,* by Florence Peterson, for *Railroad Notes* and the *New Masses.*

80. Hutchins wrote an article for *China Today* entitled "*China's Women in Struggle,*" a tribute to young Chinese women's courageous attempts for a voice in the governing of their country (April 1941).

81. GH, "Japan Wars on the U.S.," International Pamphlets (New York: International Publishers, December 1941), 4.

82. GH, "Japan's Drive for Conquest," International Pamphlets (New York: International Publishers, 1935), 11.

83. LRA, "Wages and Profits in Wartime," International Pamphlets (New York: International Publishers, 1941).

84. AR, "Farmers in Nazi Germany" (New York: Farm Research, 1942). This quote is from a flier, "Facts for Farmers." The *Farmers' Defender* reviewed it and explained how Rochester presented "the vivid story of Nazi false promises made to win farmers' support. Many were deceived by Nazi lies but they soon woke up to find themselves tied and bound as slaves in complete subjection to Nazi agents of big business" (*Farmers' Defender,* July 1942). The *New York Times* even listed the

pamphlet as *"How the Giant Food Corporation Enslaves the German Farmer"* (*New York Times*, August 9, 1942).

85. AR, "Farmers and the War" (Workers Library, 1943), 3.

86. A review by Eric Burt in the *Communist* (February 1943): 185–92, highlighted the timing of the publication of Rochester's *Lenin on the Agrarian Question* (New York: International Publishers, 1942) with the Soviet Union's membership with the democratic alliance. This highly polemical review (which declared several times in the very first page that the Soviet Union was "the most advanced social system" [p.185]), focused on the opposition between the forces of fascism and united democracy: "From this foundation [as outlined by Rochester] the Soviet workers and peasants have carried on the historic struggle against Hitlerism in behalf of all mankind, the cause of the United Nations" (186).

87. AR, *Lenin on the Agrarian Question* (New York: International Publishers, 1942), 169.

88. Ibid., 153.

89. Ibid., 164. Anna Louise Strong's pamphlet is "Democracy and Dictatorship in the Soviet Union," International Pamphlets #40 (New York: International Publishers, 1934). Rochester quotes pages 4–5 of Strong's pamphlet. Unfortunately, Strong may have been later declared a foreign spy in one of Stalin's periodic purges. Peggy Dennis, in *Autobiography of an American Communist*, wrote that "the American Communist Party remained silent, and exonerated her only after the Soviet comrades did" (119).

90. Indeed, the review of *Lenin on the Agrarian Question* in the *Communist* underscored this line of thinking, a stance that Rochester most likely would have endorsed: "The struggle for these objectives [for emancipation of the peasantry] was fought and won in struggle against the Trotskyite and Bukharinite camp of saboteurs and spies. . . . Evidence brought forth at the trials of the Trotskyite and Bukharinite traitors [known as the Moscow trials] showed indelibly that their practices were part of a well-worked out program of espionage and diversion against the Soviet Union. The sympathy they found in the kulak ranks, and the encouragement they lent to kulak terrorism were no accident" (Eric Burt, *Communist*, 190).

91. Louis Budenz to AR, September 2, 1942. His review, "From Plough to the Tractor," appeared in the *Daily Worker*, August 23, 1942.

92. This Bryn Mawr reviewer picked up on the way Rochester so easily glossed over the Bolshevik cruelty with the kulaks. "[T]he rest of the world is under the impression that these removals resulted directly or indirectly in the loss of several million lives," she said, and then added, "it seems regrettable that Miss Rochester with her keen mind and obvious desire to relate Russian experiences to our own . . . did not take time to meet the questions which inevitably rise to the lips of any ordinary reader." Nonetheless, she was taken by Rochester's prose (Elizabeth Reynolds Hapgood, review of *Lenin on the Agrarian Question*, in *The Alumnae Bookshelf* [March 1943]: 16).

93. Rochester saw Vice President Henry Wallace as the outstanding heir of Populism. He went on to become the presidential candidate of the Progressive Party in 1948, the final expression of united front politics. The CPUSA and CIO activists worked as this party's main organizing force with other non-CP groups to oppose

Truman's emerging Cold War and anti–union policies and maintain New Deal politics. The platform was not successful and its demise facilitated the anticommunism campaign in the unions and in civil and intellectual circles. See Norman D. Markowitz, *The Rise and Fall of the People's Century: Henry A. Wallace and American Liberalism, 1941–1948* (New York: Free Press, 1973).

94. AR, *The Populist Movement in the United States: The Rise, Growth, and Decline of the People's Party—A Social and Economic Interpretation* (New York: International Publishers, 1943), 122–23.

95. Ibid., 122.

Notes to Chapter Nine

1. GH, speech, "What's Past Is Prologue," Bryn Mawr College, class of 1907 fiftieth reunion, June 1957. The quote is from a letter from Deborah (Sister Deborah Margaret, formerly known as Anna Clark, who lived at St. Margaret's Convent) to GH, July 31, 1957. Hutchins received a postcard from classmate Ellen Thayer (June 1957), who also praised her speech. By all accounts Hutchins had given an excellent speech in honor of classmate Alice Hawkins at the last Bryn Mawr reunion (Cornelia "Tink" Meigs to GH, June 30, 1956).

2. Lois Rudnick, "The Life of Mabel Dodge Luhan," in *The Challenge of Feminist Biography: Writing the Lives of Modern American Women*, ed. Sara Alpern, Joyce Antler, Elisabeth Israels Perry, and Ingrid Winther Scobie (Urbana: University of Illinois Press, 1992), 136.

3. Virginia Woolf, *Three Guineas* (New York: Harcourt, Brace, 1976), 69.

4. "A New Edition of 'Nature of Capitalism,'" *Daily Worker*, February 11, 1946.

5. AR, *Capitalism and Progress* (New York: International Publishers, 1945), book jacket.

6. Ibid., 106

7. Ibid., 104.

8. Ibid., 101–2.

9. Earl Browder, *Teheran: Our Path in War and Peace* (New York: International Publishers, 1944). Rochester's review, "Teheran," was published in *Soviet Russia Today* (September 1944), 28–29.

10. AR, *Capitalism and Progress*, 99.

11. Reviews include, Ralph Bowman, "Capitalism in America," *New Masses*, May 8, 1945; "The Bandwagon," *New Republic*, March 12, 1945; "Capitalism and Progress," *San Diego Home Front News*, April 1945; and "American Capitalism Has Progressive Role," *Canadian Tribune*, May 19, 1945. A review in the *Annals of the American Academy*, by Theodore J. Kreps (September 1945): 186–87, still criticized the book as very anticapitalist.

12. Ben Levine, "Anna Rochester Gives Clear Picture of Capitalist Society," *Daily Worker*, March 19, 1945. Levine wrote: "The reader will remember that such papers [as the *New York Times*] are regularly surprised every time somebody mentions the progressive role of Peter the Great or the progressive nature of capitalism. Miss Rochester's book will help enlighten them on the consistent Marxist analysis of capitalism."

13. Letters included: Helen Hendricks to AR, March 23, 1945; Winifred Chappell to AR, March 17, 1945; Elisabeth Freudenthal to AR, March 29, 1945; Edith Klein to AR, April 6, 1945; and Florence Converse to AR, "Easter Monday" 1945. Some emphasized its value as a text book, as "required reading," and the Newark Labor School ordered it for their students (William Myles to Alexander Trachtenberg, February 9, 1945).

14. Peggy Dennis in *The Autobiography of an American Communist* (Westport, Conn.: Hill, 1977), pp. 161–63, seems to indicate this timing.

15. See, for example, Michael E. Brown, "Introduction: The History of the History of U.S. Communism," in *New Studies in the Politics and Culture of U.S. Communism*, ed. Michael E. Brown, Randy Martin, Frank Rosengarten, and George Snedeker (New York: Monthly Review Press, 1993), 15–44.

16. AR, letter to the Editor, *Daily Worker*, June 27, 1945.

17. AR, *The Nature of Capitalism* (New York: International Publishers, 1946), 89.

18. Ibid., 90.

19. "Worth Repeating," *Daily Worker*, March 16, 1946.

20. Rosalyn Baxandall makes this point in "The Question Seldom Asked: Women and the CPUSA," in Michael E. Brown, Randy Martin, Frank Rosengarten, and George Snedeker, eds., *New Studies in the Politics and Culture of U.S. Communism*, 141.

21. The HUAC had its beginnings in the late 1930s under the direction of Martin Dies and his strong anti–New Deal and anticommunist politics, but had been silenced by the Soviet alliance with the Allies during the war. Unfortunately, when the Socialist Workers Party members were indicted under the Smith Act in 1943 for criticism of U.S. policies during World War II, the Communist Party did not protest. This law would soon be used against them too.

22. In *The Cold War: A History* (New York: Henry Holt, 1993), Martin Walker writes how the Cold War became a kind of institution, that, "for all its economic and psychological burdens," was "marked by a kind of warped stability and an evolving code of acceptable behavior which helped spare humanity the devastation of a Third World War" (1).

23. Peggy Dennis, *The Autobiography of an American Communist*, 173.

24. For an excellent discussion of this point of view, see Ellen Schrecker, "McCarthyism and the Decline of Communism, 1945–1960," in Michael E. Brown, Randy Martin, Frank Rosengarten, and George Snedeker, eds., *New Studies in the Politics and Culture of U.S. Communism*, 123–40.

25. U.S. Senate Committee on the Judiciary, Subcommittee to Investigate the Administration of the Internal Security Act and Other Internal Security Laws of the Committee on the Judiciary, *The Communist Party of the United States of America, What It Is, How It Works: A Handbook for Americans* (Washington, D.C.: Government Printing Office, 1955), 2.

26. Labor Research Association, *Labor Fact Book*, vol. 9 (New York: International Publishers, 1949), 84. The twelve indicted were William Z. Foster, Eugene Dennis, John B. Williamson, Jacob Stachel, Robert G. Thompson, Benjamin J. Davis, Jr., Henry Winston, John Gates, Irving Potash, Gilbert Green, Carl Winter, and Gus Hall.

27. Foster's case was separated and postponed on account of his health so that only eleven cases were actually involved. Gus Hall, Gilbert Green, Robert G. Thompson, and Henry Winston became political refugees; Hall was arrested in Mexico City in 1951 and received an additional three years in jail. The *Labor Fact Books*, vol. 10 (1951, p. 78) and vol. 11 (1953, pp. 63–64), give interesting coverage of these events.

28. The Rosenberg's sons Robert and Michael Meeropol tried to vindicate their parents' names and wrote *We Are Your Sons* (Urbana: University of Illinois, 1986) about the case. See also Radosh and Joyce Milton, *The Rosenberg File* (London: Holt, Rinehart and Winston, 1983). While this book is critical of the Rosenbergs, it has been critiqued by Gerald E. Markowitz, "How Not to Write History: A Critique of Radosh and Milton's *The Rosenberg File*," *Science and Society* 48 (Spring 1984).

29. Max Gordon (city editor of the *Daily Worker*) to editor of the *New York Times*, April 1, 1956; printed in the *New York Times*, April 6, 1956.

30. GH to Ruth Erickson and Eleanor Stevenson, July 6, 1954. Erickson and Stevenson were a couple who lived together at "Watermill" near New Milford, Connecticut, from the 1930s to the early 1970s when Erickson died. They were socialists who "indulged in a voluminous epistolary campaign against injustice, real or apparent, in all its manifestations. They offered their opinions and advice alike to friends and world leaders" (Index to collection of Ruth Erickson and Eleanor Stevenson, Special Collections Division of University Archives, Knight Library, University of Oregon). Hutchins corresponded with the couple from 1946 to 1968, with an occasional letter from Rochester. Much of the details of Hutchins and Rochester's lives in this later period are drawn from these correspondences.

31. Maurice Isserman, *Which Side Were You On? The American Communist Party During the Second World War* (Middletown, Conn.: Wesleyan University Press, 1982), 246.

32. Draft Resolution for the 16th National Committee of the Communist Party, USA, adopted September 13, 1956 (New York: New Century Publishers, 1956), 54–55.

33. Paul Buhle, "Daily Worker," in Mari Jo Buhle, Paul Buhle, and Dan Georgakas, eds., *The Encyclopedia of the American Left* (New York: Garland, 1990), 181.

34. Diggins describes the various factions who created this "mood in search of a movement": "Originally SDS [Students for a Democratic Society] believed in the miracle of community organizing, PL [Progressive Labor Party] in the might of revolutionary struggle, YSA [Young Socialist Alliance] in the mystique of proletarian consciousness, and the DuBois Clubs [of America] in the method of coalition politics. Not surprisingly, SDS regarded PL as dangerously adventuristic, while the latter accused the former of 'bourgeois romanticism': YSA criticized DuBois members for betraying the working class, and they in turn suspected young Trotskyists [the YSA] of ideological paranoia" (John Patrick Diggins, *The Rise and Fall of the American Left* [New York: Norton, 1992], 257).

35. Ibid., 238.

36. Chambers has been characterized as a mentally unstable man who had grandiose visions, a whole series of "aliases," and thrived on perceptions of espionage and conflict. Information gleaned after the Freedom of Information Act has revealed the role of Richard Nixon and various federal agencies in falsifying evi-

dence, including the Chambers films. These films, supposed to be evidence of espionage, were actually revealed much later to be innocuous Navy footage. The political careers of Nixon and Joseph McCarthy were furthered by these events, as also was support for the FBI and new legislation to tighten national security. See William A. Reuben's account, "Richard Nixon, Whittaker Chambers, and the Hiss Case," in Mari Jo Buhle, Paul Buhle, and Dan Gorgakas, eds., *Encyclopedia of the American Left*, 534–37.

37. There are several texts that have dealt with the Alger Hiss trials and the Chambers's testimony. See, for example, Fred J. Cook's *The Unfinished Story of Alger Hiss* (New York: Morrow, 1958); John Cabot Smith's *Alger Hiss: The True Story* (New York: Holt, Rhinehart, and Winston, 1976); and Allen Weinstein, *Perjury: The Hiss–Chambers Case* (New York: Knopf, 1978). In *The Secret World of American Communism* (New Haven: Yale University Press, 1995), p. 321, Harvey Klehr, John Earle Haynes and Fridrikh Igorevich Firsov tend to believe Hiss's guilt, showing the existence of documents that support Chambers's story. For Hiss's own account, refer to *In the Court of Public Opinion* (New York: Knopf, 1957).

38. The reference to "pumpkin" refers to the story that Chambers had five rolls of microfilm (the film that eventually was revealed as innocuous) in a pumpkin patch on his Maryland farm. Chambers said it was secret State Department material handed to him by a member of the communist underground.

39. Louise Mitchell, "2 Women Debunk Pumpkin Spy Tales," *Daily Worker*, December 15, 1948.

40. Whittaker Chambers, *Witness* (New York: Random House, 1952), 268.

41. Besides the *Daily Worker* article, see also an article in the *New York Star* by Ira Wolfert and Jerome Bakst, "Chambers [*sic*] 'Threat' Tale: Woman He Accuses Tells Her Version," December 15, 1948.

42. Meyer Zeligs's *Friendship and Fratricide: An Analysis of Whittaker Chambers and Alger Hiss* (New York: Viking Press, 1967), 299. Zeligs reported that Chambers had also told State Department security officers that Hutchins had telephoned Esther Shemitz's mother in Long Island and said that "if Chambers did not return to the Party by the following Thursday, it was a question of his death." Zeligs explained that Chambers did not mention this in *Witness*, nor did the corresponding Security Office memo mention anything about Chambers's assertion.

43. Ibid., 300.

44. Ibid.

45. Louise Mitchell, "2 Women Debunk Pumpkin Spy Tales."

46. GH to AR, November 3, 1948.

47. "Rochester Notables Score Mob Attack on CP Meet," *Daily Worker*, April 16, 1948, and "First Citizen," *Chicago Standard*, April 24, 1948.

48. "McCarthy Issues Call for 10 Authors," *Baltimore Sun*, June 28, 1953.

49. GH, signed, typed statement, January 1949.

50. See, for example, Zeligs's discussion of Chambers's homosexuality in *Friendship and Fratricide*, 213–16.

51. GH to Random House editors, May 29, 1952. Hutchins also wrote to the *New York Herald Tribune* concerning a review it had made of *Witness* which Hutchins characterized as "favorable" (Lewis Gannett, book review editor, *New York Herald Tribune*, to GH, June 3, 1952).

52. Both quotations are from Chambers, *Witness*, 50.

53. Sally Cleghorn to AR, February 22, 1952. Other letters included Christmas note from section staff to GH and AR, undated; Louise Berman to GH, September 9, 1952; Vida Scudder to AR and GH, September 24, 1952.

54. AR to GH, undated.

55. GH notebook, section "books to read—books read."

56. AR to GH, February 13, 1939.

57. Charlotte Perkins Gilman, "To Labor," typed and pasted into Hutchins's notebook, undated; also sent out to friends and colleagues, Christmas 1949.

58. GH notebook, August 19, 1956.

59. Ibid., August 19, 1951, and dated every year on the same date until 1955.

60. Ibid., August 19, 1940, renewed January 1, 1941.

61. Ibid., poem, author unknown, undated (given the sequence of the notebook it is probably circa 1956).

62. AR verse to GH, August 19, undated, though probably 1944.

63. AR to GH, February 14, 1953.

64. In 1946 and 1947 Hutchins published reviews of *Trends in Collective Bargaining: A Summary of Recent Experience*, by S. T. Williamson and Herbert Harris, and *American Labor Unions: What They Are and How They Work*, and *A Survey of Labor Economics*, by Florence Peterson, for the *New Masses*. *Brotherhood of Sleep Car Porters* and *Negro Labor*, by Robert C. Weaver, and *Current Economic Problems*, by Gemmill and Blodgett, were reviewed for *Railroad Notes*. *The Future of Housing*, by Charles Abram, was reviewed for *Economic Notes*. In 1950 Hutchins reviewed *The Cost of Financing Social Security*, by the Brookings Institution, and *Railroad Monopoly*, by John G. Shott, for *Railraod Notes;* and in 1951 *Interlocking Directorates*, by the Federal Trade Commission, *Economics at Midyear, 1951*, by the Council of Economic Advisors, and *White Collar*, by C. Wright Mills, for *Economic Notes*. From 1954 onwards all reviews were for *Railroad Notes*. These included *The Negro and the Schools*, by Harry S. Ashmore, *Automation*, by John Diebold, and *Trains and the Men Who Work Them*, by Alexander Uhl. In 1955 reviews included *Unity and Diversity in European Labor*, by Adolf Sturnthal. Nineteen fifty-six reviews included *The Oppenheimer Case*, by Charles P. Curtis, *Youth in Danger*, by Robert C. Hendrickson, *Cross-Currents*, by A. Forster and B. R. Epstein, *Was Justice Done*, by Malcolm Sharp, and *On the Line*, by Harvey Swados. In 1958 Hutchins reviewed *Our Fundamental Liberties*, by Milton R. Konvitz; in 1959, *World Without War*, by J. D. Bernal; and in 1960, *1877: Year of Violence*, by Robert Bruce. Books reviewed in 1961 included *Labor's Story*, by Cole, Stein, and Sobol, *The Drug Industry*, report by the Committee on Anti-Trust and Monopoly, and *The Peace Race*, by Seymour Melman.

65. Rochester's book reviews included various essays on agriculture in *Science and Society*, a review of *Studies in the Development of Capitalism*, by Maurice Dobb, for the *New Masses* in 1947, as well as the review of Browder's book, mentioned above for *Soviet Russia Today*.

66. AR to Gerald Daniels, March 26, 1950. Rochester was replying to a letter (Gerald Daniels to Herbert Aptheker, March 19, 1950) passed on to her by Aptheker, editor of *Masses and Mainstream*, concerning a review of *American Capitalism*. Hutchins seems to have seen the letter first and had handwritten a note to

her partner on the top. Mr. Daniels also remarked that Rochester did not include Marx's *Das Kapital* in her bibliography and Hutchins responded to that: "Anna, suggest you refer Daniels to your book *The Nature of Capitalism* for quotations from Marx! He sounds very young!—a student probably."

67. David Carpenter, "The Story of U.S. Capitalism's First 200 Years," *Worker* (undated clipping); Jack Foner, "Birth of a System," *Masses and Mainstream* (February 1950): 88–89.

68. Clark Blaise, "Your Nearest Exit May Be Behind You," in *The Seductions of Biography*, ed. Mary Rhiel and David Suchoff (New York: Routledge, 1996), 201–09.

69. AR, *American Capitalism, 1607–1800* (New York: International Publishers, 1949), 115.

70. GH, *Women Who Work* (New York: International Publishers, 1952), 33.

71. Ibid., 36.

72. Mary Inman, *In Woman's Defense* (Los Angeles: Committee to Organize the Advancement of Women, 1940), 120.

73. Robert Shaffer reports this in "Women and the Communist Party, U.S.A., 1930–40," *Socialist Review* 45 (1979): 83. Note also that it was not published as a book by the mainstream CP press but by the Committee to Organize the Advancement of Women.

74. "Women Who Work," *Daily Worker*, May 28, 1953; Elizabeth M. Bacon, "America's Working Women," *Masses and Mainstream*, March 1953; "Course on Woman Question," *Daily Worker*, January 2, 1953.

75. The *Worker* articles include: "Women Workers Carry a Double Load," December 21, 1952; "It Should Have a Place on Your Reference Shelf," January 25, 1953; Betty Feldman, "Grace Hutchins Tells About Women Who Work," March 1, 1953; Betty Feldman, "The So-Called Equal Rights Amendment—It Would Torpedo Laws Safeguarding Women Workers," May 3, 1953.

76. GH, "The Struggle for Women's Political Rights in America" (review of Eleanor Flexner's *Century of Struggle: The Woman's Rights Movement in the United States* [Cambridge: Harvard University Press, 1959]), in the *Worker*, September 20, 1959.

77. GH, "Four Decades of Struggle for Women's Rights," *Worker*, March 17, 1964, and March 24, 1964.

78. LRA Staff, "East–West Trade and Jobs," in *Looking Forward: Selections of Work in Progress by Authors of International Publishers* (New York: International Publishers, 1954), 98–106. LRA staff were also featured in the article "U.S. Over Latin America," which represented forthcoming LRA pamphlets. It seems unlikely that Hutchins and Rochester were involved in the writing of these pamphlets.

79. The LRA pamphlet "Billionaire Corporations: Their Growth and Power" (New York: International Publishers, 1954) looks to have been written under Rochester's guidance.

80. GH to Ruth Erickson and Eleanor Stevenson, August 20, 1965.

81. Ibid., May 15, 1961.

82. AR to Bob Dunn concerning her resignation, April 3, 1950. Mention of her heart attacks is in a letter from GH to Ruth Erickson and Eleanor Stevenson, April 28, 1954.

83. GH to Ruth Erickson and Eleanor Stevenson, July 17, 1964.

84. AR to GH, undated; and AR to GH, October 29, 1957.

85. GH to Ruth Erickson and Eleanor Stevenson, March 31, 1962.

86. The couple had been involved in the ACLU during the thirties; Rochester had been elected to the board of directors in 1929 but had resigned as the ACLU became more conservative. Indeed, on May 13, 1940, during the ousting of Elizabeth Gurley Flynn from the ACLU board because of her communist membership, Gurley Flynn released the following statement by Rochester: "The statement by the ACLU that they had never knowingly put a Communist on the Board of Directors reveals the shortness of their memories. When I was elected to the Board about 11 years ago, the fact that I was a Communist was known to Roger Baldwin, Norman Thomas and other members of the Board. In fact, I was given to understand that one reason they wanted me on the Board was that I would represent the Communist viewpoint. I resigned on my own free will, long before they had turned into a red-baiting organization" (Elizabeth Gurley Flynn, press release, May 13, 1940). See also a letter from Robert Dunn to Roger Baldwin, May 17, 1940, that refers to Baldwin's accusation that Rochester reconstructed her memory to suit events. Dunn reminded Baldwin of his memory of a public meeting during which Baldwin said to Dunn and Rochester, "I hear you have found the Party!" Dunn explained that this incident was before Rochester's election to the ACLU Board.

87. AR to President Truman, May 19, 1947.

88. AR to Hon. Howard McGrath, November 30, 1949.

89. For example, GH to editor, *Daily Worker*, October 8, 1948.

90. For sources on Elizabeth Gurley Flynn see, for example, Rosalyn Baxandall, *Words on Fire: The Life and Writings of Elizabeth Gurley Flynn* (New Brunswick: Rutgers University Press, 1987). Gurley Flynn's autobiographies include: *The Rebel Girl, An Autobiography, My First Life (1906–1926)* (New York: International Publishers, 1955), and *The Alderson Story: My Life as a Political Prisoner* (New York: International Publishers, 1963).

91. *New York Times,* July 18, 1951.

92. Betty Feldman, "Grace Hutchins Tells About Women Who Work," *Worker,* March 1, 1953.

93. Elizabeth Gurley Flynn to GH, February 15, 1953.

94. Tom O'Connor, secretary of the Committee for the Vindication of Sacco and Vanzetti, to GH, secretary of the Elizabeth Gurley Flynn Memorial Committee, September 1964, October 6, 1964, and October 17, 1964. GH to Tom O'Connor, October 4, 1964.

95. *New York Times,* July 26, 1951.

96. *New York Times,* March 2, 1955.

97. For information on this committee see Louise Pettibone Smith, *Torch of Liberty* (New York: Dwight-King, 1959).

98. "Grace Hutchins," in *Notable American Women: The Modern Period: A Biographical Dictionary,* ed. Barbara Sicherman, Carol Hurd Green, Ilene Kantrov, and Harriette Walker (Cambridge: Harvard University Press, 1980), 364.

99. For sources on the CRC, see Gerald Horne, *Communist Front? The Civil Rights Congress, 1946–1956* (Rutherford: Fairleigh Dickinson University Press, 1987).

100. For example, in 1961 Hutchins had a model letter featured in the *Worker* to object to the refusal of the Supreme Court to review the convictions of seven de-

fendants in the Cleveland Taft–Hartley conspiracy case. She asked readers to contribute financial support to the bail fund ("A Plea from Grace Hutchins," *Worker,* April 30, 1961).

101. GH, "The Smith Act Attack on Civil Liberties," *Worker,* March 5, 1964.

102. GH to Ruth Erickson and Eleanor Stevenson, June 30, 1954, and July 17, 1964.

103. AR obituary, *New York Times,* May 12, 1966. See also Rochester's obituary in the *Worker,* May 24, 1966; and *Publishers Weekly,* June 20, 1966.

104. Program for International Women's Day celebration held in the Ballroom of Penn Garden Hotel, New York City, March 27, 1969. On the pro-Soviet aspect of the *Daily World,* Dorothy Healey, postwar leader of the Southern California CP who left the Party in 1967 after denouncing the Soviet invasion of Czechoslovakia, wrote that the *Daily World's* coverage of the Czech crisis "was designated to create an atmosphere of hysteria, spreading wild and nonsensical stories." See Healey's autobiography, *Dorothy Healey Remembers: A Life in the American Communist Party* (New York: Oxford University Press, 1990), 229.

105. Much of the information I have about Hutchins during these later years comes from letters Bob Dunn wrote to Hutchins's friends. He answered their letters and let them know how their friend was doing. The letters included Bob Dunn to Ellen Thayer, May 16, 1967, and March 8, 1968; Mary Porter, June 12, 1968; Ann Mundelein, July 26, 1968; and Francis Bliss, March 15, 1968.

106. GH, obituary, *New York Times,* July 16, 1969; also see Hutchins's obituary in the *Daily World,* July 17, 1969.

107. Clara Colon to Bob Dunn, July 27, 1969.

Index

collaboration). *See also American
Capitalism; Capitalism and Progress;
Nature of Capitalism;* Soviet Union,
workers in, compared to U.S.
workers
Capitalism and Progress, 193, 204–5,
207, 208. *See also Nature of
Capitalism*
Ceylon, 25, 133
Chambers, Whittaker, 211, 214–18,
268n15, 276–77n36, 277n42
Chappell, Winifred, 190, 269–70n43
Children's Bureau, 5, 46–51; Baby
Week campaigns of, 48–49
"Children Under Capitalism," 168
China, 6, 25, 53–70, 119, 121, 127–30,
142, 169, 198–99; Boxer rebellion
in, 247n13; history of, 247–48n14
Chinese Exclusion Act, 247n10
Christianity: Fellowship of
Reconciliation and, 105; humility
in, 155; Hutchins and, 26, 56, 183,
203–4; Hutchins and Rochester's
faith in, 3, 5, 6, 95, 147, 234,
251n20; idealism in, 102; moral
principles of, 15–16, 28, 44, 49, 75,
77, 125, 126, 137; Rochester and, 37,
40; social justice and, 80, 95, 98,
99–100, 102–3 (*see also* Christian
socialism); traditional creed of, 114.
See also Episcopal Church
Christian pacifism, 74, 97, 103, 119,
198
Christian socialism, 253n2; Fellowship
of Reconciliation and, 97–120;
Hutchins and, 69, 203–4; Hutchins
and Rochester's faith in, 2, 3, 5, 6,
75, 121, 122, 147, 151, 153;
Rochester and, 39, 40, 42. *See also
Jesus Christ and the World Today;
World Tomorrow*
Churchill, Winston, 205
Church League for Industrial
Democracy, 76, 84
C.I.O. *See* Congress of Industrial
Organizations
Citizens Committee for Constitutional
Liberties, 230

Civil Rights Congress, 229
Clark, Anna (a.k.a. Sister Deborah
Margaret), 274n1
class collaboration, 152–53, 168, 169,
172–73, 177–80, 190, 198
Cleghorn, Sarah (Sally), 81, 90–94,
100, 101–2, 116, 218, 250n11,
251–20
Cold War, 6, 208–9, 223, 225, 226,
227–30, 232, 275n22
Colon, Clara, 233–34
Colon, Jesús, 233–34
Columbia University, 35, 43, 75, 191
Comintern (Third Communist
International), 151, 152, 153, 156,
178, 193, 200, 206. *See also*
Communist Party, USA
communes, 6, 47, 78–95, 251n17. *See
also* Community House
communism, 1,3, 5, 6, 119, 130, 137,
138, 139, 141, 151–234, 259–60n1;
comradeship in, 204, 231;
discipline in, 3, 154, 155, 157, 183,
202, 204; explanations for society
of, 3, 154; faith and devotion in,
183–84, 195, 197, 203–4, 207, 220,
221, 227, 231; frugality in, 184, 220,
231; mysticism in, 154, 157, 204.
See also Bolsheviks; Bolshevism;
capitalism; Cold War; Comintern;
Communist Party, USA; Lenin, V.
I.; Marxism; socialism; Soviet
Union; Stalin, Joseph
Communist Party, USA, 6, 151–234;
bail funds for, 228–30; civil liberties
of, 211, 213, 227–30; history of,
195, 210, 259–60n1; Hutchins's
political office in, 180–82, 204, 211;
lesser evil strategy and, 268n11;
membership in, 178, 194, 197, 210,
211, 212; policy on homosexuality
of, 3, 155, 166–67, 211, 217, 236n6;
Popular Front and, 6, 153, 156,
177–80, 193, 261n10; post–World
War II and, 208–9; social fascists
and, 152, 177 (*see also* class
collaboration); Third Period of, 6,
153, 167, 169, 171, 172, 176, 190;

ABOUT THE AUTHOR

Janet Lee is associate professor and director of Women Studies at Oregon State University where she teaches a variety of courses on gender and feminism. Besides women's history and biography, her interests include feminist theory, research methodologies, and pedagogy, as well as issues concerning women and the body. She is co-author with Jennifer Sasser-Coen of *Blood Stories: Menarche and the Politics of the Female Body in Contemporary U.S. Society* (Routledge, 1996). She lives in the coastal range mountains of Oregon with her family and enjoys gardening and horseback riding.